INVESTING IN HIGHER EDUCATION

A Handbook of Leadership Development

Madeleine F. Green
Sharon A. McDade

AMERICAN COUNCIL
ON EDUCATION
Series on Higher Education
ORYX PRESS
1994

Published by The Oryx Press
4041 North Central at Indian School Road
Phoenix, AZ 85012-3397

Printed in the United States of America

Library of Congress Cataloging-in-Publication Data
Green, Madeleine F.
    Investing in higher education : a handbook of leadership
development / Madeleine F. Green, Sharon A. McDade.
        p.   cm. — (American Council on Education/Oryx series on
higher education)
    Includes bibliographical references and index.
    ISBN 0-89774-829-8
    1. Universities and colleges—United States—Administration-
-Handbooks, manuals, etc. 2. College administrators—Training of-
-United States—Handbooks, manuals, etc. 3. Leadership—United
States—Handbooks, manuals, etc. I. McDade, Sharon A. II. Title.
III. Series.
LB2341.G697 1994
378.1'00973—dc20   94-4265
                                                                    CIP

Contents

Acknowledgements

A Note to the Reader

PART ONE: THE FRAMEWORK

1. *Introduction*   3

   What is Leadership? How is Leadership Different from Management? How is Leadership Developed? What is the Handbook? Working Assumptions. How the Handbook is Organized. Conclusion. Notes. References.

2. *Leadership Development: An Institutional Investment*   13

   What's in It for Us? Benefits to the Institution. Obstacles: Myth and Reality. Getting There: Developing an Institutional Plan. Checklist of Institutional Policies and Practices. An Institutional Plan: Loyola College of Maryland. References. Resources.

3. *The Individual Perspective: Developing Leadership Capacities*   27

   Leadership Tasks and Capacities. How Do Leaders Learn? What Do Individuals Gain from Leadership Development Experiences? Conclusion. Notes. References. Resources.

PART TWO: STRATEGIES FOR DEVELOPING LEADERS

4. *Governing Boards*   41

   Responsibilities. Leadership Capacities. Strategies for Successful Boards. Strategies for Board Development. Board Evaluation as a Developmental Tool. The Role of the President in Board Development. Conclusion. Notes. References. Resources. Programs and Practices.

5. *Presidents*   59

   Career Preparation. Responsibilities. Leadership Capacities. Strategies for Development. Strategies for Boards to Foster Presidential Development. Strategies for Spouses. Conclusion. References. Resources. Programs and Practices.

6. *Senior Administrators*   **79**
   Career Preparation. Responsibilities. Leadership Capacities.
   Phases of an Administrative Position. Strategies for Develop-
   ment. Considerations for Presidents and Boards. Conclusion.
   References. Resources. Programs and Practices.

7. *Academic Deans and Mid-Level Academic Administrators*   **97**
   Career Preparation. Responsibilities. Leadership Capacities.
   Job Cycle of an Academic Dean. Strategies for Development.
   Considerations for Supervisors. Conclusion. Notes. Refer-
   ences. Resources. Programs and Practices.

8. *Administrative Managers and Professional Staff*   **119**
   Career Preparation. Responsibilities. Special Development
   Needs. Leadership Capacities. Strategies for Development.
   Conclusion. Notes. References. Programs and Practices.

9. *Department Chairs*   **137**
   Context for Departmental Leadership. Responsibilities. Lead-
   ership Capacities. Strategies for Development. Conclusion.
   Note. References. Resources. Programs and Practices.

10. *Faculty*   **155**
    Faculty as Leaders. Expanding Faculty Options. Strategies for
    Promoting Faculty Vitality and Development. Institutional
    Efforts: A Case Study. Conclusion. Notes. References.
    Resources. Programs and Practices.

11. *Team Leadership*   **175**
    Leadership Capacities. Why Teams Fail. Symptoms of a Dys-
    functional Team. Strategies for Team Building. Considerations.
    Conclusion. Resources. Programs and Practices.

12. *Evaluation: A Developmental Tool*   **189**
    The Uses of Evaluation. Strategies for a Successful Evaluation
    System. Evaluating Outcomes. Evaluating Leadership Capaci-
    ties. Linking Evaluation and Development. The Performance
    Evaluation Session. Conclusion. Notes. References.
    Resources.

PART THREE: INTEGRATING INSTITUTIONAL AND INDIVIDUAL DEVELOPMENT

13. *Getting the Most from Off-Campus Development Programs* **205**
    Selecting Off-Campus Programs. Benefiting from Confer-
    nces and Conventions. Benefiting from National Leadership

Development Programs. Conclusion. References. Selected
Off-Campus Programs.

14. *On-Campus Development: The Workplace as Learning
    Environment*   213

    How Do Leaders Learn? Strategies for Developing on the Job.
    Models of On-Campus Development Programming. Institu-
    tional Efforts: A Sampling of Approaches. Conclusion. Refer-
    ences. Resources. Programs and Practices.

15. *Inexpensive Development Ideas*   235

    Resources.

PART FOUR: APPENDIX OF PROGRAMS AND PRACTICES

Associations   247

National Programs   268

*Statewide, System-Specific, and On-Campus
Programs*   319

Participants in the Review Process   341

Index   353

About the Authors

Madeleine F. Green is Vice President of the American Council on Education and Director of the Council's Center for Leadership Development. Activities of the Center include programs for presidents and department chairs, the ACE Annual Meeting, the National Leadership Group, the ACE Fellows Program, and the national presidents' study, an ongoing research project on the backgrounds and careers of college and university presidents. In 1990–91, Green took a leave of absence from ACE to serve as interim president of Mount Vernon College in Washington, D.C. She holds a B.A. from Radcliffe College, and master's and doctoral degrees in French Literature from Columbia University. She has edited two books, *Academic Leaders as Managers* and *Leaders for a New Era: Strategies for Higher Education,* and has authored numerous articles in the area of leadership development, financial aid, and management in higher education. She is a member of the Board of Trustees of Wilson College in Pennsylvania.

Sharon A. McDade is an Assistant Professor in the Department of Higher and Adult Education and Director of Higher Education Administration Programs at Columbia University's Teachers College. Her research, teaching, and consulting focus on issues of leadership development and higher education management. In addition to working with many U.S. colleges and universities to organize and teach leadership development and management development seminars for administrators and faculty, she is involved with major consulting projects to launch similar programs for senior administrators at higher education institutions in Mexico, Nigeria, and Venezuela. She holds an Ed.D. in Administration, Planning, and Social Policy from Harvard University's Graduate School of Education, an M.F.A. in Design and Theater Technology from Ohio State University, and a B.S. from Miami University. She is the author of *Higher Education Leadership: Enhancing Skills through Professional Development Programs.*

Acknowledgements

Since its inception in 1987 with a grant from the Lilly Endowment, this project has been transformed. The *Handbook* was originally conceived as a series of papers on leadership development, but as work progressed, our commentators and colleagues were increasingly clear that a more useful contribution to higher education would be a practical publication with suggestions on the *hows* of leadership development rather than exposition on the *whys*. Ralph Lundgren, vice president at the Endowment, has been patient and supportive while the book changed and expanded into its current form. The authors and the American Council on Education are enormously grateful to Mr. Lundgren for his faith and his support.

Peggy Heim, senior researcher at TIAA-CREF, provided support for an indispensable dose of reality testing. A credible *Handbook* requires review by potential users and those who daily confront the issues about which we are writing. A grant from TIAA-CREF made it possible to convene a series of panels to critique drafts of the book and to give us valuable insights from the trenches. These sessions were essential to ensuring that we captured the reality of many different campuses. We thank the numerous individuals consulted in the development of the book, who are listed at the end.

Every writing project undertaken at ACE benefits from the expertise and good will of James J. Murray, director of the Division of Publications, Advancement, and Membership. This book is no exception, and we are in Mr. Murray's debt for his advice and assistance throughout the development of this book. The talents of other ACE colleagues were enormously helpful: Wendy Bresler's critical eye and assistance in the design and production turned a draft into a book; Jill Bogard's relentless checking saved us from our own mistakes. Colleen Allen and Mona Sutphen of the ACE staff were invaluable assistants whose careful research and cataloging produced the *Programs and Practices* sections. Kimberly Hokanson of Harvard's Graduate School of Education provided references and citations.

We also acknowledge the many alumni of ACE's Fellows Program, and of Harvard's Institute for Educational Management, Management Development Program, and Seminar for New Presidents, as well as the members of the National Leadership Group and the Commission on Leadership Development of ACE, who provided us with ideas, materials, program and practice descriptions, and critiques. The names of the many readers and contributors are listed at the end of the *Handbook*. We apologize in advance to anyone whose name we forgot to include in this very long list of helpful colleagues.

Finally, we thank the Masters John and Judy Dowling and the Resident Tutors of Leverett House (particularly Kathryn Welter, Meme Drumwright, H. W. Perry, and Elizabeth Keeney), and Donna and Michael Goldstein, who assisted with the computer problems and provided tremendous encouragement during the writing of this book. Very special thanks go to Stephen, Jessica, and Julia Green for being so patient and good humored during the nights and weekends that this book was being written.

A Note To The Reader

The authors hope that the reader will approach this book with the care and concentration that we devoted to writing it. Because this volume covers a great deal of material and is written for busy people, we know that this wish is highly unrealistic.

This *Handbook* is designed with the recognition that institutional leaders will skim most chapters and look carefully at selected ones. The dean who would like to develop some programming for department chairs will concentrate on that particular chapter; the one on governing boards may be of little interest. As an individual seeking ideas on managing her own development, she might also read the chapter on deans. We have deliberately allowed for redundancy among the chapters with the assumption that most readers will read selectively.

This book has two audiences. One is governing boards and senior administrators, who are undoubtedly reluctant to add anything else to their priority list. Yet our message to them is a simple one: investing in people must be a priority; higher education cannot afford *not* to make this investment. Readers who go beyond the introduction will do so because they accept this premise and are interested in acting upon it.

Because leadership development is a two-way process—a responsibility shared by institution and individual—we also address this book to members of the campus community: faculty and administrators who will read it with their own development in mind. We recognize that individuals must take responsibility for their own growth and leadership development, and that no one can do it for them. These readers will also scan the book selectively, matching our suggestions against their own experiences and preferences and consulting the lists of resources and programs that are helpful to them individually. Thus, each chapter is directed both to those individuals who are in a position to promote the development of someone else and to those who are the subject of the chapter.

Although we have collected information about many programs and practices for the listings that appear at the end of the chapters and in the Appendix, we recognize that we may have missed many excellent examples. Our goal was not to present a complete inventory, but rather to include a representative sampling of types, formats, and purposes.

Finally, this *Handbook* is action oriented. Its main purpose is to provide practical suggestions in a user-friendly form. If we are short on exposition and analysis, it is because we hope the reader shares our premise that leaders *can* be developed and is ready to move on to the next question: How?

Madeleine F. Green
Sharon A. McDade
February 1991

Part One:

THE

FRAMEWORK

1

INTRODUCTION

According to their catalogs and mission statements, most colleges and universities aim to develop leaders for society through the educational process. A variety of programs and co-curricular activities provide students with academic and experiential learning opportunities that are designed to expand their awareness of leadership issues and test their own leadership abilities. Discussions of how institutions can foster in their students a commitment to civic responsibilities and leadership are taking place with renewed intensity. Colleges and universities also play an active role in developing leaders for the corporate world and the government. They offer institutes, summer programs, and collaborative activities with employers to enhance the skills and abilities of corporate managers and executives.

But what about developing leaders for higher education? Ironically, we pay little attention to enhancing the ability of administrators and faculty to lead our institutions; the priority is low and our investment modest. The corporate sector, on the other hand, spends $40 billion a year on training. Surely, higher education—a $150 billion dollar enterprise—should not consider leadership development less important than the corporate sector does.[1] People are the most important resource in higher education. A campus may devote as much as 80 percent or more of its operating budget to personnel. Yet institutions invest little in the development of these valuable human resources, and when times get tough, funds for faculty and administrative development are among the first casualties. Like deferred maintenance of the physical plant, inattention to human resource development is expensive in the long run.

A college or university is as dynamic as its board, faculty, and staff; an organization *is* its people. Investing in people—providing opportunities for leadership development and professional growth—is an investment in the institution. This *Handbook* looks at how to make that investment throughout an institution in ways that are beneficial to both individual and institution.

WHAT IS LEADERSHIP?

A vast literature is devoted to answering this question. Leadership is commonly defined as the ability to produce change and to set the direction of that change (Kotter 1990, p. 104). Gardner (1990, p. 1) defines leadership as ''the process of persuasion or example by which an individual (or leadership team) induces a group to pursue objectives held by the leader or shared by the leader and his or her followers.'' Argyris and Cyert (1980, p. 63) emphasize the distinctive nature of leadership as ''the art of stimulating the human resources within the organization to concentrate on total organizational goals rather than on individual subgroup goals. . . . The art of leadership is to convince the participants to modify their goals so that they conform with those of the total organization and to put their efforts into helping the total organization achieve its goals.''

Bennis and Nanus (1985, p. 21) define ''leading'' as ''influencing, guiding in direction, course, action, opinion.'' In the most positive sense, leaders are ''transforming''; they ''engage with others in such a way that leaders and followers raise one another to higher levels of motivation and morality'' (Burns 1978, p. 20). Leadership is characterized by commitment, a strong set of values, a sense of self, and vision.

HOW IS LEADERSHIP DIFFERENT FROM MANAGEMENT?

Many writers in the field consider management more short-term and technically focused than leadership. *Leadership* implies imagination, direction, innovation, vision; *management* implies implementation, structures, routine tasks.[2] It is easy to overemphasize the differences between *management* and *leadership*; in fact, they overlap to some extent. As Gardner (1990, p. 14) puts it, ''Most managers exhibit some leadership skills, and most leaders on occasion find themselves managing.'' He enumerates the management tasks of leaders: planning and priority setting, organizing and institution building, keeping the system functioning, setting agendas and making decisions, and exercising political judgments.

In higher education, *management* often has a negative connotation, suggesting unimaginative, unacademic, and bureaucratic behaviors. (We even avoid using the word ''manager'' and instead rely on the more neutral, safer term of ''administrator.'') To be an administrator who is a ''mere manager'' is to have few redeeming features in the academic culture; to be a "good manager" is to be damned with faint praise. In this *Handbook*, management and leadership are viewed as closely related, reflecting the assumption that effective leaders are also good managers, and that management is an honorable leadership task, worthy of formal training and inclusion in the reward system. Thus, the *Handbook* focuses on the development of both *leadership* and *management,* because the skills and capacities, associated with both functions warrant deliberate development.

HOW IS LEADERSHIP DEVELOPED?

There is general agreement in the literature that leaders are made, not born. But not everyone is or can be a leader—there are some innate attributes of character and temperament that are starting points for the development of leadership potential. It is difficult to teach courage, integrity, risk taking, creativity, or innovativeness—attributes commonly associated with leaders. One might even say that it is too late to teach these at all to adults, since their characters already are well formed and subject to only marginal changes.

But the characteristics of leaders are by no means the only important factors in leadership. The principal leadership tasks outlined in Chapter 2 (providing vision, managing and decision making, working with people, shaping values and culture, and understanding oneself) can be learned through a variety of experiences. In many cases, the leader or would-be leader is the driving force in the learning experience—reflecting on leadership, watching and analyzing other leaders, finding mentors, and seeking out opportunities for growth.

Colleges and universities, as educational organizations and as employers, have a special role to play in fostering leadership by creating an environment that encourages its faculty, administrators, and staff to realize their potential and be active contributors to the life of the institution. That is where *leadership development* emerges, and that role is the main focus of this book.

Leadership development encompasses many activities and experiences that enhance the ability of individuals to make a difference, to shape the direction of their institution or unit, and to bring others along in sharing and implementing goals. It is identifying new leaders, providing people with opportunities to grow and learn, to affirm their beliefs and values, to expand their understanding of issues and people, and to improve their management skills. Leadership development may be formal or informal, structured or unstructured, deliberate or serendipitous. *Management development* is a narrower term and refers to activities that improve management skills such as decision making, planning, budgeting, and supervising. *Professional development* is also a narrower concept than *leadership development* and focuses more on enhancing job effectiveness, honing job skills, and preparing individuals for future responsibilities.

In summary, *leadership development* is a broad concept that includes but goes beyond teaching skills and enhancing career mobility. While individuals must create opportunities to develop themselves, institutions must help them do so by effectively managing human resources, by establishing a climate that encourages participation and innovation, and by actively promoting leadership development.

WHAT IS THE HANDBOOK?

Despite the tomes that have been produced on the subject, do we know what leadership really is, or how to develop it? This *Handbook* does not continue the quest for theoretical frameworks of leadership, nor does it focus on providing advice on how to be an effective leader. While it is grounded in the literature on leadership and leadership development[3] and the concepts and details verified by the hundreds of higher education leaders who participated on this project, this volume focuses on a very practical question: *How can colleges and universities develop leadership capacity and effectiveness to the fullest extent possible?*

The *Handbook* is directed to governing boards, chief executive officers, senior administrators, faculty, and others who make decisions about the duties, performance, and professional lives of faculty and staff. A major responsibility of all leaders is the identification and development of other leaders. If leadership development is to be more than a random and occasional activity, it must become an institutional commitment, supported at the highest levels and embraced as part of a culture that espouses lifelong learning by its faculty, administrators, and staff. Thus, this volume also aims to help current and emerging leaders increase their effectiveness in their current positions, prepare for greater responsibility, or think differently about their careers. Strategies and resources suggested here should help readers to enhance their own career satisfaction.

WORKING ASSUMPTIONS

The *Handbook* accepts a number of assumptions about leadership and institutional functioning. It is important to be explicit about them, because they represent a set of principles and values that shape this book. Users are encouraged to draft their own list of assumptions about leadership and compare it to this one. Doing so can illuminate personal beliefs about leadership and organizational functioning and clarify individual decisions about leadership development as both an institutional and a personal issue.

Leadership Development Is a Shared Responsibility of the Institution and the Individual.

Ultimately, people must take responsibility for their own learning and growth. They must seize and create opportunities; no one else can do it for them. Yet the institution has a responsibility to create a climate that fosters professional growth and to view leadership development as a responsibility of leaders and an effort that is integral to institutional planning and development. Because the benefits of leadership development accrue to both the individual and the institution, it is fitting that the beneficiaries share the responsibility.

Leadership Development Is Ongoing and Often Not Deliberate.

It is entirely possible to be engaged in leadership development without having deliberately embarked on a course to do so. Most learning occurs on the job—through relationships with peers and mentors, new assignments, and exposure to new ideas. Such experiences can be even richer if they are deliberately assigned or structured to be growth experiences. A faculty member who becomes the chair of a committee charged with revising the general education requirements can, with the help of a supportive dean, use the opportunity to attend national workshops, read and write on the topic, and deliberately develop a new expertise that will become a source of personal satisfaction and a resource for the institution.

Diversity Strengthens Institutional Leadership.

Effective teams include a diverse group of individuals whose different strengths complement one another. This diversity may include differences in style, temperament, and intellectual strengths, as well as race and gender. Too often, diversity is seen as an obligation—a numerical goal to be achieved or a symbolic act indicating institutional commitment to pluralism. This view obscures the real contribution that *difference* can make. Identifying promising women and minority leaders, and providing them with opportunities for growth and mobility, will both enrich the institution and help it to operate in a changing demographic environment.

Individual Power in an Institution Is Limited.

Because most decisions are made by individuals in a group context, leadership often is dispersed, and the power of any single leader is limited. This has clear implications for leadership development: communication, team building, conflict resolution, negotiation, and other collaborative skills are essential for leaders.

Leadership Is Dispersed Throughout the Institution.

We tend to equate high position with leadership, but that is an incomplete vision. Certainly, board members, presidents, and persons with significant administrative responsibilities *should* be leaders, but no title necessarily implies the ability to lead. Leadership, especially in higher education institutions, is not a function of administrative rank; it can be found at every level of the academic hierarchy. Faculty leaders are powerful individuals. Program directors and mid-level managers can shape the course of their units and ultimately influence institutional policy. Departments hire and fire faculty, decide on requirements for the major, and develop curriculum. Some program units work directly with the community, allocate resources, and determine new directions—all without specific directives from higher levels of administration. Because power and decision making are decentralized and dispersed, leadership is needed at all levels, in all parts of the institution.

A Rigid Career Movement System Inhibits the Emergence of Leadership.

Ability and performance do not ensure access to leadership positions. The absence of certain credentials can be a major obstacle. While they might not be essential to *do* a job, they are probably necessary to *get* the job. In academia, many doors are closed as a result of bias against degrees in certain fields. A professional degree, for example, may derail an individual's candidacy for an academic vice presidency or a position in a college of liberal arts.

The emergence of leadership is also stifled by the lack of movement among institutional types and across functional lines. Conventional biases dictate, for example, that experience in a private liberal arts institution is not directly relevant to a public university or to a community college. While breadth of experience and learning from new situations, new issues, and new people constitute the best preparation for leadership, academe tends to confine people to certain career boxes that thwart their development. But these narrowly construed parameters of career mobility are as damaging to the institution as to the individual. Just as these individuals are deprived of opportunities to lead, so are institutions deprived of the benefit of the talents of their faculty and staff.

Conventional Notions of "Upward Mobility" Have Limited Use in Developing Leadership.

Few people keep moving "onward and upward" from chair to dean to academic vice president, or from resident hall advisor to head of counseling to dean of students. However, attaining greater challenge or the opportunity to lead does not necessarily mean moving upward; lateral mobility and job expansion are important to leadership growth. In fact, most people reach a plateau caused by the structure of higher education institutions rather than by limitations of their abilities.

HOW THE HANDBOOK IS ORGANIZED

Part One provides the context of leadership development from the institutional and the individual perspectives. Chapter 2 outlines what institutions can hope to achieve by investing in leadership development, describes the obstacles to doing so, and suggests general strategies for launching and maintaining successful leadership development efforts. It concludes with a checklist of policies and procedures. Chapter 3 approaches the theme from the perspective of the individual, enumerates the tasks of leaders, and discusses how leadership development can help people perform those tasks more effectively.

Part Two focuses on different groups within the institution. While this approach risks reinforcing the segmentation of higher education institutions, it represents the way we normally think about leadership development: in terms of target groups. The first seven chapters in this section are organized by positions:

- Governing boards,
- Presidents,
- Vice presidents and senior administrators,
- Academic deans and mid-level academic administrators,
- Administrative managers and professional staff,
- Department chairs, and
- Faculty.

The last two chapters in this section cut across functional lines and deal with team development and the use of performance evaluation as tools for leadership development. Throughout the book, and in Part Two in particular, attention is given to diversity, noting the special needs of women and minorities who hold these positions and suggesting ways to ensure adequate gender and ethnic representation. Each chapter in this section includes:

- An inventory of important leadership skills and capacities for that particular position or function,
- Suggested strategies to develop those skills,
- A list of resources to consult, and
- A list of illustrative programs and practices.

Some of these programs are campus-based and may be replicated elsewhere. Others are national programs. Each listing includes a contact person and an address.

Part Three focuses on implementing strategies: designing in-house efforts, making deliberate use of on-the-job training, and selecting an external professional development program. This part addresses both the institution and the individual and provides information on how both can benefit and make the best use of these experiences. Finally, it contains a list of resources.

The Appendix provides information on associations and brief descriptions of the national, statewide, and on-campus programs and practices listed at the end of the various chapters.

CONCLUSION

Leaders *do* make a difference. Change, innovation, and excellence are brought about by leaders throughout the institution. Because a college or university is only as good as its faculty, staff, and administrators, their development is tied closely to institutional effectiveness. This *Handbook* is a practical guide to developing individuals who can lead institutions in their quest for excellence.

NOTES

1. Higher education spends $150 billion (U.S. Department of Education, Press Release, August 23, 1990). Corporate training totals approximately $40 billion (Neil P. Eurich, *Corporate Classrooms: The Learning Business*. A Carnegie Foundation Special Report. Princeton: Carnegie Foundation for the Advancement of Teaching, 1984, p. 6).

2. For an elaboration on the distinctions between management and leadership, see Warren Bennis, *On Becoming a Leader* (Reading, MA: Addison-Wesley, 1989), 44–9; Warren Bennis and Burt

Nanus, *Leaders: The Strategies for Taking Charge* (New York: Harper & Row, 1985); Chris Argyris and Richard M. Cyert, *Leadership in the '80s: Essays on Higher Education* (Cambridge: Institute for Educational Management, Harvard University, 1980), 63; and Lewis B. Mayhew, *Surviving the Eighties: Strategies and Procedures for Solving Fiscal and Enrollment Problems* (San Francisco: Jossey-Bass, 1979), 74–5.

3. The higher education literature on leadership *development* for faculty and administrators (as opposed to the literature on leadership in general) is sparse. Some research on the outcomes of leadership development has been conducted on national programs such as the ACE Fellows Program or Harvard's Institute for Educational Management, and these studies generally focus on the perceptions of the participants or indicators of career mobility. The authors have drawn on their previous works (Green 1988; McDade 1987) as well as on the modest amount of existing research and publication in the corporate sector on the topic of leadership development.

REFERENCES

Argyris, Chris, and Richard M. Cyert. *Leadership in the '80s: Essays on Higher Education*. Cambridge: Institute for Educational Management, Harvard University, 1980.

Bennis, Warren, and Burt Nanus. *Leaders: The Strategies for Taking Charge*. New York: Harper and Row, 1985.

Burns, James MacGregor. *Leadership*. New York: Harper and Row, 1978.

Gardner, John W. *On Leadership*. New York: Free Press, 1990.

Green, Madeleine F., ed. *Leaders for a New Era: Strategies for Higher Education*. New York: American Council on Education/Macmillan, 1988.

Kotter, John P. "What Leaders Really Do." *Harvard Business Review* 68, no. 3 (May-June 1990): 103–111.

McDade, Sharon A. *Higher Education Leadership: Enhancing Skills through Professional Development Programs*. ASHE-ERIC Higher Education Report No. 5. Washington, DC: Association for the Study of Higher Education, 1987.

LEADERSHIP DEVELOPMENT: AN INSTITUTIONAL INVESTMENT

Central to this *Handbook* is the principle that leadership development benefits the institution as well as the individual. The connection between individual development and institutional effectiveness is not always obvious. For example, presidents frequently report that they send a senior administrator to a national program such as Harvard's Institute for Educational Management as a reward or as a way to make an effective person even sharper. Rarely does the sponsoring president anticipate how that experience might benefit other individuals and the institution as a whole or follow up on the experience once the individual returns to campus. Occasionally, leadership development is seen as a remedial effort, though the time and expense involved make this an unlikely way to deal with performance problems. At most institutions, budgets are perpetually lean. While it is hard to argue that leadership development is more important than salary increases, it is certainly not a frill. Leadership development is an investment both in the short-term effectiveness of an institution—increasing job performance and satisfaction—and in its long-range health—identifying and preparing people to assume greater responsibility and increase their contribution to the institution.

WHAT'S IN IT FOR US? BENEFITS TO THE INSTITUTION

Any organization that contemplates an investment of time or money must carefully weigh the potential costs and benefits. This is especially true when many priorities clamor for resources and attention. What, then, are the positive outcomes that warrant investing in leadership development?

Ensuring and Improving Competence

For starters, effective leaders must be competent; they must understand the institution, know their jobs, keep abreast of the latest information necessary to do their jobs, and know how to access the resources they need. No one starts a job knowing how to do everything well. Job competence is learned.

Matching Individual Needs and Strengths to the Institutional Agenda

People are a resource, and their energy can be frittered away just as money can. Making the best use of people's interests and talents is analogous to using money or space or any other resource wisely.

- *Putting people in the right job.* Conventional wisdom tells us about the importance of "match" in any job. People grow into and out of jobs. The most productive individuals are those who remain challenged and fully engaged. Individuals who are stuck or mismatched inevitably will operate at a lower energy level than they would if they were in the right job.

- *Maximizing people's strengths.* Often, work can be structured to make the best use of an individual's strengths and minimize his or her weaknesses. Duties within a unit can be distributed so that those with quantitative strengths and those with "people" skills each address the kinds of work for which they are best suited. The danger of this approach is that it does not encourage people to compensate for their weaknesses or to develop a different set of skills.

- *Growing your own.* Talented people do not simply appear. Hiring from the outside has the advantage of bringing in new blood, but it is expensive and time consuming. Sometimes new employees do not fit or are not as good as expected. Grooming talent on hand is an obvious alternative that gives people room to expand their jobs or move up.

- *Reducing turnover.* Turnover of personnel is costly. The absence of a worker lessens everyone else's effectiveness, and things tend to get put on hold until a replacement is found. The costs of recruiting and training new personnel are far greater than those of investing in the development of existing employees. Experienced workers are more productive. Studies show that it can take from one to three years to fully master a new job.

Fostering Shared Goals and Common Understanding

The forces in an institution that separate units and departments are more powerful than those that unite them. Higher education institutions are often referred to as "loosely coupled" organizations; that is, the connections between and among the units are slight. Specialization and institutional size compound the problem, and the sense of shared institutional purpose can be weak indeed.

A common agenda tends to lessen conflict. However, if people do not "own" an agenda, they will find ways to avoid implementing it. Activities such as workshops, retreats, and seminars can engage people in building or supporting a communal agenda. For example, if enhancing minority participation is an important institutional objective, faculty and staff must understand the issue and feel an obligation to contribute to the success of minority students. Thus, a workshop on cross-cultural communication might teach some specific information skills and at the same time promote personal involvement in changing institutional and individual behaviors.

- *Building teams.* Institutional management is highly dependent on team efforts. Some teams are permanent entities, such as the president's cabinet or the provost's staff. Other teams are formed to complete a particular task, such as the steering committee for an institutional self-study. All participants benefit from opportunities to concentrate on their purpose and to develop personal ties. Workshops, retreats, or short off-campus sessions that focus on the particular task or issue at hand are helpful. If individuals are to function as an ongoing team, they will benefit from explicitly defining how the team functions and the roles and contributions of each member.

- *Developing linkages across the institution.* Institutional units may have remarkably little contact with one another. For example, the physicists may have closer working relationships with their counterparts at other institutions, or in other countries, than with the faculty of the English department at their own institution. Academic, student affairs, business, and administrative departments also tend to operate independently of one another. Development activities break down these barriers by helping to reinforce a common purpose and provide a common language. For example, a time-management program for faculty and administrators from all units can have the felicitous side effect of introducing people from various parts of the institution to each other and of easing their future interactions. Such linkages are most often a by-product of activities with other central purposes. For example, including individuals from various parts of the institution on a search committee provides them with exposure to the position and functional area at hand, to the workings of that unit, and to their colleagues from other parts of the campus.

- *Improving communications.* People will always grumble about the quality and quantity of communication within an institution. Improving communications requires multiple and sustained efforts. The informal atmosphere of retreats and workshops eases communications and creates personal bonds that last long after the event. The process of defining a shared agenda or a plan to implement it often creates a common vocabulary, a "lingo" that becomes a recognized shorthand, or jokes that become part of the group's history.

Promoting Institutional Renewal

Board members, faculty, and staff who are highly motivated and who see the benefits of bringing in new ideas will enliven the institution and help keep it on the cutting edge.

- *Identifying new leaders.* It is easy to overlook talented individuals already on campus. People become identified with their current job responsibilities, and it may be difficult to imagine them in a different position. We also fail to groom our own "known quantities" for leadership positions because of the usually fanciful hope that some stranger will appear with just the right qualifications and the perfect fit. The position of affirmative action officer, for example, does not clearly lead to a next step; indeed, some affirmative action officers feel trapped in their jobs. Without a conscious strategy and some help from institutional leaders, professional moves can be very difficult. If an affirmative action officer shows promise as an administrator, why not provide some training opportunities in another area, such as planning or development? If he or she has an aptitude for the "people" side of administration, a move into student affairs might be appropriate. Any of these moves would be facilitated by some preparation— perhaps an academic credential, an opportunity to exchange jobs for a brief period, or a part-time internship.

- *Introducing new ideas.* Faculty and staff who are bored or burned out will not generate new ideas or even have the energy to implement existing ones. New ideas generated by travel, sabbaticals, or opportunities to confer with colleagues keep people and their institutions vibrant and open to change.

Promoting Pluralism

The boards, faculties, and staffs of our campuses are still overwhelmingly white and male. Few of our institutions are truly pluralistic. Leadership development efforts can contribute to the diversification of the talent pool in several ways.

- *Identifying promising women and minority administrators.* Here again, the first place to look for talent is on campus. Are there faculty members who can take a leadership role in the faculty or be groomed for administrative positions? Are there lower-level administrators or entry-level professionals who could handle more responsibility with or without additional training or educational preparation? A frequent obstacle to identifying able women and minority administrators and staff is the difficulty we have in moving people out of their professional boxes and providing opportunities for them to develop new expertise. Research shows that women and minorities are usually evaluated and promoted based on past accomplishments, while white men tend to be evaluated and promoted based on perceptions of future potential. Development opportunities provide a way to turn accomplishments into potential.

- *Supporting different styles and perspectives.* As institutions make serious efforts to become pluralistic, the members of the campus community must learn to adjust to a different environment. They must become aware of their attitudes and the assumptions that govern their conduct. Some behaviors must change. Changing behaviors involves educating people and making them aware of the adjustments required to work with those who have different perspectives, life experiences, expectations, and assumptions. To assume that all of this can occur spontaneously, in the normal course of business, is to underestimate the magnitude of the task.

- *Helping faculty and administrators to serve new populations of students.* Increasingly, college students are older, part time, or minority. If institutions are to serve the needs of this "new majority," they will need to change what they teach and how they teach it, as well as the administrative structures that support learning. All this requires readjusting definitions and expectations and learning how to operate in a different environment.

Achieving Institutional Change

There is a natural tendency to resist change. For enduring change to occur, people must see the need for it; they must share the vision for any new institutional direction and participate willingly in its implementation. Leadership development can serve as a catalyst for change by introducing new ideas and creating a new perspective. Individuals who are expanding their horizons are likely to see new possibilities and to want to do things differently. Leadership development fuels both individual creativity and institutional change.

OBSTACLES: MYTH AND REALITY

If leadership development is so beneficial to institutions and to individuals, why do we do so little of it in higher education? Certainly, there are many obstacles to leadership development, and nearly as many limits to what it can accomplish. While some obstacles are real, others are more a question of attitude and priorities. Sometimes the myths are more powerful than the realities.

MYTH: The Return on Investment in Leadership Development Is Not Worth It.

The outcomes of leadership development are not easily quantifiable. In that sense, it is like liberal education: we cannot measure the results with precision. But it stands to reason that helping people become more knowledgeable and creative can only benefit the institution. Surveys of participants in professional development programs strongly indicate that they learn skills and knowledge and develop understanding of issues and problems that help them directly in their work.

MYTH: Leadership Is an Art, and Therefore Unteachable.

This belief is closely related to the "leaders are born, not made" assumption. Those who believe leadership is purely an art form maintain that it cannot be analyzed and its various components cannot be taught. While leadership is not entirely rational, neither is it totally mysterious. Some aspects of leadership can be taught through formal and informal means.

MYTH: Anyone Can Be an Administrator.

While leadership is hardly the sole province of administrators, administrative leadership is a central focus of this book. Some would call it a necessary evil; others would go further and see administration as an obstacle to the true business of education. If administration is not valued, then preparation for administration or development in that role cannot be valued. This is a popular but dangerous view—it encourages people to underestimate the difficulty of the tasks and to turn their backs on potential sources of help. How often do we hear of the excellent professor who turned out to be a disaster as a dean? Because administration requires specific abilities, excellence as a professor does not ensure the same quality as an administrator. A value system that denigrates or minimizes the importance of administrative leadership can result in costly mistakes.

MYTH: Hiring Good People Is Sufficient.

Put another way, good people will perform effectively, and ineffective people are beyond help. True, institutions need good material to develop as board members, faculty, and administrators. But this static view of people ignores the potential for human growth and change that is vital to institutional health.

MYTH: If Institutions Invest in People, They Lose Them to Better Jobs.

Though sometimes true, this statement does not have to be a reality and frequently is not. Able people inevitably seek new challenges, but those challenges are not necessarily found only in another institution. Through job expansion, new assignments, and sometimes new positions within the institution, an individual can continue to expand profession- ally and contribute to the institution. Career development can comprise lateral moves that provide new opportunities and open new career paths, as well as vertical moves, and those opportunities can be at one's own institution or elsewhere. Granted, a longer-term perspective on leadership development may be a difficult stance to take, but all higher education benefits from a pool of good leaders and well-trained people. Critics of American business decry the overemphasis on short-term gains; certainly, institutions of higher education should be in the busi- ness of taking the long view.

MYTH: It's Too Expensive.

Leadership development can be high cost, low cost, or no cost. Extended workshops and programs are admittedly expensive in time, tuition, and travel. Other efforts—on-campus programs, internships, new assignments—bear little or no cost. Whatever the out-of-pocket costs, institutions can take steps to ensure that the benefits of a particular expe- rience go beyond the individual. Part Three outlines specific ways for individuals to incorporate their professional development experiences into their working lives and into the goals of the unit. Furthermore, there are costs of *not* paying attention to leadership development: turn- over, costly searches, institutional stasis, and individual burnout.

REALITY: There Is No Plan.

Most administrators report that leadership development is conducted on an *ad hoc* basis. Few institutions have an institutional plan or money reserved for the purpose. Thus, support for any kind of leadership development (external or in-house) will depend on the information coming across administrators' desks, money left in the budget, and a variety of other unpredictable factors.

There are numerous reasons for neglecting leadership development. Most of them are rooted in short-term thinking or in acceptance of the myths that present leadership in general as unteachable and administrative leadership in particular as unworthy of deliberate preparation. The obstacles cited are familiar, reflecting the mythical notion that, by some mysterious process, leadership will emerge and flourish on its own.

The following section provides guidelines on developing a plan that will counter the tendency for leadership development to be episodic and idiosyncratic rather than integral to the institutional plan.

GETTING THERE: DEVELOPING AN INSTITUTIONAL PLAN

It is not easy to change the way we do things; it is especially difficult to *institutionalize* change. Institutionalizing a commitment to fostering leadership poses a particular problem, since everyone—and therefore no one—is responsible. Leadership development usually has no organizational home. Some large institutions have human resource departments. Sometimes, but not always, they are concerned with professional development. Frequently, their target group is administrative personnel. On the academic side of the house, the vice president and deans have responsibility for their own development and for that of their staffs; chairs oversee faculty development. Such decentralization has the advantage of promoting responsive decision making, but the price is lack of either coordination or an overarching game plan.

Strategies for Success

Any institutional leadership initiative, whether it concerns developing a strategic plan, recruiting minority students and faculty, or incorporating leadership development into the institutional agenda, will be guided by some basic principles. The following strategies should help make leadership development an ongoing institutional concern rather than an uneven and marginal undertaking.

- *Inventory current practices.* If administrators are asked what their institution does in the area of leadership development, they will often point to a series of unrelated indicators (e.g., the number of in-house programs offered, the number of people sent off to national institutes) and opportunities (e.g., a program offered for department chairs, a

faculty internship program, occasional sabbaticals for administrators).
Pulling together all this information at the school or institutional level
is an essential first step in determining if any connection among the
various opportunities and plans exists and if there is any match
between institutional goals and individual development
opportunities.

- *Incorporate leadership development into institutional planning and
decision making.* In light of the fact that leadership development is
seen as peripheral to institutional goals, it is not surprising that it is
not integrated into institutional planning. Integration requires weav-
ing new questions into the process, such as: What human resources
will be required to implement the plan? Do we currently have these
resources? Will we have them in one, two, or five years? If not, are
there persons already at the institution who can play a role in implementing the plan? What training and additional work experiences will
they need?

- *Develop a comprehensive plan.* In most institutions, leadership development takes place haphazardly. Because decision making is generally
decentralized, so are leadership development efforts. One person will
ask to be sent to a national workshop, another will decide to sign up
for a program offered on campus. Some deans will see a need to provide training for department chairs, others will not. While the structure and tradition of many institutions would not welcome centralized
decision making on leadership development, it is important to have an
explicit institutional philosophy and a plan, articulated by the president and senior officers. Department or unit plans should include
goals for faculty and staff development as well as strategies and funds
to support these goals.

- *To the extent possible, match institutional needs with individual
needs.* Organizations are untidy, and perfect synchronization between
institutional and individual needs is not always possible. A good plan
will assess the institution's needs at a given point in time and compare
them with the available talent and potential and the developmental
needs of faculty and staff. Is the faculty graying and highly tenured?
What are the implications of projected turnover for faculty leadership?
Is a capital campaign in the winds? If so, what is the current staffing in
the development office? Are there junior people who could be prepared for greater responsibility? Will new staff be needed?

- *Exercise leadership from the top.* Mobilizing a campus to overcome its
natural inertia is a central task of leaders. If leadership development is
to be an explicit institutional commitment, it should be practiced at the
highest levels and encouraged throughout the institution. Boards and
presidents must pay attention to their own effectiveness and vitality
and develop strategies for ensuring that others have opportunities to

improve their skills and to obtain new ideas and perspectives. If the president's and vice presidents' efforts (such as taking time for scholarship or attending off-campus programs) are seen as legitimate and important for the institution, the tone will be set for others to be equally serious and deliberate. On the other hand, if institutional leaders communicate the notion that professional development is a nuisance or a boondoggle, any efforts in that direction throughout the institution will be seriously hampered.

- *Ensure grass-roots involvement in leadership.* While setting the tone and establishing priorities may come from the top, implementation is the task of various units. Leadership development efforts must be suited to the needs of the participants. The more an activity is ''owned'' by those participating in it, the greater its likelihood of success.

- *Demonstrate the benefits of leadership development.* If leadership development initiatives are not beneficial to the institution or to its members, or if the costs clearly outweigh the benefits, then there is no incentive to put them on anyone's agenda. If leaders are to change the way they view leadership development, they will do so out of a combination of enlightened self-interest and a view of the benefits to the institution as a whole.

- *Make it positive, not punitive.* Leadership development should be viewed as a way of improving effectiveness and increasing job satisfaction, not as remediation. That means creating a positive climate for leadership development with enthusiastic endorsement from the top.

- *Develop appropriate goals and workable structures.* Any new direction or undertaking, including leadership development, must be consonant with an institution's history, values, and culture. Sometimes institutions are not successful in addressing a new issue or problem because the structure they develop is wrong for the campus, or the approach they take is at odds with campus culture. For example, at some institutions, forming a broad-based committee on faculty and staff development might not work. Developing consensus and moving ahead may be too cumbersome, especially in a decentralized institution. Some institutions will find it preferable to create new structures, such as a committee or task force; others will want to use existing mechanisms.

- *Allocate sufficient resources.* Some of the strategies that institutions can develop will cost money; others will not. Leadership development will have to compete with other priorities in the short term. But leadership development is not an end in itself; it is an investment that will assist in reaching other institutional goals.

- *Set explicit goals and hold people accountable.* As with any other element of planning, individual units should determine their specific objectives in concert with broader school-wide or institutional goals. A criterion for assessing the performance of supervisors should be their progress in facilitating the development of subordinates. Evaluation can ensure that plans are implemented and revised as necessary.

- *Provide incentives.* People need incentives to behave differently. If the status quo is comfortable, why change? If supervisors are rewarded for encouraging the development of others, they will be more likely to do so. Rewards might take the form of a positive factor in one's performance evaluation, public recognition, or the allocation of additional resources to further leadership development efforts. Similarly, individuals who are growing and improving can be rewarded with merit pay, additional development opportunities, and job enrichment or promotion.

- *Evaluate institutional efforts.* Multiple sources of information—evaluations of various efforts by participants and by supervisors—should be used. The various leadership development activities available (in-house programs, national institutes and programs, sabbaticals) should be assessed to determine which are more effective and which are most cost-effective.

CHECKLIST OF INSTITUTIONAL POLICIES AND PRACTICES

Policies

- Does the institution have explicit policies regarding leadership development? If yes, what are their goals?
- Are the policies disseminated broadly and often (at least annually) to faculty and administrators?
- Does the institution link leadership development to policies? For example, to the broader goal of improving minority participation on campus?
- Do individual units have leadership development plans? Are they linked to institutional goals?

Practices

- Is there a single person or office that coordinates leadership development activities throughout the institution? Are there sufficient resources and authority to be effective? If not, why not? Would designating a responsible person be a desirable option at the institution? Are there other coordinating mechanisms? How do they operate? Are academic and administrative personnel included in them? Are senior officers?

- How does the campus identify people with leadership potential? What happens to them once identified?

- How and why are people selected to participate in formal leadership development programs (either on campus or off campus)? Is the selection process succeeding in casting the net widely?

- How are people prepared to get the most out of a leadership development program? How do they share what they have learned from a program with others on campus?

- Are there special efforts in place to identify promising women and minority individuals? To ensure that they have opportunities for leadership development and job enhancement?

- Are administrators expected to engage in professional development activities? Is this expectation reflected in performance evaluation criteria?

- Is there planning for leadership development? Is it linked to the overall institutional plan? Tied to specific institutional objectives? Are there mechanisms for reviewing and modifying the plan and for assessing progress?

- Is information on leadership development activities disseminated throughout the campus? On the costs associated with these activities? Who gathers this information? How is it used?

- Is there a mechanism for evaluating the effectiveness of the leadership development plan? Have criteria of effectiveness been formulated? How?

AN INSTITUTIONAL PLAN:
LOYOLA COLLEGE OF MARYLAND

In its strategic plan developed in 1989, Loyola College specified personal and professional development as one of its seven institutional goals: "In the tradition of *cura personalis* Loyola will provide its faculty, staff, administration, and alumni with opportunities for personal and professional development and active participation in the life of the College" (Loyola College 1989). The plan specifies eight objectives to meet this goal. The first deals with setting targets for faculty, and eventually administrative compensation *vis-à-vis* its peer institutions. The second and third goals deal with the importance of teaching, scholarly research, and publication and specify ways to enhance these areas, including sabbaticals, summer research, and support for attendance at scholarly meetings.

Its fourth objective addresses staff development, affirming that it will "[p]rovide opportunities and encouragement for professional development for staff." To accomplish this goal, the college will provide funds, release time, and on-campus opportunities. In addition, the plan specifies the development of a training function within the personnel office to coordinate training opportunities for staff and administration.

The fifth objective addresses administrator development, outlining the same approaches designed for the staff. Other objectives under the general goal of providing opportunities for personal and professional development include ensuring a pleasant and productive work environment, providing avenues for all groups at the college to participate actively in the life of the institution, and providing opportunities for the alumni to remain active in the life of the institution. Contact: Kathleen Donofrio, Director of Personnel, Loyola College in Maryland, 4501 North Charles Street, Baltimore, MD 21210, (301) 323–1010.

REFERENCES

Loyola College. "Strategic Plan." Baltimore: Loyola College, 1989. Photocopy.

RESOURCES

Argyris, Chris, and Richard M. Cyert. *Leadership in the '80s: Essays on Higher Education*. Cambridge: Institute for Educational Management, Harvard University, 1980.

This slim volume of essays on leadership and management in higher education is still a classic. The Argyris essay on "Educating Administrators and Professionals" presents the author's theories on the limitations of single-loop and strengths of double-loop learning in organizations. He argues that organizations need to become learning systems. The challenges to leadership of colleges and universities in the 1980s that Cyert cites are still accurate today: leadership in uncertainty, in strategy, and for excellence. Both authors argue that for colleges and universities to be effective, they must invest in the leadership development of their faculty, staff, and administrators.

Green, Madeleine F., ed. *Leaders for a New Era: Strategies for Higher Education*. New York: American Council on Education/Macmillan, 1988.

This books faces head-on the problems of identifying and developing leaders in higher education institutions. The book covers the entire gamut of college and university leaders: faculty, department chairs, and administrators. There are also chapters on issues such as team development, use of professional development programs, selecting leaders, and leadership for women and minorities.

Harvard Business Review. *Harvard Business Review on Human Relations*. Cambridge, MA: The President and Fellows of Harvard College, 1986.

This volume includes 11 essays related to leadership within organizations from the pages of *The Harvard Business Review*. Half of the essays deal specifically with issues of leadership in relationship to people within the organization, in areas such as motivation theory, performance appraisal, and communication. The other essays deal with issues of leadership and organizations, including power, dependence, politics, and creativity. Although written entirely from the perspective of business and corporations, the essays have great relevance to the academy.

McDade, Sharon A. *Higher Education Leadership: Enhancing Skills through Professional Development Programs*. ASHE-ERIC Education Report No. 5. Washington, DC: Association for the Study of Higher Education, 1987.

This overview of leadership development in higher education explores the career paths to administration and the skills and knowledge required for executive positions. Of particular note is a section that details the benefits and problems of participation in leadership development programs and activities, for both the institution and the individual, and an extensive examination of the types of programming available in higher education. The book concludes with a discussion of the leadership development challenges that face higher education administrators.

3

THE INDIVIDUAL PERSPECTIVE: DEVELOPING LEADERSHIP CAPACITIES

W e have already noted that not all aspects of leadership can be taught. Judgment, values, courage, integrity, and creativity can be tested or nurtured but cannot be conferred on a leader or acquired at will.

However, the tasks of leadership can be described and analyzed, and we can identify the skills and capacities required to perform those tasks. We also can develop strategies for individuals to enhance their own development and for institutions to foster a climate that encourages learning.

What are the tasks of today's higher education leaders? What capacities—skills and abilities—must leaders have to be effective in the current environment? Which of these capacities are susceptible to purposeful development?

In general, all academic leaders perform the tasks described in the following section. The importance of any particular task will vary, depending on the institution and the position. This list forms the basis for future chapters that discuss the development of leaders occupying different positions in the institution.

LEADERSHIP TASKS AND CAPACITIES

Envisioning a Future

- *Tasks.* Leaders build for the future on a foundation securely rooted in the institution's history. They do not necessarily do this alone; often, they sharpen and articulate a collective vision or suggest ideas to be redefined or modified by constituents. In envisioning the future they may define a mission, set priorities, communicate a sense of direction, and empower others to take initiative.

- *Capacities.* People who can establish a vision are able to imagine possibilities, sort through large amounts of information, and make connections among disparate bits of information. These leaders can see the forest beyond the trees; they can assemble the pieces to create a whole greater than the sum of its parts. Imagination, foresight, intellectual curiosity, and risk-taking are frequently associated with vision.

- *Development.* Can people be taught to be imaginative or bold? Probably not. Can they be helped to unleash their creativity? Yes. Leaders who nurture their continued intellectual vitality, who maintain broad interests, and who develop the capacities we associate with a liberal education are likely to be able to absorb and sort through new information, make connections, and see possibilities for the future. A fertile and active mind, a finger on the pulse of the institution and the larger community, and the deliberate pursuit of new ideas and information are the underpinnings of vision.

Shaping and Interpreting Values and Culture

- *Tasks.* Shaping institutional culture is an intangible part of leadership that involves using symbolism, articulating values, and setting the tone. From department chair to university president, the leader's role is symbolic as well as functional. Faculty respond to the office of president or dean as much as to the actions of the individual in that office. Leaders live in the same culture that they are creating. To modify and reshape that culture, they must learn its rules, myths, rituals, and symbols, or they may violate the norms of the community and thus hamper their own effectiveness. Understanding the symbolic nature of leadership and the task of shaping the culture and values of an institution are central to effective leadership.

- *Capacities.* Shaping and interpreting meaning requires the ability to read the environment and learn the culture. These are largely cognitive tasks: watching, listening, asking questions, establishing a frame of reference, interpreting. More subtly, however, these tasks demand genuine willingness to understand an environment rather than impose one's wishful thinking on reality. Individuals who are learners and who can see things from several points of view are more likely to be successful at managing meaning. Leaders also must be able to make their convictions and goals real and understandable to others—to speak persuasively, to communicate their enthusiasm, and to inspire.

- *Development.* People who are genuinely interested in listening can deliberately develop and practice the capacities listed above. Soliciting feedback and encouraging dissonant points of view can enhance one's ability to decode the environment and compensate for one's blind spots. The mechanical elements of communication can be taught: people can learn to speak more clearly, to be mindful of the rhythm and cadence of their speech, and to look their audience in the eye. But the qualities of enthusiasm, hope, and conviction must be innate.

Managing and Decision Making

- *Tasks.* To turn a vision into reality, leaders must set priorities; determine directions; motivate others; establish plans, strategies, and procedures; and acquire and allocate resources. The more senior their position, the more they delegate these tasks, but they are still responsible for these functions. At every level, leaders must make decisions that move things in the desired direction. Though management is most frequently associated with operations, the aggregate of management decisions and procedures also performs leadership functions, translating a vision into practical applications.

- *Capacities.* A broad range of knowledge and skills is required to execute these management functions: knowledge of how the institution works, planning and organizing techniques, and technical mastery of relevant information such as budgeting, personnel management, collective bargaining, and fund raising.

- *Development.* Most leadership development efforts aim to develop management skills. The informational and procedural aspects of management—budgeting, planning, organizing—are reasonably concrete and easy to teach. Since information is the central business of the academy, management training that deals with acquiring needed information is generally considered a reasonable and legitimate pursuit. Learning the processes of management—organizing and decision making, for example—often carries less legitimacy, since these "mere" administrative skills "should" be easy for intelligent people to acquire.

Working With People

- *Tasks.* People are at the heart of management and leadership. Hiring people, motivating and supervising them, developing their abilities and improving their performance, resolving conflict, and providing a satisfying work environment are among the many "people" tasks of leadership. Assembling and managing an effective team is a key ability for today's leader.

- *Capacities.* Generally (but not always), leaders have good interpersonal skills and enjoy the human interaction that is central to exercising leadership. Interest in people is only a starting point, however. Leaders must communicate effectively both orally and in writing; they must understand their own strengths and weaknesses and select people who complement them. Knowing oneself, listening to and understanding others, and tolerating differences are important leadership capacities. Working effectively with people also entails an intangible capacity known as judgment—knowing when to move and when to delay, discerning what is important and what is transitory.

- *Development.* Again, this requires a combination of innate talent—an interest in and ability to understand others—and learned skills. Communication skills can be learned through practice and coaching. Workshops, seminars, and observation of others can teach such skills as negotiation, conflict resolution, and team building. Other ''people skills,'' such as supervising, providing feedback, and motivating others, are also teachable to a certain extent, but receive less attention in formal training. Academics tend to consider these skills self-evident and less worthy of study than ''hard'' information.

Understanding Oneself

- *Tasks.* The most effective individuals in the interpersonal arena know themselves, their values, and their strengths and weaknesses. They can maximize their strengths while compensating for their weaknesses. They have a clear value system that guides them in their decision making and provides a steady point of moral reference. They know where they are headed, what they can reasonably push themselves to accomplish, and what their limitations are. People who are unrealistic or confused about who they are and what they want are unlikely to be effective in their relationships with others in the workplace.

- *Capacities.* The capacities required for self-awareness are similar to those needed to be effective with others. Understanding of self starts with an ability to hear what other people are saying to us about us. Sometimes feedback is deliberate (''I wish you wouldn't keep hovering over me every time you give an assignment''); other times it is indirect or disguised (''It's just another ordinary crisis around here, business as usual''). Others tell us in many ways what we are like to work with, but we must be able to hear that message—and be willing to use that information constructively. Openness to new experiences and the ability to listen to others and to the environment are central to developing self-understanding. People who are self-aware are often willing to be vulnerable, to be open enough so that others are frank with them.

- *Development.* Bosses, peers, and subordinates are important sources of feedback on the job; friends and family are also contributors. Self-understanding also is brought about by a variety of life experiences— new situations, stress, mistakes, successes. Some leadership development programs enable participants to gain insight into their behaviors and styles, using questionnaires and other instruments to profile an individual's preferences and strengths. The Center for Creative Leadership, a nonprofit organization in Greensboro, North Carolina, that conducts research on leadership and offers leadership development programs to corporate and other executives, sponsors a number of programs that enhance self-awareness in the work setting.

HOW DO LEADERS LEARN?

We tend to equate leadership development with formal training. However, formal courses or national programs constitute only one method, one that touches relatively few administrators in any given year (though that impact is multiplied over time). Leadership development activities can be divided into three general categories: formal programs (on campus and off), on-the-job training (structured and informal), and individual initiatives.

Formal Programs

Programs sponsored by employing institutions or outside organizations permit systematic exploration of a topic in a setting that encourages learning from peers. Classroom experiences can range from a one-day workshop to a four-week residential program.

- *Short workshops and seminars.* A look at the *Chronicle of Higher Education* quickly reveals the wide array of short courses sponsored by a variety of associations, colleges and universities, consulting firms, and private companies. Many are regional or state based. Some workshops are organized by issue, such as adult learning, technology, or curriculum. Others are directed to people holding particular jobs: department chairs, deans, or financial aid officers. These programs constitute an important resource that enables individuals to obtain timely information and compare roles with colleagues who have similar interests. Sponsoring organizations include the National Association of College and University Business Officers (NACUBO), the Association of Governing Boards of Universities and Colleges (AGB), the Center for Creative Leadership, the American Management Association (AMA), and the American Council on Education (ACE).

- *Administrative conferences.* Varying from several days to less than two weeks, these programs generally are sponsored by institutions or professional associations. They are similar to the shorter seminars, and participants may be drawn from the same functional area, administrative level, or type of institution. These programs focus on management tasks and leadership responsibilities in the context of an institutional type or functional area. Some, such as the American Association of State Colleges and Universities' (AASCU's) program for academic vice presidents, the American Conference of Academic Deans' (ACAD's) seminar, or the National Association of Student Personnel Administrators' (NASPA's) Richard F. Stevens Institute, are annual events, and administrators may attend regularly or periodically for leadership renewal.

- *Conventions of national associations.* Nearly all national associations sponsor annual meetings and other periodic conferences. They generally have no restrictions on who can participate. While national meetings often have a theme, they tend to cover a broader spectrum of higher education issues than workshops or seminars and rely on panel sessions, keynote speakers, and position papers. Conferences are useful for a quick overview of new issues and the latest thinking as well as for the informal contacts and hallway conversations that characterize these meetings. Meetings of the American Association for Higher Education (AAHE), ACE, or the American Association of Community and Junior Colleges (AACJC) draw a wide variety of individuals, including presidents, deans, and faculty. Annual conferences of NASPA or the Council for Advancement and Support of Education (CASE) generally attract professionals in their respective fields.

- *National institutes and internships.* Longer than the typical workshops mentioned above, these institutes are at least two weeks in length or meet regularly as a class over a year. Sponsored by universities and higher education associations, they usually require institutional nomination or endorsement and have a competitive admissions process. Their curricula generally include higher education issues, planning and financial management, and organizational theory and skills. Examples of such programs are Harvard's Institute for Educational Management (IEM), ACE's Fellows Program, and the Higher Education Resource Service (HERS) at Bryn Mawr and Wellesley, all described in the *Programs and Practices* sections of other chapters in this handbook.

- *Programs for executives in business.* Some senior administrators find it useful to enroll in programs whose primary audiences are executives from the corporate sector. Varying in length from several weeks to an academic year, these programs enable higher education executive officers to gain a very different perspective on their positions and institutions. The curricula are geared toward chief executive officers and senior administrators and provide a corporate perspective on many of the same topics as the national institutes offer. Examples include Harvard's Advanced Management Program, Cornell's Executive Development Program, and the Massachusetts Institute of Technology's Sloan School of Management Executive Development Programs.

- *In-house courses and workshops.* Sponsoring on-campus programs for faculty and administrators can be more cost-effective and can also increase the impact of a given training activity. It is often difficult to integrate into the familiar work setting the knowledge, skills, and insights gained from off-site training, particularly when colleagues have not had the benefit of the same experience. A program for all members of a work unit can provide a common language and a shared experience, and can help establish and clarify team goals. Creating a program for the entire staff of the advancement division or for all department chairs also can have distinct advantages, in terms of time and money saved and in team building. Another option is to offer a series of classes to develop job skills, such as computer proficiency, supervision, or public speaking. Michigan State University, George Washington University, and the Maricopa Community Colleges circulate listings of such offerings to all employees.

On-the-Job Training

Formal programs such as those described above can only supplement the primary source of learning: the job. Some on-the-job learning is gained through deliberate coaching or developmental assignments, but most learning takes place in a less systematic way, through observation, experience, and mistakes. Chapter 14, *On-Campus Development: The Workplace as Learning Environment*, discusses how the workplace can be a learning environment: jobs can be used as developmental experiences by adding responsibilities, creating special assignments, providing training, rotating responsibilities, providing coaching and feedback, and creating formal or informal mentoring relationships.

Individual Initiatives

Warren Bennis (1989, p. 42) emphasizes the importance of individual initiative in leadership development, claiming that "true leaders are not born, but made, and usually self-made. Leaders invent themselves." However, there are limits to this philosophy. Leaders in organizations are products of the environment and the culture in which they lead. Institutions that do not foster or permit leadership will find themselves without it; their leaders will have moved on or failed. But to the extent that people create learning opportunities for themselves, broaden their horizons, step forward, and learn from their experiences, they are seeing to their own leadership development.

WHAT DO INDIVIDUALS GAIN FROM LEADERSHIP DEVELOPMENT EXPERIENCES?

Before embarking on a leadership development activity, it is useful to determine the benefits to be gained from the experience. With planning, it is possible to weave the lessons of experience (McCall, Lombardo, and Morrison 1988) into on-campus programming and on-the-job development to mutually benefit both the individual and the institution. Many lessons lend themselves to classroom learning and discussion; others may best be advanced through attention to on-the-job experiences. The best strategy will involve a combination of both tactics in a thoughtful, long-range human resource development plan.

Chapter 2, *Leadership Development: An Institutional Investment*, discussed the potential outcomes of leadership development that are important to the overall effectiveness of the institution. Following is an outline of what individuals can gain from various experiences.

Benefits of Leadership Development Programs

- *New skills and knowledge.* Today's administrators need a broad range of expertise ranging from planning and budgeting skills to legal savvy and computer literacy. Another set of needed competencies deals with people skills—motivating, supervising, communicating, and team building.

- *Stimulation and renewal.* Meeting new people and being exposed to new ideas are stimulating and can help people see old issues and problems in a new light. Renewal is particularly important in the academy, since upward mobility is limited for most people. People in all organizations, including colleges and universities, inevitably reach a structural career plateau, though different individuals reach it at different points in their careers. Leadership development can help in two ways. First, it can create job enrichment, so that moving "up" or "out" are not the only options. Second, by paying more attention to the relationship between career mobility and leadership development, institutions can move people laterally, shift responsibilities to keep them challenged, and provide the breadth of vision that is integral to leadership.

- *Contacts and networking.* Though not always an explicit aim of leadership development, meeting and exchanging views with one's counterparts are an important benefit. These opportunities are particularly important for presidents and senior administrators, who are unique on their campuses. Colleagues on other campuses form important support systems for information and for personal and professional assistance. The development of strong friendships and support networks is particularly notable in the longer, more intense leadership development programs.

- *Reflection and perspective.* The administrative life is one of countless meetings, deadlines, and production, leaving too little time for reading, writing, reflection, or planning. Leadership experiences away from the campus provide needed respites from pressure and routine, as well as time to consider problems thoughtfully with colleagues to see how similar issues are played out in different contexts. Certainly, programs such as the Troutbeck seminars (described in Chapter 5, *Presidents*), with their emphases on reading classical texts and reflecting on larger intellectual issues, are ideally suited to such renewal. But even the more management-oriented workshops and seminars provide new ways to conceptualize issues, gain new perspectives, and think and discuss, rather than do. Travel, time away from the job to write or reflect, and opportunities to interact with thoughtful people outside higher education are perhaps the most important avenues of self-renewal.

- *Increased self-confidence.* Academic leaders learn as they go, rarely having systematic preparation for their leadership roles. Leadership development experiences help them sort out what they know (often more than they suspected) from what they do not know. For new administrators especially, formal programs can provide a frame of reference, knowledge of resources for help and information, and the sense that their jobs are manageable.

Lessons From On-the-Job Leadership Development[1]

The most important lessons of leadership are learned on the job. Formal programs and other types of instruction can provide important information and knowledge that can be applied in the workplace. But leaders learn the most from their interactions with others, by watching successful and not-so-successful leaders in action, and from their own mistakes. Chapter 14, *On-Campus Development: The Workplace as Learning Environment*, describes ways in which jobs can be purposefully developmental. The following list outlines the lessons that can be learned from experience.

- *Setting and implementing agendas.* Creating an agenda for an institution is a central leadership task requiring an understanding of the present, a vision for the future, and the ability to envision the path between the two. Setting an institutional agenda requires understanding of the broader context in which the institution functions and the ability to think strategically about the institution and its environment. Implementing the agenda requires a different set of skills: motivating others, making decisions and taking responsibility for them, and building and using effective structures and control systems. It also includes learning about shouldering the full responsibility for projects and decisions, building and using structure and control systems specifically tied to a project, and conceiving innovative solutions and problem-solving methods under pressure.

- *Handling relationships.* Developmental programs can offer a perspective on the "people" challenges of leadership, but it is on the job that these lessons must be applied and abilities refined. Such "people skills" include handling political situations, getting people to implement solutions, negotiating, dealing with conflict, directing and motivating subordinates, and confronting staff performance problems. "People skills" also include learning how to deal with a wide range of people and how to understand their perspectives. They include students, faculty, and staff; the various internal and external constituencies of a higher education institution; former bosses and peers such as faculty colleagues; and people over whom one has no authority.

- *Basic values.* Leadership programming may play an important role in helping individuals identify and articulate their basic values, but it is on the job that these basic leadership and administrative values are tested and refined. The workplace is where the individual discovers the impossibility of managing everything alone, develops a sympathy to the human side of leadership, and cultivates a sensitivity to and knowledge of the institutional mission.

- *Leadership temperament.* On-the-job experiences teach one how to be tough when necessary, how to cope with ambiguous situations or situations beyond one's control, how to persevere through adversity, and how to use—and not abuse—power. Practical experience reinforces the lessons learned in formal training sessions.

- *Personal awareness.* While the experiences that prompt personal awareness usually happen on the job, the realization of such awareness will more often take place in conversation with mentors, supervisors, colleagues, and friends. Awareness tends to come in "aha" moments of quiet conversation and personal reflection. Leaders need to explore their personal limits and blind spots and the balance between work and personal life. Personal awareness also means knowing what really excites one about work, taking charge of one's career, and recognizing and seizing opportunities.

CONCLUSION

While leadership is greater than the sum of the tasks or attributes of a leader, it *is* possible to analyze what leaders do and to identify experiences that can prepare them for their roles.

Leadership development begins early in life with the educational process and in opportunities to take initiative and test one's abilities. And indeed, the development of leaders is a continuous process even in adult life, fostered by job challenges, intellectual stimulation, and relationships with others. Formal development activities are a small but important part of leadership development, just as attending classes represents only one component of a student's learning. A partnership in which the institution cultivates a learning environment for faculty, staff, and administrators while its employees take charge of their own growth will result in a cadre of leaders to guide that institution into the future.

NOTES

1. The Center for Creative Leadership in Greensboro, North Carolina, has conducted significant research on how and what executives learn on the job. McCall and colleagues identified five areas, titled "the potential lessons of experience," that represent the "fundamental executive skills and ways of thinking needed for effective corporate leadership" (McCall, Lombardo, and Morrison 1988, p. 7). These lessons, adapted to higher education, emphasize the basic skills and knowledge that all leaders must master, regardless of type of organization.

REFERENCES

Bennis, Warren. *On Becoming a Leader*. Reading, MA: Addison-Wesley, 1989.

McCall, Morgan W., Jr., Michael M. Lombardo, and Ann M. Morrison. *The Lessons of Experience: How Successful Executives Develop on the Job*. Lexington, MA: Lexington Books, 1988.

RESOURCES

Bennis, Warren. *On Becoming a Leader*. Reading, MA: Addison-Wesley, 1989.

Bennis, the former president of the University of Cincinnati, has built on his first-hand experiences to explore leadership through a series of provocative books and articles. Based on the premise that most people have the capacity for leadership, this book examines the process of becoming a leader. From interviews with leaders from all walks of life, he analyzes the leadership process, the ingredients of leadership, and the ways leaders can learn about themselves and their world through self-discovery and understanding. Of particular note is a final chapter on how organizations can help their members become leaders.

Gardner, John W. *On Leadership*. New York: Free Press, 1990.

Through anecdotes and historical references, Gardner explores the nature, tasks, contexts, moral dimensions, and attributes of leadership. He pays particular attention to the issues of leadership development in chapters on youth, life-long growth, and executive renewal. Other key chapters investigate leadership in the context of community, large-scale organizations, motivation, and power.

McCall, Morgan W., Jr., Michael M. Lombardo, and Ann M. Morrison. *The Lessons of Experience: How Successful Executives Develop on the Job*. Lexington, MA: Lexington Books, 1988.

Many have written about leadership development based on interviews and first-hand experience. This book is the first large-scale attempt to document leadership development through more rigorous research methods. Although not specifically cast in terms of leadership development, this book examines the experiences that had the greatest impact on the careers of successful executives in major corporations. They distilled a number of key events and experiences common to these careers that had major impact on development. They present these ideas as themes for the creation, implementation, and improvement of both organizational development programming and individual career planning. For those interested in the mechanics of this study, complimentary technical reports both detailing the research and building upon the research are available from the Center for Creative Research, 5000 Laurinda Drive, P.O. Box P-1, Greensboro, NC 27402; (919) 288–7210.

McDade, Sharon A. *Higher Education Leadership: Enhancing Skills through Professional Development Programs*. ASHE-ERIC Education Report No. 5. Washington, DC: Association for the Study of Higher Education, 1987.

This overview of leadership development in higher education explores the career paths to administration and the skills and knowledge required for executive positions. Of particular note is a section that details the benefits and problems of participation in leadership development programs and activities, for both the institution and the individual, and an extensive examination of the types of programming available in higher education. The book concludes with a discussion of the leadership development challenges that face higher education administrators.

Moore, Kathryn M., and Susan B. Twombly, eds. *Administrative Careers and the Marketplace*. New Directions for Higher Education 72. San Francisco: Jossey-Bass, 1991.

This book presents practical advice rooted in research on the career development and paths of college administrators. Chapters deal with issues such as developing a career as an insider, lessons in hiring practices, search committees, planning for career improvement, mentor relationships, career mobility, and the administrative career marketplace in the year 2000. There is also a discussion on creating strengths out of differences for women and minority administrators.

Part Two:

STRATEGIES FOR

DEVELOPING

LEADERS

GOVERNING BOARDS

Lay boards are a distinctive feature of American higher education. Other countries look with admiration at this mechanism that guards the trust of the institution, provides a buffer and a link between it and the community, supports strong presidential leadership, and bears the ultimate responsibility for the college or university's successes or failures.

While the duties of governing boards have remained fairly constant over time, the environment in which they operate has changed dramatically. Even affluent colleges and universities struggle with limited resources, and all institutions face a declining pool of high school graduates. Some institutions struggle for excellence, others for survival.

The politicization of boards in the public sector has caused some boards to become an ideological battleground and has endangered presidential tenure and effectiveness. Sunshine laws, increased authority of system boards,[1] and intrusion by legislatures have diminished the effectiveness of boards. In the private sector, the relentless pressures for enrollments and fund raising dominate the discussions and duties of the board; short-range pressures can easily obscure long-range considerations.

As the problems of higher education intensify, so does the need for responsible and imaginative governing boards. Through careful selection, education by the president or system head, and constant self-development activities, a board's effectiveness can be developed and enhanced.

RESPONSIBILITIES

The responsibilities of governing boards[2] are described in straightforward terms throughout the literature. How to carry out these responsibilities is less clear-cut, however. The gray areas are abundant: the board must support the president but not serve simply as a rubber stamp; it must constantly distinguish between policy and administration and avoid meddling in operational issues; it must balance the long-term interests of the institution with the short-term needs. The most important responsibilities of boards include:

Appointing the President

Though many constituencies may have a voice in the selection of the president, choosing the president is ultimately the responsibility of the board. Good searches begin with a realistic assessment of the institution's strengths, weaknesses, and current needs. Casting the net widely, screening carefully, and keeping a constant eye on the welfare of the college or university are but a few key elements of a search. Whom to hire as president is the single most important decision for a board.

Supporting and Evaluating the President

Since the president serves "at the pleasure of the board," a close working relationship with the board chair and other trustees is essential. Support for presidents includes feedback on their performance and concern for their well-being. Time and resources for presidents to develop their own leadership capacities are also important. Travel, time for reading and reflection, attendance at seminars and meetings, and participation in professional groups are ways to sustain leadership vitality. Also, attention to the spouse and family, who inevitably are caught up in the demands of the presidency, contributes to the well-being of the chief executive officer and his or her family.

Monitoring the president's performance includes making the president aware of his or her strengths and weaknesses in the execution of presidential responsibilities as outlined in Chapter 5. Many experts agree that continuous and informal evaluation is preferable to formal evaluation, which can involve a great deal of paper, time, and other people, and may turn into a political event.

Clarifying and Monitoring the Institution's Mission

A mission statement means more than the verbiage in official publications. Ideally, it is the guiding force behind all important decisions. The yardstick for every decision should be the following question: Is this policy, program, or expenditure consonant with this institution's mission? Is our mission still valid? Does it need to be refocused? The president and the board are in the unique position of guiding the entire institution, not simply a part or division. The central responsibilities of trusteeship are maintaining a vision of the whole and keeping an eye on the future of the institution.

Ensuring the Financial Health and Sound Management of the Institution

This responsibility includes approving a sound budget; balancing short- and long-term financial needs; managing the endowment; and ensuring prudent management of the institution's financial, physical, and human resources. Because some trustees bring special expertise in financial matters (e.g., investments, financial management, physical plant management), they traditionally have taken an active role in the oversight of this important arena.

Raising Money

Fund raising is essential to the financial health of every private institution, and is increasingly important for public institutions as well. Trustees must ensure that a sound program for fund raising is in place, including appropriate staffing and procedures for soliciting and reporting. They also have an obligation to participate themselves, contributing in accordance with their ability and working with the board chair, president, and development committee to solicit other donors. Trustees of public colleges and universities also speak for their institutions to the state legislators and county boards that decide on appropriations. In some public institutions, the boards of the university foundations play the key fund-raising role.

Overseeing the Educational Programs

It is widely accepted that faculty are the architects and keepers of the educational programs. In the last 25 years, presidents have become increasingly concerned with external relations, devoting less time to academic matters and relying on the chief academic officer to lead in academic matters. If the curriculum is the domain of the faculty, what role should the board play? Certainly, if boards have ultimate responsibility for the institution, their responsibilities must include educational programs. Yet board members are not professors, and their role is one of oversight. Boards must maintain a delicate balance of providing overall guidance and direction for educational programs while leaving the faculty in charge. Because academic decisions are not made in a vacuum, a board will want to consider issues of curriculum, new programs or departments, or discontinuing programs in light of larger institutional criteria such as the appropriateness to the mission, the financial feasibility of a proposed action, and the impact on various constituencies.

Serving as a Bridge and Buffer Between Campus and Community

Though institutions and their communities are increasingly interdependent, they still tend to focus their attention inward and to protect traditional values and practices. Board members, themselves a part of the community, should be able to bring to bear the perspective of the larger society and to interpret campus needs in a larger context. For example, a private residential college in a white rural community that draws its students from local rural and suburban areas may have a hard time focusing on the importance of recruiting minority students. A knowledgeable trustee can articulate that need and open an important dialogue. Nason (1982, p. 36) refers to trustees as the ''antennae of the institution . . . relaying back what the surrounding world is like . . . [with a] responsibility to encourage constructive change.''

Trustees are also in a position to interpret the college to the community, defend ''offensive'' films or exhibitions on the grounds of academic freedom, interpret a policy or action, or refute rumors. The board can help to enhance the institution's public image and visibility.

Preserving Institutional Autonomy

''[O]ne of the responsibilities of governing boards is to defend the institutions they govern—to defend their existence, their programs and operations, their right to manage their own affairs'' (Nason 1980, p. 41). Governing boards must guard the ability of a college or university to act as critic of society, protecting the institution from external pressure groups as well as ensuring freedom of expression on campus. Pressure from donors, politicians, businesses, and the community have the potential of infringing on the independence of the institution. Trustees of public institutions experience a particular conundrum: how does a state-appointed trustee serve the state's interest and at the same time protect the institution from the state?

Serving as a Court of Appeal

Since boards possess final legal authority, they represent the final step in decision making or dispute resolution. Ideally, established policies on faculty appointment and reappointment and on codes of conduct, reinforced by appeal procedures and sound mechanisms for due process, should take care of most contested decisions, and few disputes will reach the board for resolution. If the board is being called upon to resolve more than the occasional dispute, or if it is finding that it must overrule the president and the administration, it is a sign that the processes are not working.

LEADERSHIP CAPACITIES

Though boards have an identity and function as a group, the capacities of individual board members are the building blocks of a successful board. Thus, the following list refers to the capacities that individual board members must bring to the collective task.

The Role of the Board

Board members need to understand the nature of trusteeship and the responsibilities of board members. Board members who see themselves as undertaking the responsibilities listed above are less likely to meddle in administrative matters or otherwise envision their role as anything less than the overall stewards of the institution.

Vision

As guardians of the institution's long-term welfare, board members must always think in terms of the whole institution, considering both the present and the future. In concert with the president, the board creates a vision for the institution and the broad outline of how that vision can best be achieved. Recent research (Holland, Chait, and Taylor 1989) reveals that effective boards are future oriented and directed toward decisions of strategic magnitude.

Commitment and Participation

The sense of personal connection to an institution is an important factor in trustee effectiveness. "Members of effective boards were far more likely to have agreed to join their boards because they felt a deep sense of loyalty and even love for the college" (Taylor, Chait, and Holland 1991). This identification with the goals and values of the college and sense of personal commitment are likely to influence attendance at meetings, giving, and willingness to work on behalf of the college.

Knowledge of the Institution

It is not easy to get to know an institution in three or four meetings a year. Good decisions must be based on a thorough understanding of the institution's goals, mission, history, and operations. Acquiring such knowledge requires an investment of time and energy—reviewing written materials, visiting the campus, and speaking with various institutional constituents.

Knowledge of Higher Education

Every institution is part of a larger context of higher education. Trustees' decisions about programs, resources, and people must be informed by a

knowledge of trends in higher education (such as changing demographics and current thinking about curriculum) and of financial issues
facing higher education as a whole. Without a general knowledge of the
larger picture in higher education, boards will function in the dark, unin-
formed about the current issues that shape the course of higher
education.

Willingness to Learn

The role of the trustee is a complex one, spanning a large number of
issues and areas. Board members must be highly accomplished generalists, with a broad understanding of such diverse areas as finances, curriculum, capital projects, and the academic culture and value system. To
accomplish this understanding, board members must be learners, open
to new information and new ways of seeing things; they must understand the complexity of the institution they govern and the multiple
effects of their actions. Boards, like colleges and universities, are in process, constantly moving toward new goals, reaffirming some and modifying others. A continual learning process must undergird this forward
movement.

The Board as a Working Group

Every group has a life of its own, with activist members, quiet members,
a rhythm and chemistry among the trustees that determines the shape
and even the outcome of a meeting. It is certainly essential that the chair
be aware of the dynamics of the group, ensuring that all voices are heard
and that the group is working effectively as a team. Good relationships
among individual board members can help minimize disruptive factions
or cliques and ensure that board meetings are constructive and
productive.

Complexity

Colleges and universities are complex institutions, with multiple and
sometimes conflicting goals, decentralized power and decision making,
and subsystems within the institution that may seem to have little to do
with the larger institution. Thus, decision making can be only partially
linear, hierarchical, or even rational. Presiding over such complexity
requires understanding and acceptance, intervening with caution, and
keeping the institution on course while respecting its processes, structures, and culture.

STRATEGIES FOR SUCCESSFUL BOARDS

Make Selection of New Trustees a High Priority[3]

The self-perpetuating nature of boards of private institutions gives trustees a great deal of control over the board's future. Even though some slots may be reserved for members of the church or for alumni, the nominating committee (or committee on trustees, as it is sometimes called) has a crucial role to play in selecting trustees who will ensure continuing board effectiveness. Their role is:

- To survey the current composition of the board and to determine future needs in board membership (e.g., fund-raising assistance, legal expertise).

- To identify prospects. The board should invite suggestions from appropriate constituencies.

- To cultivate prospects. Some prospective board members will already be involved enough in the institution to receive an outright invitation. Others will have to be cultivated, brought into the life of the college or university for a period of time to develop a real interest in serving as a board member.

- To invite new board members. This may be done by the president or chair, by a team of trustees, or by some other president/trustee combination.

- To orient new board members. Even if this is done by staff, the nominating committee should oversee the process and be sure that new trustees are made welcome by the board.

- To deploy new board members. The nominating committee should recommend assignments to committees according to the new trustees' strengths and interests and find other ways to ensure that the new members' skills are being used.

A problem in public institutions stems in part from the lack of influence trustees have in suggesting or naming new members. When members of governing boards are elected or politically appointed, there is much less certainty that they will have the interests of the institution uppermost in their minds.

Ensure Effective Meetings

Ingram (1988, p. 25) points out that by definition, ''a board of trustees is a meeting, because trustees exercise their legal responsibilities only when they are convened as a corporate body.'' Though what happens between meetings is very important, the quality of committee and board meetings is central to board effectiveness. Some characteristics of good board meetings are:

- Good attendance
- Adequate preparation by trustees
- Agenda including substantial discussion of strategic issues rather than administrative or routine matters
- Varied formats and agendas
- Appropriate control over the group exercised by the chair, ensuring full participation, focus, and forward movement of the discussion
- Staff role of informing the board without dominating the meeting

Provide Adequate Staffing

Good staff support is essential to board effectiveness. The staff provides the board with meeting agendas and information between board meetings and serves as its link to the institution. The board secretary often plays an important and delicate role, but he or she is by no means the only liaison to the board. The president and senior officers are key. Good staff support includes:[4]

- Orientation for new board members (see below for additional detail on orientation)
- Ongoing provision of information about the institution and higher education (before and between board meetings)
- Preparation of a well-crafted agenda and supporting materials, and timely provision of materials to board members (at least 10 days before the meeting)
- Informal discussions by president and staff with board and committee chairs about the agenda, especially concerning difficult or controversial items
- Creation of opportunities for the board to discuss all major policy issues well in advance of any action
- Consultation by president and staff with various campus constituencies and groups on issues being brought to the board
- Responsiveness to these groups in explaining the board's action on a particular issue
- Creation of opportunities for board members to get to know students, faculty, and administrators, and to understand the institution

Create an Appropriate Committee Structure

The type of institution, the size of the board, and the frequency of its meetings will be important determinants of the committee structure; there is no ideal format. Boards of private institutions, averaging 32 members, are generally larger than those of public institutions. Boards of two- and four-year institutions generally range between five and 15 members. A five-person board will rarely have any committees. The frequency of meetings also will influence committee structure and tasks. Some states or localities mandate monthly meetings; other boards meet three or four times a year. The most common committees are the executive committee, the academic affairs committee, the student affairs committee, the nominating committee, and the development committee.

STRATEGIES FOR BOARD DEVELOPMENT

Board development is a continuous process. It begins with orienting board members to their roles and responsibilities and, for some, introducing them to issues in higher education. As we mentioned earlier, trustees are the consummate generalists; they require a working knowledge of a wide variety of issues, as well as information about the institution, the community, and the processes of higher education administration. Their continuing education and vitality are central to their ability to meet the demands of trusteeship. As links to the larger society, trustees must be well informed. As guardians of the institution's short- and long-term well-being, they must fully understand how the institution operates. And, as members of a working group, they must appreciate the need for active and constructive participation. Strategies for improving board effectiveness are discussed in the following paragraphs.

Strategies for New Trustees

In their recent study of governing boards, Kerr and Gade (1989, p. 47) found that most board members feel that they were not given adequate orientation. Elements of an effective orientation program include:

- *Essential documents.* Among the documents new board members should receive are minutes of the last several board meetings; financial information such as the operating budget and auditor's report; basic data on enrollment, departments, faculty, and curricular offerings; and the bylaws. Also useful are recent self-studies and accreditation reports. Whenever possible, brief summaries of relevant information should be provided, since it is easy to overwhelm people with paper, and trustees are unlikely to read and absorb all this information. However, documentation may be a useful resource for the future.

- *Introduction to the top campus officials.* Though new members may see these individuals at board meetings, they may have little opportunity to interact. Brief one-on-one meetings or an orientation session with several new trustees should be arranged.

- *Sense of the traditions and culture of the institution.* Although it takes time to acquire a real sense of an institution's culture, the process can be accelerated by an explicit discussion of this subject.

- *Insight into the traditions and operations of the board.* Because the board itself is an important entity of the institution, new board members will need to know how it functions and its procedures and traditions. This orientation is best provided by the board chair.

- *Overview of the trustees' legal responsibilities.* With increasing concern about litigation and liability, it is helpful to know one's legal responsibilities and potential liability. The institution's legal counsel or a knowledgeable board member can present this part of the orientation.

- *Formal orientation program.* Informational items can be part of an extended orientation spanning a few months following the appointment of the new trustees, or can be included in a formal, one-day orientation program. An orientation program does not substitute for an ongoing education that exposes new trustees to the items listed above and other information about the institution and the board. The orientation session should orient the trustees to the nature of trusteeship and provide an overview of the institution. Possible elements of a trustee orientation workshop are:

  - A tour of the campus

  - A discussion of the role of trustees

  - Briefings about the current status and the future of the institution

  - Meetings with senior administrators and faculty

  - Opportunities for social interaction with other trustees and with others in the campus community

- *Continued orientation beyond the initial workshop.* Orientation is not just a one-day undertaking. A series of activities spanning the first year or two of the trustee's term can help make the new board member feel more knowledgeable and involved. Such activities might include:

- Assigning an experienced trustee as a sponsor or mentor. The new trustee then has a person to turn to with questions and to help him or her understand the institution's history, culture, and traditions. The sponsor also benefits from the process by interpreting the institution to a newcomer.

- Encouraging trustees to attend classes (with the faculty member's prior knowledge).

- Arranging periodic meetings with faculty and administrators.

- Encouraging trustees to spend time on campus, spend a night in the residence hall, and take part in campus activities.

- Involving the new trustee by giving him or her an assignment.

Strategies for All Trustees

- *Periodic briefings and discussions of substantive issues.* As was stressed earlier, the knowledge factor is important to sustain effective trustee leadership. Trustees who are well informed about trends and practices in comparable institutions and in higher education as a whole will bring a sound perspective to their decision making and strategic thinking. Of course, trustees can keep up by reading and talking to knowledgeable individuals, but it can be especially helpful to conduct periodic briefings, perhaps as part of the regular board meetings, on issues that are relevant to the college or university. For example, for an institution seeking to heighten its profile in the research arena, information on the current availability of extramural funding and on the issues of balancing teaching and research would provide a helpful context for the board. Or, if an institution is contemplating changing its financial aid policies, a briefing on recent trends in federal, state, and institutional funding could provide important background. It is worth noting that such briefings should not overwhelm the board with data or try to make them into instant experts. Rather, the aim is to help board members become well-informed generalists.

- *Attendance at local, regional, and national meetings.* Meetings with other trustees are helpful in furthering board members' understanding of their responsibilities and the issues confronting higher education institutions. Such meetings might be local ones with trustees of similar institutions, or national workshops such as those sponsored by the Association of Governing Boards of Colleges and Universities (AGB) (see *Resource* section).

- *Visits to other institutions.* Such visits can accomplish the same purpose as meetings with other trustees. Actual campus visits provide a more concrete view of institutional practices and cultures.

- *Periodic retreats.* Boards need to be conscious of their role as a group, and should periodically assess their functioning and effectiveness. Retreats can focus on special issues as well as on self-assessment. They can have the following objectives:[5]

Long-Term Goals

- To improve the board's organization and performance, particularly in problem areas (e.g., review of the committee structure, development of strategies to increase participation)

- To enable the board to understand (or to improve) its participation in fund raising

- To encourage inactive board members to live up to their trusteeships or resign

- To solicit the board's help in refining a proposed institutional plan

- To improve relationships between the president and the board

- To improve relationships among board members

- To develop consensus on a new mission for the institution (or to regain a sense of purpose)

Short-Term Goals

- To demonstrate how other, similar types of boards are organized and function

- To present and discuss fund-raising techniques

- To ask each trustee to review his or her performance

- To conduct a self-study

- To concentrate on a particular area of the institution—the revision of academic programs, an impending accreditation visit, new construction

- To invite an expert to discuss such issues as the impact of changing demographics on higher education, projected faculty shortages, or recent developments in international education

In addition to establishing the goals of a retreat, thought must be given to its duration, timing, and setting; whether to use an outside facilitator or consultant; and how to identify that person. It is important that retreats actively engage the board members as discussants, group leaders, and problem solvers. Lectures should be used sparingly.

BOARD EVALUATION AS A DEVELOPMENTAL TOOL

Individual trustees and boards need constantly to monitor their effectiveness. If this is done with honesty, self-assessment becomes an important vehicle for self-improvement and also can serve as a measure of accountability to the larger society. A board can use a variety of methods to evaluate its own policies, practices, and structures (Paltridge 1980, p. 18).

Meetings

These may take the form of short meetings away from the regular board sessions or longer retreats. For both types of meetings, it is important that the moderator be skilled at keeping the group focused and the discussion constructive.

Questionnaires

A number of instruments exist (see *Resources* section) for boards to use in assessing their effectiveness. Because these questionnaires assess perceptions and are subject to distortions (positive and negative), they need to be used with care. However, disagreement on particular questions may be useful in pointing to problem areas. Care must be taken in designing the instrument (or adapting an existing one), getting trustee input on the nature of the questionnaire, and resolving such issues as confidentiality and ultimate uses of the information gathered. The results of the questionnaires may be discussed during retreats or shorter meetings, and can be used as a basis for action.

Consultants

Often an outsider can provide a useful perspective. AGB's Board-Mentor Service (see *Programs and Practices* section) provides an experienced, AGB-trained board member to conduct a workshop to lead the board in a self-evaluation. A consultant also can be used to indicate trouble spots and to propose solutions. In all cases, the board should participate in deciding which consultant to hire and provide all necessary information to that individual.

Ideally, board assessment should be a continual process, using a variety of approaches. Informal assessment should be interspersed with a more formal approach. For some institutions, the mixture and approach may be dictated by sunshine laws; executive sessions may be the major vehicle for assessment.

The preceding suggestions have related to the process of monitoring board assessment. Also essential to the discussion are the criteria by which boards are judged. Suggested criteria for assessing effectiveness might include the following areas: institutional mission and policy, institutional planning, physical plant, financial support and management, board membership, board organization, board–chief executive officer relations, board–faculty relations, board–student relations, and the board as a court of appeal. Some quantifiable measures of board effectiveness include (Kerr and Gade 1989, p. 86):

- Average length of term of the president. (Rapid turnover may be a sign of a dysfunctional board or board–president relationship.)
- Average rate of attendance of board members at meetings.
- Voter turnout for trustee elections (public institutions). (If fewer than 25 percent of those eligible to vote actually do so, it may indicate public apathy or lack of confidence.)
- Degree of consensus of the board on important issues.
- Percentage of time the board spends on major strategic issues, as compared with time spent on details or administrative matters.

In private institutions, the extent of financial contribution by the board would be added to this list.

Please refer to the *Resources* section for a description of the self-study criteria and questionnaires available from AGB. Instruments are also available for trustees to use in assessing their individual effectiveness. A sample developed by Richard T. Ingram can be found in Ingram and Associates (1988, p. 155).

THE ROLE OF THE PRESIDENT IN BOARD DEVELOPMENT

One of the most important jobs of the president or system head is to inform and educate the board. Keeping the board well informed and appropriately involved should be any president's top priority; the effort generally requires a substantial investment of time. Kerr and Gade (1989, p. 73) have identified the following ways that presidents can contribute to board development:

- Participate in identifying potential trustees. (This is generally not possible in public institutions.)
- Help establish a good orientation program.

- Educate board members about their roles.

- Supply a good flow of information and alert board members to crisis situations.

- Provide interesting and varied agendas for meetings and well-supported recommendations for action.

- Develop a good staff to serve the board.

- Involve board members early in the process of policy formation.

- Provide opportunities for trustees to become involved in the campus.

- Give board members a sense of appreciation for their assistance as well as a sense of accomplishment.

CONCLUSION

Developing an effective board is a continuous process requiring constant attention by the president and the board chair. It is a difficult undertaking, since board members are busy volunteers who spend relatively little time on campus or involved in their roles. Yet without a well-functioning board, the entire institution is imperiled. Presidential leadership may become so fragile that turnover accelerates and leadership is impossible; a divided board can consistently thwart progress. Investment in board development is an investment in the entire institution.

NOTES

1. This chapter encompasses boards of individual campuses (public and private) and of state systems. In a number of systems, the board interacts primarily with the system head, and the institutional presidents play quite a different role with the board. In referring to "presidents" in this chapter, we include both campus and system heads. Because the chapter covers diverse kinds of institutions and boards, some statements and recommendations will be applicable only in some situations.

2. Adapted from John W. Nason, "Responsibilities of the Governing Board," in *Handbook of College and University Trusteeship: A Practical Guide for Trustees, Chief Executives, and Other Leaders Responsible for Developing Effective Governing Boards*, by Richard T. Ingram and Associates (San Francisco: Jossey-Bass, 1980), 27–46; Clark Kerr and Marian L. Gade, *The Guardians: Boards of Trustees of American Colleges and Universities* (Washington, DC: Association of Governing Boards of Universities and Colleges, 1989), 11–12, 197; and Richard T. Ingram and Associates, *Making Trusteeship Work: A Guide to Governing Board Organization, Policies, and Practices* (Washington, DC: Association of Governing Boards of Universities and Colleges, 1988).

3. See *Recommendations for Improving Trustee Selection in Public Colleges and Universities* (Washington, DC: Association of Governing Boards of Universities and Colleges, 1980).

4. Adapted from Clark Kerr and Marian L. Gade, *The Guardians: Boards of Trustees of American Colleges and Universities* (Washington, DC: Association of Governing Boards of Universities and Colleges, 1989), 97.

5. Adapted from Richard T. Ingram and Associates, *Handbook of College and University Trusteeship: A Practical Guide for Trustees, Chief Executives, and Other Leaders Responsible for Developing Effective Governing Boards* (San Francisco: Jossey-Bass, 1980), 95.

REFERENCES

Holland, Thomas P., Richard P. Chait, and Barbara E. Taylor. *Institutional Governance: Identifying and Measuring Board Competencies.* Final Report on Research Project Submitted to the United States Department of Education. [College Park]: National Center for Postsecondary Governance and Finance, University of Maryland, 1989. Photocopy.

Ingram, Richard T., and Associates. *Handbook of College and University Trusteeship: A Practical Guide for Trustees, Chief Executives, and Other Leaders Responsible for Developing Effective Governing Boards.* San Francisco: Jossey-Bass, 1980.

———. *Making Trusteeship Work: A Guide to Governing Board Organization, Policies, and Practices.* Washington, DC: Association of Governing Boards of Universities and Colleges, 1988.

Kerr, Clark, and Marian L. Gade. *The Guardians: Boards of Trustees of American Colleges and Universities.* Washington, DC: Association of Governing Boards of Universities and Colleges, 1989.

Nason, John W. "Responsibilities of the Governing Board." In *Handbook of College and University Trusteeship: A Practical Guide for Trustees, Chief Executives, and Other Leaders Responsible for Developing Effective Governing Boards,* by Richard T. Ingram and Associates. San Francisco: Jossey-Bass, 1980.

———. *The Nature of Trusteeship: The Role and Responsibilities of College and University Boards.* Washington, DC: Association of Governing Boards of Universities and Colleges, 1982.

Paltridge, James Gilbert. "Studying Board Effectiveness." In *Handbook of College and University Trusteeship: A Practical Guide for Trustees, Chief Executives, and Other Leaders Responsible for Developing Effective Boards,* by Richard T. Ingram and Associates. San Francisco: Jossey-Bass, 1980.

Recommendations for Improving Trustee Selection in Public Colleges and Universities. Washington, DC: Association of Governing Boards of Universities and Colleges, 1980.

Taylor, Barbara E., Richard P. Chait, and Thomas P. Holland. "Trustee Selection and Board Effectiveness." *Nonprofit and Voluntary Sector Quarterly*, forthcoming 1991.

RESOURCES

Board Self-Study and User's Guide Kit. Washington, DC: Association of Governing Boards of Universities and Colleges, 1987.

Designed to help governing boards assess their own performance and organization, these kits help elicit the objective information required for board self-study and self-evaluation. Each of these six kits includes a copy of the *User's Guide to Self-Study Criteria for Governing Boards* and one of the following titles: *Independent College and University Governing Boards; Community College Governing Boards; Public College and University Governing Boards; Governing Boards of Public Multicampus Higher Education Systems; Boards of State Postsecondary Education Planning and Coordinating Agencies;* or *Governing Boards of Theological Schools.*

Houle, Cyril O. *Governing Boards: Their Nature and Nurture*. San Francisco: Jossey-Bass, 1989.

This text provides guidance on improving the effectiveness of governing boards in nonprofit and public organizations. The book discusses the operation and external relationships of the board and provides insight into the requirements for an effective governing mechanism. Drawing on the latest information in the field and on personal experience, Houle demonstrates how to handle successfully the full range of challenges facing board members.

Ingram, Richard T., and Associates. *Handbook of College and University Trusteeship: A Practical Guide for Trustees, Chief Executives, and Other Leaders Responsible for Developing Effective Governing Boards*. San Francisco: Jossey-Bass, 1980.

This comprehensive text addresses all issues relating to college and university trusteeship and provides insight into the traditional and new responsibilities of the board member. The book includes information on governing board operation, institutional oversight, resource development, and policy issues facing trustees and administrators, and is a comprehensive resource for all trustees, chief executives, and administrators who work closely with the board.

———. *Making Trusteeship Work: A Guide to Governing Board Organization, Policies, and Practices*. Washington, DC: Association of Governing Boards of Universities and Colleges, 1988.

This resource guide provides insight into trusteeship by offering advice on board effectiveness. Ingram begins the book with a look into the organizational structure of the board and its link to the CEO. The remainder of the book includes 13 sections that address the various board committees. It also includes a useful annotated bibliography and appendix.

Kerr, Clark, and Marian L. Gade. *The Guardians: Boards of Trustees of American Colleges and Universities:* Washington, DC: Association of Governing Boards of Universities and Colleges, 1989.

This book describes contemporary issues related to the complex and diverse roles of boards. The guiding principles behind this study are that (1) trustees are essential to the effective functioning of American higher education, (2) boards do not work as effectively as they could, and (3) their roles very often erode over time. The authors offer several recommendations about the effective use of governing boards.

Nason, John W. *The Nature of Trusteeship: The Role and Responsibilities of College and University Boards*. Washington, DC: Association of Governing Boards of Universities and Colleges, 1982.

This text is a revision of the series of essays published in 1975 on the problems affecting the future of trusteeship. The revision focuses on an updated list of the major trustee responsibilities and 14 conditions necessary for board effectiveness. By drawing on the new scholarly material that has become available in the past seven years, Nason describes the dramatic broadening and altering of the role and responsibilities of the trustee. The book also includes an assessment of state system and coordinating board needs and discusses the legal liabilities of the trustee.

Wood, Miriam Mason. *Trusteeship in the Private College*. Baltimore: Johns Hopkins University Press, 1985.

This report is the result of in-depth, confidential interviews with trustees and presidents from 10 private liberal arts colleges from four states. Wood describes what trustees actually do in relation to the governance of the institution, and gives some insight into the decision-making process, power structure, and relationships of the trustee.

Zwingle, J. L. *Effective Trusteeship: Guidelines for Board Members*, third ed. Washington, DC: Association of Governing Boards of Universities and Colleges, 1985.

This booklet is a quick introduction and guide to college and university trusteeship. Divided into basic sections, these guidelines discuss the basic relationships and problems facing academic trusteeship and the procedures and bylaws that direct the operation of the board. There is also a short section on the future of trusteeship and a useful compendium of checklists, audits, and an annotated bibliography.

PROGRAMS AND PRACTICES

Complete information on each listing is provided in the *Appendix*. The letter and number in the parentheses correspond to the section and entry number in the *Appendix*.

National Associations

While trustees are welcome at the annual meetings and conventions of any of the presidential associations (See Chapter 4, *Presidents*) and may join any of the individual higher education associations, there are several associations that specifically address their needs as members of governing boards.

Association of Community College Trustees (ACCT) (A100)

Association of Governing Boards of Universities and Colleges (AGB) (A105)

National Programs

The following list provides a sampling of the range and variety of off-campus programs available to members of governing boards and is not meant to be an inventory of all programs and activities available to these leaders. Note that many programs offered by associations are available only to member institutions.

Association of Community College Trustees (ACCT) (P14)

National Legislative Seminar and Regional Seminars *(P14a)*

Association of Governing Boards of Universities and Colleges (AGB)(P15)

Board-Mentor Service *(P15a)*
Improving Board Performance *(P15b)*
Institute for Trustee Leadership: Program for Board Chairs and Chief Executive Officers of
 Independent Institutions *(P15c)*
Introduction to AGB Services During National Conference on Trusteeship *(P15d)*
On-Campus Fundraising Workshop *(P15e)*
Program for Academic Affairs Committee Chairpersons and Senior Academic Officers *(P15f)*
Seminar for Chairpersons and Chief Executives of Theological Schools and Seminaries *(P15g)*
Seminar on Endowment Management *(P15h)*
Speaker Service *(P15i)*
Strategic Planning for Theological Schools *(P15j)*
Trustee Responsibility for Financial Affairs *(P15k)*
Workshop for New Trustees *(P15l)*

Association of Governing Boards of Universities and Colleges in Cooperation with the National Association of System Heads (P16)

Governing the Public Multicampus System *(P16a)*

Council for Advancement and Support of Education (CASE) (P26)

Presidential and Trustee Leadership in Fund Raising *(P26b)*

Williamsburg Development Institute (P72)

Williamsburg Development Institute *(P72a)*

5

PRESIDENTS

This chapter is concerned with people who head colleges and universities, systems of institutions, and campuses within systems. Although usually identified as "presidents," they may also be titled "chancellors" or "superintendents." Campus heads in a multicampus system may be titled "directors" or "deans." The term "president" is used here to refer to individuals in all these roles.

There are two schools of thought regarding preparation for the presidency. One view suggests that college and university presidents, like members of Congress and other elected government officials, cannot prepare specifically for these jobs as do leaders of corporations and the military. The processes of selection are too capricious, the chances of selection too remote. Like congressional posts, college presidencies are temporary jobs to which many aspire but for which few are actually chosen. Although some presidents may serve long terms like some elected officials, it is difficult to plan an entire career around the expectation of such a position (Kauffman 1980).

A second view is that academic leaders acquire valuable decision-making experience as they move up through the ranks of higher education administration. In these positions, leaders acquire a solid basis for taking on the ultimate decision-making responsibilities of the presidency. Whatever view one takes, preparation for the presidency is difficult and often circumstantial.

In the past it may have been possible for presidents to get by as role models, good intuitive managers, and seat-of-the-pants leaders. But the complexity of the presidential job today makes this more difficult. George B. Vaughan, a long-time observer of the community college presidency, has studied events leading to the exit of presidents as a way to investigate topics of presidential preparation and effectiveness. He theorized that presidents likely to leave early are most often those who do not have the "organizational skills required today; they make costly blunders that would be avoidable if they had the necessary skills" (Vaughan 1986, p. 203).

Given the position's demands and the lack of formal preparation, how can a president acquire the skills and abilities needed to lead in today's complex environment? The answers are varied, but finding them is vital to the success of institutional leaders.

CAREER PREPARATION

Kerr and Gade, in their massive study of the American college presidency (1986), noted that 10,000 individuals will serve as college and university presidents in any given decade. (Approximately 3,200 institutions average about one-and-one-half presidents per decade.) Unlike lightbulbs, Kerr and Gade explained, college and university presidents are not interchangeable. Instead, they are products of heredity, environment, training, and chance, varying enormously by time and place.

The study also revealed many different reasons for people's interest in the presidency: to take on a personal challenge; to grow personally, learn new skills, meet new people, see new places, do new things, experience excitement, and try new ideas; to serve a religion or help a gender, racial, or ethnic group; to work with young people; to fulfill an obligation to the institution and its community; to take the next step on the ladder; to escape from an increasingly unsatisfactory life of teaching and research; to get more money, more prestige, a bigger house, and travel; and to accept the recognition of work well done, contributions made—as an honor, a vote of confidence.

It is not surprising that the paths leading to the presidency are as varied as the reasons for serving. In the past, "serendipity often played a major role in deciding who became a president . . . . Today, however, the presidency is often viewed as the culminating point of a career that has been years in the making" (Vaughan 1986, p. 9). Still, the components of that career are no longer as homogeneous or as predictable as in the past. Where presidents once typically followed a predictable progression to their post, their backgrounds now vary increasingly, ensuring that each brings a unique set of experiences to the presidency. Furthermore, it is impossible to determine the extent to which prior experiences directly prepare an individual for a presidency.

Statistics demonstrate the variety of experience of people in the position of president (Green 1988; Moore et al. 1983):

- Seventeen percent had previously served as presidents and nearly 6 percent had served as presidents twice before. Men were more than twice as likely as women to have been presidents previously. Universities that grant doctorates were nearly twice as likely as other institutions to hire a previous president.

- Forty-two percent came directly from vice presidencies. The position of provost/vice president for academic affairs is the principal entry portal to the presidency.

- Only one-fifth lacked faculty experience.

- Only 3 percent followed the traditional academic career ladder (faculty, department chair, dean, provost, president). Ninety-five percent served in at least one of the ladder positions, while 32 percent skipped as many as three rungs, usually the department chair and deanship positions. Other positions often substituted for these two positions.

- More than two-thirds had served in the same or similar institutions. Thirty-two percent were internal candidates; another 36 percent came from the same type of institution. Specialized institutions were more likely to recruit internally. There was limited mobility across sectors.

- The average tenure of the presidency is seven years.

It is also interesting to observe the careers of community college presidents, who are often omitted from such studies. There were once considerable differences in backgrounds between presidents of four-year institutions and presidents of community colleges. As more community colleges mature as institutions, these differences seem to be narrowing. Founding presidents of community colleges have retired, opening leadership to a new breed of presidents with higher education rather than K—12 backgrounds. In contrast with the very long tenures of founding presidents, these new presidents typically serve for five years or less.

RESPONSIBILITIES

Presidents fulfill many responsibilities that are highly dependent upon the type of institution, its mission, its position in a system, the timing within the institution's development, and the nature of its faculty and students. The following list of responsibilities is drawn from the works of Vaughan (1986), Kauffman (1980), Fisher (1984), and Kerr and Gade (1986).

Providing Leadership for Varied and Conflicting Constituencies

The president's primary job is to provide leadership and direction in defining and adapting the mission, goals, and objectives of the institution. A president creates a specific, overall vision and strategy for the institution while keeping both internal and external constituencies aware of the broader central purpose, values, and social worth of higher education. To accomplish this, the president must first create and maintain an effective relationship with the board. The president also tries to accommodate the varied and sometimes conflicting constituents who expect to participate in directing the institution.

Overseeing Education and Instruction

Presidents lead the development and implementation of policies that enhance teaching and research and are responsive to societal and student needs. They foster the development of academic programs adequate to the needs of the institution's target population by encouraging curriculum development and improvement. Presidents also set appropriate standards for teaching and research while fostering an academic environment in which free inquiry and discourse can thrive.

Defining the Working Environment for Faculty, Administrators, and Staff

The president holds ultimate responsibility for selecting and retaining qualified personnel. Presidents do not usually hire faculty, administrators, or staff personally; however they do establish hiring and personnel policies. The development and effective implementation of these policies enable the president to create and maintain effective relationships with the faculty, staff, and other administrators, and to organize the institution's staff for maximum performance.

As the president of a community college stated, ''Through policy and example, the president establishes the working culture of an institution. Everything a president does, or doesn't do, is watched—and either copied or criticized—but has an impact on the institution's culture.'' The president sets the tone and the structure of the campus by encouraging the professional growth and leadership development of all employees; initiating a cooperative environment for faculty bargaining and facilitating adherence to bargaining agreements; and resolving conflicts and grievances satisfactorily, as well as initiating action to reduce the causes for grievances. Some recent scholarship on female leadership styles may be helpful when considering ways to move away from the traditionally hierarchical and competitive model of college organization to a more collaborative environment.

At a discussion among presidents of several types of institutions, there was agreement when one president stated, ''More than any other individual, a president establishes the importance of diversity in all staffing areas and particularly among the students. Diversity cannot be achieved unless presidents make it clear that they are committed and working actively to ensure the acceptance and integration of new campus constituencies and the development of a truly multicultural organizational model.''

Establishing an Appropriate Climate for Student Development

Education takes place both inside and outside the classroom. Through policy and programming, presidents can ensure that the best interests of each student are satisfied. This requires developing academic, personnel, financial, physical, and student admissions plans that reflect the institution's unique mission or, within a system, the assigned mission of the campus.

Relating the Institution to its External Constituencies

A president speaks for the institution to the many publics that it serves and upon which it must depend for support. Presidents participate in and influence the decision making, coordination, and control of higher education agencies and executive and legislative branches; represent the institution to surrounding educational institutions and in local, state, and national professional and educational organizations; and take part in public activities to gain the respect of the community. In all these arenas, it is important that the president communicate the values, mission, and contributions of the institution.

Other presidents agreed with the president of a major urban university who stated, "Presidents represent not only their own individual institutions, but also all of higher education. We serve as advocates for education and as defenders of institutional autonomy and academic freedom. Whenever we speak or write, we represent all of education."

Securing Resources and Overseeing Their Use

The president is the institution's best agent to acquire, manage, and monitor the resources necessary to carry out the mission of the institution. While many tasks—controlling costs and productivity, establishing priorities and realistic controls to meet institutional needs while maintaining a balanced budget—may be delegated to others, the final responsibility for oversight lies with the president.

Ensuring the Smooth Management of the Institution

While many management responsibilities are delegated to other members of the management team, the president has ultimate responsibility for oversight. The president can initiate and ensure adequate and accurate planning; launch studies, reviews, and evaluations of policies and procedures and ensure their implementation; and ensure compliance with all federal, state, and local rules. The management challenge to presidents is to provide dynamic leadership and smooth administration that support the president's agenda while observing the constraints imposed by external forces and limited resources.

LEADERSHIP CAPACITIES

While the basic leadership *capacities* needed by successful college presidents have remained constant over the decades, today's leaders also must possess new *skills* to deal with the increased complexities of the modern university. As higher education leadership has become more technical, political, and complex, the balance has tipped: educational and intellectual leadership has receded, while other factors of management, politics, and fund raising have increased in importance. This shift reflects the gradual transformation of the college president from a leader/scholar into a leader/manager.

This section discusses the leadership capacities college or university presidents need to be effective today.

Providing Vision

As in the past, the president remains the chief interpreter of mission, indicator of priorities, and communicator of direction. To move an institution ahead, presidents must address the social, economic, demographic, and cultural changes of the surrounding world and cope with forces in dynamic and shifting conflict. Harlan Cleveland, a seasoned observer of American colleges and universities, has described the president as the one person who must see the "situation as a whole, . . . who does not lose sight of the institution's goals. The president should constantly influence the shaping and reshaping of those goals" (cited by Kauffman 1980, p. 14).

A truly effective president combines vision and management synergistically to ensure that the vision becomes reality. Often, the line between leadership and management is blurred; changing the campus culture or influencing and articulating its values frequently is accomplished through routine management decisions.

Managing and Decision Making

An important part of the president's leadership capacity is the ability to design an organizational structure that addresses the full range of management functions. This structure should ensure the smooth operation of the college so that the educational mission can be accomplished. An important, and often overlooked, leadership corollary is the capacity to use this structure effectively, to delegate not only responsibility but also authority for tasks, to provide adequate support, and to ensure a positive environment so that the leadership within the structure is effective.

Working With People

It is likely that there never existed a time when a president could make a decision without much questioning or challenge, but it is easy to understand why higher education leaders might yearn for those mythic days of yore. Today the reality is that other people are the key to success and an essential element of every leadership action.

A major aspect of the ability to work with people is the president's role as the chief link with most of the institution's publics. Although a president may have acquired skills in handling faculty, students, staff, and administrators while in other senior leadership roles, the presidency is the only place for extensive interaction with groups such as the board of trustees, legislators, and the external community. Also, campus heads are the major interface with the system head. "There is no doubt in my mind that the whole area of dealing with public relations—the general public, the business public, and . . . the legislature—is a whole new set of skills that were not really required by my predecessor" (Vaughan 1986, p. 60).

Accordingly, the leadership capacity for working with people goes beyond interpersonal dynamics to include a larger responsibility for setting a campus environment or mood for institutional vitality. The president is thus responsible for motivating others, bringing out their best, and working with and through them.

Maintaining Vigor and Vitality

A longtime college president observed, "Being a college or university president requires substantial physical and psychological stamina. It means having the ability to handle high levels of frustration, fragmentation of time and task, loss of anonymity, and a life constantly in the center of conflict. It dictates [the] capacity . . . to accept the separation between the leader and the rest of the community and the loneliness of making the final decision."

Presidents tend, for practical and political reasons, to invest in people around them but to leave themselves until last. When they get around to addressing their own needs, resources and time are often exhausted. Many studies show that presidents average 60- to 80-hour work weeks, including many evenings and most weekends; that they rarely take all their vacation time; and that the vacation time they do take is typically spent working.

These difficulties emphasize that understanding oneself is an important capacity of leadership. This includes understanding one's leadership and management styles as well as one's physical and psychological limits.

STRATEGIES FOR DEVELOPMENT

Why invest in leadership development for a president? While a candidate for the presidency feels an obligation during the interview to assert his or her leadership abilities, in fact, presidents, both new and experienced, have a wide range of development needs. Initially, they need orientation to their new jobs and opportunities to learn new skills and to supplement their experiences. Later, development opportunities help presidents develop vision, broaden perspectives, and understand the environment. Throughout their careers, but especially at the later stages, presidents need opportunities for personal renewal, stimulation, and motivation.

Strategies for New Presidents

Whereas 80 percent of business and industry chief executive officers come from within, bringing with them an average of 24 years in the same company (Heidrick and Struggles 1987), an equal percentage of college or university presidents come from other institutions. Unlike most presidents of business and industry, college and university presidents must learn not only the business of being president but also about operating in a new organization.

One strategy to help prepare potential presidents is for colleges and universities to provide senior executives (presumably at the vice-presidential level) with on-the-job training for presidential responsibilities. Although not all senior executives will serve as president in the particular institution at which they began training, the benefits of such an investment would serve the larger higher education community.

Listed below are more conventional development opportunities for new presidents.

- *Formal programs.* Besides the Harvard Seminar for New Presidents, there are few formal opportunities designed specifically for newly appointed presidents who have not yet entered the presidency or for presidents in their first months of service. Various institutes and seminars for new presidents (listed at the end of this chapter) are available to presidents after their appointment. Presidents often attend these programs a year after they assume office, since the programs are usually scheduled in the summer. Such programs are particularly useful for initiating new presidents into the network of presidents in their institutional sector, for providing colleagueship, and for providing insights into problem solving.

- *Informal activities.* For many presidents, the tasks at hand when taking on a new job do not allow the time to attend formal programs, or the formal programs are not offered at a time that works well for the new president. Many presidents create their own "preparation" programs; these often involve personal visits with trusted friends and visits to organizations that can serve as resources. Most of the Washington, DC, based presidential associations will host a new president for a personal orientation to services and resources.

Mentoring relationships can be very important during the first weeks of a presidency. If a new president does not have a friend with the experience to fill this role, it may be possible to locate such a mentor through one of the national or institutional-sector associations. A president at the end of his first year in office remembered, "I visited established presidents at institutions similar to mine, meeting with more senior presidents to discuss issues of entry, problems they might have in common, and ways to handle their particular type of institution. These visits were particularly helpful for me and my spouse, because they provided an opportunity to explore with others the issues related to the stress on presidential families."

Consultants also can provide a helpful outside perspective to new presidents. Increasingly, boards of trustees are making available funds for new presidents to hire consultants during these crucial first months to serve as private and confidential sounding boards and supportive strategists.

Strategies for All Presidents

As presidents gain experience, they develop a better understanding of their strengths and weaknesses. A smart president will embark immediately on self-improvement through leadership development opportunities.

- *National associations and institutional networks.* Many national associations, such as the American Council on Education (ACE), the American Association of State Colleges and Universities (AASCU), and the American Association of Community and Junior Colleges (AACJC), design annual meetings with the needs of presidents in mind. They often include specific sessions for CEOs. Some presidential organizations, such as those for Catholic colleges (the Association of Catholic Colleges and Universities) and urban institutions (the Association of Urban Universities), provide more focused discussions of the problems faced by specific groups of institutions. Both types of organizations provide ample opportunities for new and experienced presidents to meet and mix and to share problems, solutions, and information.

- *General programs for senior administrators.* Presidents have available to them the full range of developmental opportunities described in other chapters. These include conventions, seminars, national institutes, and administrative seminars. Presidents may bring specific needs to such sessions and derive benefits different from other senior officers. Attending these programs provides insight into higher education issues and into policy and management problem solving. Another benefit of these sessions and presentations is the interaction with colleagues who share similar positions and problems.

- *Specific programs for presidents.* Presidents often find that while a broad array of programs is useful for addressing particular substantive areas, they derive greater benefit from programs targeted to presidents. Many programs exist to assist presidents with the particular tasks of their jobs. Examples include the Council for Advancement and Support of Education (CASE) programs specifically geared to teach presidents about fund raising, and the annual National Association of Independent Colleges and Universities (NAICU) program that briefs presidents on the federal education agenda. Other programs provide team-building and problem-solving opportunities for presidents and key members of the senior staff.

- *Consultants.* An often overlooked but powerful tool for on-the-job development of the president is that provided by consultants and other resource persons. Although some presidential development needs are specific to time, place, and issue, consultants can develop training to address these specific needs. Examples of such assistance are coaching for public speaking or media interviewing and strategy sessions with an expert on collective bargaining negotiations.

- *Team building.* Programs exist to develop campus teams, particularly the president and key officers. For example, the Association of Governing Boards of Universities and Colleges (AGB) offers many programs for the president and key members of the board of trustees. Other organizations, such as CASE, sponsor programs for groups such as the financial management team (including the president) to address specific campus problems.

Strategies for Renewal

In the stressful job of the president, renewal is particularly important. A president celebrating her first anniversary in office observed, ''Although a president may begin with high levels of energy and ideas, these dissipate all too quickly. Presidents have to quickly learn that to sustain ourselves in a demanding job like this, we must plan regular opportunities to refresh ourselves personally and professionally. This was one of the toughest lessons I had to learn to survive in this job.'' Regularly scheduled renewal and rest opportunities are a vital way to stave off excessive psychological strain and physical manifestations of stress.

- *National programs.* National institutes and administrative seminars are the most widely known examples of programs for renewal. Most provide opportunities for presidents to step out of their work routines and to reenter the world of study and reflection, to sit back and put it all into perspective, and to achieve a broader understanding of principles and theories. In addition, national programs provide important opportunities to identify and develop colleagues on whom a president can call for advice and consultation.

- *Programs for business executives.* For even stronger doses of management theory, college and university presidents can join the classes of business-management institutes. Many top business schools run executive education seminars, some specifically for CEOs of businesses and corporations but also open to college and university presidents. An example is the Advanced Management Program of Harvard's Graduate School of Business Administration. Other top business schools, such as the Massachusetts Institute of Technology's Sloan School and Northwestern University, offer executive management institutes.

- *Seminars in the liberal arts.* While the programs mentioned above stress leadership and management, another set of programs explores the liberal arts. The Troutbeck Program, designed especially for college and university presidents, is a prime example of this type of programming. In these programs, presidents explore philosophy, history, and politics, and reflect upon the enduring values of society. The goals of these seminars are rethinking and expanding the vision of the academic mission, renewing intellectual confidence, overcoming presidential isolation, and deepening an understanding of leadership.

- *On-the-job renewal.* Many presidents have found that they can turn activities required of them on a regular basis into developmental opportunities. The president of a major state university explained, ''Early in my presidency I learned a trick from an old pro president. I incorporate a theme or common subject into my speeches and writing for a year. This gives me the opportunity to delve into a topic in depth and to explore its nuances using the techniques of research and scholarship that characterized my academic life before becoming an administrator.''

  Some associations, including the AASCU, organize study forums and travel abroad for presidents. These trips provide a break from the campus routine, opportunities for interaction with other presidents, formal investigation of other educational systems and foreign cultures, and entry to relationships with international institutions. Such trips blend work, intellectual stimulation, and relaxation.

- *Reading, Writing, and Reflection.* The presidency drains energy— physical, mental, and emotional. The president of an independent university in the southwest commented, ''In a culture of academic reflection, hushed libraries, and scholarly discussions on philosophical points, it's surprising how often the president's life is just the opposite—action oriented, energized, always in motion.'' It is important for a president to read, write, and reflect. Some of this activity may relate to maintaining a broad perspective on higher education issues, such as keeping up with the *Chronicle of Higher Education*, association newsletters, and the like. Presidents can broaden their perspective of their jobs by reading the many books available on the topic, or personal reflections by other presidents. Most presidents feel a strong need to cultivate intellectual interests outside of higher education, keeping abreast of developments in their discipline, being knowledgeable about world events, or reading a variety of books, magazines, and journals, including fiction and poetry. Finding even small amounts of time to disengage from the daily concerns of the presidency and to connect with the world of ideas is essential to the vitality of most academic leaders.

David Riesman, a long-time student of the college presidency, has said that he wishes every president could have a cabin on a lake, far removed from the campus. Such a cabin may be the only place where the president can retreat to think, unwind, and pursue personal interests.

- *Service on committees and boards.* Presidents can derive developmental benefit as well as personal challenge from serving on committees and boards. In most higher education associations and organizations, presidents fill the positions on the board of directors and serve as chairs of major committees. These positions provide an opportunity to explore higher education issues, to exchange views with top educational leaders, and to give direction to important higher education enterprises that can affect national education policy.

Presidents often are called upon to serve on or chair local, state, and national task forces, committees, blue-ribbon panels, and organizations. Such positions can provide stimulating points of contact with other types of groups. In addition, presidents often are called upon to serve on the boards of area corporations and businesses. This kind of service offers opportunities to see how other organizations are run, to observe other leaders solving problems, to develop larger networks, to meet colleagues in new areas, and to exercise leadership in other venues. Service on editorial boards for higher education publications, journals, and book series can help a president stay on the cutting edge of current college and university issues.

- *Other personal development programs and opportunities.* Other categories of personal development programs, geared more specifically to business executives, are often open to college presidents. Such programs include executive adventure programs such as Outward Bound, study trips abroad, and public service programs both in the United States and abroad.

Preparing for the Next Step

Key problems faced by every president are when to leave the presidency and where to go afterward. Kerr and Gade's studies of presidents (1986) showed that 15 percent moved to another presidency, 20 percent returned to the faculty, 15 percent moved into other administrative positions in higher education (usually in state or system offices or associations), 25 percent went into retirement or semiretirement, and 25 percent left academic life.

Presidents who anticipate a return to teaching and research need to invest time throughout their presidential tenures in keeping up with their disciplines. A former president turned teacher remembered, ''Like many presidents, when I started the job I intended to stay current in my field, but like those others, I found the task impossible. I advise any president facing a return to teaching and research to dedicate specific time to catch up with research and to acquire new expertise.'' After years in the presidency, some may decide to forgo their old field and declare a new expertise in higher education. But this, too, requires a deliberate effort to acquire the conceptual and theoretical tools of higher education through readings, attendance at professional meetings, and participation in research associations such as the American Educational Research Association (AERA) and the Association for the Study of Higher Education (ASHE).

In preparation for leaving the presidency, many attempt to establish a particular skill or area of expertise for consulting. This may require intense study to develop a full range of expertise in addition to that acquired on the job.

STRATEGIES FOR BOARDS TO FOSTER PRESIDENTIAL DEVELOPMENT

The board of trustees, and particularly the chair of the board, plays a crucial role in ensuring the ongoing development of a president. A president will not pursue development in spite of a board, and even a president inclined to development needs the support of the board to ensure that this is seen as important for the president and the institution. The board's responsibilities include three primary areas:

Encourage the President to Seek Development Opportunities

The board should not only encourage a president to pursue development opportunities but also should actively work with the president to identify and evaluate such opportunities. Many institutions include consideration of future development activities in the president's annual review.

Provide Sufficient Resources

Programs for presidents may be more costly than those directed at other campus administrators because of the unique needs of presidents, the higher visibility (and thus fees) of speakers, and the greater selectivity of meeting sites. The president is in a unique symbolic situation: since every move and expenditure may be monitored by the community, it can be difficult to use resources that are not made available to others. Programs outside of academe (those specifically designed for corporate executives) charge corporate prices, although some offer scholarships for college officers. The board should make sufficient resources available for the president's participation in these programs.

Set an Example of Active Leadership Development

The board must indicate the value it places on leadership development by actively pursuing its own development. This may include board retreats, periodic self-assessment, and attendance at programs designed to help boards understand higher education issues and board effectiveness. (See Chapter 4, *Governing Boards*, for further detail.)

STRATEGIES FOR SPOUSES

The spouses of college and university presidents have become a topic of increased discussion, in terms of both their expected roles in relation to the institution and the support that the institution should provide. The number of models that the presidential spouse can now follow has expanded dramatically since the days of the "minister's wife" and the "southern belle who knows her place" (Kerr and Gade 1986, p. 113). The expanded number of models means that presidents and their spouses each need their own sources of development, first to choose among the many models for the one that best suits their situation, and second for continued support as the presidency continues.

Many programs for presidents also include options for spouses. These range from integration of the spouse into the program as an equal learning partner to parallel but separate programming for presidents and spouses. Some programs provide opportunities for spouses to investigate the higher education issues in which the president is immersed; others provide opportunities to explore the unique situation and stresses of the presidency. The appendix of the programs and practices listed at the end of this chapter includes notations about spouse participation.

In the past five years, increased research has focused on the presidential spouse. The situation of the presidential spouse is now a common topic in most books on presidencies and is itself the primary topic of books. There are now enough articles and books on the subject of the presidential spouse to fill the spouse's own bookshelf.

Many presidential associations offer networks and support groups for spouses. Typically, these groups meet during the association's annual meetings and keep in contact through newsletters.

CONCLUSION

Presidents have special and unique developmental needs that change over the course of their tenure. Although many programs exist to address these changing developmental needs, presidents also must creatively take advantage of everyday tasks to ensure ongoing intellectual stimulation and personal growth. Like other members of the academy, the president must carefully analyze developmental needs and plan to address them. The board plays a crucial role in ensuring that the president actively pursues his or her personal and leadership development.

REFERENCES

Fisher, James L. *Power of the Presidency*. New York: American Council on Education/Macmillan, 1984.

Green, Madeleine. *The American College President: A Contemporary Profile*. Washington, DC: American Council on Education, 1988.

Heidrick and Struggles, Inc. *Chief Executive Officer*. Chicago: Heidrick and Struggles, Inc., 1987.

Kauffman, Joseph F. *At the Pleasure of the Board: The Service of the College and University President*. Washington, DC: American Council on Education, 1980.

Kerr, Clark, and Marian L. Gade. *The Many Lives of Academic Presidents: Time, Place and Character*. Washington, DC: Association of Governing Boards of Universities and Colleges, 1986.

Moore, Kathryn M., Ann M. Salimbene, Joyce D. Marlier, and Stephen M. Bragg. ''The Structure of Presidents' and Deans' Careers.'' *Journal of Higher Education* 54, no. 5 (September/October 1983): 500–515.

Vaughan, George B. *The Community College Presidency*. New York: American Council on Education/Macmillan, 1986.

RESOURCES

Bensimon, Estela Mara, Marian L. Gade, and Joseph F. Kauffman. *On Assuming a College or University Presidency: Lessons and Advice from the Field*. Washington, DC: American Association for Higher Education, 1989.

>   Essays on lessons learned from experienced presidents, the president-trustee relationship, and strategies for an effective presidency. The book ends with a resource guide written by Sharon A. McDade on leadership development programs appropriate for new and seasoned presidents, and an annotated list of references.

Clodius, Joan E., and Diane Skomars Magrath, eds. *The President's Spouse: Volunteer or Volunteered*. Washington, DC: National Association of State Universities and Land-Grant Colleges, 1984.

>   One of the first and still among the best of the anthologies of essays about aspects of the spousal role. The book includes essays by wives of presidents of state universities and land-grant colleges on the issues and challenges of this unique role.

Cohen, Michael D., and James G. March. *Leadership and Ambiguity: The American College President*, Second ed. Boston: Harvard Business School Press, 1986.

>   Classic higher education book sharing insights from a survey on the careers of college and university presidents. Its greatest contribution is the concept of the university as an ''organized anarchy'' in which presidents can make little impact.

Fisher, James L. *Power of the Presidency*. New York: American Council on Education/Macmillan, 1984.

>   Analyzes the types of power—coercive, rewards, expert, legitimate, and charismatic—that presidents can use to accomplish objectives. Concentrates on knowing when, where, why, and how to use them. It also includes helpful and often humorous tips for success. A controversial treatise on power and the presidency.

Fisher, James L., and Martha W. Tack, eds. *Leaders on Leadership: The College Presidency*. New Directions for Higher Education 61. San Francisco: Jossey-Bass, 1988.

>   A sourcebook of advice on the college presidency from 18 individuals who know the job first-hand. Provides insight into the nature of college leadership—the problems and the opportunities, the challenges and the rewards. The institutions represented span the higher education spectrum.

Kauffman, Joseph F. *At the Pleasure of the Board: The Service of the College and University President*. Washington, DC: American Council on Education, 1980.

>   One of the best descriptions of the problems, challenges, and opportunities of the college presidency. Emphasizes ''service'' as a major responsibility.

Kerr, Clark. *Presidents Make a Difference: Strengthening Leadership in Colleges and Universities*. Washington, DC: Association of Governing Boards of Universities and Colleges, 1984.

>   Results of a three-year study on the college presidency. Through a series of recommendations and suggested actions directed to trustees, the book covers topics of trustee support, presidential review, determining how long to stay (and when to leave), and governance issues.

Kerr, Clark, and Marian L. Gade. *The Many Lives of Academic Presidents: Time, Place and Character*. Washington, DC: Association of Governing Boards of Universities and Colleges, 1986.

>   Comprehensive study of the academic presidency and those who fill it. Sequel to *Presidents Make a Difference*. Examines the reality of decision making in higher education and the impact of leadership on a college campus. Sections on the relevance of power and influence are particularly helpful. Annotated bibliography of books on higher education leadership and governance.

McCall, Morgan W., Jr., Michael M. Lombardo, and Ann M. Morrison. *The Lessons of Experience: How Successful Executives Develop on the Job*. Lexington, MA: Lexington Books, 1988.

An in-depth survey of how top managers of business and industry developed their management and leadership skills. The survey asked for experiences that had the greatest impact on their careers and the lessons they took from those experiences. The book reports on the key elements that can maximize the skill development potential of on-site job assignments, the arena in which they found the most benefit for leadership and management development.

Ostar, Roberta H. *Public Roles, Private Lives: The Representational Role of College and University Presidents*. Washington, DC: Association of Governing Boards of Universities and Colleges, 1991.

This special report of the AGB examines the personal roles of the presidents of colleges and universities in their own right. It focuses on the social responsibilities of the presidents and their spouses. Use of personal quotes and anecdotes adds to the discussion of subjects which include attending social events, raising funds and friends, organizing parties, maintaining privacy, identifying the roles of the spouse and supporting the president and his or her spouse. Charts and graphs outline the data appearing in this work.

Taylor, Barbara E. *Working Effectively with Trustees: Building Cooperative Campus Leadership*. ASHE-ERIC Higher Education Report No. 2. Washington, DC: Association for the Study of Higher Education, 1987.

Examines the board from the perspective of the president. Particularly valuable for its insights on how administrators and faculty can share authority with trustees.

PROGRAMS AND PRACTICES

Complete information on each listing is provided in the *Appendix*. The letter and number in the parentheses correspond to the section and entry number in the *Appendix*.

National Associations

The following are considered "presidential" associations because the president is either the member or the official voting delegate for the institution. All of these associations sponsor annual meetings or conventions, typically with special sessions designated for presidents. Many also have specific tracks or sessions for new presidents. Selected development programs offered by some of these associations are described following this list.

American Association of Community and Junior Colleges (AACJC) (A19)

American Association of State Colleges and Universities (AASCU) (A25)

American Council on Education (ACE) (A40)

Association of American Colleges (AAC) (A86)

Association of American Universities (AAU) (A90)

Council of Independent Colleges (CIC) (A132)

National Association for Equal Opportunity in Higher Education (NAFEO) (A155)

National Association of Independent Colleges and Universities (NAICU) (A169)

National Association of State Universities and Land-Grant Colleges (NASULGC) (A173)

Specialized Associations

American Association of Bible Colleges (AABC) (A14)

American Association of Colleges of Osteopathic Medicine (AACOM) (A17)

American Association of Presidents of Independent Colleges and Universities (AAPICU) (A24)

American Indian Higher Education Consortium (AIHEC) (A46)

Association of Catholic Colleges and Universities (ACCU) (A93)

Association of Community College Trustees (ACCT) (A100)

Association of Episcopal Colleges (AEC) (A104)

Association of Governing Boards of Universities and Colleges (AGB) (A105)

Association of Independent Colleges and Schools (AICS) (A106)

Association of Jesuit Colleges and Universities (AJCU) (A107)

Association of Military Colleges and Schools of the United States (AMCS) (A108)

Association of Southern Baptist Colleges and Schools (ASBCS) (A112)

Association of Theological Schools in the United States and Canada (ATS) (A115)

Association of Urban Universities (AUU) (A117)

Council of 1890 College Presidents (CCP) (A129)

Hispanic Association of Colleges and Universities (HACU) (A142)

Lutheran Educational Conference of North America (LECNA) (A149)

National Association of Schools and Colleges of the United Methodist Church (NASCUMC) (A171)

National Association of Trade and Technical Schools (NATTS) (A176)

United Negro College Fund (UNCF) (A189)

National Programs

The following list provides a sampling of the range and variety of off-campus programs available to presidents and is not meant to be an inventory of all programs and activities available to these leaders. Note that many programs offered by associations are available only to presidents of member institutions.

American Association of Community and Junior Colleges (AACJC) (P5)

  Presidents Academy Workshop *(P5b)*

American Association of State Colleges and Universities (AASCU) (P6)

  New Presidents Sessions *(P6b)*
  Presidents' Academy *(P6c)*
  Summer Council of Presidents *(P6d)*
  Workshop for New Member Presidents/Spouses During Annual Meeting *(P6e)*

American Council on Education (ACE) (P7)

  The Fellows Program *(P7b)*
  Occasional colloquia for presidents *(P7c)*
  Sessions during annual meeting for presidents *(P7d)*

American Management Association (AMA) (P8)

Aspen Institute (P9)

  The Executive Seminar *(P9a)*
  21st Century Leaders Program *(P9b)*

Association of American Colleges (AAC) (P10)

Specially designated presidential sessions at annual meetings *(P10a)*

Association of Community College Trustees (ACCT) (P14)

National Legislative Seminar and Regional Seminars *(P14a)*

Association of Governing Boards of Universities and Colleges (AGB) (P15)

Improving Board Performance *(P15b)*
Institute for Trustee Leadership: Program for Board Chairs and Chief Executive Officers of
   Independent Institutions *(P15c)*
Introduction to AGB Services during National Conference on Trusteeship *(P15d)*
Seminar for Chairpersons and Chief Executives of Theological Schools and Seminaries *(P15g)*
Seminar on Endowment Management *(P15h)*
Strategic Planning for Theological Schools *(P15j)*
Trustee Responsibility for Financial Affairs *(P15k)*

*Association of Governing Boards of Universities and Colleges (AGB) in Cooperation with the
National Association of System Heads (P16)*

Governing the Public Multicampus System *(P16a)*

The Bush Foundation (P18)

Leadership Program for Midcareer Development *(P18a)*

Christian A. Johnson Endeavor Foundation (P23)

Troutbeck Program/Educational Leadership Project *(P23a)*

Council for Advancement and Support of Education (CASE) (P26)

Presidential and Trustee Leadership in Fund Raising *(P26b)*
Presidents' Colloquium on Institutional Advancement *(P26c)*

Council for International Exchange of Scholars (CIES) (P28)

Fulbright Scholar Program *(P28a)*

Council of Independent Colleges (CIC) (P32)

New Presidents Workshop preceding Annual Presidents Institute *(P32a)*
Presidents Institute *(P32b)*

Harvard University/Graduate School of Business Administration (P36)

Advanced Management Program (AMP) *(P36a)*

Harvard University/Graduate School of Education (P37)

Harvard Seminar for New Presidents *(P37a)*
Institute for Educational Management (IEM) *(P37b)*

Massachusetts Institute of Technology (MIT)/Sloan School of Management (P48)

Alfred P. Sloan Fellows Program *(P48a)*

National Association of Independent Colleges and Universities (NAICU) (P54)

Public Policy Seminar for New Presidents *(P54a)*

National Association of State Universities and Land-Grant Colleges (NASULGC) (P55)

Council of Presidents *(P55a)*

National Institute for Leadership Development (P59)

Workshop for Women Presidents *(P59e)*

Society for Values in Higher Education (P64)

The Fellows Meeting *(P64a)*

University of Georgia/Institute of Higher Education and The Georgia Center for Continuing Education (P69)

Annual Conference on Higher Education and the Law *(P69a)*

Williamsburg Development Institute (P72)

Williamsburg Development Institute *(P72a)*

Statewide, System-Specific and On-Campus Programs

Arizona State University (ASU) (S2)

President's Breakfast Series *(S2d)*

6

SENIOR ADMINISTRATORS

While the president is the leader most visible to the public, the other senior administrators are usually the most visible leaders to those who work within the institution. These leaders usually carry the title of vice president; some institutions, particularly liberal arts colleges and community colleges, use the title of dean for these senior officers.

Traditionally, even the smallest college includes senior officers in the areas of academic affairs, student services, institutional advancement, business, and administration. The vice president for academic affairs is often titled provost. In community colleges the comparable title is often dean of instruction, while in a liberal arts college the title is dean of the faculty. The purview of the vice president for institutional advancement may include fund raising, development, alumni relations, public relations, marketing, and government and legislative relations. The realm of vice president for administration usually includes operations, physical plant, and personnel.

At larger institutions, the number of senior officers multiplies to provide specialized attention to more areas. There may be additional senior officers in research or legal affairs, areas that in smaller schools are handled by consultants.

In some institutions, the academic vice president is considered the first among the vice presidents and is responsible for the institution in the president's absence. Another model includes an executive vice president to whom the other vice presidents report.

CAREER PREPARATION

Academic Vice Presidents/Provosts

Like presidents, academic vice presidents usually do not begin their careers intending to be administrators. The move into administration is rarely a deliberate act, and takes on meaning as a career transition only in retrospect (Alexander et al. 1989, McDade 1986). As a chief academic officer at a major research university commented, ''In retrospect, my *vita* suggests that I was accumulating experiences and leadership lessons at each job that pointed directly to this provostship. But in reality, those experiences and lessons could have taken me in a dozen different directions, including continued tenure as a professor and leadership roles on an international level within my discipline.''

Unlike other vice presidents, chief academic officers almost always began their careers as faculty members intending to pursue a career of teaching and research. The first administrative job—as chair or associate dean, for example—may turn out to be the first unplanned step into an administrative career.

At some time during that first administrative job, a few decide that the world of administration offers significant challenges and rewards. The fledgling administrator then begins to scale the administrative career ladder, perhaps to a deanship, then to an academic vice presidency. While a majority of academic vice presidents follow this path, the permutations and variations have expanded. Compared to a decade or more ago, today academic vice presidents have spent fewer years in faculty positions. They have experimented with more ''off-ladder positions,'' e.g., director of centers, manager of nonacademic areas, and even positions outside of the academy (Moore 1983, Poskozim 1984). Yet, in comparison to the presidency, which increasingly draws candidates from the full range of institutional positions, the ladder to becoming the chief academic officer is somewhat more traditional.

The customary career steps provide valuable training in preparation, organization, and management, as well as the development of strong communication abilities. Faculty experience provides invaluable socialization for academic leadership positions. Although faculty search committees recognize that the academic vice presidency requires many skills besides those of teacher and researcher, they consistently demand an academic background to prove that candidates are ''one of us'' and understand the lives of professors.

Student Services, Institutional Advancement, and Administrative Senior Officers

The other main areas of institutional leadership—student services and personnel, development and fund raising, business and administration—have their own individual career paths. For many, however, the routes to these positions are idiosyncratic and unpredictable. Recently, graduate programs directed at each of these administrative positions have evolved. For example, an increasing number of senior administrative officers have business degrees with a specialization in nonprofit organizations, while student affairs officers increasingly have doctorates in student services.

Each area has developed its own entry and ladder positions. It is most common for chief student affairs officers to have started their careers in counseling or residence hall management and for chief institutional advancement officers to have started on fund raising or alumni affairs staffs. Traditionally, few administrative senior officers have had faculty experience, but increasingly, faculty ranks are fertile recruiting grounds for administrative leadership positions. Several studies have shown the faculty as a source second only to the combined count of entry-level management positions for nonacademic senior officers (McDade 1987, Twombly 1986, Moore et al. 1985, Rickard 1985).

At each rung on the career ladder, administrators are exposed to the tasks and responsibilities of their chosen area and socialized into that administrative world. Since few managers cross administrative areas or transfer from one to another, it is not until attaining a senior position that one has substantial programmatic and policy exchange with other areas.

RESPONSIBILITIES

Each vice president directs the operations of his or her area and acts as the principal liaison between that unit and the rest of the institution. As members of the senior leadership team, vice presidents share with the president the responsibilities for the health and well-being of the institution, the development of policy, and planning for its future. Responsibilities of senior officers can be grouped as follows:

Creating Vision

A vice president's primary duty is to create an overall vision for the unit and develop a strategy for implementing that vision.

Directing Operations

From that vision should flow the structure and operations of the unit. This includes providing unit leadership and a sense of direction for faculty and staff, defining the unit's tasks, and planning for the most efficient and effective use of resources.

Forging Links With the Senior Leadership Team

The many areas of the college officially come together at the vice-presidential level. While there may be many types of formal and informal interchanges at lower levels, the senior officers provide official linkages, integrated planning, and comprehensive policies. Beyond solving the day-to-day problems of operations, this senior leadership team typically shares the overall responsibility for long-range planning. As a team, this group establishes the tone of operations, as well as the goals for those operations, for the entire institution. In turn, senior officers create leadership teams of the officers within their own units.

Securing Resources and Overseeing Their Use

While the president has ultimate responsibility for budgets and resources, operationally these are shared responsibilities of the senior officers. Individually, vice presidents prepare budgets for their units, but together with the president they create an institutional budget that takes into consideration the needs and goals of each unit. Since many units do not have their own revenue sources, vice presidents have varying responsibilities for securing resources. As funds from traditional sources (tuition, fees, government support) decline, it will be necessary for all senior officers—not just the vice president for development—to be involved in the solicitation of outside funds. This will include proposing grants, going on fund-raising trips, meeting with donors, and lobbying government and supporting organizations.

Creating the Working Environment for Administrators and Staff

Typically, the president's responsibility for the selection and retention of qualified personnel is delegated to senior officers. Vice presidents design and implement personnel policies, create and maintain effective relationships with all workers in their areas, and establish the working culture for their units. If there is a strong institutional commitment to diversity, the vice presidents must make it clear that they are committed to promoting a pluralistic campus and are working actively to find, hire, support, and promote women and minorities within their areas. The academic vice president of a public comprehensive university observed, ''While the president is the role model for the entire campus, the vice presidents are even more powerful role models to the members of our units because of our proximity. What I do about pluralism is noted—and followed.''

Linking the Unit to the Institution's Mission

All administrative areas must be linked to and support the institution's mission. Vice presidents interpret the institutional mission to their areas and shape their areas' contributions to the overall mission. Working with the president, vice presidents design the structures and strategies to achieve the individual components of the mission.

Relating the Unit to the Institution and the Community

A vice president represents his or her unit to the rest of the institution. This includes attending ceremonial events; serving on key committees; and addressing student, faculty, and staff gatherings. Although the president is typically the representative of the institution to the outside world, vice presidents are often deputized to represent the institution when the president is unavailable. In addition, vice presidents may have regular and assigned external roles, such as serving on the Chamber of Commerce or representing the college to the local town board.

LEADERSHIP CAPACITIES

Vice presidential leadership capacities combine the management responsibilities usually associated with mid-level managers and the leadership roles of presidents. While the capacities are similar across senior positions, the mix varies for each specific position.

Providing Vision and Setting Goals

The president may be the chief definer of vision, but vice presidents work collaboratively with the president to shape the vision. They are also the chief interpreters. This interpretive role includes setting the operational goals for their units.

Understanding Higher Education

Senior officers serve as important links between an institution and the larger higher education community. To help staff members better understand their roles and tasks, vice presidents need to interpret them in the context and goals of higher education. It is within this broader context that senior officers develop the policies and organizational structures that shape individual institutions.

Working With People

As leader of a major unit within the college or university, the senior officer is responsible for the well-being and productivity of many people. The executive vice president of a liberal arts college notes, ''People issues—large, small, insignificant, crucial—take up most of each of my days. A senior officer has to be able to work with a very wide range of people, many from different academic or administrative backgrounds, and meld them all into a productive team.''

Managing and Decision Making

It is within the vice presidential units that the business of a college or university actually takes place. Thus, a vice president needs to be a good manager to make the unit function productively. In large institutions, management at the senior levels probably is not as oriented toward detail and implementation as at lower levels of administration, but instead includes a greater emphasis on strategy, planning, and decision making. In smaller institutions, senior officers are responsible for both policy formation and policy implementation. These responsibilities are further fragmented by the number of hats that senior officers must wear. The chief student affairs officer of a small college commented, ''I serve as chief judicial officer for students, personnel officer for members of the student services staff, chief advisor to all student organizations, head of student orientation programming, chief formulator and implementer of student affairs policy, as well as key adviser to the president on student-related issues. And, oh yes, supervisor of dormitories and food services and collector of all complaints on these. And that's just a few of my hats!''

Maintaining Mental Vigor and Physical Vitality

A college leader, no matter the job level, cannot make a long-term and substantial contribution to the organization unless he or she maintains the mental vigor and physical vitality needed to run the long race. An institutional advancement vice president explained, ''There's never a down part of the cycle, a quiet period. The pace is unrelenting. It's a marathon, not a sprint.''

PHASES OF AN ADMINISTRATIVE POSITION

On every job, an administrator goes through a learning cycle. Understanding this job cycle can help administrators understand their own development needs and enhance the development they offer the members of their staffs.

Entry Phase

While many mid-level administrators move into their jobs from within the institution, most senior officers enter their positions from other institutions. Thus, upon taking a new job, senior officers must first learn about the institution, the community, and the region. The new officer must become familiar with demographic, economic, and political trends affecting the institution, while homing in on the institution's specific qualities. For an officer new to senior ranks, there is also a learning curve for the task of heading a major institutional unit. A chief student affairs officer explained, ''During this learning period, a wise senior officer will follow a plan of entry to ensure meeting all the important people with whom he or she must interact. It's best to touch all the bases early.''

Growth Phase

After two to three years, an administrator settles into the ''midlife'' of a position, becoming comfortable with the role and its responsibilities. There is enough accumulated information to enable the senior officer to make decisions within a context without having to research each situation. In this stage, administrators will settle on some issues of vital importance to the organization and to themselves and begin to work hard on them. The senior officer also will begin to reach out beyond the institution to become active in the community and to renew previous development activities at higher levels of responsibility. Also, senior officers start to become involved in other areas not directly related to their units, such as fund raising. They experience a growing need for information on process and on new, unexplored areas less obviously related to the unit.

Mature Phase

During this stage, the administrator has mastered the job and no longer needs to devote as much time as before to details and operations. More routine work can be delegated, leaving the senior officer more time for planning, integrating programs with the other units, and assuming additional responsibilities assigned by the president. Issues that the officer began to address in earlier phases may begin to bear fruit or become clearly impossible to solve. As a chief academic affairs officer of a community college described it, ''Because of the increased flexibility of time, senior officers can take on major roles in the community and in their professional associations and begin to mentor junior officers.''

The mature stage of the cycle presents several key challenges. Some senior officers will begin to feel burnout during this phase, especially if major initiatives have taken substantial time and energy but are not showing much progress. Others, seemingly successful in the previous cycles, may find their attention beginning to wander and will require new stimuli to stay engaged and energized. Solving the problems of

derailed projects and finding new stimuli are crucial development challenges for this phase. If senior officers are successful in addressing these
needs, they are likely to stay with the institution longer and recycle back
to the growth phase. If not, they are likely to begin thinking about new
jobs.

STRATEGIES FOR DEVELOPMENT

Different support strategies may be appropriate for the different
phases of administrative development.

Strategies for New Senior Administrators

In some institutions and in some fields, mid-level administrators are
groomed for senior-level positions. This grooming is found more often
in the administrative offices than in the academic ranks and in smaller
institutions rather than larger ones. A chief financial officer of a small
comprehensive college notes, "It's not unusual in smaller institutions
for someone in the finance area to be identified and groomed to take
over the chief administrative position upon the retirement of the incumbent." But in general, new administrators enter the senior ranks with little preparation beyond a job well done in a more junior position that
may have provided insight into the role, personality, and responsibilities
of at least one senior supervisor. The following strategies can help senior
officers orient themselves to their new roles.

- *Formal programs.* The few formal programs for new senior administrators are found primarily in the administrative fields. Many administrative associations offer introductory programs for the major
  transition points. The National Association of Student Personnel
  Administrators (NASPA) provides a program for senior student affairs
  officers, and the Council for Advancement and Support of Education
  (CASE) provides a program for chief institutional advancement
  officers.

- *Informal activities.* Many senior officers create their own entry development programs by visiting their counterparts at sister institutions.
  The new chief academic officer of an institution within a major state
  system noted, "One of the best things I did when I started this job
  was to visit systematically my counterparts on . . . all our sister campuses, which helped me to understand where they were coming from
  in discussions." Others plan systematic visits to the many units
  within their own institutions.

Strategies for All Senior Administrators

- *Networks and interactions with other people.* It is useful to discuss problems with peers. Each senior officer is unique on a campus. While a general counsel and a vice president for research may have institutional interests in common, they approach those interests from very different perspectives. Thus, it is important to have a well-developed and -maintained network within which to share problems, polish strategies, interact with people facing like problems under similar conditions, acquire outside opinions on institutional issues, and participate in introspective discussions on career and institutional goals. Usually, senior officers shift from the networks of colleagues from discipline bases associated with their former jobs to networks of peers sharing an administrative base. A general counsel explained, "To build and maintain useful networks requires a lot of work to keep in touch with colleagues and to track their activities, problems, and institutional situations. You've got to give equally so those colleagues are ready to give when you need information and assistance."

- *Reading on issues.* Senior officers need to know not only their own area, but also about all the rest of the institution and about a variety of issues as different as demographic trends, facilities maintenance, and telecommunications. While on-the-job experience contributes substantially to such wide-ranging information, a broad-based knowledge of educational issues comes only from keeping up with the news and literature. Senior officers may find it useful to expand their reading beyond higher education to include economics, management, leadership, political science, history, the sciences, and the humanities.

- *Association meetings.* The conventions and annual meetings of associations provide a forum where senior officers can gain perspective and stimulation away from the pressures of campus demands. Association meetings vary significantly in their format and content. It is worth shopping around to find the type of association meeting that meets one's needs at a specific time; it is also important to recognize that those needs may change over time. Associations and their conventions can provide friendships, collegiality, and moral support as well as skills development. A chief student affairs officer observed, "The regular attenders at a NASPA or ACPA [American College Personnel Association] convention find as much, if not more, value in comparing notes with their friends as in the sessions themselves. You know who is going to be there and you go out of your way to find time to talk shop."

Associations also provide important opportunities for leadership roles and national visibility. Through participation on national boards and task forces, senior administrators can keep on the cutting edge of their fields.

Many academic officers also try to keep in touch or stay active in their disciplinary associations. A chief academic officer of a liberal arts college stated, ''It's tough to keep up, but continued contact with my discipline has provided intellectual sustenance and relief from my steady diet of 'administrivia.'''

- *National leadership development programs.* A number of leadership development programs are designed for senior administrators with the goal of perfecting their leadership and management skills. Some of these programs are held in resort locations and schedule free time for family activities and sports to enable participants to combine work and pleasure. A major leadership development program such as the Institute for Educational Management (IEM) may be valuable, depending on when it comes in the individual's career, its relevance to that career, the individual's goals, and considerations of institutional timing. Participation also may satisfy the need to reenter the learning world after a long time in the management world.

- *Specialized seminars and workshops.* In the growth and mature stages of the job cycle, senior officers need to stretch beyond their own areas of expertise to understand better the specific offices in their units or in other parts of the institution. For these reasons, senior officers may seek programs on specialized topics besides the more generalized leadership development programs discussed above. Programs of interest to senior officers might include the management and policy implications of admissions, economic trends, assessment, or international education.

- *Learning from institutional crises.* As one senior officer put it, another pronunciation of ''crisis'' is ''opportunity.'' There is no faster or greater learning opportunity than an institutional crisis, no matter the size or cause. Because of their very time-pressured natures, crises force administrators to collect information, perform analysis, and produce solutions in ways different from those used under normal circumstances. Networks are especially crucial for ideas and advice. Extraordinary conditions require unusual combinations of ideas and strategies, all providing learning opportunities. While the key learning benefits come from personally living through the crisis, learning also comes from evaluating the crisis after the fact and assessing actions and results. This concept of learning from the crises of others forms the premise of the case-study method of instruction.

- *Travel.* While many associations offer travel/study trips abroad for senior officers in that field, travel does not have to take one far or for very long to be productive. A side-trip to visit another campus while participating in a convention may produce new stimulation and ideas. Service on accreditation teams is another way to see other institutions and explore how they function.

Increasingly, senior officers also need to know about issues of international education. International travel, often organized by associations or state economic organizations, provides an avenue to this knowledge as well as important contacts at foreign educational institutions.

- *Sabbaticals and exchanges.* Gradually, institutions are beginning to provide administrative sabbatical programs, usually of short duration. During such sabbaticals, a senior administrator may work at another institution or in an association for a change of scenery and challenge, or may undertake a special short-term job for the university system or state education office. Exchanges of senior officers for short-term projects and sabbaticals are sometimes arranged through system offices, consortia, and associations. Sabbaticals can also provide an opportunity for international travel and study, or to focus on scholarship in one's discipline. While senior faculty have long benefitted from programs such as the Fulbright, some international exchanges, albeit of shorter duration, are now available for senior administrators, too.

- *In-depth study of an issue and consulting.* Often, senior officers develop a special area of focus in higher education about which they can research, write, or consult. Research and writing provide opportunities for introspection and clarification; consulting provides the opportunity to work with other institutions. A chief academic officer of a community college observed, ''Consulting provides an opportunity for me to see how other institutions function; I always learn as much from a project as do the administrators and institutions with which I consult.'' Thus, institutions that allow their vice presidents to do some consulting can benefit more from the information and insights brought back home than they lose from the periodic absence of the senior officers.

Some senior administrators find it useful to stretch their knowledge by identifying a specific ''issue for the year'' for reading and research. The issue typically is chosen in relation to some project or challenge on campus—for example, diversity or assessment. Then, reading, conference attendance, and networking activities for the year can center on the issue. This is a challenging yet time-efficient way to explore issues in sufficient depth to become proficient, while providing a significant variety of stimuli over the years.

- *Teaching.* Although the daily demands of a senior administrative position may not allow for regular teaching duties, it may be possible and desirable to teach a few classes or to deliver lectures as part of courses organized by regular faculty. Such forays into teaching, though limited in scale, provide the opportunity to keep one's hand in teaching and stay in touch with students. In some institutions, administrators teach one course each semester or year. For nonacademic senior officers, teaching an occasional class or course provides important credibility with faculty and first-hand experience in the academic enterprise.

- *Mentoring.* Mentoring is a natural outreach of senior roles and responsibilities. Mentoring may occur spontaneously and informally or be part of a formal institutional program. Informal mentoring includes the typical senior officer tasks of explaining, coaching, evaluating, and stimulating the work of staff members. In a formal mentoring effort, the Fellows programs of the American Council on Education (ACE) and the California State University System assign faculty and mid-level administrators to senior officers in a prescribed relationship that can be equally stimulating to mentor and protege. Mentoring puts into practice the adage that one learns the most from teaching another.

- *Professional service.* Senior officers often are called upon to provide assistance to the higher education community—for example, by serving on accreditation teams or on the committees and boards of associations. While these activities take time away from institutional business, they provide insight into the operations of other institutions and exposure to new content areas.

- *Nonacademic activities.* Because of their visibility within the institution and to the community, vice presidents have increased opportunities to participate in community and state activities. Some of these, such as serving on a governor's task force on education, may be natural outgrowths of the job; others may ostensibly be unrelated. Participation in community activities provides interaction with people other than those typically encountered in academia. Service on the board of directors for the local bank provides a fascinating look into business operations and the local economy. Volunteer activities—from serving ''meals on wheels'' to the elderly to helping with the local recycling operation—provide stimulation in new and different directions. All offer potential returns to the institution and individual in terms of expanded networks and new vistas. A vice president of planning at a major research university commented, ''Such outside activities provide a counterweight to the vicissitudes of the major leadership burdens of a vice presidency. For me, serving an occasional meal at the local homeless shelter helps to put institutional problems and politics into perspective very quickly and emphatically.''

- *Maintaining quality of life.* The demands on a vice president can be all-consuming. There is always more to do and better ways to do it. A senior officer is expected to be sensitive to the growth, development, and renewal needs of all members of the unit's staff, but only the president worries about the senior officers in this regard. Thus, senior leaders must address their own development, devise their own renewal strategies, and exert control over their own lives to create a healthy and balanced quality of life. In a discussion among chief academic officers, all echoed the sentiment expressed by one, that ''It is important to ask oneself what gives personal pleasure, with what kinds of people does one want to spend time, what does one look forward to—and then act on these.''

- *Balancing personal and professional life.* In senior positions, allocation of time changes dramatically over the years. It becomes increasingly difficult to separate personal interests and needs from institutional ones. For example, to help make the institution known, senior officers become involved in national activities; to smooth ''town/gown'' relations, vice presidents participate in community projects and organizations. In such activities, personal and professional interests may overlap, providing challenge, benefit, and pleasure. A vice president for research at a major comprehensive university explained, ''It is also important to develop or maintain an area of activity that provides purely personal pleasure—be it watercolor painting, tennis, or gardening. The hours spent in such pursuits can provide needed distance from the job, an arena of satisfaction and accomplishment separate from the ebb and flow of institutional politics, and quiet moments for reflection.''

As administrators reach senior levels of responsibility with their attendant strains and demands, personal lives—marriages, families, elderly parents—provide new challenges and demands. This balance becomes much harder as jobs become more public oriented and as evenings fill with meetings, dinners, and speeches. At the same time, children may be reaching adolescence and needing increased attention. A move to a new institution may uproot the entire family, forcing children to change schools just as they are settling into high school and spouses to give up meaningful jobs and support networks. Both married and single administrators must reestablish networks and support systems in the new town, a difficult task to squeeze among the demands of a new job.

Balancing job and private life is particularly difficult for a single administrator who does not have the entree into the local community that is provided by spouse and children. A single female chief academic officer of a public institution in the midwest explained, ''Single administrators have to work doubly hard to find and develop friendships, to maintain contacts with family and friends located in disparate places, and to carve out private time. 'After all,' many unconsciously rationalize, 'single administrators can stay late/attend the meeting/go to the dinner because they do not have families waiting at home.'''

It is at the vice presidential level that most administrators first encounter loss of anonymity. More than one senior administrator recounts the first shock of this loss, usually described in terms of engaging in a friendly conversation at the end of the grocery store aisle and suddenly realizing that the other person is silently analyzing the contents of the shopping cart.

This balancing act of personal and professional life requires constant monitoring and initiative. Networks provide insights and advice. Many association programs combine business with vacations. The wise senior administrator will pay the same attention to mental and physical health as to leadership and management development.

CONSIDERATIONS FOR PRESIDENTS AND BOARDS

In terms of their own development, vice presidents are caught in the middle. Much of the focus of leadership development is downward, as vice presidents are expected to pay attention to the development of staffs. President and boards need to pay similar attention to the developmental needs of senior officers. This includes assessing individual development needs and providing sufficient funds to address them.

Many institutions have procedures for a formal, annual evaluation of vice presidents. Few of these procedures also include the assessment of development goals and the annual design of development plans. Identifying specific goals and detailing strategies to accomplish these goals would couple individual development to the mission and challenges of the institution.

CONCLUSION

Both the job and the development needs of vice presidents and senior officers change over time in office. The needs of a new vice president are decidedly different from those of a seasoned veteran. Although associations, conventions, and general education programs continue to provide developmental opportunities, seasoned vice presidents also must experiment with new and different stimuli appropriate to their changing needs and unique circumstances. The president and the board of trustees play an important role in ensuring that senior officers plan for continual development and that this development is coupled to the needs and goals of the institution.

REFERENCES

Alexander, Paula B., Jane S. Norton, Suzann B. Goldstein, Elizabeth S. Becker, Jane H. Degnan, and Joseph Hobbs. ''Career Management of Leaders in Higher Education.'' South Orange, NJ: Seton Hall University, January 1989. Photocopy.

McDade, Sharon A. ''Professional Development of Senior-Level Administrators of Colleges and Universities.'' Ed.D. dissertation, Harvard University, 1986.

———. *Higher Education Leadership: Enhancing Skills through Professional Development Programs*. ASHE-ERIC Higher Education Report No. 5. Washington, DC: Association for the Study of Higher Education, 1987.

Moore, Kathryn M., Ann M. Salimbene, Joyce D. Marlier, and Stephen M. Bragg. ''The Structure of Presidents' and Deans' Careers.'' *Journal of Higher Education* 54, no. 5 (September/October 1983): 500–515.

Moore, Kathryn M., Susan B. Twombly, and S. V. Martorana. *Today's Academic Leaders: A National Study of Administrators in Community and Junior Colleges*. University Park, PA: Center for the Study of Higher Education, Pennsylvania State University, 1985.

Poskozim, Paul S. ''New Administrators: A Statistical Look at Movement within the Ranks, 1982–83.'' *Change* 16, no. 7 (October 1984): 55–59.

Rickard, Scott T. ''Career Pathways of Chief Student Affairs Officers: Making Room at the Top for Females and Minorities.'' *NASPA Journal* 22, no. 4 (Spring 1985): 52–60.

Twombly, Susan B. ''Career Lines of Top-Level Two-Year College Administrators: Implications for Leadership in a New Era.'' Paper presented at the annual meeting of the Association for the Study of Higher Education, San Antonio, TX, 20–23 February, 1986.

RESOURCES

Allen, Louise H. ''On Being a Vice President for Academic Affairs.'' *Journal of the National Association of Women Deans, Administrators, and Counselors* (Summer 1984): 8–15.

This is an informative exploration of the job of academic vice president (AVP). The article includes a profile of the typical AVP (and a more specialized description of the typical female AVP), a useful description of an AVP's typical day, and hints for those aspiring to the position.

Brown, David G., ed. *Leadership Roles of Chief Academic Officers*. New Directions for Higher Education 47. San Francisco: Jossey-Bass, 1984.

This book overviews the roles and responsibilities of the chief academic officer, including essays on participatory leadership strategy, strategies for faculty development, sustaining faculty leadership, academic governance, using the budget to maintain quality, taking advantage of emerging educational technologies, and academic goals. The book also includes much advice on being a successful chief academic officer.

Ehrle, Elwood B., and John B. Bennett. *Managing the Academic Enterprise: Case Studies for Deans and Provosts*. New York: American Council on Education/Macmillan, 1987.

This book presents 25 case studies focusing on issues of finance, personnel, organizational structure, curriculum, academic freedom, and standards. The authors provide a variety of possible options for action with each case.

Houle, Cyril O. *Continuing Learning in the Professions*. San Francisco: Jossey-Bass, 1980.

This foundation book describes the evolution of professions. Houle discusses the needs of professions, including those such as student affairs in colleges and universities, for life-long learning to grow continually with the needs and challenges of the field, the job, and the professional. He discusses three modes of continuous learning, including instruction, inquiry, and performance.

Moore, Leila V., and Robert B. Young, eds. *Expanding Opportunities for Professional Education*. New Directions for Student Services 37. San Francisco: Jossey-Bass, 1987.

Focuses on issues of the professionalization of the student services function. Separate essays by leading student services leaders focus on the development of the student services administrator at various stages on the career ladder. These include graduate education, on-the-job professional education, and the role of professional associations.

PROGRAMS AND PRACTICES

Complete information on each listing is provided in the *Appendix*. The letter and number in the parentheses correspond to the section and entry number in the *Appendix*.

Associations

There are no associations for vice presidents in general, or even for specific types of vice presidents. Instead, vice presidents typically participate in the national associations of the areas in which they play senior leadership roles. Increasingly, vice presidents participate in the associations that represent their institutional sector, taking on secondary leadership roles behind their presidents.

National Programs

The following list provides a sampling of the range and variety of off-campus programs available to vice presidents and is not meant to be an inventory of all programs and activities available to these leaders. Note that many programs offered by associations are available only to vice presidents serving at member institutions.

American Association of Community and Junior Colleges (AACJC) (P5)

Fellows Program *(P5a)*
Professional Development Workshop *(P5c)*

American Association of State Colleges and Universities (AASCU) (P6)

Academic Leadership Institute *(P6a)*

American Council on Education (ACE) (P7)

Department Leadership Program *(P7a)*
The Fellows Program *(P7b)*

American Management Association (AMA) (P8)

Aspen Institute *(P19)*

21st Century Leaders Program *(P19a)*

Association of Governing Boards of Universities and Colleges (AGB) (P15)

Program for Academic Affairs Committee Chairpersons and Senior Academic Officers *(P15f)*
Seminar on Endowment Management *(P15h)*
Trustee Responsibility for Financial Affairs *(P15k)*

The Bush Foundation *(P18)*

Leadership Program for Midcareer Development *(P18a)*

Carnegie Mellon University/School of Urban and Public Affairs (P19)

Academic Leadership Institute *(P19a)*
College Management Program *(P19b)*

Center for Creative Leadership (P20)

Dynamics of Strategy: Goals into Action *(P20a)*
Executive Women Workshop *(P20b)*
Leadership and Teamwork: Increasing Team Leadership Capabilities *(P20c)*
Leadership Development Program *(P20d)*

Central Association of College and University Business Officers (CACUBO) (P22)

Management Institute *(P22a)*

Council for Advancement and Support of Education (CASE) (P26)

Forums for Women and Minority Institutional Advancement *(P26a)*
Summer Institute in Executive Management *(P26d)*

Council for International Exchange of Scholars (CIES) (P28)

Fulbright Scholar Program *(P28a)*

Council on International Educational Exchange (CIEE) (P33)

Development Seminars *(P33a)*

Harvard University/Graduate School of Education (P37)

Institute for Educational Management (IEM) *(P37b)*
Institute for the Management of Lifelong Education (MLE) *(P37c)*
Management Development Program (MDP) *(P37d)*

Higher Education Resource Services (HERS) Mid-America/Bryn Mawr College (P39)

HERS Summer Institute for Women/Bryn Mawr Institute *(P39a)*

Higher Education Resource Services (HERS) New England/Wellesley College (P40)

HERS Institute for Women/Wellesley Institute *(P40a)*

League for Innovation in the Community College (P45)

Executive Leadership Institute *(P45a)*
Leadership 2000 *(P45b)*

Massachusetts Institute of Technology (MIT)/Sloan School of Management (P48)

Alfred P. Sloan Fellows Program *(P48a)*

National Association of College and University Business Officers (NACUBO) (P52)

Senior Financial Officers Conference *(P52a)*

National Association of College and University Business Officers (NACUBO)/Marriott Education Services (P53)

Executive Leadership Institute *(P53a)*

National Association of Student Personnel Administrators (NASPA) (P56)

Richard F. Stevens NASPA Institute *(P56a)*

National Center for Higher Education Management Systems (NCHEMS) (P57)

National Institute for Leadership Development (P59)

Leaders for Change *(P59b)*

North Carolina State University (P60)

Community College Leadership Institute *(P60a)*

NTL Institute (P61)

Human Interaction Laboratory *(P61a)*
Management Work Conference *(P61b)*
Senior Executive's Conference *(P61c)*
Other programs *(P61d)*

Society for Values in Higher Education (P64)

The Fellows Meeting *(P64a)*

Southern Association of College and University Business Officers (SACUBO)/University of Kentucky *(P65)*

College Management Business Institute (CMBI) *(P65a)*

Texas A&M University/College of Education (P66)

Summer Seminar on Academic Administration *(P66a)*

University of Central Florida (P68)

Financial Management for Women in Higher Education *(P68a)*

University of Georgia/Institute of Higher Education and the Georgia Center for Continuing Education *(P69)*

Annual Conference on Higher Education and the Law *(P69a)*

Western Association of College and University Business Officers (WACUBO) (P71)

Business Management Institute *(P71b)*
Executive Leadership and Management Institute *(P71a)*

Williamsburg Development Institute (P72)

Williamsburg Development Institute *(P72a)*

Statewide, System-Specific, and On-Campus Programs

Arizona State University (ASU) (S2)

Management Development Program (MDP) *(S2a)*
President's Breakfast Series *(S2d)*

Colorado Women in Higher Education Administration and the American Council on Education National Identification Program (ACE/NIP) (S11)

Academic Management Institute for Women *(S11a)*

University of Tennessee (S36)

Institute for Leadership Effectiveness *(S36a)*

7

ACADEMIC DEANS AND MID-LEVEL ACADEMIC ADMINISTRATORS

Academic deans are the quintessential mid-level administrators.[1] They exist partway between the professorate and the president, with roles, responsibilities, and identities in both worlds. Most academic deans preside over broad academic units that join related (although sometimes only loosely) academic disciplines and are typically called colleges, schools, or divisions. Such units may include humanities and sciences, education, business, fine arts, health sciences, home economics, academic development, libraries, engineering, law, technologies, and agriculture. They also may include graduate and professional studies, continuing education, and undergraduate education. The range and depth of responsibilities may vary dramatically by the size of the unit and the size of the institution.

While this chapter focuses on deans, it is also appropriate for other mid-level academic administrators such as assistant and associate vice presidents for academic affairs, assistant and associate provosts, assistant and associate deans, and directors of major academic units such as research centers or libraries. The "assistant" and "associate" positions, while including key and significant responsibilities of their own, are often perceived as training positions or stepping-stones to deanships or academic vice presidencies. In community colleges, a dean is often the chief academic officer while associate deans or division heads lead general academic units.

Actual responsibilities and scope of operations may vary across these positions and across institutional sectors, but all participate in the basic leadership of academic affairs. In this chapter, the term "dean" will be used to refer to this entire group of academic administrators.

CAREER PREPARATION

Usually, academic deans begin as professors. They often move into administration as chairs of their academic departments. Having had some success in management and showing an inclination toward the tasks of administration, they are selected to move up the ladder to a deanship to provide leadership for a larger academic unit.

Increasingly, not all deans ascend through this traditional pathway. Variations are particularly noticeable within professional schools and in areas such as freshman programs, continuing education, and adult education. These deans may come from the profession served by the school, business, or other nonprofit organizations or through other unique career paths. Some deans, such as leaders of graduate programs or deans of undergraduate studies, relate very differently to the institution's organizational structure in that they often supervise no faculty and control budgets and projects in different ways.

Few receive more than an orientation for their jobs as department chairs; even fewer receive orientation or training for the job of dean. As is true for the positions of president and academic vice president, a deanship is difficult to anticipate and even more difficult to prepare for. While a department chair position provides exposure to the tasks and responsibilities of administration, the lessons may not apply at the next level of leadership or may be significantly altered through collective bargaining rules. Yet to faculty, who typically dominate the search committees that select academic middle managers, evidence that the candidate has experience as a member of the faculty, and preferably as a department chair, is essential. For many search committee members, such experiences provide important credibility because they indicate socialization into the complex culture of academia.

Increasingly, academic deans spend some years of their development in academic-related areas such as the library, media resources, or computing services. As the definition of education broadens in an increasingly technological world, classroom and teaching extend into these nontraditional venues. Deans supervising these areas take on increasing significance in the academic leadership hierarchy.

Typically, deans learn their jobs by doing them. Learning is driven by the tasks that appear on one's desk each morning. Unfortunately, these opportunities appear in a somewhat random stream, not in an organized flow. A dean needs a clear mental agenda to survive and, more important, to make an imprint of leadership on these random events. Systematic leadership development efforts can help to provide and refresh the context for that mental agenda.

The job of an academic dean is highly people-intensive. After all, the inventory of an academic school or college is its faculty, staff, and students. Many deans concur with the sentiment, ''I spend a major part of the day with people, working through processes—and that means meetings and more meetings.''

Some deans advance from the faculty into academic administration ranks within their present institutions. They may have known or worked closely with only two or three academic vice presidents and presidents. Thus, most deans have had few examples of different leaders, either to learn from or to measure themselves against.

RESPONSIBILITIES

Like the department chair, the academic dean faces in two directions. The dean is both an academician and an administrator, leading faculty and department chairs on the one hand and answering to senior officers on the other. The administrative responsibilities typically support the academic ones, but there can be tension when it is unclear where a dean's loyalties should lie. Tucker and Bryan's (1988) research suggests the following array of duties:

Providing Academic Leadership

- *Setting academic priorities.* Deans oversee education in their units by leading the development and implementation of policies for teaching, research, and service. Working with faculty governance committees, deans need to establish (usually through an extensive negotiation process through the faculty governance system) the academic priorities of their units within the institution's context, and to ensure that those priorities are met.

- *Building and maintaining an academic program.* Although formal responsibility for the creation of academic programs and curricula may reside with the faculty, deans are instrumental in proposing and facilitating programmatic development. The actual academic role of the dean may vary across institutions and even across units in an institution, but the dean generally retains the administrative responsibility and oversight for building and maintaining programs. This includes authorizing new programs, terminating old programs, and overseeing the hiring of faculty.

- *Ensuring academic quality and creating a community of scholars.* While department chairs hold the primary responsibility for the operation and quality of instructional and research programs, the dean is often the only person who is in a position to compare and evaluate courses across the entire unit. The dean affects academic quality through such concrete steps as the promotion and tenure process or the allocation of human and financial resources, and through less tangible means such as leadership in the development of programs, setting standards, and serving as a role model.

- *Ensuring the best faculty and students.* Although faculty recruitment is more in the province of individual departments, the dean may establish priorities, monitor process, and have a voice in hiring decisions. A dean's influence at these points of entry can be very important to the unit and institutional character. Several deans concurred that "the dean must serve as a catalyst for securing diversity and pluralism within the unit. Leadership for pluralism must come from the top, and for most faculty and students, the dean is the top."

   Although the actual recruitment of students may be conducted by the office of admissions or enrollment management, the dean of each unit may be involved with the establishment of admissions criteria and policies. At many institutions, deans are also actively involved in outreach to and recruitment of students.

- *Participating in the faculty tenure and promotion process.* Department faculty committees typically make the primary decisions concerning promotion and tenure. Department chairs and deans then work together to implement these decisions. In some institutions, deans can veto committees' decisions; in most, they forward decisions with recommendations to the academic vice president. Although the role of a dean in the promotion and tenure process may be more symbolic than actual, a dean does have influence in the way search committees and tenure committees are formed.

Managing the Unit

- *Directing operations.* The dean oversees the operations of his or her unit: conducting meetings, making committee appointments, developing goals, organizing and directing operations, and coordinating activities. The list of management responsibilities seems endless to many deans. Often, the dean must work with and through committees; other times, she or he is directly involved. Because the administrative duties are so numerous, deans must delegate many responsibilities to their staffs (if they have assistant or associate deans), as well as to chairs and faculty. The briefness of the above listing belies the enormity of the tasks; entire books are devoted to each individual responsibility.

- *Securing resources and budgeting for their use.* The involvement of deans in securing resources may vary dramatically across units, but the centrality of deans to the budget process is a constant. Deans establish the academic and operational priorities of the unit through the budgets they create in consultation with the faculty, department chairs, appropriate committees, and the senior management team. Typically, once a budget is established, deans are involved in periodic checkups that are done on a prescribed schedule.

Increasingly, fund raising and development are also part of a dean's job. A dean of humanities noted, ''I've had to become entrepreneurial. Fund raising is a whole new world for me, for all the deans at my [public] institution. Sometimes I think I spend all my extra time in the office of the development director.'' Another dean noted, ''One of the most important development lessons I ever learned was how to use overhead from grants to benefit my unit. Resource acquisition comes in many small but important ways.''

- *Supervising and developing support staff and faculty.* Although academic deans are typically thought of as leaders of faculties, they are also supervisors of many and various types of support staff. A dean of fine arts explained, ''My music school has a large number of support technicians whose jobs are distant and generally unknown to me, and yet I have to be concerned about their general welfare and job satisfaction.'' This job responsibility includes developing the leadership abilities and management skills of support staff members as well as faculty. It also includes mentoring department chairs to enhance their leadership abilities and to help them grow in their jobs. Often deans serve as consultants to chairpersons who are trying to work through difficult situations. Another important part of a dean's function is to forge a management team from the assistant and associate deans, directors, and department chairs in the unit.

- *Resolving personnel conflicts.* Deans spend a great deal of time on personnel problems, and especially on resolving conflicts among faculty, chairs, students, and parents. Conflict resolution skills are vital to the dean. One dean commented, ''I do my most important work behind closed doors and can't brag about it to anyone, to preserve confidentiality. The successes of this work include the suit or grievance not filed and the incident that did not become a crisis.''

- *Creating the working environment.* Deans set the tone for the working environment of a unit through their actions, both large and small. A dean who communicates primarily through memos and reports establishes a very different tone from one who deals mostly in person-to-person conversations. A dean of arts and sciences at a major private institution remarked, ''One of my biggest surprises was the degree to which department chairs, faculty, and staff all take their work performance cues from my management and leadership style. I've learned that every action, no matter how small, contributes to setting the tone.''

- *Supervising facilities, space, and equipment.* While chairs typically retain responsibility for departmental facilities and equipment, the dean has oversight responsibilities. This usually manifests itself by making a dean the arbitrator of space disputes and the reconciler of competing demands.

- *Planning.* A great deal of the job of any leader is planning. Any unit, no matter what its size, needs to consider its future and to plan for it in a comprehensive, organized way. Such planning cannot be done in isolation, but must be undertaken in the general context of the institution.

  Accreditation processes are an increasingly important aspect of planning. To many deans, accreditation literature and processes are foreign and confusing worlds that must be dealt with more and more frequently. "My unit deals with six different accrediting associations," commented a dean of graduate and professional studies. "Accreditation requirements are the driving force behind our planning processes."

Relating to the Institutional Mission

- *Linking the institution and the unit.* Part of the dual responsibilities of deans is representing the institution to the unit and the unit to the institution. It is the dean's responsibility to minimize conflict by maintaining a constant flow of information between the unit and the institution and constantly making clear the institution's mission, goals, and plans to members of the unit.

  The dean is the principal representative of and advocate for the unit to senior leaders. Deans may be members of a deans' council that considers campus-wide issues and formulates decisions or recommendations that are communicated upward in the administrative hierarchy. Similarly, as members of the senior administration, deans must both communicate and promote administrative decisions among members of their unit.

- *Linking the disciplines within the unit.* As leader of the unit, the dean bridges the gaps among disciplines. A dean must learn enough about each discipline in the unit and its academic culture to be able to communicate well with all faculty about their teaching and research. Increasingly, deans also coordinate and serve as architects for interdisciplinary efforts such as centers, institutes, programs, and projects.

- *Addressing needs and concerns of related constituencies.* Every unit has its own collection of related constituencies to which the dean must tend. Internally, these constituencies include the heads of other academic units, students, and the senior officers of the institution. Externally, these groups include alumni, advisory boards, community supporters, corporations, foundations, legislators, accrediting agencies, regulatory bodies, professional associations, and donor friends. The dean must keep these groups informed of the activities of the unit, attend to the particular interests of each group, and provide each group access to its areas of interest within the unit, as well as market the unit to these many constituencies.

Coda

While faculty may complain about the perceived power of deans, and senior officers complain that deans do not do enough, deans often feel powerless, caught between a rock and a hard place. As a dean of arts and sciences at a medium-sized public institution observed, ''You can determine your power by figuring out how many things can take place with just your signature or when your signature is the last one. It's very humbling to realize that there is very little that requires my signature to make it happen. That's a statement of my 'power.''' Another dean replied, ''I probably only make four or five significant decisions each year, but they are truly significant decisions. The rest of the time I'm a problem solver, crisis avoider, representative, and go-between.''

LEADERSHIP CAPACITIES

This brief description of the leadership capacities needed by deans reflects both the unique responsibilities of deans and the requirements of academic administration at many levels in the institution.

Providing Vision and Setting Goals

Vision is a capacity needed by all leaders. The term implies seeing the unit in a context beyond its day-to-day operations and establishing goals to change that vision into reality.

Understanding Higher Education

To best fulfill their responsibilities to the unit and the institution, deans must place their campuses in the general context of higher education. This capacity includes the ability to interpret that context within the framework of the unit's goals and structure.

Working With People

Deans spend most of their days working with people. Their success as leaders depends upon their ability to work effectively with faculty, students, support staff, and other administrators.

Managing and Decision Making

Deans, like administrators at every level, must make decisions. While the academy emphasizes consensual decision making, ultimately someone must make an operational decision and be responsible for it. That someone is typically the dean.

Maintaining Intellectual Vigor

While deans live at the gateway to their academic units, it is difficult to maintain their intellectual vigor in the face of the unrelenting demands on their time and energies. Maintaining intellectual vigor is key to a dean's ability to maintain credibility and relevance with faculty and students as well as with those in other units and colleges within the institution. A dean sets an example by his or her level of intellectual activity. This may include teaching an occasional class or course, as a way to both keep close to the students and maintain credibility with other faculty.

Dealing With Stress

The hours and demands of administration increase as one assumes increasing levels of responsibility. The stress experienced at the department chair level compounds at the dean level as public visibility and involvement increases. Dealing with stress and managing it in a productive way are crucial balancing acts for all individuals. Deans can improve the success of this balancing act through careful monitoring of the relationship of personal and professional life, training in stress-reduction techniques, and periodic comparison of short-term activities with long-term personal and career objectives.

JOB CYCLE OF AN ACADEMIC DEAN

The concept of job cycles was introduced in the previous chapter. Academic deans face very definite cycles that have important implications for professional development. The cycles have as much to do with learning the job as with coping with changes in one's identity and relationship to an academic discipline. The direction and pace of the cycles also have much to do with upward mobility. The ladder from dean to academic vice president is steep. Where do deans go? And what preparation is needed to get there?

Entry Phase

At a recent discussion involving academic deans, one dean summarized the entry phase of his job as having three definite steps. During the first part (approximately the first three months), he found himself saying under his breath, "This is easy. I can do this." At the second step, starting at approximately the third month (or first crisis, whichever comes first), he found himself muttering, "This is impossible. I'll never be able to do this." As he entered his second year, he found himself thinking, "This is hard work, but I can do it if I try hard enough." The other deans at the discussion concurred with his analysis of the entry phase: it took approximately two years to feel really in control of the job in a proactive rather than reactive way.

- *Learning the job.* As is typical of administrative positions in higher education, the job of dean is learned while doing it. While there are increasing numbers of assistant and associate dean positions where one can learn parts of the job of being dean, most deans still do not have the experience provided by these intermediary positions. In the best of circumstances, the academic vice president or another dean may serve as a coach. As one dean explained, "I learned the job by sitting with the provost and going over materials. The provost's guidance was critical in my learning the job."

  Deans can benefit from substantial work on management development in the early years in their positions, to help them to put some structure into their jobs. Formal training, mentoring, and interaction with other deans can help to ensure that a dean has the necessary information to address the important problems and avoid overemphasizing the trivial or superficial.

- *Establishing an identity.* New deans live with one leg still firmly planted in the faculty and the other just stepping into administration. Typically, they are finishing research and writing assignments started before entering the deanship. More than one dean echoed the sentiment, "It became increasingly difficult to find time and attention for my scholarly pursuits, and their purposes became dimmer as more pressing administrative responsibilities took precedence."

  For many new deans, these tensions provoke guilty feelings of defection from their disciplines. They begin to shed old models of faculty success before finding acceptable models of administrative and leadership success.

Growth Phase

- *Feeling comfortable in the job.* During their first two to four years, deans master the details of their jobs and may even begin to feel comfortable in them. By this phase, a dean may either feel energized and challenged by the job or depressed by the demands and process.

- *Switching orientations.* During this phase, deans begin to define themselves differently, first to themselves and then to others. They often face a crucial decision: to go on in administration or to return to the faculty. To be able to return to a discipline, one must continue to define one's role in that discipline, perhaps by moving to areas of the discipline that do not change as rapidly. To move ahead in administration, one must start defining oneself differently.

Maturation Phase

- *Mastering the job.* Deans who have stayed at the task to this stage (four to eight years) may be regarded as "old hands" by others. They know how to make things happen and how to get the job done. In addition to having learned their unit, the chairpersons within that unit, and their institution, they may have begun to establish themselves in regional or even national associations. A longtime dean of a college of arts and sciences observed, "I realized that I had reached a certain stage in my career when I began to serve as mentor to all the new deans . . . within the institution and to many others in the wider higher education community." Many deans at this stage develop an area of expertise in administration and begin to publish, speak, and consult.

- *Making career decisions.* After five to eight years it may be difficult to return to a discipline without substantial "retooling." It is often too late for scientists and others in fields that change rapidly; even in fields such as history, it is necessary to go back and reimmerse in the discipline. At this point, a dean needs to decide whether to go on to a higher level in administration, to remain at the dean's level, or to return to the faculty.

  Examples of career options are as varied as the number of deans. A microbiologist-turned-dean of arts and sciences lamented that after only three years in this job it was already too late to return to her laboratory; there was no other career option for her but to move into higher levels of administration. A drama expert, while serving as dean of graduate studies, had continued regular research and publications in his field of German existential theater. His credibility remained such that he was able to consider moving to academic vice presidencies as well as tenured faculty positions.

STRATEGIES FOR DEVELOPMENT

There are a variety of strategies that can enhance the management and leadership development of deans and mid-level academic administrators.

Learning the Basics—Managing and Leading

- *Reading.* Academic deans are steeped in the tradition of research and scholarship; the natural way for them to learn about the job is to read about it. As one dean jokingly remarked, "I immediately put together my own Deaning 101 course. Isn't that what a good academic is supposed to do?"

- *On-campus opportunities.* Deans need opportunities and ways to meet others on their campuses so that they can do their jobs better. Campuses differ in the amount of formal and informal interactions available at the dean level. The more formal and structured the campus relationships, the more vital it is for the dean to get to know as many people as possible.

- *Programs specifically for deans.* Although there are no specific associations encompassing all deans, some professional organizations provide subgroupings for deans. There are several organizations for academic deans, such as the Council of Colleges of Arts and Sciences and the American Conference of Academic Deans. These organizations provide excellent introductions to the roles of deans, including orientation programs, with opportunities for more extensive involvement for longer-tenured deans. They also offer regional and sector groupings that may be very useful and supportive.

- *Off-campus programs.* Throughout a dean's tenure, off-campus programs of all types serve as key resources for information specific to the issues of the campus and details on what is happening at peer institutions. Seasoned deans suggest that the greatest benefits are accrued when off-campus programs are attended with clear goals in mind; for example, seeking information on faculty handbooks or strategies for evaluating teaching performance, and engaging in informal discussions with other participants at a higher education convention. Participation in off-campus programs provides opportunities to step back from the daily grind and reflect on the larger issues and goals of the unit and institution. Because off-campus programs are an expensive form of leadership development, the institution needs to make sufficient funds available.

- *Networking.* Virtually all programs and events become sources for network building. For new deans, the emphasis is on meeting peers; seasoned deans seek to maintain already existing networks. Networks are useful for collecting problem-solving ideas, for obtaining information, and for identifying resources. As deans settle into their jobs, they use their telephones more frequently as networking links to secure copies of materials such as faculty handbooks and tenure guidelines that they can compare to their programs. Seasoned deans also report using their networks more extensively to solve individual and specific problems—personal, professional, and institutional.

An important lesson of networking is that there are many models of deaning and many paths to success at the job. "One of the best things I did as a new dean was to visit each of the other deans on my campus to ask them how they did their job," remembered a dean of education on a major land-grant campus. "None of the specifics stayed with me, but the biggest lesson was how differently each approached the job. And the visits were the foundation of considerable networking later."

Usually networking is considered an external activity, but deans also need networks within the institution. Successful deans have extensive networks into all areas of the institution, with as many contacts on the nonacademic side of the house as on the academic side. There need to be substantial linkages between middle managers in an institution, no matter what their responsibilities. In many ways, the success of the institution depends upon the networks forged at this level.

Shifting From Discipline to General Higher Education

- *General leadership and higher education management programs.* National institutes (longer programs of two or more weeks), such as Harvard's Management Development Program (MDP), Carnegie Mellon's College Management Program, and Higher Education Resource Service (HERS) programs at Bryn Mawr and Wellesley Colleges and in Colorado, provide opportunities to expand one's knowledge base and to enhance management skills and leadership performance. Besides a focus on higher education issues, such programs provide deans with the opportunity to form deep friendships with their peers. Knowing others in similar positions enables academic middle managers to learn about leadership and measure personal growth. National institutes typically provide alumni activities that further reinforce the learning and networks.

- *Exposure to the wider world of higher education.* The world of higher education begins to open to deans as they become more aware of and involved in general education issues. Deans describe their desire to explore the national environment, to learn about national issues, to investigate wider challenges. At a recent meeting of academic deans, there was general agreement that, ''you read the *Chronicle* in an entirely different way after you become a dean. Suddenly all the stories have immediate relevance in one way or another—each issue is either on your desk or going to be on your desk or should be on your desk.''

■ *General higher education associations.* While maintaining membership in disciplinary associations, deans begin to explore the benefits of the more generalized higher education associations. From these associations—their annual meetings, publications, and networks— deans can learn about cutting-edge issues, the language and literature of higher education, and the names of innovators. Many deans cite the annual meetings of general higher education associations as excellent hunting grounds for speakers and consultants to bring back to campus.

Some associations are more useful than others in meeting the needs of deans. More broadly based organizations such as the American Association for Higher Education (AAHE) and the American Association of Colleges (AAC) tend to be more useful to deans than sector associations, which are directed more to senior officers (although many of these associations are beginning to reach out to deans). Many of these broadly based associations provide orientation programs for new attenders to make it easier for them to get into the swing of the conference. Deans also report high satisfaction with consortia, regional and state networks, and system networks that bring together deans from peer and geographically linked institutions.

■ *Other discipline-based conferences.* It also may be useful to sample disciplinary conferences. As a dean of arts and sciences at a large comprehensive institution reported, ''After listening to the presentations and meeting the key scholars at several disciplinary conferences, it was easier for me to relate to faculty from the other disciplines in the academic unit and to evaluate their work for promotion decisions.''

■ *Reaching out on behalf of others.* After several years, deans begin to realize that when attending meetings and conferences, they are searching as much for information for their department chairs as for themselves. More seasoned deans begin to see themselves as consultants to the campus, collecting ideas for all their campus colleagues. They find themselves beginning to think in terms of institutional development, not just discipline or unit development.

Taking Responsibility for One's Own Development

■ *Finding on-campus opportunities.* A seasoned dean of research observed, ''After becoming comfortable with the daily routine, I found that I needed to take responsibility for my development by seeking campus opportunities for new challenges.'' Examples include participation in campus-wide fund-raising activities, institutional long-range planning, and system-wide programming. Any of these provide a reason to explore new areas of management and leadership.

- *Mentoring others.* Deans have much to learn and much to teach. Typically, the provost is the key mentor for deans, facilitating the learning process, although other deans also play key roles. But there is also a great deal to be learned by helping others (especially department chairs and associate and assistant deans) learn the ropes of higher education administration and leadership.

- *Developing areas of expertise.* Many deans derive satisfaction from developing an area of expertise within higher education administration. Because this expertise is used on the job, it is easier to justify the time and energy needed for research and writing. Such an area may fill the void left by the loss of close contact with an academic discipline.

- *Learning alternative problem-solving techniques.* Deans, steeped in the problem-solving techniques of their disciplines, soon learn that any single such method is limited and begin to seek multiple problem-solving techniques and frames of reference. Business-school-sponsored executive education programs that provide training in decision-making techniques provide interesting development options.

- *Teaching.* Throughout the early years in their position, deans spend a great deal of time thinking about how to balance their jobs, their personal lives, and their careers. While department chairs may continue to teach and conduct research, albeit sometimes at reduced levels, these academic supports usually do not exist at the deans' level. (This may not be the case in medical schools, where chairs may be expected to continue teaching and researching at previous levels.) An education dean commented, ''I found that I needed to relate my disciplinary background to my deaning roles by finding new ways to express my discipline or to relate it to my new higher education responsibilities. I met that need by guest lecturing on general education issues, management topics, and then on leadership in a wide range of courses.''

- *Stress reduction.* Stress becomes an increasing problem for mid-level managers, no matter what their roles in the organization. Those who have risen from the faculty ranks may be particularly affected by the loss of freedom and control. Deans used to the constant stimulation of teaching and research may become extremely stressed when these stimuli are replaced with endless meetings, memos, and ceremonial occasions. It is useful to learn some stress-reduction strategies, both for short-term release of daily tensions and for the longer-term dissipation of job-related anxiety. Deans need to find alternative intellectual stimulation and food for the mind: for example, by participating in interdisciplinary scholarly discussions, regularly attending guest lectures in other disciplines, and pursing higher education and administration research and writing.

CONSIDERATIONS FOR SUPERVISORS

Academic vice presidents can play an important role in the development of the deans and assistant and associate vice presidents who report to them. Deans need assistance from their supervisors in discovering and then analyzing their leadership strengths and weaknesses and in devising plans for addressing them.

In their early years on the job, deans benefit from the guidance of supervisors in choosing appropriate programs to attend and from introductions to a wider range of peers. For example, a dean could take an associate dean along to a convention and provide introductions and guidance into the network instead of just turning that individual loose to navigate the convention alone. Deans also benefit from ongoing advice about appropriate programs and activities as their abilities and interests evolve and as they gain expertise in their jobs. Academic vice presidents and presidents also can help deans deal with the transition from faculty to administration by being sensitive to the ideological dilemma of discipline versus administration and providing support for the passage. They can help deans discover alternative forms of intellectual stimulation and establish other areas of expertise in higher education.

Supervisors and presidents can support deans by recognizing their achievements and accomplishments, both on and off campus. Recognition of participation in professional development activities and especially of leadership roles in higher education organizations legitimizes these activities. While any recognition is helpful, it is particularly useful to note such activities at faculty meetings and in campus publications.

Supervisors can make a significant difference in the development of those who report to them by building significant learning opportunities into each job. This includes steering deans and assistant and associate deans toward experiences necessary to be prepared for the next level of responsibility.

People in assistant and associate positions require special attention and mentoring to help enhance their visibility within the institution. Since the assistant/associate positions can be ''safe'' positions, mentors can help by urging the taking of risks and the undertaking of difficult projects. A long-time academic vice president observed, ''If I'm doing my job well in this respect, it is something like managing a minor league baseball team—I keep losing the good people who move up into better positions because of my mentoring.''

Finally, academic vice presidents and presidents can nurture the development of deans by fostering good relationships among the deans at the institution and at peer institutions. Even this small step can provide an important foundation for networks and problem solving.

CONCLUSION

Besides requiring new technical and leadership skills, academic deans need assistance in managing the transition from faculty to administration. This transition includes professional needs such as acquiring networks and developing higher education knowledge, as well as personal needs for reconciling the demands of academics and administration. Leadership development needs evolve as the dean acquires expertise. The academic vice president plays an important role in helping deans to evaluate their developmental needs, in identifying appropriate opportunities, and in integrating new lessons back into the deans' jobs.

NOTES

1. Academic deans who report directly to the president and who serve as chief academic officers are included in the chapter on senior administrators.

REFERENCES

Tucker, Allan, and Robert A. Bryan. *The Academic Dean: Dove, Dragon, and Diplomat*. New York: American Council on Education/Macmillan, 1988.

RESOURCES

Gould, John Wesley. *The Academic Deanship*. New York: Teachers College, 1964.

The seminal work on the subject referenced by all the more recent authors.

Morris, Van Cleve. *Deaning: Middle Management in Academe*. Urbana: University of Illinois Press, 1981.

An insider's view of the role of the academic dean. Covers most of the bases—the faculty and its politics; salary, promotion, and tenure; institutional outreach; affirmative action; money (how to get it and how to spend it); governance; and evaluating the dean. Morris includes appendices focusing on evaluation criteria.

Murphy, Jerome T. "The Unheroic Side of Leadership: Notes from the Swamp." *Phi Delta Kappan* 69, no. 9 (May 1988): 654–59.

From the vantage point of a researcher-turned-administrator, Murphy offers some observations on educational leadership, noting at the outset that "the popular view as hero fails to capture the character of leadership in a world of grand designs and daily problems." In the article, Murphy balances the traditional characteristics of the leader as hero with six dimensions characterizing the unheroic side of leadership.

Rosovsky, Henry. *The University: An Owner's Manual*. New York: Norton, 1990.

The book by Harvard University's former Dean of Arts and Sciences reviews the mission and mores of America's colleges and universities with special consideration to each of its "owners"—students and their families, alumni, faculty, donors, trustees, the press, and the general public. Of particular interest are the specific chapters on deaning, including a litany of a typical day as dean and a chapter of reflections on the job as well as a series of amusing but on-target "helpful hints," including "never be surprised by anything"; "learn the value of being vague"; and "never underestimate the difficulty of changing false beliefs by facts."

Tucker, Allan, and Robert A. Bryan. *The Academic Dean: Dove, Dragon, and Diplomat*. New York: American Council on Education/Macmillan, 1988.

This is the basic course on how to be an academic dean. The book is a handbook of the roles and responsibilities of the dean, including in-depth discussions of budgeting and programming. The book discusses the many aspects of the relationship of dean to faculty, department chairs, academic vice president, president, students and staff.

PROGRAMS AND PRACTICES

Complete information on each listing is provided in the *Appendix*. The letter and number in parentheses correspond to the section and entry number in the *Appendix*.

National Associations

The following list provides a sampling of the associations that serve deans and mid-level academic administrators. There are also many regional associations for deans; for example, organizations such as the Colorado Council of Deans of Education. Many associations, such as the AAHE and the American Association of Community and Junior Colleges (AACJC), sponsor caucuses for women, minorities, faculty, and other groups that cut across functional lines.

American Assembly of Collegiate Schools of Business (AACSB) (A8)

American Association for Adult and Continuing Education (AAACE) (A9)

American Association for Higher Education (AAHE) (A11)

American Association of Colleges for Teacher Education (AACTE) (A15)

American Association of Colleges of Nursing (AACN) (A16)

American Association of Colleges of Osteopathic Medicine (AACOM) (A17)

American Association of Community and Junior Colleges (AACJC) (A19)

American Association of Dental Schools (AADS) (A20)

American Association of University Administrators (AAUA) (A30)

American Association of University Women (AAUW) (A32)

American Association of Women in Community and Junior Colleges (AAWCJC) (A33)

American Conference of Academic Deans (ACAD) (A39)

American Council on Education/National Identification Program for the Advancement of Women in Higher Education (ACE/NIP) (A41)

Association for Continuing Higher Education (ACHE) (A79)

Association of American Law Schools (AALS) (A88)

Association of American Medical Colleges (AAMC) (A89)

Association of Collegiate Schools of Architecture (ACSA) (A98)

Association of Collegiate Schools of Planning (ACSP) (A99)

Association of Research Libraries (ARL) (A110)

Association of Schools of Journalism and Mass Communication (ASJMC) (A111)

Association of University Summer Sessions (AUSS) (A116)

Council of Colleges of Arts and Sciences (CCAS) (A130)

Council of Graduate Schools (CGS) (A131)

Higher Education Resource Service (HERS) (A141)

International Council of Fine Arts Deans (ICFAD) (A145)

National Association for Core Curriculum (NACC) (A154)

National Association for Women in Education (NAWE) (A157)
Formerly National Association for Women Deans, Administrators, and Counselors (NAWDAC)

National Association of Academic Affairs Administrators (AcAfAd) (A158)

National Association of Schools of Art and Design (NASAD) (A172)

National Association of Schools of Dance (NASD) (A172)

National Association of Schools of Music (NASM) (A172)

National Association of Schools of Theater (NAST) (A172)

North American Association of Summer Sessions (NAASS) (A184)

University Council for Educational Administrators (UCEA) (A190)

National Programs

Programs listed in Chapter 8, *Administrative Managers and Professional Staff,* also may be applicable for focused exploration of management skills in areas such as personnel management, planning, financial management, labor ralations, fund raising and development, etc. The following list provides a sampling of the range and variety of off-campus programs available to mid-level academic administrators and is not meant to be an inventory of all programs and activities available to these leaders. Note that many programs offered by associations are available only to deans and academic administrators of member institutions.

American Assembly of Collegiate Schools of Business (AACSB) (P1)

Associate Deans Seminar *(P1b)*
New Deans Seminar *(P1a)*

American Association of Colleges for Teacher Education (AACTE) (P3)

New Deans Institute *(P3a)*

American Association of Colleges of Nursing (AACN) (P4)

Executive Development Series *(P4a)*

American Association of Community and Junior Colleges (AACJC) (P5)

Fellows Program *(P5a)*
Professional Development Workshop *(P5c)*

American Council on Education (ACE) (P7)

Department Leadership Program *(P7a)*
The Fellows Program *(P7b)*

American Management Association (AMA) (P8)

Association of American Law Schools (AALS) (P10)

Deans and Librarians Workshop *(P10a)*
Senior Administrators Workshop *(P10b)*

Association of American Medical Colleges (AAMC) (P11)

Executive Development Seminar for Deans *(P11a)*

Association of Collegiate Schools of Architecture (ACSA) (P12)

Administrators Conference *(P12a)*

Association of Research Libraries (ARL) (P16)

Advanced Management Skills Institute *(P16a)*
Basic Management Skills Institute *(P16b)*
Creativity to Innovation Workshop *(P16c)*
Project Planning Workshop *(P16d)*
Resources Management Institute *(P16e)*
Training Skills Institute *(P16f)*

The Bush Foundation (P18)

Leadership Program for Midcareer Development *(P18a)*

Carnegie Mellon University/School of Urban and Public Affairs (P19)

Academic Leadership Institute *(P19a)*
College Management Program *(P19b)*

Center for Creative Leadership (P20)

Dynamics of Strategy: Goals into Action *(P20a)*
Executive Women Workshop *(P20b)*
Leadership and Teamwork: Increasing Team Leadership Capabilities *(P20c)*
Leadership Development Program *(P20d)*

Council for Advancement and Support of Education (CASE) (P27)

Summer Institute in Executive Management *(P27d)*

Council for International Exchange of Scholars (CIES) (P26)

Fulbright Scholar Program *(P26a)*
Seminars for International Education Administrators in Germany and Japan *(P26b)*
U.S./United Kingdom College and Unversity Academic Administrator Award *(P26c)*

Council of Colleges of Arts and Sciences (CCAS) *(P29)*

   Annual Seminars *(P29a)*

Council of Colleges of Arts and Sciences (CCAS) and American Conference of Academic Deans (ACAD) *(P30)*

   Seminar for New Deans *(P30a)*

Council of Graduate Schools (CGS) *(P31)*

   Summer Workshops for Graduate Deans *(P31a)*

Council on International Educational Exchange (CIEE) *(P33)*

   Development Seminars *(P33a)*

Harvard University/Graduate School of Education *(P37)*

   Institute for Educational Management (IEM) *(P37b)*
   Institute for the Management of Lifelong Education (MLE) *(P37c)*
   Management Development Program (MDP) *(P37d)*

Higher Education Resource Services (HERS) Mid-American/Bryn Mawr College *(P39)*

   HERS Summer Institute for Women/Bryn Mawr Institute *(P39a)*

Higher Education Resource Services (HERS) New England/Wellesley College *(P40)*

   HERS Institute for Women/Wellesley Institute *(P40a)*

Institute for Educational Leadership (IEL) *(P41)*

   Educational Policy Fellowship Program *(P41a)*

League for Innovation in the Community College *(P45)*

   Leadership 2000 *(P45b)*

League for Innovation in the Community College, the University of Texas–Austin, and the W. K. Kellogg Foundation *(P46)*

   Expanding Leadership Diversity in Community Colleges *(P46a)*

Lilly Endowment, Inc *(P47)*

   Workshop on the Liberal Arts *(P47a)*

Massachusetts Institute of Technology (MIT)/Sloan School of Management *(P48)*

   Alfred P. Sloan Fellows Program *(P48a)*

National Association of Academic Affairs Administrators (AcAfAd) *(P50)*

   Management Development Seminar for Assistant and Associate Deans *(P50a)*

National Center for Higher Education Management Systems (NCHEMS) *(P57)*

National Institute for Leadership Development *(P59)*

   Building a Better Team on Campus: Understanding Gender Issues *(P59a)*
   Leaders for Change *(P59b)*
   Leaders Project *(P59d)*
   Leadership for a New Century *(P59c)*

North Carolina State University *(P60)*

   Community College Leadership Institute *(P60a)*

NTL Institute *(P61)*

   Human Interaction Laboratory *(P61a)*
   Management Work Conference *(P61b)*
   Other Programs *(P61d)*

Oklahoma State University (P62)

   Annual National Conference of Academic Deans *(P62a)*

Professional and Organizational Development Network in Higher Education (POD) (P63)

Society for Values in Higher Education (P64)

   The Fellows Meeting *(P64a)*

Texas A&M University/College of Education (P66)

   Summer Seminar on Academic Administration *(P66a)*

University of Central Florida (P68)

   Financial Management for Women in Higher Education *(P68a)*

University of Georgia/Institute of Higher Education and the Georgia Center for Continuing Education (P69)

   Annual Conference on Higher Education and the Law *(P69a)*

W. K. Kellogg Foundation (P73)

   National Fellowship Program *(P73a)*

Statewide, System-Specific, and On-Campus Programs

Arizona State University (ASU) (S2)

   Leadership Academy *(S2c)*
   President's Breakfast Series *(S2d)*

Association of California Community College Administrators (ACCCA) (S3)

   Mentor Program *(S3a)*

Board of Governors of State Colleges and Universities (Illinois) (S5)

   Affirmative Action Administrative Fellows Program *(S5a)*

City University of New York (CUNY) (S9)

   Women's Leadership Institute *(S9b)*

Colorado State University (S10)

   The Administrative Women's Network *(S10d)*
   Leadership Series *(S10c)*
   Professional Development Institute *(S10b)*

Colorado Women in Higher Education Administration and the American Council on Education National Identification Program (ACE/NIP) (S11)

   Academic Management Institute for Women *(S11a)*

Lansing Community College (S19)

   Community Leadership Development Academy *(S19a)*

Maricopa Community College District (S20)

   Professional Group Program *(S20c)*
   Visions Career Development Program *(S20a)*

University of Tennessee (S36)

   Institute for Leadership Effectiveness *(S36a)*

University of Wisconsin System (S39)

   Administrative Associate Program *(S39a)*

8

ADMINISTRATIVE MANAGERS AND PROFESSIONAL STAFF

Complementing, supporting, and reinforcing the work of faculty and academic administrators is a large and important group of administrative managers and professional staff: '''the people in the middle' between the faculty and the executive decisionmakers'' (Kraus 1983, p. 29).[1] This broad and diverse group is sometimes called ''middle management,'' ''administrative staff,'' ''nonacademic personnel,'' or ''managerial professionals,'' but no label quite covers the entire range of responsibilities.

Administrative managers include registrars and comptrollers, admissions and financial aid officers, heads of counseling centers, and directors of learning resources, media centers, alumni activities, and publications. Their positions generally fall in the areas of public affairs, fund raising, student affairs, or business and administrative affairs. However, some are academic, such as internship coordinators, directors of off-campus programs, or directors of noncredit programs. Rarely are they members of the faculty, though some may have teaching experience and hold doctorates.

The supervisory responsibilities they carry also vary tremendously— from the large staff of a student counseling center to one or two support staff in a small office—depending in part on the size of the institution. Professional staff such as computer specialists or institutional researchers may have little or no supervisory responsibilities.

One characteristic shared by the members of this eclectic group is the fact that their jobs often require a specialized and up-to-date body of knowledge. Benefits managers, media specialists, purchasing officers, and directors of planned giving each bring specific expertise to their jobs and must continue to learn new skills and information relevant to their particular areas. This poses a special challenge to their professional growth, since the development of expertise may preclude the development of breadth. As a result, administrative managers may get typecast and miss the opportunity to play a different role, carry out different responsibilities, or assume leadership on campus.

CAREER PREPARATION

People in administrative management often follow idiosyncratic career paths and face limited options for upward or even lateral mobility. In many institutions, their lack of faculty credentials and status diminishes their standing and limits the positions to which they can aspire. As a staff member in a counseling service put it, ''I see a lot more of certain students than their professors ever will, but faculty can hardly imagine that I could affect a student's life as much as they do.''

Yet administrative managers and professional staff are often the historical memory of an institution, and many spend their entire careers in the same college or university. While institutional loyalty and historical memory bring real advantages, administrative managers also may feel stuck, and therefore be less satisfied with their work, less creative, less innovative, and less productive.

Scott (1978, p. 31) points out that middle managers are a frequently ignored group, noting that they achieve ''their status almost in spite of their institutions or, at least, without conscious institutional support. They suffer, and yet they prosper. They have a high degree of institutional loyalty, but most look off campus, mostly to their associations, for training, guidance, recognition, colleagueship, and rewards.''

The specialization that permeates higher education is particularly visible in the jobs of administrative managers. A sense of turf can lead to a sense of isolation, an inability to see how one's job relates to the whole. Thus, it is especially important in planning leadership development for administrative managers to provide a wider vision of the institution's mission and functioning.

Many of the liabilities described above are also potential strengths. Their unpredictable career paths and distinctive status often enable administrative mangers to make many positive contributions to their institutions:

- Transfer of expertise—Skills in financial management, public relations, marketing, and human resources can be applied in many settings. This cross-fertilization can provide new perspectives and real contributions to a different part of the institution while offering new challenges to the individual.

- Service to other programs—Often the expertise sought outside the institution is available right at home. The director of continuing education programs may have marketing expertise that would benefit the admissions office; the director of human resources might consult with the deans or faculty on faculty development.

■ Service to students—Staff members in student services, the registrar's office, and learning resource centers have much contact with students. The same is true for financial aid counselors, food service managers, and persons in the business office. Thus, administrative managers serve as bearers of the institution's image, confirming or negating the institution's professed commitment to serving students.

RESPONSIBILITIES

The job responsibilities of administrative managers and professional staff vary significantly according to the particular position and its relevant expertise. Still, most positions have in common the compound responsibilities of manager, professional, expert, and leader. Indeed, many administrative managers perform the tasks common to all academic leaders: envisioning a future, shaping the environment, making decisions, working with people, planning, and implementing. The common responsibilities of administrative managers are similar to those of academic deans and mid-level academic administrators described in the preceding chapter.

Like others in mid-level positions, administrative managers relate to several organizational layers: supervisors, peers, and subordinates. Uyterhoeven's (1989, p. 138) observation about middle managers in the corporate sector is applicable to their counterparts in academe: "They are both delegators and doers, both strategists and operators, or, to use [a] sports analogy, both coaches and players. In contrast, their superiors are usually coaches and their subordinates are normally players." Achieving a workable balance among these sometimes conflicting roles is a delicate task for administrative managers. These individuals have the pivotal role of translating the more general and abstract goals articulated by senior executives into concrete action.

Setting Priorities

Administrative managers develop and implement policies for their units. Working with supervisors and oversight committees, they establish the management priorities of their units within the institution's context and ensure that those priorities are met. The head of the public relations unit for a large university commented, "Unlike my colleagues in corporations, here we must invest more time in the process of setting priorities through the extensive negotiation process of consensus building that permeates the academy.''

Supporting Academic Programs

Although formal responsibility for the creation of academic programs and curricula resides with the faculty and academic administrators, administrative managers are still instrumental to building and maintaining academic programs. While the direct impact of an administrative manager's support on the institution's academic program may vary, all contribute in some large or small way to the general functioning of the operation. The academic programs would not exist without the students recruited and processed by the admissions office. It is just as important that the finance office process the bills and the benefits office keep track of salaries. ''We take care of the operational details so that the faculty can really concentrate on their teaching and research. Can you imagine how few books would get written by those professors if they had to process every bill associated with their research grants, order every test tube themselves, or keep their FICA withdrawals straight with the government?'' remarked the personnel officer of a Big 10 university.

Managing the Unit

An administrative supervisor must oversee the operations of his or her unit by conducting meetings, developing goals, organizing and directing operations, and coordinating activities, to cite only a few duties. It may be possible to delegate many responsibilities to staff members for actual implementation. Making connections across units to solve a problem or achieve a goal takes time and energy, but those connections are investments with high payoffs.

Securing Resources and Budgeting for Their Use

While administrative managers may not be as involved in fund-raising for the support of their unit as are their academic counterparts, they still must participate in the negotiations process that allocates funds across institutional units. They also have comparable responsibilities in establishing budgets and monitoring their implementation.

Linking Operations

Just as a dean links various academic departments, so many administrative managers link the operational areas of their units. It is typical for admissions and financial aid to be combined, or for the operations of government and media relations to be linked. The mid-level administrative supervisor must provide linkages for these sometimes disparate operations and provide a cohesive whole for their activities. Such a supervisor affects administrative quality through choices in the promotion and evaluation process, through the allocation of human and financial resources, or, less tangibly, through leadership in the development of programs, setting standards, and serving as a role model.

Securing and Ensuring the Best Employees

Although nonacademic employee recruitment may be more centralized in a personnel office than faculty recruitment, an administrative supervisor usually makes the final selection of the best person for the job. In addition to finding the best person for a job and shaping the focus of the unit, the administrator's choice also should reflect the institution's goal of employee diversity.

Evaluating Employees

Most institutions have an evaluation and promotion process for administrative employees that is parallel to that used for faculty. Administrative supervisors must spend much time in this evaluation process to ensure the development of employees and the best match of their abilities to their jobs.

Forming an Administrative Team and Creating a Working Environment

To ensure smooth operations, an administrative supervisor will benefit from investing in the efforts of team building with members of the unit. Depending on the span of control in the unit and the similarity of operations performed by the various members of the unit, such a task may vary in difficulty. Team building also means resolving conflicts among employees and creating a positive working environment. A development officer commented, "Resolving conflicts among my staff sometime seems to take more time out of my day than do the actual activities of fund-raising. But we would not be able to raise the funds if the staff was not a cohesive team and if our time was wasted in dealing with stress and fighting among ourselves. My biggest job is creating a peaceful working environment in which my experts can do their best jobs."

Supervising Facilities, Space, and Equipment

While students may think of facilities, space, and equipment as possessions of academic units, typically these fall under the purview of administrative managers. Tasks such as ordering and repairing equipment or maintaining facilities are typically responsibilities of administrative managers.

Planning

Planning is a key task of any leader, regardless of the size or purpose of the unit. Every unit needs to consider its future and to plan for it in a comprehensive, organized way. Such planning cannot be done in isolation, but must be undertaken in the general context of the institution. Strategic and long-range planning are important vehicles for moving a unit forward.

SPECIAL DEVELOPMENT NEEDS

As noted earlier, the special circumstances of administrative managers and professional staff and their lack of academic credentials and faculty status can raise issues of credibility and prestige: long service may lead to a feeling of stagnation; a high degree of specialization can result in a sense of isolation. Leadership development strategies for this group should address the following issues:

Introduction to General Management

Newly appointed administrative managers will need help in making the transition from specialist to administrative head. The move into one's first position as an administrative manager is like the transition from faculty member to department chair. It requires the development of new skills in managing complex relationships, planning, budgeting, and supervising.

Increasing Career Mobility

Development strategies can help administrative managers break out of the career boxes in which they find themselves. Exposing people to different parts of the institution, providing internships, and assigning work that stretches people beyond their particular expertise are all ways of preparing individuals to move in new directions. Additional education also can help administrators redirect their careers. It should be noted that for some administrative managers, moving on may mean leaving the institution or higher education altogether.

Overcoming Isolation

The more people are involved with other offices and tasks, the more they will see the relevance of their work to the rest of the institution. Committee assignments, participation in task forces, and projects that cut across divisional lines are useful means of lowering barriers and diminishing isolation.

Identifying New Leaders

Identifying leadership from the middle ranks presents special challenges for institutions, especially the larger ones. Middle managers tend to get lost, and supervisors need to work actively to identify emerging leaders as well as to encourage their development.

LEADERSHIP CAPACITIES

The following leadership capacities cut across the different fields and jobs of administrative managers and professional staff. Each position will require a different mix. A computer specialist must be extremely knowledgeable about a technical area and may have fewer people to supervise, while the director of the annual fund works with many volunteers and needs well-honed interpersonal skills.

Vision and Goal-Setting

Vision and goal-setting are leadership tasks at every level in the institution, requiring an understanding of the whole, a sense of the future, and the ability to project beyond the day-to-day operations of the unit. This is a particularly important issue for administrative managers and professional staff, who may have few opportunities to broaden their vision, to relate their work to the whole of the institution, and to interact with others beyond their unit.

Mastery of Specialized Information

As higher education has become a more sophisticated enterprise, so has the administrative manager's job become highly information-intensive and specialized. Fund accounting, financial aid, and computer services are all complicated content areas; professionals must have complete mastery of the substance of their particular areas.

Team Building

Team building within a manager's unit requires maintaining effective communication both within the unit and with other offices in the institution. Relationships with faculty are also very important but perhaps more problematic because of status issues and the need for administrative managers to earn the trust and respect of people with whom they do not regularly work. Relationships with other administrative managers may require similar efforts to overcome some of the turf divisions that frequently hamper communication and cooperation.

Understanding the Institutional Context

Expertise alone will not make an administrative manager effective. A registrar must understand both faculty concerns about awarding credit for prior learning and student concerns about scheduling; a director of the student center plays a role in the larger institutional effort to understand and reduce attrition. Understanding the institutional context and issues that shape a particular unit's agenda is essential to dealing effectively with the many interrelated activities.

Leadership and Management Skills

Because administrative managers' jobs are both strategic and operational, development should address both aspects of their work. Leadership development opportunities to broaden the manager's vision of the institution, to encourage innovation and risk taking, to shift the individual's perspective from specialist to generalist, will enhance the strategic and visionary capacities of the administrative manager. Training in budgeting, communication, and supervisory skills and in the technical aspects of the job will assist administrative managers in their day-to-day operations.

STRATEGIES FOR DEVELOPMENT

How Senior Administrators can Foster the Development of Administrative Managers[2]

As a first step, senior administrators must simply pay attention to the development of administrative managers. Leadership development opportunities often are more available to senior officers or clerical and technical personnel; administrative managers tend to be the forgotten group. Supervisors of middle managers should consider the following approaches:

- *Create opportunities for development on the job.* Since upward mobility is not always feasible or desirable as a primary vehicle for professional growth for administrative managers and professional staff, it is important to use the job itself to provide developmental opportunities. An important way to accomplish this is to give people new assignments that stretch their capacities and test them in new areas and to provide guidance and feedback during this assignment.

- *Encourage leadership and innovation from the ranks.* A climate in which new ideas can flourish is a climate for innovation. Creating such an environment involves letting people experiment, take risks, and sometimes fail. If people genuinely believe that their ideas will be heard, they are more likely to be innovative.

- *View middle management as a talent pool.* Given the opportunity, talented people will contribute in areas beyond the "boxes" in which their job descriptions put them. Traditionally, the higher education culture has valued new blood over known quantities, believing that greater talent is to be found outside the institution. Hence, administrative managers may be an underutilized pool of people who are frequently capable of assuming greater responsibility. A bright young personnel officer may be ready to move into the senior position in that area in a few years; similarly, a mid-level person in that office could be retrained to move into other areas such as governmental relations or financial management.

  Administrative managers and professional staff make up an especially important pool of women and minority administrators. Institutions committed to fostering leadership among women and minorities will want to look to this group as a resource for more senior positions.

- *Provide opportunities for participation in institution-wide activities.* Including administrators from a variety of areas on institution-wide task forces and committees benefits both the institution and the individual. They bring a variety of perspectives on such issues as planning, student life, or the search process; they also bring skills in managing the group process. Some may have valuable contributions to make to subjects long thought the unique province of the professorate. For example, a middle manager with international experience could be a useful part of the debate on internationalizing the curriculum. Mixing people from various parts of the institution creates personal bonds and networks that break down traditional barriers and helps build a sense of shared purpose. Exposure to individuals and issues beyond their particular domain serves to broaden the horizons of administrative managers and gives them perspective and insights that they could not gain in their departments.

- *Use interim positions as developmental opportunities.* Units sometimes need to replace people quickly, if only as a temporary measure.

The opportunity to fill an ''acting'' position can provide an unparalleled opportunity for people to test their abilities and learn new skills. These opportunities can be deliberately structured as a developmental experience, with careful supervision and feedback integral parts of the learning process.

- *Provide job rotation opportunities.* Even a short stint in another office can be a highly energizing experience. (Though longer experiences in other areas may be even more useful, practical obstacles of job coverage may make them infeasible.) A one- or two-month internship in another area can provide useful exposure to institutional operations and help people think through their career options. In more closely related areas—within student affairs or administrative operations—it is more feasible to move people for a longer period, or even permanently.

- *Provide sabbaticals.* Unfortunately, most campuses provide sabbaticals only to faculty and senior academic officers. Yet the need to retool, to gain fresh perspectives, is equally strong (if not stronger) in middle management. Long tenure and lack of mobility make these opportunities especially important to the continued professional well-being of administrative managers.

- *Conduct retreats or workshops for administrative managers.* In spite of apparent differences in job descriptions, common responsibilities of managing human and financial resources can provide sufficient links to form the basis of sound team building, a planning effort, or the development of particular leadership skills. Retreats or workshops designed around the special needs or capacities of participants can facilitate such exchanges in an environment free of the day-to-day pressures of the administrative job.

- *Support participation in professional associations.* The professional associations listed at the end of this chapter are excellent sources of information and professional development opportunities. They provide important links to colleagues in the same field, access to timely information, and a sense of professional identity that is a source of pride.

- *Encourage visits to counterparts in other institutions.* A visit to another institution can yield useful insights into how the same issues and operations are handled in another context. Sometimes such contacts will be impeded by the perception that the institutions are competitors, but that obstacle can be overcome by the choice of institution. These visits can last from a few days to a few weeks.

Taking Responsibility for One's Own Development

The following suggestions can help administrative managers and professional staff attend to their development:

- *Seek opportunities to participate in institutional deliberations.* Committee work and task forces can provide opportunities to learn about the institution and meet colleagues. Because of the specialized expertise that administrative managers offer, their participation should have a reciprocal benefit.

- *Develop breadth.* It is easy for an administrative manager or professional staff member to become more and more specialized in one field. But knowledge of other areas of the institution helps develop skills as a generalist and prepares individuals for a broader spectrum of future opportunities. Skills in oral and written communication, problem solving, and decision making are highly portable and are great assets in seeking new responsibilities or jobs. It is also very useful to keep abreast of institutional developments and higher education issues within the state and nationally.

- *Seek relevant development experiences outside higher education.* Exposure to an analogous operation in a nonprofit organization or in business can be a useful development opportunity. Job changes are also significant learning opportunities. An assistant registrar reported the benefits of moving to a corporate setting for a few years. He brought a proficiency in information systems to the corporation, where he learned an additional set of skills and perspectives that in turn proved useful when he returned to academe.

- *Take an active role in creating future opportunities.* Institutional and professional colleagues can be helpful sources of advice and information. A supportive supervisor can provide help in developing a plan and in supplying needed feedback.

- *Become active in professional organizations.* At a minimum, attendance at meetings and occasional workshops will keep people informed. An active role in a professional association can be a source of satisfaction in itself; moreover, it can offer the opportunity to use a different set of skills and interact with people different from those on the job.

- *Seek leadership responsibilities outside the institution.* Leadership roles in civic and community affairs and professional associations provide windows on a different and larger world as well as the satisfaction of service.

CONCLUSION

Understanding the role of administrative managers and professional staff in the context of institutional goals and priorities is the first step to utilizing this untapped source of energy on campus. With institutional support and opportunities for development, administrative managers can provide effective leadership within the university and can add their unique perspective to the campus decision-making process. While administrative managers and professional staff face the dangers of over-specialization, isolation, and career dead ends, these are not inevitable. Addressing the development needs of administrative managers takes little effort on the part of the institution and brings the inestimable benefit of maintaining a vital and productive cadre of middle managers.

NOTES

1. Much of the material in the preceding chapter describing academic deans and mid-level academic administrators is relevant to administrative managers and professional staff. Thus, this section focuses largely on those aspects of the positions of administrative managers that are *different* from those of academic administrators. Readers are advised to consult this chapter in conjunction with the preceding one for full coverage of relevant material.

2. Many of the recommendations in this section and the following one are adapted from Robert A. Scott, *The Development of Competence: Administrative Needs and Training Goals in American Higher Education* (n.p.: 1978). ERIC ED179143.

REFERENCES

Kraus, John D. "Middle Management in Higher Education: A Dog's Life?" *Journal of the College and University Personnel Association* 34, no. 4 (Winter 1983): 29–35.

Scott, Robert A. *The Development of Competence: Administrative Needs and Training Goals in American Higher Education*. N.p.: 1978. Photocopy. ERIC ED179143.

Uyterhoeven, Hugo. "General Managers in the Middle." *Harvard Business Review* 67, no. 5 (September-October 1989): 136–45.

RESOURCES

Scott, Robert A. *Lords, Squires, and Yeomen: Collegiate Middle Managers and Their Organizations*. Research Report No. 7. Washington, DC: AAHE-ERIC, 1978.

The classic book about middle level administrators in the college and university setting. Scott reviews the characteristics and challenges faced by middle managers, the implications of their positions within the higher education organization, and the levers of power and influence available to them.

PROGRAMS AND PRACTICES

The following lists identify some of the associations and development programs that serve administrative managers and professional staff. The numbers in parentheses following each entry refer to the detailed descriptions of these programs that appear in the appendix, *Programs and Practices.*

National Associations

The following list provides a sampling of the associations and programs that serve administrative managers. There are also many regional associations for administrative managers; for example, organizations such as the National Association of Student Personnel Administrators (NASPA) and the Council for the Advancement and Support of Education (CASE) support regional organizations. Many associations, such as the AAHE and the American Association of Community and Junior Colleges (AACJC) sponsor caucuses for women, minorities, faculty, and other groups that cut across functional lines.

American Association for Adult and Continuing Education (AAACE) (A9)

American Association for Counseling and Development (AACD) (A10)

American Association for Higher Education (AAHE) (A11)

American Association of Collegiate Registrars and Admissions Officers (AACRAO) (A18)

American Association of University Administrators (AAUA) (A30)

American Association of University Women (AAUW) (A32)

American Association of Women in Community and Junior Colleges (AAWCJC) (A33)

American College Personnel Association (ACPA) (A37)

American Council on Education/National Identification Program for the Advancement of Women in Higher Education (ACE/NIP) (A41)

American Library Association (ALA) (A50)

American Society for Training and Development (ASTD) (A62)

Association for Continuing Higher Education (ACHE) (A79)

Association for Institutional Research (AIR) (A80)

Association for School, College, and University Staffing, Inc. (ASCUS) (A82)

Association of American University Presses (AAUP) (A91)

Association of College and University Auditors (ACUA) (A95)

Association of College and University Housing Officers—International (ACUHO-I) (A96)

Association of College Unions—International (ACU-I) (A97)

Association of Conference and Events Directors—International (ACED-I) (A101)

Association of Physical Plant Administrators of Universities and Colleges (APPA) (A109)

Association of Research Libraries (ARL) (A110)

Association of University Summer Sessions (AUSS) (A116)

CAUSE (Association for the Management of Information Technology) (A119)

College and University Computer Users Conference (CUCUC) (A120)

College and University Personnel Association (CUPA) (A121)

College Media Advisers (CMA) (A123)

College Placement Council (CPC) (A124)

Cooperative Education Association (CEA) (A125)

Council for Adult and Experiential Learning (CAEL) (A126)

Council for Advancement and Support of Education (CASE) (A127)

Council on Governmental Relations (COGR) (A134)

Higher Education Resource Service (HERS) (A141)

International Association of Campus Law Enforcement Administrators (IACLEA) (A144)

Jesuit Association of Student Personnel Administrators (JASPA) (A147)

National Academic Advising Association (NAcAdA) (A153)

National Association for Equal Opportunity in Higher Education (NAFEO) (A155)

National Association for Women in Education (NAWE) (A157)
   Formerly National Association for Women Deans, Administrators, and Counselors (NAWDAC)

National Association of College Admission Counselors (NACAC) (A160)

National Association of College and University Attorneys (NACUA) (A161)

National Association of College and University Business Officers (NACUBO) (A162)

National Association of College and University Food Services (NACUFS) (A163)

National Association of College Deans, Registrars, and Admissions Officers (NACDRAO) (A164)

National Association of Education Office Personnel (NAEOP) (A166)

National Association of Educational Buyers, Inc. (NAEB) (A167)

National Association of Personnel Workers (NAPW) (A170)

National Association of Student Financial Aid Administrators (NASFAA) (A174)

National Association of Student Personnel Administrators (NASPA) (A175)

National Collegiate Athletic Association (NCAA) (A178)

National Council of University Research Administrators (NCURA) (A180)

National Orientation Directors Association (NODA) (A182)

National University Continuing Education Association (NUCEA) (A183)

North American Association of Summer Sessions (NAASS) (A184)

Society for College and University Planning (SCUP) (A185)

Special Interest Group for University and College Computing Services (SIGUCCS) (A187)

University Council for Educational Administrators (UCEA) (A190)

National Programs

Programs listed in Chapter 7, *Academic Deans, and Mid-Level Academic Administrators,* also may be applicable for exploration of general management skills and higher education issues. The following list provides a sampling of the range and variety of off-campus programs available to administrative managers and professional staff and is not meant to be an inventory of all programs and activities available to these leaders. Note that many programs offered by associations are available only to administrators from member institutions.

American Association of Community and Junior Colleges (AACJC) (P5)

Fellows Program *(P5a)*
Professional Development Workshop *(P5c)*

American Council on Education (ACE) (P7)

The Fellows Program *(P7b)*

American Management Association (AMA) (P8)

Association of Research Libraries (ARL) (P17)

Advanced Management Skills Institute *(P17a)*
Basic Management Skills Institute *(P17b)*
Creativity to Innovation Workshop *(P17c)*
Project Planning Workshop *(P17d)*
Resources Management Institute *(P17e)*
Training Skills Institute *(P17f)*

The Bush Foundation (P18)

Leadership Program for Midcareer Development *(P18a)*

Carnegie Mellon University/School of Urban and Public Affairs (P19)

College Management Program *(P19b)*

Center for Creative Leadership (P20)

Leadership Development Program *(P20d)*

Central Association of College and University Business Officers (CACUBO) (P22)

Management Institute *(P22a)*

College and University Personnel Association (CUPA) (P24)

Council for Advancement and Support of Education (CASE) (P26)

Forums for Women and Minorities in Institutional Advancement *(P26a)*
Summer Institute in Executive Management *(P26d)*

Council for Advancement and Support of Education (CASE), and Snelling, Kolb & Kuhnle (P27)

Skills for Success: A Workshop for Getting Ahead *(P27a)*

Council for International Exchange of Scholars (CIES) (P28)

Fulbright Scholar Program *(P28a)*
Seminars for International Education Administrators in Germany and Japan *(P28b)*
U.S./United Kingdom College and University Academic Administrator Award *(P28c)*

Council on International Educational Exchange (CIEE) (P33)

Development Seminars *(P33a)*

Harvard University and the College Board (P38)

Summer Institute on College Admissions *(P38a)*

Harvard University/Graduate School of Education (P37)

Institute for the Management of Lifelong Education (MLE) *(P37c)*
Management Development Program (MDP) *(P37d)*

Higher Education Resource Services (HERS) Mid-America/Bryn Mawr College (P39)

HERS Summer Institute for Women/Bryn Mawr Institute *(P39a)*

Higher Education Resource Services (HERS) New England/Wellesley College (P40)

HERS Institute for Women/Wellesley Institute *(P40a)*

Institute for Educational Leadership (IEL) (P41)

  Educational Policy Fellowship Program *(P41a)*

League for Innovation in the Community College (P45)

  Minority Leadership Program *(P45c)*

League for Innovation in the Community College, the University of Texas—Austin, and the W.K. Kellogg Foundation (P46)

  Expanding Leadership Diversity in Community Colleges *(P46a)*

National Association of College Admission Counselors (NACAC) (P51)

  Admission Middle Management Institute *(P51a)*

National Association of Student Personnel Administrators (NASPA) (P56)

  Richard F. Stevens Institute *(P56a)*

National Center for Higher Education Management Systems (NCHEMS) (P57)

National Institute for Leadership Development (P59)

  Building a Better Team on Campus: Understanding Gender Issues *(P59a)*
  Leaders for Change *(P59b)*
  Leadership for a New Century *(P59c)*
  Leaders Project *(P59d)*

NTL Institute (P61)

  Human Interaction Laboratory *(P61a)*
  Management Work Conference *(P61b)*
  Other Programs *(P61d)*

Southern Association of College and University Business Officers (SACUBO)/University of Kentucky (P65)

  College Management Business Institute (CMBI) *(P65a)*

University of Central Florida (P68)

  Financial Management for Women in Higher Education *(P68a)*

University of Georgia/Institute of Higher Education and the Georgia Center for Continuing Education (P69)

  Annual Conference on Higher Education and the Law *(P69a)*

University of Maryland (P70)

  Student Affairs Conference *(P70a)*

Western Association of College and University Business Officers (WACUBO) (P71)

  Business Management Institute *(P71b)*
  Executive Leadership and Management Institute *(P71a)*

W.K. Kellogg Foundation (P73)

  National Fellowship Program *(P73a)*

Williamsburg Development Institute (P72)

  Williamsburg Development Institute *(P72a)*

Woodrow Wilson National Fellowship Foundation (P74)

  Administrative Fellows Program *(P74a)*

Statewide, System-Specifics, and On-Campus Programs

Programs and activities on the following list typically are restricted to members of the sponsoring institution or organization.

The American University (AU) (S1)

Office of Training and Development Programs *(S1a)*

Arizona State University (ASU) (S2)

Internship *(S2b)*
Leadership Academy *(S2C)*
Management Development Program (MDP) *(S2a)*

Association of California Community College Administrators (ACCCA) (S3)

Mentor Program *(S3a)*

Board of Governors of State Colleges and Universities (Illinois) (S5)

Affirmative Action Administrative Fellows Program *(S5a)*

Boston College (S6)

Professional Development Program *(S6a)*

California State University System (CSU) (S7)

Administrative Fellows Program *(S7a)*

City University of New York (CUNY) (S9)

Women's Leadership Institute *(S9b)*

Colorado State University (CSU) (S10)

Administrative Women's Network *(S10d)*
Leadership Series *(S10c)*
Professional Development Institute *(S10b)*

Colorado Women in Higher Education Administration and the American Council on Educational National Identification Program (ACE/NIP) (S11)

Academic Management Institute for Women *(S11a)*

Columbia University (S12)

Connections *(S12b)*
Front Line Leadership Program *(S12c)*
Middle Management Development Program *(S12d)*
Professional Development Programs *(S12a)*

Eastern Illinois University (S14)

Programs for Professional Enrichment (PPE) *(S14a)*

George Washington University (S15)

The Training Division of Personnel Services *(S15a)*

Lansing Community College (S19)

Community Leadership Development Academy *(S19a)*

Maricopa Community College District (S20)

M&O/Crafts Training Program *(S20b)*
Professional Group Program *(S20c)*
Visions Career Development Program *(S20a)*

Pennsylvania State University (S21)

Administrative Fellows Program *(S21a)*

Rochester Institute of Technology (RIT) *(S22)*

Executive Leadership in an Academic Setting *(S22a)*

Stanford University *(S23)*

Administrative Development Program *(S23b)*
Human Resources Development Programs *(S23a)*
Management Development Program *(S23c)*
Stanford Supervision and You *(S23d)*

Tennessee Board of Regents *(S26)*

Minority Management Development Program *(S26a)*

University of California—Los Angeles (UCLA) *(S27)*

Management Enhancement Program *(S27a)*

University of Iowa *(S30)*

Administrative Seminar Program *(S30a)*

University of Kansas *(S31)*

Office of Personnel Services *(S31a)*

University of Massachusetts—Boston *(S32)*

Staff Exchange Program *(S32a)*

University of Nebraska—Lincoln/Institute of Agriculture and Natural Resources *(S33)*

Administrative Development Map *(S33e)*
Office of Professional and Organizational Development (OPOD) *(S33a)*

University of South Carolina *(S34)*

Minority Administrative Fellowship *(S34a)*

University of Tennessee *(S36)*

Institute for Leadership Effectiveness *(S36a)*

University of Texas—El Paso *(S37)*

New Faculty and Staff Orientation Program *(S37a)*

9

DEPARTMENT CHAIRS

Delicately and sometimes precariously positioned between faculty and administration, department chairs play a pivotal role in delivering educational services. They are higher education's first-line academic leaders, making important decisions in the trenches that directly affect the quality of an institution—decisions about hiring, about evaluating and developing faculty, about curriculum, and about students. They are "leaders among peers" (Tucker 1984), sometimes elected by their colleagues, and generally blessed with much responsibility but little formal power. The power they do have derives largely from the relationships they are able to build and the trust they establish among faculty and other administrators. Such power is not inconsequential; the confidence of the dean, for example, can be an especially important source of authority for the chair.

Most department chairs have no preparation for their administrative responsibilities, although they may enter the position from jobs entailing many different tasks and requiring a wide range of skills and abilities. Some faculty accept the position because of an interest in administration; they see the job as an opportunity to accomplish something—to move their department, to make some changes, to improve quality. Some serve only because it is their turn and eagerly await the expiration of their term. Though reluctant initially, they may rise to the challenge and profit from training and development. A rarer breed—the "adversarial chair," described by John Bennett (1989)—takes on the position to do battle with the dean or the administration, viewing the department's problems as externally induced. These are the most difficult chairs for deans to work with; an important first step is to get them to accept responsibility for the department's fate.

In spite—or perhaps because—of the difficulties of performing a complex job with no preparation, some department chairs develop a stronger interest in administration and seek further administrative responsibilities as deans and academic vice presidents. Department chairs constitute an important talent pool for other administrative positions. They are a vital link in the chain of academic quality, yet they may have the least formal preparation of the many "amateur" managers in academic administration. Enhancing their effectiveness brings both short- and long-term payoffs to the institution.

CONTEXT FOR DEPARTMENTAL LEADERSHIP

This chapter presents only a snapshot of the department chair; its fixed picture obscures a more fluid reality. As is the case for other administrators and faculty, the development of a chair is determined by many variables.

Length of Tenure as Chair

The development of a department chair is a progression of several stages. A faculty member may be thinking of serving as chair, moving into the position, in the early stages, or contemplating a move back to the faculty or into administration. Career development is never static, and that of the chair is no exception.

Size of Department

The size of the department is an important determinant of workload, department culture, and the issues a department faces. The paperwork associated with a department of 25 full-time faculty and 30 part-timers is substantially greater than that associated with a five-person department. Moving a sizeable number of faculty members in the same direction toward shared goals presents a different challenge from developing consensus in a small department. By the same token, a small department has fewer resources to shuffle, and the debate on any issue easily becomes personalized because of the small number of participants.

Department Culture

Just as each institution has a distinctive culture, so may departments. A department's shared history, its way of conducting business, its reputation, and its relationship with the college or institution (a stepchild? a center of excellence?) are key factors in the chair's job. Does the department have a history of acrimonious factionalism? Do the department's members consider themselves the institution's premier entrepreneurs? The resident intellectuals? To be effective, a chair must be attuned to these and similar questions of department culture.

Discipline

The responsibilities of the chair also vary with the discipline and with the school in which the department is located. A chair of a professional department will generally have greater external duties, representing the department to the professional community in a variety of capacities.

Method of Selection and Length of Term

A chair elected by the faculty has a different concept of the job than one appointed by the dean. An elected chair generally identifies with the faculty role and sees the job as a diversion from a faculty career. That individual is less likely to see the chair's role as an agent of change, since his or her eventual return to the faculty is more significant than the temporary stint as chair. This rotation has other effects as well. It is much more difficult for a chair to make changes when several other members of the department's faculty are former chairs, each with well-known stances on issues and problems. An appointed head, who may have an indefinite term, is likely to identify much more strongly with administration and to take a greater interest in learning how to be effective.

RESPONSIBILITIES

Though most department chairs are part-time administrators, they have a staggering array of responsibilities and tasks.[1]

Governing the Department

Leading a department includes developing and implementing the structures needed to conduct its business. These responsibilities include conducting department meetings, establishing department committees, establishing and implementing department plans and goals in collaboration with the faculty, preparing the department for accreditation and evaluation, and serving as an advocate for the department to higher administration. Most of these functions involve collaboration with the faculty and delegation of administrative responsibilities to individuals and committees.

Managing Instruction

Overseeing instruction involves a combination of housekeeping and educational leadership. On the administrative side, chairs schedule

classes, manage off-campus programs, supervise and schedule department examinations, and manage space and the budget. More substantive responsibilities include advising majors, monitoring dissertations
and programs of study for graduate students, and keeping department
curriculum and programs vigorous and up-to-date.

Managing Faculty Personnel Issues

Department chairs recruit and select faculty members, assign faculty
responsibilities (teaching, committee work), initiate and manage faculty
development activities, evaluate faculty performance, supervise promotion and tenure recommendations, invoke termination proceedings, participate in grievance hearings, make merit recommendations, deal with
unsatisfactory faculty and staff performance, keep faculty members
informed of department and college activities, prevent and resolve conflict among faculty members, and promote affirmative action.

Promoting Faculty Development

Chairs are the most important agents of faculty development. Their
responsibilities include fostering good teaching, helping faculty formu-
late their professional development plans, stimulating research and publication, encouraging and supporting faculty participation in
professional activities, and representing the department at professional
meetings. (See Chapter 10, *Faculty*, for elaboration of strategies for chairs
to promote faculty development.)

Working With Students and Student Issues

Department chairs recruit, select, and advise students, work with the
student government, and encourage student participation in department
governance. In departments with graduate programs, chairs oversee
admissions and financial aid.

Representing the Department to the Institution

Even when the department chair speaks as an individual, he or she is
perceived as speaking for the department. The chair serves as the primary interpreter of the discipline to the rest of the institution. The chair
also represents the department to the administration and faculty governance bodies and works to build and maintain the department's
reputation.

Serving as Link to External Groups

Besides representing the department to the university, the chair
coordinates activities with outside groups—for example, other

departments, high school teachers in the discipline, and funding agencies. This function may include ceremonial obligations, appearance at community functions, or attendance at meetings of relevant professional groups. Chairs also process department correspondence and requests for information and complete forms and surveys.

Managing the Budget and Resources

The scope of a chair's financial responsibility varies widely. In some departments, there is little discretionary money, while in others, chairs function more like deans and have a great deal of latitude to raise and allocate funds. Chairs generally prepare and propose department budgets, seek outside funding, encourage faculty to write proposals, administer the department budget, set priorities for use of travel funds, and prepare annual reports.

Supervising the Departmental Office

Like all administrators, department chairs manage human and other resources. They manage department facilities and equipment, including maintenance and control of inventory, and monitor building security and maintenance. Management of the office invariably entails responsibility for correspondence, files, and paper flow. Chairs deal with paperwork generated by faculty, administrators, and external groups. In addition to overseeing faculty personnel issues, chairs also supervise and evaluate the clerical and technical staff.

LEADERSHIP CAPACITIES

What leadership skills and capacities are required of the successful department chair? The list is a familiar one, similar to those required of other academic administrators: understanding their unique role, creating a vision, managing people, communicating effectively, and managing financial resources. Yet each of these plays out in a special way for department chairs, who occupy an ambiguous position with much more influence than authority. As a first among equals, a chair may find that leadership is perhaps more subtle than for other administrators, whose formal authority provides a foundation for leadership. Also, because few chairs spend most of their careers in this position, they retain a strong dual identity—one foot in the faculty, one in administration.

Creating a Vision

Vision is of crucial importance to the most senior people in an institution, yet because the totality of the organization is at stake, creating a vision and working to realize it are also important at the department level. Creating a vision is a shared task: while the chair may provide leadership, ideally the faculty are active participants. Creating a vision includes developing departmental goals and then building sufficient unity within the department to move toward them. As the bridge between faculty and upper-level administrators, chairs need to root their vision for the department in a broader understanding of the entire discipline and institution. They must ensure that the department's goals are compatible with the institution's, and they must be able to communicate that understanding to their faculty. But chairs do not automatically have this window on the institution; they need opportunities to broaden their horizons. Likewise, an understanding of higher education at the state and national levels is also extremely helpful.

Chairs can significantly influence the direction of their departments through the faculty hired, courses offered, outside monies raised, and the encouragement of faculty excellence. Or they can spend their terms as caretakers or paper shufflers and leave the department much as they found it. Turning a vision into reality is a difficult task for department chairs, since much of their work is accomplished through persuasion, negotiation, and cheerleading.

Understanding the Role of Department Chair

Their shift in role and identity is a frequent source of difficulty for chairs. The move from faculty member to department chair requires several important transitions (Bennett 1989). The first transition is from academic to manager: the life of teaching and scholarship is replaced by one of meetings, phone calls, and paperwork, which crowd out professorial pursuits. Another transition is from specialist to generalist: the skills required to specialize in 18th century architecture are different from those needed to build a broad curriculum and make decisions about a wide variety of issues. A third transition is from solo flyer to team player, working with students, faculty, administrators, alumni, and outside groups, often in committees or through delegation.

If department chairs are to master these important transitions, they will need to understand the stresses and strains of the new job, and decide how they want to spend their time and define their role. It is easy (and sometimes tempting) to get caught in the maelstrom of administrative work. Time management is especially difficult for new chairs, who must decide what they are willing to give up to perform their new role—research? teaching excellence? personal time?

Issues of self-awareness vary with length of service as chair. New chairs will need to assess their strengths and weaknesses and determine how to get help when it is needed. More experienced chairs need to recognize when they have done all they can, when it is time to step down, and what new avenues exist for professional renewal.

Managing and Decision Making

Management and decision making constitute a significant proportion of the chair's job. Keeping the department running smoothly is essential, and provides a necessary base for growth and innovation. Department chairs are generally not prepared to prepare a budget, handle paper, run meetings, or supervise personnel. Like most academic administrators, department chairs generally learn their jobs as they go, asking questions of colleagues and especially department secretaries, trying out ideas, and making mistakes. While some department chairs receive some training in the first few years of their tenure, few receive any preparation prior to assuming the job.

Working With People

People skills are at the heart of the department chair's job. Chairs hire faculty and staff and have a full spectrum of personnel responsibilities: evaluating, mentoring, dealing with unsatisfactory performance, and resolving conflict. They serve as the liaison between faculty and administrators, and often between faculty and the rest of the institution. They represent the department to the institution and to the external public. All these responsibilities are exercised in the delicate context of being a leader among peers, with relatively little real power. The skills of communication, persuasion, and negotiation, of using influence, motivating people, and building trust, are central to the chair's effectiveness.

STRATEGIES FOR DEVELOPMENT

How Deans Can Foster the Development of Department Chairs

Deans play an important role in fostering a climate that encourages the development of chairs, by serving as teachers and mentors to chairs, by encouraging and legitimizing efforts to enhance their leadership, and by providing financial support for their professional development. Without the dean's moral and financial support, each chair must learn the job independently—a laborious and certainly less effective process. New department chairs need help getting oriented to their roles, understanding the institution's expectations, learning the institution's policies and procedures, sharpening their interpersonal skills for the responsibilities of the job, and managing their time. Deans should consider the following strategies:

- *Provide an orientation program for all new chairs.* Such a program can take many forms: an intensive one- or two-day workshop or a semester-long series of two-hour sessions. It could be taught by a combination of experienced chairs, deans, and other institutional administrators and cover such topics as roles and responsibilities of the chair, relevant institutional policies, the budget process, and procedures for procurement and contracts. The frequency with which the program is offered will depend on the size of the institution or college within it and the number of new chairs in any given year.

- *Support new chairs' participation in off-campus programs.* Programs offered by the American Council on Education (ACE) and Kansas State University (see *Programs and Practices*, below) can help new chairs gain a better understanding of their job through interaction with colleagues from other institutions. Such workshops provide useful information about faculty development, evaluation, performance counseling, and time management.

- *Develop a system for new chairs to gain access to senior faculty advisors.* People are often reluctant to seek advice, and constructing such a mechanism may make it easier for them. The process can be informal or structured. For example, new chairs might select a "mentor" from a list of experienced chairs who have been provided with a list of guidelines. Several such teams then might meet regularly for group discussion.

- *Pair new chairs.* Often the most bewildering aspect of a new job is the sense of aloneness, of struggling through problems unknown to anyone else. Pairing new chairs can allow them to share common experiences. While more experienced chairs may be better able to offer advice, a companion who is learning the same lessons at the same time can offer great encouragement and support.

- *Ensure that new chairs have access to information they need and know where to get help.* The dean plays an important role as facilitator, helping new chairs help themselves. This may include putting them in touch with consultants or identifying sources of information on such varied topics as institutional policies, faculty workload, search procedures, and software packages.

- *Be explicit about expectations.* Deans need to communicate their expectations, both those regarding the routine of running a department as well as those specific to issues within the department. Discussions of expectations and goals are important for all chairs, but it is essential that the new chair start out armed with this information. Similarly, regular feedback about progress toward these goals is essential.

Leadership development is an ongoing process. Deans can make a variety of development strategies available throughout the chair's tenure.

- *Develop a "Council of Department Chairs" or other mechanism for chairs to meet regularly.* Such a group can be a working group, a problem-solving group, and a source of new ideas and advice. Meetings may be devoted to discussions of topics important to the department chair's job, such as negotiation, dealing with unsatisfactory employees, combatting substance abuse, or recruiting minority faculty. In-house resources or outside speakers can be used. These meetings are also an opportunity for deans to get feedback from the chairs on important issues.

- *Conduct an annual workshop for department chairs.* While time and expenses are involved here, especially if the workshop is held at an off-campus site, annual workshops can provide an important opportunity for chairs to focus on their jobs and their effectiveness. The program may be planned and run by an outside consultant or facilitator, or it can be done entirely in-house. It is often helpful to have outsiders present as experts and facilitators, but it is also important not to overlook the resources present on campus. The chairs should play an active role in determining the design of the program. Two days usually provide enough time to delve into issues and to give chairs an opportunity to chat informally. Longer programs permit greater depth and provide more opportunities for informal interaction. However, if there is significant resistance to the time involved, deans should consider a biannual event, or two or three half-day sessions.

- *Meet regularly with chairs to review departmental and personal goals.* Every chair has different needs, and individual meetings are essential to understanding them. These meetings also will enable the dean to make activities and meetings for all chairs responsive to their articulated needs.

- *Help chairs stay active in their field.* Too often, at the end of their terms, department chairs feel that they have lost touch with their discipline while in office. Release time that is commensurate with the responsibility of the chair helps, as does the availability of summer grants, clerical help, and the assignment of a co-chair or deputy chair in larger departments.

- *Evaluate institutional policies and procedures on the selection and term of department chairs.* Is the method of selection working in favor of departmental leadership or against it? Is the term of office long enough to accomplish something? Short enough to ensure the vitality of the department and the chair? The answers to these questions will differ from one context to another.

- *Use self-assessments, professional development plans, and performance appraisals to assist chairs in their development.* Setting one's own goals and monitoring one's own performance are essential to ongoing development. An annual self-appraisal can be the point of departure for a discussion of the chair's plans, aspirations, and developmental needs. It is useful to separate planning for professional development from performance appraisal, in spite of the relationship between the two.

- *Set aside funds to allow chairs to attend off-campus programs that will meet their professional development needs.* Such activities may include a wide range of opportunities—courses to hone management skills, travel or research that helps chairs stay active in their fields, or conferences or travel to other campuses to learn about enhancing the curriculum through scholarship on women and minorities.

Taking Responsibility for One's Own Development

There is much that new chairs can do for themselves to ease their transition into their new roles.

- *Invest time in learning the culture of the institution and the department.* The temptation to plunge in is great, given the workload facing chairs. Yet a period of transition, beginning before assuming the job, can allow the new chair to gather valuable information that will inform all subsequent decisions. Most people will intuitively know to conduct such a study, but a conscious and deliberate process will produce richer and more useful results. Some questions that can guide such an inquiry are:

    - What are the distinctive features of this institution? How is it the same or different from other institutions of its type?

    - What are the explicit values of this institution? To what extent are they congruent with actual policies, procedures, and ways of doing business?

    - What are the important symbols and traditions of the institution? Of the college or school in which the department is located? Of the department?

    - How does the college or school in which the department is located relate to the larger institution? Has it always been this way?

- What are the dean's goals for the department? For this school? What is the dean's style of decision making, of communication?

- What styles of decision making and communication predominate in the institution? In the college or school? In the department?

- What is the image of my department in this institution? Why is this so? How do faculty members outside the department view it?

Established chairs will soon discover that their most precious resource is time. Implementing the following actions will undeniably add to the chair's already full schedule, but the payoffs in the short and long term can be substantial.

- *Develop a network of chairs in one's discipline.* A network of colleagues is a rich source of information, moral support, and professional development.

- *Manage time with an eye on the future.* It is all too easy after a three- or five-year term as chair to feel disconnected from one's research or other faculty interests. Chairs must set aside time to continue those interests or to cultivate new interests to pursue upon returning to the faculty.

- *Become familiar with the literature on department chairs.* There are many helpful insights to be gained from books, articles, and newsletters. A little reading can go a long way.

- *Become familiar with higher education issues.* Knowing the larger context in which chairs operate is important. At a minimum, regular perusal of the *Chronicle of Higher Education* will provide an overview of current issues and trends. Membership in an association such as the American Association for Higher Education (AAHE) provides a way to learn about broader educational issues.

- *Use evaluation as an opportunity to set goals.* Goal setting should be an important part of every evaluation system. Chairs can use their evaluations by the dean to set personal and professional goals for the future. These goals should be explicitly discussed with the dean as a basis for future evaluation as well as for individual growth.

CONCLUSION

While department chairs play complex and delicate roles as leaders among peers, their potential for exercising leadership is enormous. They have a direct impact upon institutional quality through the decisions they make concerning faculty, the teaching and learning process, the curriculum, and students. In spite of the importance of the chair's job and the difficulties surrounding the transition from faculty to chair, preparation for the position and development while in it are often overlooked. Deans can make a significant difference in helping chairs develop their leadership capacities and in fostering continuous professional growth. Similarly, chairs who see themselves in leadership roles can take a number of steps to broaden their vision of the department and the institution and to develop the capacities required to serve as a leader of the departmental faculty.

NOTE

1. The list of responsibilities of chairpersons is adapted from Allan Tucker, *Chairing the Academic Department: Leadership Among Peers*, 2nd ed. (New York: American Council on Education/Macmillan, 1984), 2–3.

REFERENCES

Bennett, John B. "Department Chairs: Leadership in the Trenches." In *Leaders for a New Era: Strategies for Higher Education*, edited by Madeleine F. Green. New York: American Council on Education/Macmillan, 1984.

———. "About Department Chairs." *AAHE Bulletin* 42, no. 2 (October 1989): 9–11.

Tucker, Allan. *Chairing the Academic Department: Leadership Among Peers*, 2nd ed. New York: American Council on Education/Macmillan, 1984.

RESOURCES

Bennett, John B. *Managing the Academic Department: Cases and Notes*. New York: American Council on Education/Macmillan, 1983.

A case study approach to the management of departments. Covers analysis of the chair's role, conflict resolution, faculty performance issues, departmental policy making, and new issues in higher education. The entrepreneurial, political, and academic responsibilities of the chair are also considered.

Bennett, John B., and David J. Figuli, eds. *Enhancing Departmental Leadership: The Roles of the Chairperson*. New York: American Council on Education/Macmillan, 1990.

This book is a compilation of several essays from ''The Department Advisor'' that focus on issues facing department chairs. The essays are divided into five sections: roles and responsibilities of chairs, faculty and staff hiring and evaluation, faculty development, legal issues, and determining departmental priorities.

Booth, David B. ''Department and Chairperson Development.'' In *Developing and Evaluating Administrative Leadership,* edited by Charles F. Fisher. New Directions in Higher Education 22. San Francisco: Jossey-Bass, 1978.

In this brief article, Booth stresses the need for regular interaction with faculty members in order to facilitate department development. Booth focuses on the case history of a department chair who succeeded in transforming his department as a result of his commitment to the faculty.

———. *The Department Chair: Professional Development and Role Conflict.* AAHE-ERIC/Higher Education Research Report No. 10. Washington, DC: American Association for Higher Education, 1982.

The role of the department chair as the interface between the faculty and administration is the primary focus of this text. Attention is also given to the selection, orientation, socialization, and evaluation of the chair. The monograph discusses the constraints experienced by chairs, the academic leadership model, and institutional and disciplinary influences on the department.

Creswell, John W. et al. *The Academic Chairperson's Handbook.* Lincoln: University of Nebraska Press, 1990.

This handbook draws on interviews with 200 academic chairpersons from 70 campuses who discuss their solutions to typical problems that occur in bridging relations among faculty, administrators, and students. The text is divided into two sections; the first presents 15 strategies for developing a department, exercising leadership, and reaching out to faculty. The second part applies these strategies to the day-to-day business of the department chair.

DECAD: Departmental Evaluation of Chairperson Activities for Development. Information and materials available from Kansas State University, Center for Faculty Evaluation and Development, 1615 Anderson Avenue, Manhattan, KS 66502, (800) 255–2757.

DECAD is a comprehensive system to assess the effectiveness of the department chairperson using ratings by faculty members as well as the chairperson's self-ratings. Once the DECAD survey instrument is completed by the department head and faculty members in the department, a computerized summary and interpretation of results is generated with comparisons based on the DECAD national database of over 300 departments.

The Department Chair: A Newsletter for Academic Administrators. Bolton, MA: Anker Publishing Company, v. 1– , 1990– .

A quarterly newsletter designed to aid department chairs with the tasks and challenges of leadership. Issues feature articles on topics ranging from salary policies to faculty workload, copyright tips to budgeting. The newsletter regularly features data useful for chairs presented in tables and graphs. Each issue also includes a listing of new books with particular application to department chairs.

The Department Advisor. Denver: Higher Education Executive Publications, Inc., in affiliation with the American Council on Education, Center for Leadership Development, v. 1– , 1985–.

A national quarterly newsletter whose aim is to provide department chairpersons with concrete assistance on the variety of tasks for which they have responsibility. Each issue features several essays written by chairpersons, presidents, deans, and legal experts on topics of interest and importance to deans.

Tucker, Allan. *Chairing the Academic Department: Leadership among Peers,* 2nd ed. New York: American Council on Education/Macmillan, 1984.

This book is a practical ''how-to'' guide covering roles and responsibilities of the department chairperson. Topics covered include: leadership style, delegation and department committees, decision making and change, encouraging faculty development, faculty evaluation, performance counseling, grievances and unions, conflict, setting goals, preparing department budgets, assigning and reporting faculty activities, and managing department resources.

PROGRAMS AND PRACTICES

National Associations

Many disciplinary associations have informal or even formal subgroupings for chairs and provide support through newsletters or other communications. (See Chapter 10, *Faculty*, for a representative listing of disciplinary associations.) The following list provides a sampling of the associations that specifically serve department chairs. Many associations, such as the AAHE and the American Association of Community and Junior Colleges (AACJC) sponsor caucuses for women, minorities, and other groups that cut across functional lines. Department chairs also may be interested in the newsletters and support materials supplied by many of the institutional organizations listed in Chapter 5, *Presidents*. The annual meetings of some of these associations, such as the Council of Independent Colleges (CIC) and the Association of American Colleges (AAC), are regularly attended by deans, department chairs, and faculty. Department chairs may also find supporting materials from the collegiate associations listed in Chapter 7, *Academic Deans and Mid-Level Academic Administrators*.

Complete information on each listing is provided in the *Appendix*. The letter and number in parentheses correspond to the section and entry number in the *Appendix*.

Administrators and Teachers of English as a Second Language (ATESL) (A4)

American Association for Higher Education (AAHE) (A11)

American Association of Community and Junior Colleges (AACJC) (A19)

American Association of University Administrators (AAUA) (A30)

American Association of University Women (AAUW) (A32)

American Association of Women in Community and Junior Colleges (AAWCJC) (A33)

American Council on Education/National Identification Program for the Advancement of Women in Higher Education (ACE/NIP) (A41)

Association of Chairmen of Departments of Mechanics (ACDM) (A94)

Association of Departments of English (ADE) (A102)

Association of Departments of Foreign Languages (ADFL) (A103)

Council of Writing Program Administrators (CWPA) (A133)

Higher Education Resource Service (HERS) (A141)

National Association for Women in Education (NAWE) (A157)
Formerly National Association for Women Deans, Administrators, and Counselors (NAWDAC)

National Association of Academic Affairs Administrators (AcAfAd) (A158)

National Programs

Programs listed in Chapter 10, *Faculty*, also may be applicable for exploration of issues of teaching and scholarship. Programs listed in Chapter 7, *Academic Deans and Mid-Level Academic Administrators*, may be useful for exploration of general management skills and higher education issues. The following list provides a sampling of the range and variety of programs available to these leaders. Note that many programs offered by associations are available only to administrators and faculty of member institutions.

American Association for Higher Education (AAHE) (P2)

    Annual Meeting *(P2a)*
    Conference on Assessment in Higher Education *(P2b)*

American Association of Colleges of Nursing (AACN) (P4)

    Executive Development Series *(P4a)*

American Association of Community and Junior Colleges (AACJC) (P5)

Fellows Program *(P5a)*
Professional Development Workshop *(P5c)*

American Council on Education (ACE) (P7)

Department Leadership Program *(P7a)*
The Fellows Program *(P7b)*

American Management Association (AMA) (P8)

Association of Collegiate Schools of Architecture (ACSA) (P13)

Administrators Conference *(P13a)*

The Bush Foundation (P18)

Leadership Program for Midcareer Development *(P18a)*

Carnegie Mellon University/School of Urban and Public Affairs (P19)

College Management Program *(P19b)*

Center for Creative Leadership (P20)

Leadership Development Program *(P20d)*

Council for International Exchange of Scholars (CIES) (P28)

Fulbright Scholar Program *(P28a)*
Seminars for International Education Administrators in Germany and Japan *(P28b)*
U.S./United Kingdom College and University Academic Administrator Award *(P28c)*

Council on International Educational Exchange (CIEE) (P33)

Development Seminars *(P33a)*

Harvard University/Graduate School of Education (P37)

Institute for the Management of Lifelong Education (MLE) *(P37c)*
Management Development Program (MDP) *(P37d)*

Higher Education Resource Services (HERS) Mid-America/Bryn Mawr College (P39)

HERS Summer Institute for Women/Bryn Mawr Institute *(P39a)*

Higher Education Resource Services (HERS) New England/Wellesley College (P40)

HERS Institute for Women/Wellesley Institute *(P40a)*

Institute for Educational Leadership (IEL) (P41)

Educational Policy Fellowship Program *(P41a)*

Kansas State University/Center for Faculty Evaluation and Development (P44)

Annual Conference for Academic Chairpersons *(P44a)*

League for Innovation in the Community College (P45c)

Minority Leadership Program *(P45c)*

League for Innovation in the Community College, the University of Texas–Austin, and the W. K. Kellogg Foundation (P46)

Expanding Leadership Diversity in Community Colleges *(P46a)*

Lilly Endowment, Inc (P47)

Workshop on the Liberal Arts *(P47a)*

Modern Language Association (MLA) (P49)

Association of Departments of English (ADE) Summer Seminars *(P49a)*
Association of Departments of Foreign Languages (ADFL) Summer Seminars *(P49b)*

National Center for Higher Education Management Systems (NCHEMS) (P57)

National Institute for Leadership Development (P59)

Building a Better Team on Campus: Understanding Gender Issues *(P59a)*
Leadership for a New Century *(P59c)*
Leaders Project *(P59d)*

North Carolina State University (P60)

Community College Leadership Institute *(P60a)*

NTL Institute (P61)

Human Interaction Laboratory *(P61a)*
Management Work Conference *(P61b)*
Other Programs *(P61d)*

Professional and Organizational Development Network in Higher Education (POD) (P63)

Society for Values in Higher Education (P64)

The Fellows Meeting *(P64a)*

Texas A&M University/College of Education (P66)

Summer Seminar on Academic Administration *(P66a)*

University of Central Florida (P68)

Financial Management for Women in Higher Education *(P68a)*

W. K. Kellogg Foundation (P73)

National Fellowship Program *(P73a)*

Statewide, System-Specific, and On-Campus Programs

Typically, the programs and activities in the following list are restricted to faculty members of the sponsoring institution or organization. Programs listed in Chapter 10, *Faculty,* also may be applicable to address the teaching and scholarship aspects of the lives of department chairs.

Arizona State University (ASU) (S2)

Academic Chairs Group *(S2e)*
Internship *(S2b)*
Leadership Academy *(S2c)*
Management Development Program (MDP) *(S2a)*

Association of California Community College Administrators (ACCCA) (S3)

Mentor Program *(S3a)*

Board of Governors of State Colleges and Universities (Illinois) (S5)

Affirmative Action Administrative Fellows Program *(S5a)*

California State University System (CSU) (S7)

Administrative Fellows Program *(S7a)*

Chicago State University (S8)

Minority Administrative Fellow Program *(S8a)*

City University of New York (CUNY) (S9)

Women's Leadership Institute *(S9b)*

Colorado State University (S10)

The Administrative Women's Network *(S10d)*
Leadership Series *(S10c)*
Professional Development Institute *(S10b)*
Professional Development Programming *(S10a)*

Colorado Women in Higher Education Administration and the American Council on Education National Identification Program (ACE/NIP) (S11)

Academic Management Institute for Women *(S11a)*

Columbia University (S12)

Connections *(S12b)*
Middle Management Development Program *(S12d)*
Professional Development Programs *(S12a)*

Eastern Illinois University (S14)

Programs for Professional Enrichment (PPE) *(S14a)*

George Washington University (S15)

Training Division of Personnel Services *(S15a)*

Indiana University—Bloomington (S17)

Faculty Development Resources *(S17a)*

Kennesaw College (S18)

Leadership Kennesaw College *(S18a)*

Lansing Community College (S19)

Community Leadership Development Academy *(S19a)*

Maricopa Community College District (S20)

Professional Group Program *(S20c)*
Visions Career Development Program *(S20a)*

Rochester Institute of Technology (RIT) (S22)

Executive Leadership in an Academic Setting *(S22a)*

University of Kansas (S31)

Office of Personnel Services *(S31a)*
Workshops for University Managers *(S31c)*

University of Nebraska–Lincoln/Institute of Agriculture and Natural Resources (S33)

Administrative Development Map *(S33e)*
NUPROF *(S33d)*
Office of Professional and Organizational Development (OPOD) *(S33a)*
Pre-Tenure Support Group *(S33b)*

University of Texas–El Paso (S37)

New Faculty and Staff Orientation Program *(S37a)*

University of Wisconsin–Eau Claire (S38)

School for Graduate Studies and Office of University Research *(S38a)*

University of Wisconsin System (S39)

Administrative Associate Program *(S39a)*

10

FACULTY

For faculty more than any other academics, leadership development cannot be separated from professional development. Faculty who feel challenged and encouraged in their academic careers will contribute their vitality to the institution as a whole. Those who do not may still emerge as leaders—but often as gadflies or leaders of the opposition. Hence, it is profoundly important for administrators to establish an institutional culture conducive to meaningful faculty growth and participation.

The *Handbook's* theme of shared responsibility for leadership development is central to this chapter. Effective faculty development efforts require support from top-level administrators as well as leadership by the affected individuals.

FACULTY AS LEADERS

The cultivation of faculty leadership[1] is less straightforward than the development of administrative leadership. Administrative leadership derives from the authority of the position; faculty leadership emerges. Also, generalizations can be made about the skills and capacities needed to perform various administrative jobs, and suggestions can be proffered to develop the required leadership capacities. But faculty leadership roles are complex and ambiguous, linked as much to the character of the individual and to the campus context as to any inherent job requirements.

Faculty leaders are often self-appointed; if they are elected by their peers, that election may represent the culmination of a process of self-identification. While there are inevitable forces that impede the emergence of leadership, the opportunities for faculty to lead are numerous. On campus, they may serve on committees or task forces, on the faculty senate or the faculty union negotiating team, as directors of special projects, and as opinion leaders. As role models, they function as teachers, researchers, citizens, mentors to other faculty, innovators of new courses and programs, and department chairs. In professional or disciplinary associations, they may serve on committees and task forces or be members of the executive board. They may exercise leadership in the community on agency boards, as activists in civic affairs, or as experts or resources in their fields.

Obstacles to Faculty Leadership

Every college and university harbors potential leaders. But they do not always emerge: structural or cultural obstacles may stifle leadership altogether or ensure that it will be exercised only off campus.

Faculty leadership in the governance process is essential to creating a sense of shared destiny. Yet professors often are unwilling to take on these responsibilities and administrators may be equally unwilling to share them. Some administrators see their roles as *the* decision makers; some faculty prefer to be left alone to teach and do research. A faculty-administration standoff may be tolerable when the institution is in equilibrium, but it may become dysfunctional when the institution is unbalanced by external pressures, cutbacks, or some transgression of the established division of labor. A dean who suddenly overrules departmental recommendations on tenure may meet faculty resistance and hostility not only on that issue but on others as well.

While faculty leadership may emerge from a negative climate, it flourishes more often in a campus culture that recognizes, rewards, and supports it. However, a number of conditions can prevent faculty leadership from emerging on campus.

- *When the limits of faculty decision making are narrow.* The traditional sphere of faculty decision making—promotion, tenure, curriculum, and student progress—is vital but limited. Activities like strategic planning, resource allocation, and fund raising are also opportunities for faculty influence. The challenge is to achieve expanded faculty participation without impeding or overly complicating the decision-making process.

- *When faculty leadership is not valued.* In some institutions, faculty view active participation in the governance system as tasks for those who are less successful at teaching and research. This value system creates a climate in which faculty leadership is not an honorable task.

- *When faculty leadership is not rewarded.* Service is an almost universally stated criterion for promotion and tenure. However, in some institutions it runs a distant third to teaching and research. In such an environment, it is self-destructive to do significant committee work. Moreover, ineffective faculty committees whose reports languish on the shelf contribute to the perception that leadership is a futile endeavor. Unless there is a real possibility of making a difference through leadership, faculty will grow discouraged and cynical.

- *When there is administrative resistance to faculty leadership.* There may be truth to the belief that administrators do not want faculty participation. Administrators get frustrated by the perceived "tunnel vision" of faculty and by the time it takes to collaborate in decision making. As a result, they may resist faculty leadership by avoiding faculty, trivializing their involvement, or simply making decisions without faculty input.

- *When there exists a divisive institutional culture.* The "we-they" mentality is a fact of life at some institutions. It may stem from struggles over resources, a faculty union, decisions and policies that have angered the faculty over time, or any number of historical incidents that shape the institutional environment. A climate of distrust may result in faculty withdrawing from governance, or in combative behaviors where the rhetoric and the struggle preclude the possibility of meaningful collaboration.

Creating a Climate for Growth

Administrators play an important role in fostering faculty leadership. Institutional culture determines how faculty leadership emerges and whether it is sustained. A negative environment spawns faculty leadership that aims to protect the faculty from its administrative adversaries. Similarly, administrators who equate power with control (rather than with shared responsibility) will thwart faculty leadership. But those who see the workplace as a learning environment can draw on the talents and expertise of faculty and see the development of leadership in others as a way to improve the institution. By creating a positive climate, administrators can encourage faculty leadership toward shared goals. This can be accomplished in many ways:

- *Communicate openly and often.* Real information delivered regularly will not guarantee that faculty will recognize and understand the institution's situation, but it certainly will improve the odds. Frequent and open communication is the cornerstone of trust.

- *Encourage faculty initiative.* Some faculty will identify solutions as well as problems. Encourage them to investigate these solutions and consider their suggestions carefully.

- *Make faculty involvement meaningful.* It is rarely productive to expend faculty resources on administrative tasks or meetings without a clear purpose. The physical presence of a faculty member does not guarantee meaningful involvement, and faculty will become resentful or apathetic if their time is routinely wasted.

- *Provide development opportunities beyond the department.* Narrow vision is often a result of lack of exposure. Administrative internships and special assignments (chairing a planning effort or developing an assessment plan) are excellent ways to give faculty a window on the rest of the institution.

- *Reward faculty leadership.* Faculty leadership is more likely to flourish if it is rewarded through recognition and is a real criterion for promotion and tenure.

- *Support participation in leadership development programs.* National programs, such as the American Council on Education (ACE) Fellows Program, the ACE National Identification Program, and the Higher Education Resource Service (HERS)-Bryn Mawr, as well as on-campus workshops, can help faculty expand their understanding of higher education, hone their leadership skills, and clarify career goals.

Administrators must make a deliberate effort to identify potential faculty leaders, to help them develop their leadership skills, and to pay special attention to women and minority faculty. Administrators frequently have opportunities to identify faculty leaders through their participation in the governance process or in other campus activities. The evaluation process is another way to identify those with leadership ability. Using ''growth contracts'' or similar planning tools, the development of faculty leadership can be fostered through significant governance assignments, internships on campus, and participation in external programs.

Taking Responsibility for One's Own Leadership Development

While it is incumbent on administrators to create an environment in which leadership opportunities can flourish, the long tradition of faculty tending to their personal and professional development should not be ignored. Leadership means acting on one's commitment, seeing opportunities to make a difference, and seizing the opportunity to contribute. Faculty leadership also requires breadth: becoming informed about institutional issues and understanding the state and national issues that affect the campus. Faculty members who read widely and attend meetings that provide a broad base of knowledge obtain the vision that is important for any leader.

Also, faculty leadership is an opportunity for personal and professional growth. Leading a curriculum revision or an assessment effort presents an opportunity to learn about new issues and to develop a network beyond one's institution. Faculty can take a leadership role to gain expertise in a new area and to become involved in new professional organizations, consulting, and research.

EXPANDING FACULTY OPTIONS

The choice of a career as a faculty member has traditionally implied a lifetime commitment to the profession, and sometimes to a single institution. It is not surprising, then, that it can be difficult for professors to create a sense of movement within these static parameters. Yet, faculty members do have options within their jobs—in leadership roles, on campus or externally, and through their scholarship, teaching, consulting, and professional associations. Through their initiative, and through the efforts of administrative leaders, professors can remain vital and productive.

Many forces and attitudes exist that constrict rather than expand possibilities for faculty. Dealing directly with these obstacles, perceived and real, is the essential first step in overcoming them. On the one hand, lack of administrative commitment will prevent meaningful efforts to develop faculty leadership. By the same token, faculty attitudes may create obstacles to leadership development. Chief among these is the notion that the professorate is a lifetime commitment—a calling, rather than a profession. Lovett (1980, p. 64) compares the rules of academe to those of the clergy. The first tenet, she says, is ''that true intellectual discourse and activity ('the life of the mind') are only possible in academe.'' The second ''is that the academic monastic order provides the only secure shelter from a materialistic, corrupt, Philistine culture.''

The insularity engendered by this attitude diminishes options. It discourages movement in and out of the professorate, creating dependency on the institution and a reluctance by administrators to develop policies that will loosen the bonds (Furniss 1984). From this arises the myth that faculty respond only to an internal reward system, and that the administration can safely ignore faculty's development needs.

Yet another obstacle to launching effective faculty development and renewal activities is the failure of faculty to become actively involved in leading the effort. A faculty development program that is identified as the administration's rather than the faculty's is doomed. Support, of course, is necessary, and perhaps even quiet behind-the-scenes leadership. In the final analysis, a program for faculty must be *by* and *of* and *for* the faculty.

The Nature of Faculty Careers

While the pattern of a faculty career is somewhat predictable—attaining a Ph.D., entering the profession, and achieving the various milestones of tenure and promotion—there are important variations. Superstar professors have always had greater mobility than their less dynamic counterparts. Faculty in fields such as business and the sciences may move among academe, government, and industry, or have active consulting practices. Women's careers may take on a different rhythm, with some women stopping out early and others reentering higher education later in their careers.

Reaching a career plateau or simply feeling stuck are constant dangers for faculty. Sometimes, the plateau is structural. At institutions that do not have faculty ranks, there are no career ladders to climb. Or a faculty member may get stuck at the associate professor level because the reward system changed midstream and research is now essential. Other times, the plateau is psychological. Even reaching the capstone rank of full professor may have its negative side. There are no more goals toward which to aim, with the prospect looming ahead of 25 or 30 years of doing the same thing.

The challenges for faculty to remain vital are even greater than those facing administrators who have more options to make lateral moves, to expand their jobs, or to move on. Faculty vitality requires creating opportunities within the sphere of one's existing position: finding new interests within one's field or venturing into another one, becoming a faculty leader, or taking on responsibility within one's professional association.

Adapting Development to Evolving Faculty Careers

To be effective, a leadership development activity must respond to an individual's needs at various stages in his or her life and career. Beginning faculty face a very different set of problems from those nearing retirement. The following scheme of the stages of a faculty career and the ensuing development needs are adapted from Roger Baldwin's paradigm (1990).

- *Entry and early career.* A faculty member's first job is a time of growth and adjustment. Finishing the dissertation, preparing courses, learning how to teach, juggling time, embarking on research, and learning the institutional culture are all important tasks for new professors. Personal responsibilities must be juggled with the considerable professional load. Following the initial adjustment, faculty members enter a probationary period and are integrated into the academic profession by establishing themselves with students and colleagues, conducting and publishing research, and developing professional networks beyond the institution. Faculty in this career stage have the following development needs:

  - Orientation to the institution—New faculty members need to learn the ropes. What are the policies and procedures that govern the

institution? How do you get things done? On a more subtle level,
what are the informal processes that are important to the life of the
institution? Who are the informal leaders and opinion-makers?
What is the culture and history of the college or university?

- Assistance in completing the dissertation—Faculty members can be
  assisted in completing their dissertations by minimizing their
  involvement in assignments that will distract them. Adjusting
  teaching schedules to allow sufficient blocks of time for writing is a
  useful strategy.

- Clear understanding of the expectations of the department and
  institution for promotion and tenure—The criteria of teaching,
  research, and service need clarification. What kind of research is valued for promotion and tenure? In what kind of journals? What is the
  best balance of the three? How has it changed over time, if at all?

- Regular feedback on teaching, and progress toward tenure based on
  established criteria.

- Support for teaching improvement—Chairs and deans must continually articulate, reinforce, and reward teaching improvement.

- Support for the establishment of a research agenda.

- *Mid-Career.* This phase may include consolidation or new directions.
  For some faculty members, this is the period of finding one's stride,
  going for or achieving full professor status, and earning a reputation
  in one's field or on one's campus. Others may begin to feel bored and
  look for new challenges, diversifying their interests, contemplating a
  move into administration, and taking on faculty leadership roles. Mid-
  career faculty pose special developmental challenges. On the one
  hand, they have experience and expertise that can be enormously beneficial to the institution. On the other, they may see the rest of their
  faculty careers stretching out ahead of them with little promise for
  new challenges. Some are at risk of becoming "deadwood." At this
  point in their lives, faculty can benefit greatly from a system or program that enables them to question their career goals in a nonthreatening environment. They also can use assistance in exploring options.
  For some, new research interests will be of paramount interest, while
  others may direct energy to faculty leadership roles in curriculum
  reform or planning efforts. These options also may include a different
  role in the institution, such as heading a program, taking a temporary
  administrative assignment, or moving outside higher education.

- *Late Career.* During the years preceding retirement, a different set of
  developmental issues are presented. Some professors remain active
  and energetic in their fields; others may feel that the new generation

of faculty has left them behind. With the uncapping of retirement, continued vitality will be the central issue for some professors. Some faculty will need the same support as those in mid-career. Others will need assistance as they make the transition into retirement and consider early retirement options, financial planning, pursuing new interests, and adjusting to a new life.

Creating an Environment that Supports Faculty Vitality

A crucial leadership role of institutional administrators is to create a climate that fosters learning. Faculty members, like their students, ought to be lifelong learners. A positive culture will enable faculty to take the initiative to foster their own development.

The following strategies can help create that environment:[2]

- Ensure that faculty development programs are owned and led by faculty.
- Make participation voluntary.
- Link faculty, administrators, and institutional development in the planning process.
- Ensure that the person responsible for faculty development activities has authority as well as responsibility.
- Make faculty development an explicit responsibility of chairs and deans; evaluate them on their efforts and successes in this area.
- Provide hard money to keep a core program going; use grants and other soft money to innovate.
- Create flexible personnel policies that encourage faculty to experiment. Extending leave time and development funds can help faculty discover and pursue new options. Faculty are understandably reluctant to leave a position entirely, but through "toe-dipping," as Furniss (1981, p. 106) calls it, professors can find alternate career interests.
- Develop consortia arrangements to pool resources and multiply capacity. Institutions can cooperate to exchange faculty and administrators or provide short-term placements, to co-sponsor workshops, and to undertake jointly what they could not afford to do alone.
- Provide workshops on personal and leadership development.
- Reward participation in faculty development activities; link participation to promotion, tenure, and compensation.
- Create opportunities for on-campus administrative internships and other special assignments that will expose faculty members to institutional operations.

A Note on Minority Faculty

These developmental needs are applicable to all faculty. However, minority faculty in majority institutions have special burdens placed upon them. They are called to serve on many committees; minority students and the community also place special expectations on them. Considering these extra burdens, department chairs and deans must make additional efforts to ensure the success of minority faculty. These efforts should include the strategies outlined later in this chapter, as well as personal attention to anticipating problems and providing assistance in resolving them. Institutions can encourage peer support groups. Also, they should take steps to ensure that the tenure process does not discriminate against minority faculty members. Faculty members who conduct research on minority issues and who publish in minority-focused journals may be disadvantaged in the tenure review process by their colleagues' lack of familiarity with these research areas and publications, or by their devaluation of different scholarly endeavors.

STRATEGIES FOR PROMOTING FACULTY VITALITY AND DEVELOPMENT

Department chairs and individual faculty members can pursue a number of specific strategies that will help faculty be successful as they move through their careers and as they seek to expand their leadership options.

Departmental Support

The department chair plays a key role in fostering faculty development and helping faculty explore options. In dealing with tenured faculty, the department chair serves as a discreet guide, since post-tenure evaluation is rare. Persuasion, encouragement, and modeling the desired behaviors are the principal tools for chairs in this effort. Here are some suggested steps:

- *Link faculty development to curricular planning and change.* Departmental efforts to shape the curriculum offer a number of opportunities for faculty development: creating a new course outside one's general teaching area, team teaching, or taking on a piece of the revised core curriculum.

- *Work with each faculty member to develop a yearly plan for development.* Articulating dreams and goals is the first step toward achieving them. Chairs can work with faculty to determine realistic objectives and examine appropriate development options.

- *Consider differential staff assignments.* Everyone has different strengths and needs. Using people's strengths as teachers or researchers helps make intelligent use of human resources. Some faculty members will be invigorated by preparing new courses, while others will benefit from free time for research or special projects.

- *Bring in speakers and organize workshops on new developments in the discipline and in higher education.* Provide a forum for faculty to talk about the substance of their work and engage colleagues in dialogue. Speakers can be invited from neighboring institutions to talk about a new course, research in progress, or a new project. By the same token, workshops, guest speakers, and brown-bag lunches can be used to enhance faculty members' understanding of new students and multicultural issues.

- *Help faculty prepare grant proposals.* Workshops, advice, and technical assistance make the process of developing grant proposals more manageable and improve the quality of the proposals.

- *Explore the possibility of joint development activities with departments of your discipline in other institutions.* Joint development of a small-scale exchange program or a series of symposia pools the resources of several institutions.

Taking Initiative for One's Own Development

Faculty, like all professionals, bear a great deal of the responsibility for their own well-being and future. Furniss (1981, p. 11) suggests that faculty members should think of themselves as professionals and of the institution as their primary client. However, the view of the faculty member as "freelance professional" may create an environment where faculty members teach their classes and disappear, feeling little obligation to the institutional community.

On the positive side, this model encourages personal and professional planning and self-reliance. Institutions can only provide opportunities; it is the responsibility of the resourceful faculty member to take advantage of those opportunities and to encourage their less motivated colleagues.

Faculty members should take full advantage of development opportunities. Faculty may learn useful information and techniques by participating in programs or taking advantage of other opportunities offered by the institution. National and regional organizations also provide development opportunities. In the best possible world, deans and department chairs would actively encourage faculty to participate; the reality is that faculty more often will learn about various opportunities and then convince their deans and department heads that they should participate.

Taking on new challenges will often require an increased workload. But a new assignment or a leadership role on campus or in a professional association will be a source of invigoration as well. Here are some other suggestions for taking charge of one's own leadership development:

- *Take an active role in creating opportunities.* Professors who match their talents to new initiatives both in the institution and in professional associations can create opportunities for themselves while serving their institutions. Personal and professional networks are helpful in alerting people to further opportunities.

- *Stay active with colleagues in the discipline.* This takes some work, but corresponding, visiting, and exchanging work in progress is enlivening.

- *Develop a contract for personal and leadership development.* Even if the institution does not subscribe to this mechanism for promoting personal development, faculty members may want to develop their own written plans.

- *Take action.* Faculty and administrators each complain about the indifference of the other. Creating a healthy institutional climate is the responsibility of faculty as well as administrators. If the faculty is determined to stonewall administrators' efforts to bridge the gulf, they generally will succeed. Faculty members will find it more rewarding to be a part of the solution.

INSTITUTIONAL EFFORTS: A CASE STUDY

Like many colleges, St. Norbert's in De Pere, Wisconsin, supported traditional faculty development practices, including sabbaticals and travel funding. Ten years of general discussion regarding faculty development culminated in the creation of a new position, Director of Faculty Development (a two-thirds release time faculty position), to supervise existing initiatives and weld them into a comprehensive program.

The new director, Kenneth J. Zahorski, surveyed faculty for their concerns and needs. From their suggestions, he and a newly elected Ad Hoc Faculty Development Planning Committee crafted a multi-part program that received unanimous support from the faculty assembly and administration. The program's goal was ''to provide pedagogical, professional, and personal renewal and growth to faculty in all stages of their careers" by creating "a wide range of opportunities, and then provid[ing] the help faculty need to take full advantage of these opportunities."

The program's foundation is a Resource Center that "provides faculty easy access to a variety of professional materials" while also serving as a teaching-learning laboratory. Besides nearly 1,000 texts and periodicals on pedagogical, curricular, and professional concerns (to which faculty actively contribute as they come across materials in their research and travels), the Center also houses videotapes and files of external sources of financial support information. New faculty are introduced to the Center, the faculty development programs, and the college through an orientation and mentor program. A late-summer acclimation session provides new faculty with a forum for exchanging ideas about teaching and advising, and acquaints them with facilities and services; this session is followed by three fall-semester roundtable discussions on topics such as building a syllabus. Through the mentor program, new instructors, both full- and part-time, work with senior faculty who provide support and advice.

All faculty, administrators, and staff may attend the informal lunchtime "Food for Thought" and other discussion series. Faculty make presentations on topics such as their research, sabbatical work, and higher education issues. These discussions promote an "exchange of ideas about teaching and scholarship." A leitmotif of the presentations has been collegial cooperation in scholarship and teaching.

Beyond these more traditional programs, St. Norbert's supports several less common endeavors. It is a member of the Faculty Exchange Center and supports the participation of St. Norbert faculty in exchanges. To facilitate greater cooperation and interaction among Wisconsin's liberal arts colleges, especially in the area of faculty development, St. Norbert's took the initiative in creating a statewide faculty development network to facilitate the sharing of expertise, ideas, and resources. The network operates through the structure of the Wisconsin Association of Independent Colleges and Universities (WAICU).

The faculty development office keeps faculty apprised of its topical sessions and workshops, grant programs, counseling services, annual faculty development conference, faculty resource inventory, and other events through its newsletter, *The Beacon*. It features stories on sabbatical experiences, essays on scholarly activities, teaching tips, lists of publications and presentations by faculty, and new materials in the resource center. Its goal is to provide a medium for exchanging ideas about teaching, scholarship, and professional development.

St. Norbert's points to the significantly increased number of publications from faculty, particularly in areas of classroom research and pedagogy, as the most obvious benefit from these efforts. There has been increased interest in interdisciplinary courses and team teaching growing from associations started at the discussion series. Less tangible, but of greater importance for the institution, is the increased sense of community and a new sense of connection among faculty, their research interests, and their teaching responsibilities. On the most basic level, the efforts have ''raised the veil of silence on teaching and made it a valid and valuable topic for faculty and community discussion'' (Zahorski [no date], 1990, 1991). Contact: Dr. Kenneth J. Zahorski, Director, Office of Faculty Development, St. Norbert College, 320 Boyle Hall, De Pere, WI 54115, (414) 337–3093.

CONCLUSION

Faculty exercise leadership in many ways, both on and off the campus. Faculty leadership is essential not only in areas such as curriculum and academic standards, but also in areas that go beyond the traditional province of faculty. Constructive faculty leadership thrives through partnerships in which administrators share information and power and faculty step forward to assume responsibility and take on leadership roles.

Faculty leadership goes hand-in-hand with faculty vitality. Professors who are actively engaged with their own work and with the life of the institution can lead their peers. A combination of motivated individuals and an institution that respects and fosters faculty leadership will produce a richness of talent.

NOTES

1. For discussions of faculty leadership, see Patricia R. Plante, ''In Support of Faculty Leadership: An Administrator's Perspective,'' and Rose-Marie Oster, ''Developing Faculty Leadership: A Faculty Perspective,'' in Madeleine Green, ed., *Leaders for a New Era: Strategies for Higher Education* (New York: American Council on Education/Macmillan, 1988).

2. A number of the recommended strategies in this section are drawn from a comprehensive review of the literature, as presented by Carole J. Bland and Constance C. Schmitz, ''An Overview of Research on Faculty and Institutional Vitality,'' in Jack H. Schuster, Daniel W. Wheeler, and Associates, *Enhancing Faculty Careers: Strategies for Development and Renewal* (San Francisco: Jossey-Bass, 1990).

3. Many of the strategies pertaining to mid- and later-career professors and those recommended for individual faculty are adapted from Brian Copp, *Full Professor Status: Milestone or Millstone* (River Falls: University of Wisconsin, Dean's Office, College of Arts and Sciences, 1989). Photocopy.

REFERENCES

Baldwin, Roger G. "Faculty Career Stages and Implications for Professional Development." In Jack H. Schuster, Daniel W. Wheeler, and Associates, *Enhancing Faculty Careers: Strategies for Development and Renewal*. San Francisco: Jossey-Bass, 1990.

Bland, Carole J., and Constance C. Schmitz. "An Overview of Research on Faculty and Institutional Vitality." In *Enhancing Faculty Careers: Strategies for Development and Renewal*, by Jack H. Schuster, Daniel W. Wheeler, and Associates. San Francisco: Jossey-Bass, 1990.

Furniss, W. Todd. *Reshaping Faculty Careers*. Washington, DC: American Council on Education, 1981.

———. *The Self-Reliant Academic*. Washington, DC: American Council on Education, 1984.

Lovett, Clara. "Breaking the Vows of the Academic Monastic Order." *Chronicle of Higher Education*, 4 February 1980, 64.

Zahorski, Kenneth J. Telephone interview with Sharon A. McDade. 27 November 1990.

———. Letter to Sharon A. McDade. 6 March 1991.

———. "Third Annual Report: 1987–88." [De Pere, WI]: St. Norbert College, Office of Faculty Development. [No date]. Photocopied.

RESOURCES

Baldwin, Roger, Louis Brakeman, Russell Edgerton, Janet Hagberg, and Thomas Maher. *Expanding Faculty Options: Career Development Projects at Colleges and Universities*. Washington, DC: American Association for Higher Education, 1981.

This report charts the range of faculty career development efforts, and raises questions that need to be considered by those interested in developing their own projects and programs.

Baldwin, Roger G., ed. *Incentives for Faculty Vitality*. New Directions in Higher Education 51. San Francisco: Jossey-Bass, 1985.

This book studies the issue of incentives to enhance faculty vitality from several useful perspectives. Chapters discuss the psychological and sociological foundations of effective incentives, and discuss incentives from the practical perspective of what works, what does not work, and why.

Bardwick, Judith M. *The Plateauing Trap: How to Avoid It in Your Career . . . and Your Life*. New York: AMACOM, 1986.

The author, a psychologist and management consultant, offers practical strategies for escaping the pitfalls of the "plateauing trap," described as the feeling that one's career is at a standstill, that work has lost its challenge, and that life has become a tedious routine.

Bergquist, William H., and Steven R. Phillips. *A Handbook for Faculty Development*, v. 1–3. Washington, DC: Council for Advancement of Small Colleges in association with the College Center of the Finger Lakes, 1975–81.

Volume 1 (1975), designed as a self-contained guide to faculty development, presents a brief overview of the topic followed by sections on instructional, organizational, and personal development. Volume 2 (1977) expands on concepts and practices discussed in the previous volume, such as course design, life planning, and values clarification, and introduces new topics, such as portfolio and program evaluation. Discussion in Volume 3 (1981) is couched in a deeper appreciation of the linkage between faculty development and the career development of individual faculty and the long-term planning and institutional research initiatives of colleges and universities.

Clark, Shirley M., and Darrell R. Lewis, eds. *Faculty Vitality and Institutional Productivity: Critical Perspectives for Higher Education*. New York: Teachers College Press, 1985.

This book considers theoretical issues, empirical questions, institutional policy options, and external and demographic influences that affect faculty vitality.

Furniss, W. Todd. *Reshaping Faculty Careers*. Washington, DC: American Council on Education, 1981.

This book examines academic life in the context of the institutions in which it occurs and of a society that has changed socially and economically. It seeks ways to restore lost harmony or to find new harmonies and suggests means for faculty members, institutions, and the society to pursue the most promising of these ways toward optimally satisfactory and productive changes.

Hall, Douglas T., and Associates. *Career Development in Organizations*. San Francisco: Jossey-Bass, 1986.

Focusing on the rapidly developing field of organizational career development, this volume details methods of updating career development techniques for individuals. It further discusses using these techniques to improve career management programs within corporations and other organizations.

Schuster, Jack H., Daniel W. Wheeler, and Associates. *Enhancing Faculty Careers: Strategies for Development and Renewal*. San Francisco: Jossey-Bass, 1990.

A comprehensive guide to the strategies, programs, and supports that institutions can implement to enhance faculty members' career and personal development. This book examines the key factors that bear on professional growth, including the role of professional schools in the preparation of prospective faculty, career consulting for faculty, wellness programs, employee assistance programs to help deal with substance abuse, and strategies for instituting early retirement programs. It shows how professional development relates to the larger context of higher education issues.

PROGRAMS AND PRACTICES

Complete information on each listing is provided in the *Appendix*. The letter and number in parentheses correspond to the section and entry number in the *Appendix*.

National Associations

Many disciplinary associations have informal or even formal subgroupings for faculty of related academic areas. Many associations, such as the American Association for Higher Education (AAHE) and the American Association of Community and Junior Colleges (AACJC), sponsor caucuses for women, minorities, and other groups that cut across disciplinary lines. Department chairs also may be interested in the newsletters and support materials supplied by many of the institutional organizations listed in Chapter 5, *Presidents*. The annual meetings of some of these associations, such as the Council of Independent Colleges (CIC) and the Association of American Colleges (AAC), are regularly attended by deans, department chairs, and faculty. Department chairs may also find supporting materials from the collegiate associations listed in Chapter 7, *Academic Deans and Mid-Level Academic Administrators*.

Academy of International Business (AIB) (A1)

Academy of Management (AM) (A2)

Academy of Marketing Science (AMS) (A3)

Administrators and Teachers of English as a Second Language (ATESL) (A4)

American Academy of Religion (AAR) (A5)

American Alliance for Health, Physical Education, Recreation, and Dance (AAHPERD) (A6)

American Anthropological Association (AAA) (A7)

American Association for Higher Education (AAHE) (A11)

American Association for the Advancement of Science (AAAS) (A12)

American Association for the Advancement of Slavic Studies (AAASS) (A13)

American Association of Philosophy Teachers (AAPT) (A21)

American Association of Phonetic Sciences (AAPS) (A22)

American Association of Physics Teachers (AAPT) (A23)

American Association of Teachers of Arabic (AATA) (A26)

American Association of Teachers of German (AATG) (A27)

American Association of Teachers of Slavic and East European Languages (AATSEEL) (A28)

American Association of Teachers of Spanish and Portugese (AATSP) (A29)

American Association of University Professors (AAUP) (A31)

American Association of University Women (AAUW) (A32)

American Astronomical Society (AAS) (A34)

American Business Law Association (ABLA) (A35)

American Chemical Society (ACS) (A36)

American Comparative Literature Association (ACLA) (A38)

American Economic Association (AEA) (A42)

American Educational Research Association (AERA) (A43)

American Forensic Association (AFA) (A44)

American Historical Association (AHA) (A45)

American Institute of Biological Sciences (AIBS) (A47)

American Institute of Nutrition (AIN) (A48)

American Legal Studies Association (ALSA) (A49)

American Mathematical Association of Two Year Colleges (AMATYC) (A51)

American Mathematical Society (AMS) (A52)

American Medical Association, Council of Medical Education (CME-AMA) (A53)

American Musicological Society (AMS) (A54)

American Philosophical Society (APA) (A55)

American Physical Society (APS) (A56)

American Political Science Association (APSA) (A57)

American Psychological Association (APA) (A58)

American Society for Engineering Education (ASEE) (A59)

American Society for Microbiology (ASM) (A60)

American Society for Theatre Research (ASTR) (A61)

American Society of Allied Health Professions (ASAHP) (A63)

American Society of Cytology (ASC) (A64)

American Society of International Law (ASIL) (A65)

American Society of Parasitologists (ASP) (A66)

American Society of Zoologists (ASZ) (A67)

American Sociological Association (ASA) (A68)

American Speech-Language-Hearing Association (ASLHA) (A69)

American Statistical Association (ASA) (A70)

American Studies Association (ASA) (A71)

American Veterinary Medical Association (AVMA) (A72)

American Vocational Association (AVA) (A73)

Archaeological Institute of America (AIA) (A74)

Association for Asian Studies (AAS) (A75)

Association for Biology Laboratory Education (ABLE) (A76)

Association for Business Communications (ABC) (A77)

Association for Communication Administration (ACA) (A78)

Association for Library and Information Science Education (ALISE) (A81)

Association for Theater in Higher Education (ATHE) (A83)

Association for the Study of Higher Education (ASHE) (A84)

Association of African Studies Programs (AASP) (A85)

Association of American Geographers (AAG) (A87)

Association of Caribbean Studies (ACS) (A92)

Association of Education of Journalism and Mass Communication (AEJMC) (A111)

Association of Teacher Educators (ATE) (A113)

Association of Teachers of Technical Writing (A114)

Broadcast Education Association (BEA) (A118)

College English Association (CEA) (A122)

Cooperative Education Association (CEA) (A125)

Council for Adult and Experiential Learning (CAEL) (A126)

Council for Agricultural Science and Technology (CAST) (A128)

Council on Social Work Education (CSWE) (A135)

Ecological Society of America (ESA) (A136)

Economic History Association (EHA) (A137)

Entomological Society of America (ESA) (A138)

Financial Management Association (FMA) (A139)

Geological Society of America (GSA) (A140)

History of Science Society (HSS) (A143)

International Technology Education Association (ITEA) (A146)

Linguistic Society of America (LSA) (A148)

Mathematical Association of America (MAA) (A150)

Modern Language Association of America (MLA) (A151)

Music Educators National Conference (MENC) (A152)

National Association for Ethnic Studies (NAES) (A156)

National Association for Women in Education (NAWE) (A157)
formerly National Association for Women Deans, Administrators, and Counselors (NAWDAC)

National Association of Biology Teachers (NABT) (A159)

National Association of Colleges and Teachers of Agriculture (NACTA) (A165)

National Association of Geology Teachers (NAGT) (A168)

National Business Education Association (NBEA) (A177)

National Council for Geographic Education (NCGE) (A179)

National Education Association (NEA) (A181)

Society of Ethnic and Special Studies (SESS) (A186)

Speech Communication Association (SCA) (A188)

National Programs

Programs listed in Chapter 9, *Department Chairs*, also may be applicable for exploration of higher education issues in support of their faculty leadership roles or with an eye toward their own movement into administration. The following list provides a sampling of the range and variety of off-campus programs available to faculty and is not meant to be an inventory of all programs and activities available to these leaders.

American Association for Higher Education (AAHE) (P2)

　Annual Meeting *(P2a)*
　Conference on Assessment in Higher Education *(P2b)*
　Faculty Senate Leadership Retreat *(P2c)*
　Forum on Exemplary Teaching *(P2d)*

American Association of Community and Junior Colleges (AACJC) (P5)

　Fellows Program *(P5a)*

American Council on Education (ACE) (P7)

　The Fellows Program *(P7b)*

Council for International Exchange of Scholars (CIES) (P28)

　Fulbright Scholar Program *(P28a)*

Council on International Educational Exchange (CIEE) (P33)

　Development Seminars *(P33a)*

Faculty Exchange Center (P34)

Higher Education Resource Services (HERS) Mid-America/Bryn Mawr College (P39)

　HERS Summer Institute for Women/Bryn Mawr Institute *(P39a)*

Higher Education Resource Services (HERS) New England/Wellesley College (P40)

　HERS Institute for Women/Wellesley Institute *(P40a)*

Institute for Educational Leadership (IEL) (P41)

　Educational Policy Fellowship Program *(P41a)*

League for Innovation in the Community College (P45)

　Minority Leadership Program *(P45c)*

League for Innovation in the Community College, the University of Texas–Austin, and the W. K. Kellogg Foundation (P46)

　Expanding Leadership Diversity in Community Colleges *(P46a)*

Lilly Endowment, Inc (P47)

　Workshop on the Liberal Arts *(P47a)*

National Faculty Exchange (NFE) (P58)

National Institute for Leadership Development (P59)

　Building a Better Team on Campus: Understanding Gender Issues *(P59a)*
　Leadership for a New Century *(P59c)*
　Leaders Project *(P59d)*

North Carolina State University (P60)

Community College Leadership Institute *(P60a)*

Professional and Organizational Development Network in Higher Education (POD) (P63)

Society for Values in Higher Education (P64)

The Fellows Meeting *(P64a)*

W. K. Kellogg Foundation (P73)

National Fellowship Program *(P73a)*

Statewide, System-Specific, and On-Campus Programs

Typically, the programs in the following list are restricted to faculty members of the sponsoring institution or organization.

Arizona State University (ASU) (S2)

Internship *(S2b)*
Leadership Academy *(S2c)*
Management Development Program (MDP) *(S2a)*

Beaver College (S4)

Faculty Fellow in Academic Affairs *(S4a)*

Board of Governors of State Colleges and Universities (Illinois) (S5)

Affirmative Action Administrative Fellows Program *(S5a)*

California State University System (CSU) (S7)

Administrative Fellows Program *(S7a)*

Chicago State University (S8)

Minority Administrative Fellow Program *(S8a)*

City University of New York (CUNY) (S9)

Chancellor's Academic Affairs Faculty Fellowship Program *(S9a)*
Women's Leadership Institute *(S9b)*

Colorado State University (S10)

The Administrative Women's Network *(S10d)*
Leadership Series *(S10c)*
Professional Development Institute *(S10b)*
Professional Development Programming *(S10a)*

Committee for Institutional Cooperation (CIC) (S13)

Academic Leadership Fellows Program *(S13a)*

Eastern Illinois University (S14)

Programs for Professional Enrichment (PPE) *(S14a)*

George Washington University (S15)

Training Division of Personnel Services *(S15a)*

Gordon College (S16)

Professional Development Through Growth Plans *(S16a)*

Indiana University–Bloomington (S17)

Faculty Development Resources *(S17a)*

Kennesaw College (S18)

Leadership Kennesaw College *(S18a)*

Lansing Community College (S19)

Community Leadership Development Academy *(S19a)*

Maricopa Community College District (S20)

Professional Group Program *(S20c)*
Visions Career Development Program *(S20a)*

Pennsylvania State University (S21)

Administrative Fellows Program *(S21a)*

Rochester Institute of Technology (RIT) (S22)

Executive Leadership in an Academic Setting *(S22a)*

St. Norbert College (S25)

Faculty Development Program *(S25a)*

State University of New York (SUNY) (S24)

Affirmative Action Leave Program *(S24a)*

Tennessee Board of Regents (S26a)

Minority Management Development Program *(S26a)*

University of California–Riverside (S28)

Office of Instructional Development *(S28a)*

University of Kansas (S31)

Faculty Fellows Program *(S31b)*
Office of Personnel Services *(S31a)*

University of Nebraska–Lincoln/Institute of Agriculture and Natural Resources (S33)

NUPAGE *(S33C)*
NUPROF *(S33d)*
Office of Professional and Organizational Development (OPOD) *(S33a)*
Pre-Tenure Support Group *(S33b)*

University of South Carolina (S34)

Minority Administrative Fellowship *(S34a)*

University of Southern Colorado (S35)

Faculty Directors Program *(S35a)*

University of Texas–El Paso (S37)

New Faculty and Staff Orientation Program *(S37a)*

University of Wisconsin–Eau Claire (S38)

School for Graduate Studies and Office of University Research *(S38a)*

University of Wisconsin System (S39)

Administrative Associate Program *(S39a)*

Washington State University (S40)

Faculty Development and Support Services *(S40a)*

11

TEAM LEADERSHIP

Although leadership is generally associated with individuals—their positions, capacities, and relationships with constituents—the functioning of most colleges and universities is highly dependent upon groups. The president's cabinet, the curriculum committee, and the publications staff are examples of teams that meet regularly, share information, and make decisions. In this chapter, the term "team" is used to denote any work group that shares a common agenda. It may be the president's cabinet, the department chairs who report to a dean, a standing group, a work unit, or an ad-hoc committee. Although the team leader plays a pivotal role in ensuring the effectiveness of the group, as noted in earlier chapters, he or she is not solely responsible for its success.

The model of shared leadership that underlies this *Handbook* recognizes that individual leaders *do* matter and that not every decision should be subject to collective deliberation or decision making. But groups and teams are central to higher education institutions, and thus the development of effective teams is at least as important as the development of individuals.

While work groups can be a source of great energy, synergy, and innovation, they can also be dysfunctional—paralyzed by individual agendas, politics, poor leadership, or lack of trust. Later in this chapter, we review why some teams fail.

What, then, are the leadership capacities of teams? What skills and abilities must the *group* possess for the team to achieve its goals?

LEADERSHIP CAPACITIES

Trust

Trust among team members is the essential foundation for effective team leadership. Without it, personal agendas transcend common ones, competition strangles cooperation, and information becomes a bartered commodity. Trust allows the group to function as a unit and keeps the members' sights fixed firmly on the common good.

Common Language

Words have different meanings in different areas of an institution. Someone from academic affairs defines problems and solutions in terms different from those used by someone in institutional advancement or student services. Teams need to build a common language. This requires allowing time during which team members can discuss issues, question the meaning of ideas and words, and hammer out common definitions that have meaning for all team members.

Bridges Over Functional Boundaries

Teams must build bridges across the boundaries that separate different functions. Administrators rise through their own functional areas; rarely, for example, does someone from student affairs work in fund raising or an academic officer in the business office. The people within a profession develop their own mindset, ways of analyzing problems, and tools for devising solutions; usually these are sufficiently different from those of any other functional area to ensure confused communication and unconnected work. Thus, when a group of professionals, each from a different part of the institution, get together on a team, their outlook and interests are quite different. They need to build intellectual bridges across the boundaries that separate each from the other. The ability to find conceptual commonalities is a leadership task of teams.

Shared Agenda and Vision

A committee is not necessarily a team; it becomes one only when individual agendas are subordinate to the team's task, when the members operate from a shared agenda and a common view of their assignment. A shared agenda can be forged by a leader who makes a particular vision so compelling that all team members *want* to be involved, or by a team that works together long enough that their interests and agendas merge.

Common Experiences

A successful team shares experiences. The coach of a successful sports team drills the team in basic maneuvers and plays until they are part of the common experience of each individual team member. When a particular play is called, all the team members play their parts without even thinking. A successful work team builds a repertoire of similar ''plays'' through the accumulation of experiences. Each new situation becomes part of the team's common history and colors the team's responses to all future experiences. Programs to foster such common experiences can make a significant contribution to team unity.

Common Rewards

A well-functioning team shares rewards. Just as the entire team is rewarded when the trophy in the school lobby is inscribed with the members' names, so does a work team benefit from group rewards and recognition. A well-functioning management team will find a way to turn group rewards and recognition into group celebrations that become part of their common history, language, and experiences.

Diverse Memberships

Research supports the general expectation that teams composed of similar types will show cohesion early, but that cohesion may be limited in scope. Groups of diverse types take longer to ''become a team,'' but solve problems more successfully. ''Types'' can be defined in various ways; for example, the cabinet of the vice president for student affairs probably will gel faster than the cabinet of the president, because the student affairs officers share common traditions and experiences. Many teams explore the diversity of their member types through the Myers-Briggs Type Indicator (MBTI) test or other instruments that can reveal styles and preferences. The MBTI points out differences in how people identify and solve problems and relate to other people. Team members report that a knowledge of type leads to better appreciation of differences and more productive teamwork.

Shared Information

Within a well-functioning team, information is shared; it is not the property of any individual. The free flow of information enhances effectiveness of both individual team members and the entire group.

WHY TEAMS FAIL

Academe is full of solo flyers. The most difficult aspect of the transition from professor to administrator often is that administrators must achieve their goals with and through other people. It is no wonder that building an effective team is especially difficult in colleges and universities. The following reasons why teams in colleges and universities fail are adapted from discussions in Heany (1989), Varney (1989), and Rosen (1989).

Specialization

By definition, professionals are specialists who can claim certain areas of expertise, knowledge, and experience. Special knowledge and skills are a source of pride to the professional, whose expertise is a job asset. However, specialization also can breed poor communication, isolation, tunnel vision, and turf battles. When each team member represents a different unit of the organization or an entirely different discipline or expertise, no one may completely understand the work of any of the other members. This specialization is compounded in higher education by the pecking order of various functions. While academic affairs is clearly the driving force in every institution, its dominance may drown other voices. Representatives of dominant units may be ill-disposed to collaborate with members of less prestigious units.

Competitive Culture

Competition is a dominant cultural theme in the United States. Traditional American values prize individual achievement more than group cohesion. It is no wonder that competition triumphs over collaboration as a value in the classroom, on the playing field, and in committee meetings.

Organizational Structure

Most organizational structures reflect individual responsibilities and recognize individual accomplishments. Consequently, most professionals strive to contribute a solo performance that will draw attention to their individual accomplishments. And in turn, supervisors recognize and emphasize individual performance because, among the diverse job responsibilities and multiple involvements of individuals within the typical organizational structure, it is easier to identify individual contributions.

Reward Structures

Individual performance is far easier to recognize and quantify—and therefore to reward—than is team performance. The work of teams may produce less tangible results than that of individuals, and thus can be more difficult to evaluate. The goal of many institutional committees is not to take a specific action but to study a situation. In addition, one academic may serve on several committees and teams that present different and sometimes unclear objectives and results. It is nearly impossible to quantify the participation of one person on the many committees on which he or she may serve, and then to quantify the results of each team to determine the reward (promotion or salary increase) that should go to each employee at the end of the year.

Turf and Power

Power in higher education often is commensurate with the ability to defend one's turf. Turf and power issues can generate coalitions that in turn create ''party lines'' of policies to which the faction must adhere. When a team meeting breaks down into posturing and inflexibility, it is generally a symptom of turf protection and power politics. These situations tend to deteriorate into rehashes of the same debates.

Egos

Teams are successful when individual members can subordinate their ego needs to the larger purposes of the team. In team sports, members are taught that they can succeed (win) through team playing rather than through individual grandstanding. Because success is much harder to define and quantify for the leadership teams of colleges and universities, the necessity to submerge individual egos is less clear. Committee leaders, deans, and presidents would benefit from schooling in the dynamics of team development.

Tension Between Personal and Organizational Goals

Many academics tend to be more preoccupied with their careers than with the long-term success of their institution. As the dean of fine arts at a western state college explained, ''If my institution won't worry about my career, then I will have to.'' Career advancement is based on individual accomplishments, not on the health of the institution or the contributions of a team. It is individual accomplishments that fill a *vita* and entice a search committee.

Change

To some extent, all organizations are in a constant state of change. Each successive institutional or unit leader typically wants to organize to suit his or her own perspective of the unit and its purposes. Staff turnover is a constant at the higher levels. Since teams work best after relationships and trust have been forged among colleagues, any change in the composition of a team requires a recalibration of the group. Restructuring and turnover unbalances existing relationships and forces people to reestablish trust with new people. Change also may cause the incumbent team members to feel vulnerable. In the wake of change, teamwork must be recreated and reconfigured.

SYMPTOMS OF A DYSFUNCTIONAL TEAM

The following checklist of clues for a dysfunctional team is adapted to higher education from Heany (p 27–28).

- Do team members view their work as stand-alone tasks?

- Does work proceed like a relay race—that is, one function must complete its move before another begins?

- Can representatives of one functional area contribute to work underway in another area? Or is work completed independently and recounted at a meeting or in a formal report?

- Are written memos the favored method of communicating among functional areas? Do members pick up the phone when they have questions, or do they send a letter?

- Does information take the great circle route from one area to another? Does it have to be sent upward through a dean before it can go back down to another department chair, up through the president before it can go back down to another vice president?

- How fast do messages move between areas?

- Do problems of quality ignite a search for the guilty party?

- Are finger-pointing and raucous debates common? Do those with the loudest voices dominate meetings? How often do all members of the group speak at a meeting? Are there some members who never seem to speak? Have all members "found their voice" to be able to express their ideas in group discussions?

- Are team members overly concerned with avoiding criticism?

- Do the potential long-term effects of decisions generate little interest? Does the team often discuss the long-term effects of decisions or does it make decisions only considering the here-and-now?

- Are members especially conscious of their ranks and positions? Are members unwilling to accept anyone without long tenure in the job and in the institution?

- How well attended are team meetings? Are members often "too busy" to attend sessions, thus signaling a lack of interest in the group?

- How well defined is the immediate task, the long-term task? Can everyone in the group explain the task clearly and succinctly? Can everyone articulate the mission of the institution and how the task relates to that mission?

- How often is the "standard approach" offered as the solution to a problem? How often does a variation of the phrase "that's the way we always do it here" enter conversation? How often are ideas dropped because they do not fit the standard approach? How freely do group members question the fundamental concepts of issues?

STRATEGIES FOR TEAM BUILDING

Building a team, regardless of the level at which the team functions, is accomplished by acknowledging the importance of the group as a team and by providing opportunities for team members to develop or reinforce a sense of shared purpose. Team leaders need to create opportunities for the members to share common experiences, focus on common topics, and share interests, both professional and personal. Team-building opportunities need to be both large and small—weekend retreats as well as 10–minute breaks for shared snacks before a meeting. Both activities serve different but equally useful purposes and contribute toward team building. Most important, team building is not a one-time effort; it takes constant effort and tending. Particular strategies for team building include the following:

Group Attendance at Events

Many organizations provide discounts when several representatives from the same institution attend an event. The American Association for Higher Education (AAHE) also offers special programming for teams attending its conventions.

Programs for Teams

Several programs are designed specifically for teams. For example, the programs for trustee development of the Association of Governing Boards (AGB) are organized for a team of president and chair of the board of trustees, or of academic vice president and trustee chair of the committee on academics. The American Council on Education's (ACE's) on-campus programs for deans and department chairs help participants to focus on roles and responsibilities in the context of their particular institution. Other programs are designed so that a team of administrators can focus on an institutional problem and develop plans to address that problem with the benefit of critique from the program's faculty and other participants.

Programs for Team Leaders

In a culture that fosters individualism and enterprise, few faculty or administrators have had specific training in managing a team, let alone in the dynamics of team building. While programs for the development of team leaders do exist, they are difficult to find and typically are not designed for higher education. Such programs are more readily found in corporations or are offered by other organizations specifically for leaders from business and industry. Organizations such as the National Training Laboratories (NTL), the Center for Creative Leadership in Greensboro, North Carolina, and the American Management Association in New York are also useful sources.

Common Leadership Development Experiences

Sending members of the team to national institutes over a period of years provides another route to team building. Over several years, senior administrative officers of several institutions have attended Harvard's Institute for Educational Management (IEM). Although each participant develops individually, the experience provides a shared set of concepts and information. The vice president for student personnel at an institution that used IEM in this way felt that the participants "brought back a common vocabulary and context for discussion that can give a common vision of management. It helped to mold us into a stable and visionary team. . . . We have a common bond." A president who used IEM to build her senior administrative team explained that as a result of their participation, her senior officers were able to "think institutionally. Since their IEM exposure, I can share with my vice presidents more of the work of advocating for the institution." (Professional Development . . . 1987.)

Retreats

Retreats of work groups can concentrate on process issues such as the team's communication or work styles, or on the team's tasks, such as developing a yearly plan, planning an event or project, or redesigning a program. A well-conceived event builds trust, encourages informal interaction, and focuses team members' attention on a communal task.

Positive outcomes include greater cohesion, stronger personal relationships upon which to build better professional rapport, and greater individual investment in a shared agenda.

Programs Focused on Common Topics

While team building often is concerned with the process, it also needs to address the tasks of the group. Thus, participation in programs that address important topics of mutual concern also can contribute to team building. A committee considering assessment issues may find that attending AAHE's Conference on Assessment in Higher Education will advance the knowledge of the group, develop common language, and support the decision-making process.

Process Evaluation

Often groups are simply not aware of how they work together. They immerse themselves so quickly and completely in the task assignment that they do not take the time to develop a working style, build a common language, or create a shared agenda or vision. A permanent or rotating process evaluator, who is called upon at the end of each meeting to comment on the development of the team and the quality of its interactions, can be useful in this regard. Every campus has people whose disciplines trained them for such process evaluation; these skills should be considered when appointing members to a committee. A team that lacks such skills (for example, the president's cabinet rarely has latitude to include someone specifically because of his or her process evaluation skills) may wish to train one member or even the entire team in process evaluation skills as part of team development activities.

Consultants

Many consultants have specific training in the skills of team development. Again, these skills may be found on your campus in a professor who has developed expertise from working with businesses, schools, or nonprofit organizations. When a group has existed for a long time, has had a significant turnover of members, or has had a change of leadership, a consultant can help to build a bridge to a new way of doing business. The president of a research university noted, ''Half of our trustees come from a business background, while the other half come from campus and alumni or are just eminent people. It's a terrific challenge to bring such a disparate group together to function as a team. A team-building consultant used every several years is a great way to weld such an odd group of people into a functioning group.''

Finding team-building consultants appropriate to higher education can be difficult. While many independent consultants and firms specialize in team-building diagnosis and development for business and industry, few have extensive experience in the very different world of higher education. Higher education experts who supply team-building support often were hired for other expertise, such as planning, and were pressed into team-building service when intervention became necessary to accomplish the team's task. A potential consultant's expertise in team building should be investigated. Education, psychology, and business faculties are a good source for consultants and information on consultants.

Social Interaction

The longer a team works together (particularly if the team structure is permanent) or the more intensively a team must work together over a short time, the more important it is that the team function on both a task and social level. People who share outside interests are more likely to work well together as a team. Thus, it is important to provide formal and informal social opportunities. Granted, most schedules are so full that yet another event, even if it is social, often elicits a collective groan. Yet social interaction can make a significant improvement in the ability of a team to function together.

Simulations

The cast of a play does not become an "ensemble" until they have rehearsed the script so thoroughly that actors know each other's parts. Similarly, a leadership team needs to rehearse situations so that all members know their roles and the roles of others. Rehearsals are particularly useful for crisis situations: the residence hall leadership team will find it useful to rehearse what it should do if a student in the hall attempts suicide; the president's cabinet needs to rehearse its actions in case of an institutional crisis such as a fire, racial incident, or serious crime. Besides preparing the team for the situation, such simulations also provide opportunities to discuss appropriate strategies, uncover the strengths of team members, and prepare for contingencies. They are team-building activities that create bonds, develop common language, and build bridges across disciplines.

CONSIDERATIONS

Whether and how to build a team usually is the choice of the group's leader: a dean may organize department chairs as a team, while the provost's cabinet remains a group of individuals. But for individual teams to be most effective, team management and team building must permeate the institutional culture. Research on team building, though derived almost entirely from business, government, and military settings, indicates several considerations for presidents and senior officers.

- For team development to be successful throughout the institution, there must be commitment to team management at the most senior levels. If the senior group exhibits team leadership, other groups are likely to follow.

- Team leadership and building require sustained commitment. A one-shot workshop can often be more destructive than doing nothing at all because it raises expectations but offers little or no subsequent payoff.

- Team building is potentially a change agent. Any change of leadership style will cause confusion and turmoil for those who do not adapt readily to a new process. Team building, like any type of change, requires the investment of time.

- Team building involves risk, especially for the leader who institutes the change. The risk is just as real, although perhaps less obvious, for the other members of the team who are asked to share themselves and trust others in new and different ways.

- Although consultants can speed the process and help a team surmount difficulties, a team-building effort is successful only if the members of the team feel they own the process. Consultants come and go, but team members must live with the process every time they meet and interact. Ensure that the consultant provides support and direction for what happens after he or she leaves.

- Those who take the risk to develop teams and to practice team management should be recognized and rewarded, particularly during the fledgling stage when the team may miss as often as hit in the success of its process. Coaching someone who volunteers to serve as team leader for a committee or management group may take more time because the problems are different and more complex than those of a hierarchical group.

- Conversely, the purpose of team building is to develop an effective working group that can make better and faster decisions. Although a group needs time to become a team, it must continue to produce during the process, whether that entails meeting interim task force goals or making budget decisions.

- An overall institutional commitment to team building will have a ripple effect as various teams develop. The development of one team will affect other teams. In the best of all worlds, senior leaders will manage this process to foster synergy across tandem developments.

CONCLUSION

The role of the individual leader is esteemed in higher education, as in much of the rest of American society, but does not necessarily guarantee the best results. Although higher education touts its collegial environment, the processes of team building are often very different in reality. An effective leadership team takes work, time, and commitment. For a team to cohere, development efforts must be multiple and ongoing. Equally important are the evaluation of the process of team building and the effects of the changes wrought, and the diagnosis of new needs based on the changing status of the group and the demands placed upon it. Although the supervisor or chair of a team bears the greatest responsibility for team building, all members must share in development efforts to ensure success.

REFERENCES

Heany, Donald F. *Cutthroat Teammates: Achieving Effective Treatment Among Professionals.* Homewood, IL: Dow-Jones Irwin, 1989.

Rosen, Ned. *Teamwork and the Bottom Line: Groups Make a Difference.* Hillsdale, NJ: L. Erlbaum Associates, 1989.

"Professional Development at Longwood and Dowling Colleges." *IEM Newsletter.* Vol. 3; Issue 1. Cambridge, MA: Institute for Educational Management, Spring, 1987.

Varney, Glenn H. *Building Productive Teams: An Action Guide and Resource Book.* San Francisco: Jossey-Bass, 1989.

RESOURCES

Heany, Donald F. *Cutthroat Teammates: Achieving Effective Teamwork Among Professionals.* Homewood, IL: Dow-Jones Irwin, 1989.

Although this book is written for an audience in business and industry, it is relevant to higher education because it addresses the idea of teamwork among professionals—that is, mid- to senior-level administrators who have specialized areas of expertise. Brief case studies include scripts of interactions among team members to illustrate the developments and problems that Heany discusses and to enable readers to construct parallels in higher education. The author describes team building on a variety of levels: between line and staff officers, between organizations, and between units within an organization.

Parker, Glenn M. *Team Players and Teamwork: The New Competitive Business Strategy.* San Francisco: Jossey-Bass, 1990.

While most books on the topic of teams focus on the leadership issues of building a team, this book asks, "what makes a good team player?" Parker identifies four styles of team players—

contributors, collaborators, communicators, and challengers—who are critical to the effective, dynamic team. The book also explores issues such as ineffective team players, the strengths and weaknesses of teams, team leaders, and developing a team culture. The last chapter is particularly instructive on ways in which management, the human resources unit, training and development programming, and individuals can contribute to team building. The book draws on stories from more than 50 team-driven organizations to illustrate concepts.

Rosen, Ned. *Teamwork and the Bottom Line: Groups Make a Difference*. Hillsdale, NJ: L. Erlbaum Associates, 1989.

This book investigates the theories and issues of teamwork from a psychological perspective. It focuses on such issues as how groups affect their members, the by-products of group process, motivation in task groups, issues of recognition and reward, group development, participation in decision making, and the renewal process.

Varney, Glenn H. *Building Productive Teams: An Action Guide and Resource Book*. San Francisco: Jossey-Bass, 1989.

Varney provides a solid theoretical basis useful for understanding the dynamics of teams, with chapters on recognizing unproductive teams, methods for diagnosing team problems, and planning team improvement. The subtitle is apt: there are pages of resource sheets, checklists, and diagnostic instruments. Case studies and scripts of team interactions illustrate the theoretical points in a practical way. This is a real "how-to" book for any leader who wants to transform a working group into a well-functioning team.

PROGRAMS AND PRACTICES

The following list provides a sampling of the range and variety of off-campus programs available to administrators and faculty for team-building and is not meant to be an inventory of all programs and activities available to these leaders. Some programs are specifically designed for participation by campus teams; others address team-building as a component within their curricula.

Complete information on each listing is provided in the *Appendix*. The letter and number in parentheses correspond to the section and entry number in the *Appendix*.

American Association for Higher Education (AAHE) (P2)

Annual Meeting *(P2a)*
Conference on Assessment in Higher Education *(P2b)*

American Council on Education (ACE) (P7)

Department Leadership Program *(P7a)*

Association of Governing Boards of Universities and Colleges (AGB) (P15)

Board-Mentor Service *(P15a)*
Improving Board Performance *(P15b)*
Institute for Trustee Leadership: Program for Board Chairs and Chief Executive Officers of Independent Institutions *(P15c)*
On-Campus Fundraising Workshop *(P15e)*
Program for Academic Affairs Committee Chairpersons and Senior Academic Officers *(P15f)*
Seminar for Chairpersons and Chief Executives of Theological Schools and Seminaries *(P15g)*
Seminar on Endowment Management *(P15h)*
Strategic Planning for Theological Schools *(P15j)*
Trustee Responsibility for Financial Affairs *(P15k)*

Association of Governing Boards of Universities and Colleges in Cooperation with the National Association of System Heads *(P16)*

Governing the Public Multicampus System *(P16a)*

Association of Research Libraries (ARL) *(P17)*

Advanced Management Skills Institute *(P17a)*

Center for Creative Leadership *(P20)*

Leadership and Teamwork: Increasing Team Leadership Capabilities *(P20c)*

Council for Advancement and Support of Education (CASE) *(P26)*

Presidential and Trustee Leadership in Fund Raising *(P26b)*

Harvard University/Graduate School of Education *(P37)*

Institute for Educational Management (IEM) *(P37b)*

League for Innovation in the Community College *(P45)*

Leadership 2000 *(P45b)*

Lilly Endowment, Inc. *(P47)*

Workshop on the Liberal Arts *(P47a)*

National Institute for Leadership Development *(P59)*

Building a Better Team on Campus: Understanding Gender Issues *(P59a)*

12

EVALUATION: A DEVELOPMENTAL TOOL

Faculty and administrative evaluation are rich and complicated topics. Each has spawned a literature as well as debate and discussion on campuses around the country. This chapter focuses on one aspect of evaluation—the relationship between evaluation and development. How can evaluation be used to help people improve their performance and develop their leadership capacities? The resources listed at the end of this chapter can give readers a broader view of evaluation and advice on how to develop and administer an evaluation system.

THE USES OF EVALUATION

Faculty and administrative evaluation has multiple applications:

- Personnel decisions such as promotion and tenure
- Salary decisions
- Accountability
- Improved individual performance
- Improved organizational functioning

The last two purposes—facilitating individual growth, thereby improving the overall functioning of the institution—receive far less attention in the literature and in practice than the others. Rarely is a meaningful connection drawn between evaluation and development. The role of coach and mentor is more difficult than that of supervisor; it is generally easier to assess someone's performance than to work out a mutually agreeable plan to improve it. Still, feedback from various individuals enables people to assess their strengths and weaknesses and provides a basis for growth and improvement.

Evaluation is a complex and often controversial subject. For example, faculty evaluation as it relates to the promotion and tenure process is accepted widely, but the role of student and peer evaluations, the mix of criteria used in arriving at judgments, the role of post-tenure evaluation, and the confidentiality of evaluations are continuing sources of dispute. Similarly, many object to the evaluation of administrators. Fisher (1987) notes that many objections are based on the potential side effects of the process. Some critics maintain that administrative roles are too diffuse and different to evaluate; others insist that the evaluation systems are so imperfect as to render the exercise invalid or that they invariably are tainted by political considerations (Seldin 1988). Yet it is also important to note, as Nordvall (1979, p. 13) does, that whether or not a formal evaluation system is in place, ''[e]valuation always takes place. People have opinions about the quality of work of others, and these are expressed. Organizations must make decisions about hiring, retention, promotion, and salary. Where there is no formal evaluation system, the informal evaluation provides at least part of the basis for these decisions. So the question is not whether the evaluation will take place but how it takes place.''

Whatever the shortcomings or imperfections of formal evaluative processes, many institutions have used them successfully. With the incorporation of sufficient flexibility and safeguards, the process can work. The many potential uses of evaluation to help individuals and the institution are described in the following paragraphs:

Attune Supervisors to Faculty and Staff Performance

Supervisors who are more aware of an employee's strengths and weaknesses can make a concerted effort to bolster those strengths and work with the individual to remedy the weaknesses. A staff member who shows talent in writing can be given more assignments to hone those skills. By the same token, if that individual is weak in budgetary skills, the supervisor will know to provide more guidance and feedback on budget-related assignments.

Improve Supervisors' Ability to Counsel and Coach

Developing other people is an important part of any leadership position. A performance evaluation system provides structured opportunities to serve as coach and help others to develop their potential.

Help Identify People With Potential for Greater Responsibility and Leadership

Identifying and cultivating a talent pool is essential for all institutions. Evaluation can be especially useful for identifying talented women and minority individuals who can be prepared to assume greater responsibility within the organization. This applies to faculty who may be potential administrators as well as to administrators who can assume different and more responsible positions.

Help Match Individual Goals and Talents With Institutional Needs

Job "fit" and satisfaction are key elements of effectiveness. Performance evaluation can identify untapped strengths or areas of interest that can be helpful to the institution.

STRATEGIES FOR A SUCCESSFUL EVALUATION SYSTEM

This section is drawn from Seldin's checklist for developing a successful evaluation system.[1] The list encompasses suggestions applicable to faculty and administrators, though not all will apply to both groups.

Make the Process Compatible With the Institutional Culture

Institutions have different ways of doing things, different traditions, values, and symbols. Furthermore, the culture of a particular school or department may be different from the overall institutional culture. An evaluation system must "feel right" to the faculty and staff it serves. The culture will determine the environment for evaluation: How much trust surrounds the process? To what extent is it a shared undertaking? Does the institution place a high value on teamwork or on solo performance? To what extent do rewards or the lack thereof dominate the evaluation process? These and other variables will have a noticeable effect on the structure and type of evaluation system developed as well as on its implementation.

Use Formal, Objective Standards

Because evaluation is a human process, it will always be subjective to some degree. Nevertheless, every effort should be made to base evaluation on objective standards. Examples of objective criteria are research productivity, committee service, service to disciplinary organizations, and teaching evaluations by peers and students. Criteria for administrators might include communication skills, monies raised, and successful completion of specific assignments. To the greatest extent possible, performance standards should be specific and criterion-based—for example: holds classes and office hours as expected, demonstrates current knowledge of the academic discipline, uses effective writing skills, consults others in decision making, and shows consistent followup once decisions are made.

Make the Appraisal System as Simple as Possible

The evaluation process must not be so complicated that it is unworkable or is perceived as an additional burden. People will always figure out how to shortcut or ignore a process that seems overly cumbersome. Keep assessment instruments short and limit the number of people involved.

Use Multiple Sources of Information

Everyone on a campus or in an organization has multiple constituents. Faculty interact with students, chairs, and administrators; the dean's constituents are faculty, chairs, and the chief academic officer. A true picture of performance can be formulated only by asking a number of individuals for their perspectives.

Gather First-Hand Knowledge of the Person Being Evaluated

Individuals who do not know first-hand the person being evaluated cannot provide useful evaluative data. Hearsay is never a productive addition to the evaluation process. (In the evaluation of scholarship, however, faculty from other institutions who do not personally know the person being evaluated often are called upon to serve as objective commentators.) At the same time, be aware that evaluation by friends presents an equal problem—one that sometimes is unavoidable on a small campus.

Use Explicit Criteria and Explain Them Thoroughly

Both faculty and administrators need to have a clear sense of the criteria by which they are being assessed. What is the relative importance of scholarship versus teaching excellence in the tenure process? Is the chair expected to be an entrepreneur and to develop relationships and programs that serve the wider community? Some criteria for evaluation will change with time, depending on the priorities of the school or college in a given year. When changes occur, faculty and administrators need to be informed of these shifts.

Give Feedback and Make Specific Suggestions for Improvement

Too often, performance evaluation is a hit-and-run, once-a-year phenomenon. Ideally, formal sessions are complemented by informal conversations, including positive feedback as appropriate and suggestions for improvement tied to specific incidents and examples of performance.

Offer Techniques for Improvement, Not Punishment

The goal of evaluation sessions should be to help people, to point out areas of excellence and areas of weakness. Nothing constructive is accomplished by berating or demoralizing people. Chairs and supervisors often need assistance in the techniques of this coaching role, and workshops on conducting performance evaluations can be very useful.

Adapt the Evaluation Procedure to the Position

No two positions are the same, and administrative evaluations can be both "generic" and tailored to the specific position. (Of course, faculty evaluation is significantly different from administrative evaluation.) An evaluation must be tailored to the job responsibilities of the individual. Thus, administrators can be rated on the same general areas (e.g., planning and managing, supervisory skills, goal setting) but for each person the definition of these areas and the expectations will be significantly different.

Involve the Affected Groups in the Design of the Evaluation Program

This is a basic principle of instituting any system in the academy, especially one that can be perceived as threatening. If faculty and staff do not have a hand in designing or adapting the system, it is likely to fail.

Set Up a Mechanism to Review the Evaluation System

Every system needs periodic fine-tuning and revision. Consult users frequently on the adequacy of the system and conduct a regular formal review.

Ensure That the Process Is Legally Sound

Evaluation processes must be nondiscriminatory and provide due process. Title VII of the Civil Rights Act of 1964, made applicable to colleges and universities in 1972, prohibits discrimination in employment on the basis of race, color, religion, sex, or national origin. An evaluation system that does not bear a valid relationship to job performance violates Title VII. Thus, a good evaluative system clearly states evaluation criteria and adheres to them throughout the evaluation process. This minimalist approach to compliance, however, ignores the potential of a good evaluation system to help the institution become fairer and more diverse. A good system will ensure equal consideration of women and minorities for raises and advancement. A system also must include mechanisms to ensure due process, as protected by the 14th Amendment. This entails following written procedures and ensuring the right to a hearing on personnel decisions. (See Seldin 1988, p. 138–140, for advice on constructing a legally sound evaluation system.)

EVALUATING OUTCOMES

An objective performance evaluation is based on demonstrated accomplishment of desired goals. Those goals should be clearly stated, and the faculty member or administrator should agree with the supervisor that the objectives are appropriate. The annual statement of goals then becomes the basis for the next evaluation. This technique helps people to focus on what they want to accomplish, and permits the evaluation to focus on the achievement of those goals. The evaluation should be an opportunity to understand why certain goals were not met and to either revise the goals or devise a new plan for achieving them. Bland (1990) suggests six areas in which objectives can be written, adding one to Harvey's (1976) five:

Routine Responsibilities

These are the tasks that are the core of the position and are repeated from year to year. The majority of an individual's objectives will fall into this category. Examples for department chairs would include scheduling classes, conducting faculty evaluations, and guiding curriculum development.

Problem Solving

Every unit faces different problems at different times. Thus, the objective for the registrar for a given year may be to review the computer system to address efficiency problems, while a department chair may place a high priority on increasing external funding.

Innovative or Developmental Accomplishments

While the previous objective is geared toward remedies for existing problems, a developmental objective takes the department or unit in new directions. Examples are developing new activities to expand alumni involvement or working with the faculty to revise the departmental curriculum to be more inclusive of new scholarship.

Professional Growth

These are the goals that form the link between evaluation and development. A faculty member might decide to learn more about computerized instruction, or a dean might plan to develop a better understanding of international education.

Community Service

When community service is expected of faculty and administrators, annual objectives should be written in this area.

Institutional Priorities

To the greatest extent possible, individual goals and priorities need to be consonant with institutional objectives. Thus, if major institutional priorities are to attract more international students or increase the participation and success of minority students and faculty, they must be incorporated into unit goal-setting and evaluation systems.

EVALUATING LEADERSHIP CAPACITIES

Different positions require different leadership capacities. The ability to articulate a vision and build unity around it is central to presidential effectiveness, while the capacity to organize and delegate tasks is more important to the success of a chief advancement officer. It is more difficult to be objective in this arena, since some capacities are not easily measured. Evaluation experts recommend that leadership abilities be measured in terms of behaviors that can be observed and defined.

This is not to say that an evaluation process is ever completely scientific or objective. Indeed, an individual's style and personal characteristics may be important determinants of effectiveness. But to state that a person is "abrasive" or "not a good colleague" is far less helpful than to say that he or she "does not listen" or "disregards the opinions of others," and to cite specific examples of those behaviors. Similarly, to describe someone as charismatic is less revealing than to note instances where that individual succeeded in building consensus against the odds or introduced a profound change without creating unproductive conflict. Here, then, is a sampling of leadership capacities translated into measurable behaviors:

Leadership

- Provides a sense of direction for the department, school, or unit
- Achieves sufficient unity within the group to permit forward movement
- Demonstrates good judgment
- Shows innovativeness, flexibility, honesty, and integrity
- Serves as a positive role model to others
- Is committed to the goals of the institution and advances them
- Is committed to professional growth and development

Planning

- Establishes goals consonant with the institution's or school's mission
- Formulates plans to meet the goals
- Monitors progress toward the goals

Managing

- Understands the job
- Meets deadlines
- Makes timely decisions
- Follows through
- Manages resources prudently
- Delegates tasks well

Working With People

- Consults appropriately in decision making
- Motivates subordinates

- Encourages leadership development
- Is sensitive to needs of subordinates and colleagues
- Communicates effectively orally and in writing

The importance of each of these skills or capacities may be rated, as well as the individual's effectiveness in each. Numerical scales can be elaborated upon with explanatory comments.

LINKING EVALUATION AND DEVELOPMENT

Once an evaluation system is in place, how can it best serve development? Seldin (1988, p. 157) points out that evaluation will not automatically result in improved performance. He cites three factors that determine whether evaluation will lead to improvement: whether the evaluation points out information that is new to the individual, whether the individual is motivated to improve, and whether the individual knows how to improve. He goes on to cite several conditions under which individuals will improve their performance (p.156):

- When they are aware of alternative ways of behaving or performing
- When they accept that change is desirable
- When they believe that change is feasible
- When they receive supportive feedback on their behavior
- When they personally are engaged in the developmental process
- When they are rewarded for improvement

How can an evaluation system help meet these criteria? The following considerations are relevant to faculty and administrative evaluation:

Recognize That It Is Often Difficult to Separate the Multiple Purposes of Evaluation

The distinctions among the multiple purposes of evaluation are difficult to maintain. While a department chair may be thinking in terms of the faculty member's development, the faculty member may be preoccupied with promotion or compensation. Relationships built on trust and frequent feedback can provide some help in dealing with this knotty issue.

Include Specific Suggestions on Improving Performance

It's one thing to gather data on an individual's performance and another to interpret it and use it as the basis for action. A performance evaluation that only reports the data is useless for development. A session with one's supervisor is an essential part of the evaluation process. It should include suggested actions, a timetable, and a mechanism for followup, which may be as simple as regular informal conversations.

Help Supervisors Develop Their Evaluation Skills

Giving feedback and performance counseling are not easy, and people usually need some instruction. Providing written information on the process and encouraging evaluators to attend workshops can help them to learn active listening techniques, give feedback in a constructive and nonthreatening way, and deal with the possible emotional fallout of the process.

Use a Development Plan or "Growth Contract"

This may seem like a corny device to some, but it can be a very successful way to focus on particular strategies and long-term goals. A plan or contract becomes a point of reference to guide developmental activities and can serve as a benchmark in future evaluations.

Support Development

If an institution is serious about using evaluation to foster development, it must support that philosophy with resources and policies. Summer stipends for scholarly work or funds for attendance at workshops are obvious examples. Support also can be nonmonetary: an institutional attitude that development is positive rather than remedial and that it is a necessary component of professional growth.

Reward Those Who Pursue Professional Development

If development is seen as a positive force and a person's performance does indeed improve, then rewards are in order. For administrators, these may include raises, travel funds, expanded responsibilities, and interesting assignments. For faculty, rewards may be travel funds, release time, and raises.

Include Career Planning in the Evaluation and Development Process

Performance evaluation should go beyond the "how am I doing?" questions. Equally important, especially for those in mid and late career, is the "where am I going?" issue. This issue is treated at some length in

Chapter 10, *Faculty*, but it is an important one for administrators as well, especially as many administrators lack clear career paths.

THE PERFORMANCE EVALUATION SESSION

The face-to-face session between faculty and chair or administrator and supervisor is the focal point in any evaluation system. It is the culmination of the data-gathering process. Performance evaluation sessions can be emotionally charged, and the temptation to avoid painful encounters can be powerful. As important as it is, the performance appraisal session should be part of a continuum, preceded by regular feedback on performance, and followed by periodic assessment of the individual's progress toward new goals. Consider the following pointers to ensure the effectiveness of the performance evaluation session:

Chairs and Supervisors

- Determine the main points to cover in the session.

- Determine the one or two most important areas for improvement. Supervisors should avoid overloading the individual with a long list of needed improvements. This trivializes the process and makes the suggestions overwhelming.

- Listen, listen, listen.

- Do not personalize the interview session. Confine observations to performance, objective standards, and criteria.

- Whether or not a self-assessment instrument is part of the process, individuals should be encouraged to reflect on their perceptions of strengths and weaknesses. A discussion of these varying perceptions can be useful.

- Explore job satisfaction and discuss ways to enhance it.

- Never rush. Sufficient time (perhaps an hour) should be set aside without interruptions. If the individual needs more time, schedule another session.

- Encourage discussion on the adequacy of supervision.

- Set a problem-solving tone.

- Provide feedback in terms of behaviors, not traits. Describe what the person has done, not what he or she *is*.

Individuals Being Evaluated

- Before the session, clarify mutual understanding of job responsibilities and objectives and seek regular feedback from supervisor and colleagues.

- Determine the main points to cover in the appraisal session.

- Be an active participant. Evaluation is a mutual process.

- Understand that the person evaluating you may lack skill and thus find the task difficult. Give the evaluator the benefit of the doubt. Most supervisors want to be helpful; some are better at it than others.

- Precede the evaluation with a thorough self-appraisal. Most people who do this are not surprised by what they hear in the evaluation session.

- Avoid being defensive; view evaluation as an opportunity for growth. Avoid taking criticism personally.

- Use the session as an opportunity to discuss professional goals, both short and long term.

- Ask for negative feedback if the evaluator offers only positive comments.

- Take notes to remember things. The act of note taking provides emotional detachment from the session.

- Be sure that you are hearing what the evaluator is saying: restate his or her main points in your words (a technique of ''active listening'').

CONCLUSION

A successful evaluation system promotes individual growth and improvement and can help institutional leaders identify emerging talent. A well-constructed system is rooted in the culture of the institution and involves faculty and staff in the development of the evaluation program. Although evaluation has multiple objectives and may be linked to promotion and salary raises, it is also a useful tool to enhance performance and contribute to leadership development.

NOTES

1. For complete listing, see Peter Seldin, *Evaluating and Developing Administrative Performance: A Practical Guide for Academic Leaders* (San Francisco: Jossey-Bass, 1988) 11–12.

REFERENCES

Bland, Carole J. *Annual Academic Administrator Evaluation at the University of Minnesota*. Minneapolis: University of Minnesota, Office of the Vice President for Academic Affairs and Provost, 1990. Photocopy.

Fisher, Charles F. "Leadership Selection, Evaluation, and Development," in Marvin W. Peterson and Lisa A. Mets, eds., *Key Resources on Higher Education Governance, Management, and Leadership: A Guide to the Literature*. San Francisco: Jossey-Bass, 1987.

Harvey, L. James. *Managing Colleges and Universities by Objectives: A Concise Guide to Understanding and Implementing MBO in Higher Education*. Littleton, CO: Ireland Educational Corp., 1976.

Nordvall, Robert C. *Evaluation and Development of Administrators*. AAHE-ERIC/Higher Education Research Report No. 6. Washington, DC: American Association for Higher Education, 1979.

Seldin, Peter. *Evaluating and Developing Administrative Performance: A Practical Guide for Academic Leaders*. San Francisco: Jossey-Bass, 1988.

RESOURCES

Centra, John A. *Determining Faculty Effectiveness: Assessing Teaching, Research, and Service for Personnel Decisions and Improvement*. San Francisco: Jossey-Bass, 1981.

> Discusses the general principles and guidelines behind developing successful evaluation forms and procedures. Centra uses research findings to formulate the suggestions outlined in the book. Topics addressed include the uses and limitations of student ratings, self-assessment, evaluation by peers, and legal considerations and personnel decisions.

Farmer, Charles H. *Administrator Evaluation: Concepts, Methods, Cases in Higher Education*. Richmond, VA: Higher Education Leadership and Management Society, Inc., 1979.

> A still-useful text on the subject of administrative evaluation, this book is organized into four sections designed to explore the development, techniques, and processes of successful administrative evaluation systems. Basic management theories are outlined in relation to higher education, and Farmer provides case studies and suggestions on the process of developing a program. Besides a selected bibliography, there are several case studies of evaluation programs used at several campuses across the country.

Fisher, Charles F., ed. *Developing and Evaluating Administrative Leadership*. New Directions in Higher Education No. 22. San Francisco: Jossey-Bass, 1978.

> Throughout this collection of short essays, the authors suggest that professional development and personnel evaluation are two sides of the same integral process for the improvement of both individual and institutional performance. The chapters move sequentially from a focus on administrative evaluation to the implications for professional and personal development and renewal.

Miller, Richard I. *Evaluating Faculty for Promotion and Tenure*. San Francisco: Jossey-Bass, 1987.

> The book contends that the quality of a promotion and tenure system depends on the quality of faculty evaluation. The author discusses the nature and processes involved in yearly evaluations of faculty performance for purposes other than promotion and tenure.

Nordvall, Robert C. *Evaluation and Development of Administrators*. AAHE-ERIC/Higher Education Research Report No. 6. Washington, DC: American Association for Higher Education, 1979.

> This compact monograph provides an overview of the issues surrounding evaluation of administrators: reasons for undertaking evaluation, its relationship to organizational development,

approaches to developing evaluation systems, the selection and implementation of an evaluation program, and the uses of administrative development programs. The concluding chapter deals with the evaluation and development of college presidents.

Seldin, Peter. *Changing Practices in Faculty Evaluation: A Critical Assessment and Recommendations for Improvement*. San Francisco: Jossey-Bass, 1984.

This book is intended for faculty and administrators involved in the evaluation and tenure process. Seldin considers the changes and emerging trends in policies and practices in assessing faculty performance, based on a national study. The text compares current evaluation practices.

———. *Successful Faculty Evaluation Programs: A Practical Guide to Improve Faculty Performance and Promotion/Tenure Decisions*. Crugers, NY: Coventry Press, 1980.

This book provides an in-depth understanding of the faculty evaluation process. By providing practical strategies and guidelines, the text helps faculty and administrators avoid the common pitfalls when developing a successful evaluation program.

———. *Evaluating and Developing Administrative Performance*. San Francisco: Jossey-Bass, 1988.

This book is a comprehensive guide to developing a fair and accurate evaluation and structured development of academic administrators. Seldin highlights the complete process of initiating and monitoring an evaluation program, and suggests how to use evaluation results in an equitable and legally sound manner. The text is a ''how-to'' guide, and it provides numerous resources, including evaluation forms, performance rating questionnaires, and interview guidelines.

Part Three:

INTEGRATING INSTITUTIONAL AND INDIVIDUAL DEVELOPMENT

13

GETTING THE MOST FROM OFF-CAMPUS DEVELOPMENT PROGRAMS

Leadership development consists of far more than attending work-shops, seminars, and conferences, but these experiences are extremely useful in improving administrative skills and acquiring up-to-date information. Because off-campus programs are so widely attended and constitute the major financial investment in development for most institutions, they warrant special attention. The value of these programs can be enhanced by careful selection and organized follow-through. "Only through designing and implementing a seminar investment strategy . . . can returns be maximized" (Van Auken and Ireland 1980, p. 21).

Unfortunately, few administrators actually prepare for or follow through after an institute or seminar, and few institutions provide or require structure for such follow-through. Typically, administrators sign up for an activity, attend, and then file the materials in that growing stack of "I'll get to it someday" papers in the corner of their office. The reasons administrators give for not preparing or following up are real; constraints of time and energy and the immediate demands of the job are always preeminent. Nonetheless, basic attention can pay off in increased dividends. The strategies outlined in this chapter, based on the work of Fisher (March 1977; June 1977), McDade (1987), Seldin (1988), and Van Auken and Ireland (1980), can help individuals and sponsoring institutions receive the maximum return on their investment in a professional development program.

SELECTING OFF-CAMPUS PROGRAMS

The *Chronicle of Higher Education* and other publications list hundreds of institutes, seminars, conferences, annual meetings, and workshops offered in any given year. The following checklists provide guidelines to determine the best match of a program to individual and institutional goals.

Checklist for Individuals

- Does the program address the individual's career development needs? Is it at the appropriate level?

- Are the topics congruent with the individual's interests?

- Who are the speakers or program faculty? What are their backgrounds and areas of expertise?

- What are the instructional methods? Are they suited to the individual's learning style and preferences?

- Does the length and format suit the individual's needs and learning styles? Is it a compact, information-intensive session or a program designed to promote more leisurely dialogue? How much informal interaction with colleagues does the participant seek and how much does the program provide?

- What types of administrative positions and institutions will be represented? Is the individual seeking diversity of participants for cross-fertilization or commonality of interests to facilitate information swapping and "how-to" conversations?

- Is there an opportunity for the individual to serve as a speaker or panelist?

- Is the program affordable? Are the timing and location right? Will the participant need to pay some expenses personally to supplement the institution's contribution?

- Is there provision for the participants to evaluate the learning experience at the program's conclusion or at a later point?

- Is there provision for the participants to benefit from program follow-up or alumni activities that can extend the learning experience?

Checklist for Institutions

- Does the program speak directly to the short- or long-term needs and goals of the institution?

- Will the program introduce new information and ideas that will help address a specific institutional problem, goal, or activity?

- Who are the speakers and program faculty? What are their backgrounds? Are any of the presenters potential resources, speakers, consultants, or employees for the institution?

- What are the instructional methods? Will they help the participants apply what they have learned?

- What types of administrative positions and institutions will be represented? Will other participants be potential resources, either for the individual in the fulfillment of his or her job or for the institution?

- Can the institution afford the program's time and cost? Are there less-expensive alternatives?

BENEFITING FROM CONFERENCES AND CONVENTIONS

Many administrators rely on conventions and conferences as their major (and sometimes only) professional development experiences. The annual meetings of associations are among the most accessible off-campus development activities. Most associations actively court attendees; a number also solicit proposals for presentations. While there are many benefits from being an observer, presenters can reap even greater rewards from the preparation process, the interaction with other presenters and the event planners, the visibility during and after the convention, and the recognition at home.

The following suggestions can help maximize the return on an investment in the meetings, conferences, workshops, institutes, and seminars.

Become Involved in a Professional Organization and Its Meetings

The first step to becoming professionally active is joining an organization or association. Some presidential organizations such as the American Council on Education (ACE) or the Council of Independent Colleges (CIC), offer institutional membership. The annual meetings of most professional associations generally are open to anyone; nonpresidents are welcome at the conventions of most presidential associations. Other associations, such as the American Association for Higher Education (AAHE) or the American Educational Research Association (AERA), have individual memberships.

An individual who stays current with their literature and researches their program themes can take the opportunity to develop and propose appropriate sessions for upcoming meetings. Even if proposals have not been solicited, a good unsolicited suggestion often will be given serious consideration.

Use Conferences to Network

The action at most conventions is in the halls. Most conference attendees expect to hear a few informative sessions and take away a few good ideas. But the overriding value for many is the interaction with colleagues: comparing notes on a particular topic, renewing old acquaintances, and meeting new people with similar interests and problems. Social events, roundtable discussions, scheduling appointments with particular individuals at the convention, and engaging with the speakers are among the many ways of reaching out to new people.

Collect New Information and Ideas

Participants can compound the value of a conference by collecting materials that will be useful to their colleagues at home, attending a session or buying a tape that would interest someone else on campus. It is helpful to review the program at the beginning of the meeting, to target sessions one particularly wants to hear and plan other activities around those sessions.

Attend as a Team

A drawback of attending national conferences or seminars often is the absence of others from the institution who can share the experience. Many conferences offer special prices for teams, thus encouraging the development of a shared language and joint problem-solving initiatives. For example, sending several department chairs to a conference on leading the department will help them develop a shared understanding of the position and facilitate future conversations among them. Or, a more diverse team of faculty leaders, department chairs, academic administrators, and presidents might attend a conference on assessment or on internationalizing the curriculum.

Follow Up

One often returns from a conference with a pile of calling cards and good intentions of following up on conversations. Notes to remind people of information requested or promised should be sent off quickly, before the memories get vague or the information less useful. An hour devoted to going through the conference materials, writing follow-up letters, and distributing information to colleagues on campus is a useful investment in continuing the dialogue. Another way to prolong the conversation is to organize a breakfast or lunch session with other conference attendees from the same area.

A report to one's supervisor helps crystallize the valuable points of the conference. It also helps the writer relate the event to the institution and the job and helps the supervisor understand the potential payoff to the institution. Sharing materials with supervisors and colleagues is an important means of broadening the impact of individual attendance.

BENEFITING FROM NATIONAL LEADERSHIP DEVELOPMENT PROGRAMS

National leadership development programs offer more extensive development opportunities and set more ambitious goals. They aim to widen horizons, consider policy issues, provide an integrative vision of institutional functioning, and enhance personal leadership skills. Many of these programs, such as Harvard's Institute for Educational Management (IEM), the ACE Fellows Program, and the Higher Education Resource Services (HERS)-Bryn Mawr program, require significant personal and institutional investments of time and money. They range from two weeks (Carnegie Mellon and Harvard's Management Development Program [MDP]) to four weeks (IEM and HERS-Bryn Mawr) to an academic year (ACE Fellows Program). However, greater investment should produce greater dividends, and administrators and institutions may find that careful planning and integration of the experience into institutional goals can maximize the benefits of participation. In addition to the suggestions made in the previous section, the following points are specifically relevant to national leadership development programs.

Plan for the Investment

Previous participants can be helpful in selecting and preparing for a program. (Most programs will share rosters of recent participants.) What were the strengths and weaknesses of the program? What would the participant have done differently to have a better experience? Would any particular preparations have made the program more productive? What can be done to get the most benefit from the experience?

Before leaving for the program, plan the best way to document learning. Besides taking notes, it may be useful to keep a journal or to dictate observations and reflections. Generally, participants receive the curriculum and reading assignments before the program. Review these in advance, to determine if other resources or institutional documents should be brought to the program or if any questions should be asked on campus relevant to the program's coverage. All too often, participants find themselves wishing they had read a particular article or brought along the institution's budget or strategic plan. Putting off preparation until the last minute results only in frantic calls to the office for overnight mail, or in the more serious consequence of missed opportunities.

Finally, before attending a leadership development program, commit in advance to a post-activity feedback session with colleagues and supervisors. Ideally, participants will bring home insights and ideas for change to be shared with others.

Follow Up

A written report helps participants digest the experience and reflect on it. It also helps supervisors see the potential benefit to the institution, and helps colleagues benefit from the ideas and information that the participant gathered.

A follow-up session with colleagues and supervisors should be designed to enlist interest and support, not to inundate others with data in which they have little interest. Copying and distributing materials of potential interest is a useful first step. A debriefing meeting should concentrate on aspects of the program that are applicable to the institution and that will appeal to colleagues. This session must be handled with care, to avoid delivering newly found wisdom and truth to unwilling listeners.

Periodic reviews of program materials and personal notes help recapture insights, evaluate progress on plans, and measure the effect of the program on individual performance and development. The program also can be tied to one's work through a concrete proposal for a new activity or a new way of approaching an issue that stems from the program, documenting how the lessons from the program will help with the new project. Individuals can incorporate lessons and new goals derived from the program into their annual performance evaluations.

CONCLUSION

The bottom line for evaluating the usefulness of professional and leadership development programs is performance. Admittedly, it is difficult to correlate development activities with performance in a direct way. Specific objectives can be formulated, and off-campus conferences, seminars, and leadership development programs can be used in a deliberate way to achieve these objectives.

The professional development activities described in this chapter are an important antidote to the insularity of campus life. Exposure to issues, new information, and other people's perspectives is in itself useful. Greater dividends will be reaped if these investments are carefully selected, prepared for, and followed up.

REFERENCES

Fisher, Charles F. "The Evaluation and Development of College and University Administrators." *ERIC/Higher Education Research Currents* (March 1977).

———. "The Evaluation and Development of College and University Administrators, Part Two: Professional Development of Administrators." *ERIC/Higher Education Research Currents* (June 1977): 3–6.

McDade, Sharon A. *Higher Education Leadership: Enhancing Skills through Professional Development Programs.* ASHE-ERIC Higher Education Report No. 5. Washington, DC: Association for the Study of Higher Education, 1987.

Seldin, Peter. *Evaluating and Developing Administrative Performance: A Practical Guide for Academic Leaders.* San Francisco: Jossey-Bass, 1988.

Van Auken, Philip M., and R. Diane Ireland. "How Small Businesses Can Gain the Most From Employee Seminars." *Journal of Small Business Management* 18, no. 4 (October 1980): 18–21.

SELECTED OFF-CAMPUS PROGRAMS

The following list provides a sampling of the range and variety of off-campus programs that draw higher education leader participants from the entire national higher education scene. This is not meant to be an inventory of all programs and activities available to these leaders. These programs were specifically mentioned in the preceding text or are listed because of the large number of annual participants or long history.

Complete information on each program is provided in the *Appendix.* The letter and number in parentheses correspond to the section and entry number in the *Appendix.*

American Association of Community and Junior Colleges (AACJC) (P5)

   Professional Development Workshop *(P5c)*

American Council on Education (ACE) (P7)

   Department Leadership Program *(P7a)*
   The Fellows Program*(P7b)*

Carnegie Mellon University/School of Urban and Public Affairs (P19)

   Academic Leadership Institute *(P19a)*
   College Management Program *(P19b)*

Center for Creative Leadership (P20)

   Leadership Development Program *(P20d)*

Central Association of College and University Business Officers (CACUBO) (P22)

   Management Institute *(P22a)*

Council for International Exchange of Scholars (CIES) (P28)

   Fulbright Scholar Program *(P28a)*
   Seminars for International Education Administrators in Germany and Japan *(P28b)*
   U.S./United Kingdom College and University Academic Administrator Award *(P28c)*

Harvard University/Graduate School of Education (P37)

   Institute for Educational Management (IEM) *(P37b)*
   Institute for the Management of Lifelong Education (MLE) *(P37c)*
   Management Development Program (MDP) *(P37d)*

Higher Education Resource Services (HERS) Mid-America/Bryn Mawr College (P39)

    HERS Summer Institute for Women/Bryn Mawr Institute *(P39a)*

Higher Education Resource Services (HERS) New England/Wellesley College (P40)

    HERS Institute for Women/Wellesley Institute *(P40a)*

Institute for Educational Leadership (IEL) (P41)

    Educational Policy Fellowship Program *(P41a)*

National Association of College and University Business Officers (NACUBO)/Marriott Education Services (P53)

    Executive Leadership Institute *(P53a)*

National Association of Student Personnel Administrators (NASPA) (P56)

    Richard F. Stevens NASPA Institute *(P56a)*

National Center for Higher Education Management Systems (NCHEMS) (P57)

National Institute for Leadership Development (P59)

    Building a Better Team on Campus: Understanding Gender Issues *(P59a)*
    Leaders for Change *(P59b)*
    Leadership for a New Century *(P59c)*
    Leaders Project *(P59d)*

Southern Association of College and University Business Officers (SACUBO)/University of Kentucky (P65)

    College Management Business Institute (CMBI) *(P65a)*

W. K. Kellogg Foundation (P73)

    National Fellowship Program *(P73a)*

Williamsburg Development Institute (P72)

    Williamsburg Development Institute *(P72a)*

14

ON-CAMPUS DEVELOPMENT: THE WORKPLACE AS LEARNING ENVIRONMENT

Higher education usually equates leadership development with attendance at off-campus learning events, generally in formal training situations such as national workshops, seminars, and institutes. Yet in other fields, such as business, government, and the military, leadership development includes a full array of on-site learning opportunities and programs as well as on-the-job development.

Many of America's best-run businesses routinely provide in-house development programs for their executives. These typically address a broad range of topics, from time management and computer skills to business strategy and international relations. The corporate campuses of Xerox, International Business Machines (IBM), and National Cash Register (NCR) are well-known as training and educational centers. Some now have degree-granting status. These and other businesses also put great effort into systematically developing their employees in and through their jobs. IBM is well-known for rotating its employees through jobs so that they learn many facets of the organization and its business. Similarly, the Armed Services use job rotation to ensure that officers experience many areas of military operations.

Within the academy, as well, there is widespread recognition that most learning occurs in one's work environment, and that the job itself is the richest, most constant source of development. Still, colleges and universities lag far behind in the support of on-site programming and on-the-job development. But the recent increase in the number of on-campus fellowships, job exchanges, team-building activities, and formal courses may indicate that some institutions are beginning to see the benefits of providing developmental programming for their employees. Those that have experimented with formalized on-campus learning experiences can point to the effect on job performance and career mobility, and thus on institutional effectiveness.

HOW DO LEADERS LEARN?

Other chapters in this handbook have touched on developmental stages within various higher education positions. Regrettably, higher education does not have a tradition of grooming people from within to take on jobs of greater responsibility; it is up to the individual to make the job a learning experience.

It is one thing to understand that the job itself is potentially the richest source of learning, and another to translate that understanding into a series of deliberate strategies and developmental experiences. Perhaps more organizations do not provide formalized structures for on-the-job learning because this type of learning is messy, hard to diagnose, and difficult to program. Some people are more likely to learn from their experiences than others, and different people will learn different things from the same experience; this further complicates the challenge of developing such learning experiences. The workplace is not a controlled learning laboratory.

Formalized on-the-job learning again raises the concept of shared responsibility between individual and institution for leadership development. Fostering a positive learning climate requires a partnership of individuals who want to learn and institutions that will create appropriate learning opportunities. Before designing deliberate workplace learning strategies, institutional leaders should analyze the various sources of learning on the job and what people can learn from different experiences. The research of Kotter (1988), McCauley (1986), McCall (1988), and McCall, Lombardo, and Morrison (1988) forms the basis for the following discussion on learning strategies.

New Assignments

A new assignment promotes learning, whether it is a totally new job or a new responsibility within a current job. "In retrospect, one of my best on-the-job learning experiences was revising the freshman advising system," an associate dean remembered. "I dug into the research on advising and freshmen, then called around the country to identify issues and national trends of advising. Then I had to determine the strengths and weaknesses of our current system. I needed to envision a new system, develop a plan, and mobilize others—which taught me to interact with new groups and to develop further my interpersonal skills. It was the first time I took a major leadership project from start to finish and managed all aspects by myself." As the associate dean's story suggests, there are as many learning benefits from involvement with new assignments as there are types of new assignments.

- *Starting from scratch.* Building a team, program, or any new activity uses several important skills, including vision, planning, organizing, motivating others, and working with new constituencies.

- *Turning it around.* The difficulties associated with a troubled or failing operation are frequently great teachers. Administrators who try to turn around a tough situation diagnose problems, make hard decisions, and deal with difficult interpersonal issues such as conflict resolution, negotiations, and trust building. These experiences can be as painful as they are instructive.

- *Assuming increased responsibility.* Adding more responsibility to an individual's portfolio usually entails managing additional people, money, and functions. Increased complexity (and perhaps workload) requires individuals to manage more effectively, think more broadly, and interact more with peers, bosses, and subordinates.

- *Joining projects, committees, and task forces.* There is great learning potential in new projects and temporary assignments. A department chair confessed, ''Although committees often seem the bane of my work existence, I've learned a great deal from them about how organizations and people work, not to mention about crucial higher education issues. I've learned that task forces can be deliberately structured to add an extra dimension of learning to the experience.'' Involvement in committees provides exposure to how other institutional operations work and gives people a different perspective on their environment and their jobs.

- *Switching between staff and line responsibilities.* The conventional wisdom holds that jobs with line responsibility (e.g., director of a unit, with supervisory responsibility and budget authority) are the most important and professionally satisfying. Staff jobs (often titled ''assistant to'') are also excellent learning experiences and can provide more breadth of vision than a line job. Experiencing both changes one's perspective on an institution and increases one's range of skills. Line jobs teach decision making about personnel and money while challenging supervisory and motivational skills. Staff positions are likely to hone negotiating skills and the ability to get things done through persuasion rather than authority. They also provide a broader overview of the entire unit or institution than do line jobs.

Other People

As we work, we watch others and learn from them. Exposure to bosses, colleagues, and subordinates reveals different ways of doing things, conceptualizing issues, and interacting with others.

- *Bosses.* Ideally, bosses are positive role models as well as teachers. Subordinates learn from watching them in action and analyzing what they do and why. When bosses are serious about the development of others, they take an active role in coaching, sharing information, explaining their decisions and actions, and providing feedback. If both subordinate and boss share the vision of being in a learning situation, learning is more likely to occur. Even a difficult boss can offer valuable—albeit painful—experience in coping with stress, in accommodating value or style dissonance, and in preserving one's sense of self in the face of conflict or disapproval.

- *Peers.* Peers also can serve as teachers and role models. They can provide information on various issues as well as on the values and culture of the institution. Their feedback is generally less threatening than that of a boss, and they can be helpful in developing career strategies and learning about different job options.

- *Mentors.* Mentoring, whether informal or part of a planned effort, has received much attention lately, especially in the popular literature. A mentor supports a protege in a variety of ways: serving as sponsor and advocate, showing the more junior person the ropes and explaining the system, providing career counseling, and helping to develop a sense of confidence and competence. Good mentors provide feedback and actively coach the protege, pointing out mistakes and suggesting improvements. Research shows that mentors are particularly helpful for minority and women faculty and administrators, who benefit from a sense of personal connection and the affiliation with an individual who can help navigate unfamiliar and sometimes inhospitable territory. Some institutions have formal mentoring programs for all new faculty, while others have them for minority students, faculty, and administrators. For example, the American Council on Education (ACE) Fellows Program designates the president and senior officers of an institution as mentors to the Fellow.

- *Others.* Working with different people—within or outside the institution—enables individuals to broaden their repertoire of interpersonal skills and deepen their appreciation of different perspectives and styles. Opportunities for a junior administrator to present information and interact with senior people, or for faculty to interact with board members, are potential learning experiences. Chairing a committee composed of unfamiliar individuals, with the attendant tasks of creating a working team and keeping people on track through persuasion and negotiation, is also an opportunity for development. Even negative role models can serve to illustrate bad management or repugnant values, teaching others what *not* to do or be.

STRATEGIES FOR DEVELOPING ON THE JOB

The following list of strategies can be used by individuals and institutions to foster learning on the job.

Strategies for Individuals

- *Conduct a self-assessment.* It is useful periodically to take stock of one's strengths and weaknesses, identify areas for further development, and determine preparation needed for additional or different responsibilities. Areas to assess include technical job knowledge, understanding of the broad scope of the institution, interpersonal skills and relationships, and record of accomplishments. Several instruments exist to guide this type of self-assessment.

- *Conduct a job assessment.* Considering the self-assessment, how well does one's current job fit career objectives? What competencies are most/least used in this job? What is liked most/least about the job? What developmental opportunities does it present? What opportunities could be created? Ideally, this assessment should be conducted with a supervisor, whose help is instrumental in any development plan.

- *Create short- and long-term development plans.* Many people dream of career-crowning jobs without thinking through the necessary interim objectives. It is useful to outline regularly one or two manageable short-term objectives (attainable in six months to a year) in the context of a long-term development plan. Such short-term objectives should be directly linked to one's current job; learning opportunities are a supplement to, not a substitute for, getting one's job done. Thus, it is unrealistic to create a laundry list of new areas to master or skills to develop; one or two goals are plenty for most mortals. Examples of manageable short-term goals are to improve public speaking skills, to learn more about international education, or to learn how to use a computer spreadsheet.

- *Seek assignments that will offer new skills and information.* Committees, task forces, and professional organizations offer many different learning opportunities. Participation on a search committee, a task force on general education, or a strategic planning committee can be a learning experience for faculty and administrators. In deciding whether to take on a new assignment or participate in a given activity, assess what can be learned and whether that learning matches current interests and goals.

- *Keep an eye on the future.* Personal and professional planning can be approached many different ways, depending on one's values and philosophy. Most people in leadership positions have not adhered to a detailed long-range plan, but instead followed a loosely conceived plan that allowed for permutations and side trips. Being open to new opportunities and new directions is an important part of leadership. If one's roadmap is too clearly delineated, one may miss important turns in the road.

Strategies for Institutions

- *Require annual development plans from all employees.* Make leadership development the rule, not the exception. When everyone takes part, learning becomes a joint responsibility of the individual and the institution. Keep the process low-key and manageable, and separate the development plan from the performance evaluation to make it nonthreatening and self-directed. (Adherence to the plan will most likely improve performance, however.)

- *Make development of subordinates part of supervisory evaluation.* Developing others is a normal part of an administrator's job. If leadership development is an institutional commitment, then it ought to be a part of every supervisor's job description, and the responsibilities for development should be included in the performance appraisal process.

- *Initiate formal mentoring programs.* A formal mentoring program for faculty or administrators is a common form of on-campus development. Payoffs can be high if the matches between mentors and proteges have been sensitively made. Such a program typically provides mentors and proteges the opportunity to meet regularly to reinforce the process.

- *Encourage and support participation in training opportunities.* Financial support is important; so is ensuring adequate job coverage while someone participates in a leadership development experience. Sometimes this simply means encouraging all team members to pitch in when one has such an opportunity. As Chapter 13 on the use of off-campus programs elaborates, formal development programs are most useful when they are part of a larger individual plan and when they are directly relevant to the job. Conversations with supervisors and colleagues before and after the program are particularly helpful, both for the individual and for the institution.

MODELS FOR ON-CAMPUS DEVELOPMENT PROGRAMMING

There are as many variations on the basic models of on-campus development programs as there are colleges and universities.

Temporary Experience in Another Job or Place

There are many ways to give faculty and administrators temporary seasoning in another job. Traditionally, fellowships have denoted experiences at another college or higher education organization. Usually, these are sponsored by external organizations (such as the ACE Fellows Program) or systems offices (such as the California State University Administrative Fellows Program), and often include extra financial support, such as providing funds for travel or attendance at professional development meetings.

However, institutions increasingly offer fellowships, job rotations, and exchanges, particularly for faculty, in the offices of senior executives. For example, some institutions have identified special short-term positions within key offices such as student affairs, development, academic affairs, and finance. Typically, candidates are identified for these positions through nominations or applications, and serve for an academic term or year. They gain a new perspective on the unit and learn some of its details, then return to their regular positions having gained a broader understanding of how the institution works. Tasks typically include special projects and research that support the regular work of the office but do not require specialized expertise or long-term commitment.

Exchanges can incorporate both on- and off-campus jobs. The National Faculty Exchange brokers faculty exchanges, but many others are arranged privately. In such an exchange, faculty who teach similar courses at sister institutions simply swap places for a term or year, continuing to draw their salary and benefits from the home institution, while experiencing academic life at another institution. In direct exchanges, two professors simply switch jobs; they may even live in each other's home for the term, thus saving housing costs. Some institutions allow job exchanges among their employees. Typically, these exchanges involve mid-level administrators. The goal is for administrators to gain new skills without leaving the campus. The exchanges may be within a particular unit, such as personnel, or between similar positions in different units.

Networks

Every professor and administrator can claim a network of colleagues. Institutions can further develop these networks by creating links between people involved in similar jobs and responsibilities or with interests in common issues. Despite the informality of many of these networks, institutions can realize a substantial payoff for the price of coffee and postage. An academic vice president explains, ''Several years ago, a group of women started to meet once a month over brown-bag lunches to discuss common job problems. Soon we gave ourselves a name, began to reach out systematically to other women in similar situations, regularized the date and place, and eventually elected officers. From that network have grown many positive initiatives and new policies. We've been instrumental in moving women into more senior positions and in attracting and keeping women faculty.''

Institutions can build networks to advance specific objectives: for example, a network of professors interested in case-study teaching with support through the office of academic affairs, or a network of faculty and administrators involved in supporting issues of diversity on campus with joint support from admissions, financial aid, advising, student affairs, academic affairs, and residential life. Networks often come and go according to the needs of employees. Support may vary from an office that keeps a mailing list to an infrastructure that books speakers and organizes workshops for network members.

Orientation Programs

Many institutions offer new employee orientation programs: general introductions to the institution, its history, its policies and practices, and its educational mission, with senior officers explaining the goals and operations of their units. In addition, some institutions offer orientation programs for employees who move to new levels of responsibility: for example, for those employees who are beginning to supervise other employees and handle their units' budgets.

Skills Development Programming

Skills development programs are usually organized through the personnel or human resources office. The complexity of these offices varies dramatically, depending upon the size of the institution, the number of potential participants, the definition of participants (faculty only, professional staff/administrators only, support staff only, or some combination of these groups), and the history and evolution of the unit. Typically, an institution tries to provide an array of short programs, each addressing a specific audience or a particular management problem or issue. Programs might include weekly seminars for new supervisors, a one-day introduction to a software program, or an afternoon session on the challenges of supervising work-study students.

Longer Seminars

Some institutions are experimenting with longer seminars that focus on management and leadership issues and are directed to specific groups of administrators or faculty. For example, Metropolitan State University offers an ongoing series of programs for department chairs that focuses on their particular leadership challenges.

INSTITUTIONAL EFFORTS: A SAMPLING OF APPROACHES

A look at the history and goals of some on-campus development activities can explain their growth and relationships to their institutions.

Arizona State University

The Management Development Program (MDP) is the general title applied to the professional development efforts targeted toward academic and operations administrators by the human resources department at Arizona State University (ASU). The program was born from the suggestions of a presidential task force on management development and has received total commitment from former and current presidents. It complements a comprehensive staff development program.

The MDP comprises four tiers: a speaker series for senior officers, a luncheon series and retreats for academic department chairs, an academy for mid-level managers, and internships for potential managers and managers with growth potential. The speaker series, informally titled "The President's Breakfast Series," brings nationally and internationally known speakers to ASU to address issues related to institutional goals. By-invitation-only participants include senior-level officers (vice presidents, deans, and senior officers of comparable rank).

Academic department chairs participate in a largely self-directed group that determines its own needs and designs programming to address those needs. Besides monthly lunch meetings at which the speaker from the president's breakfast series may address the chairs, there are annual retreats that focus on departmental problems and challenges. Participants range from new chairs to veterans and span the spectrum of disciplines, sharing common problems and possible solutions, and supporting each other in the tug-of-war between administrative responsibilities and scholarly interests.

The Leadership Academy for mid-level management personnel meets twice a month throughout the academic year. The curriculum is designed to cover management and higher education topics, with the goals of communicating the ASU management philosophy and providing participants with a broader view of the university. Participants are chosen through a process of nominations and applications. A related program offers management internships that provide exposure and experience to potential managers and managers with growth potential. The internship positions are posted and internal candidates apply and compete for them. Internships in vice presidents' offices provide exposure to institutional issues and operations. For example, at the vice presidential level, interns have assisted with minority faculty recruitment efforts, the institutional budgeting process, and preparing materials for board of regents action. Interns placed at department levels have developed proposals to assist spouses of new faculty or administrators identify employment possibilities, have served as liaisons with state agencies to encourage wider use of mass transit by members of the campus community, and have developed benefits summaries for retirees and those terminating from ASU.

The number of internal promotions among program participants is high. Alumni of the Academy and former interns find they have increased career mobility that comes from improved strengths and new areas of expertise. The institution benefits from an enlarged pool of skilled people, including increasing numbers of women and people of color, who are known quantities on whom it can draw for promotions. ASU benefits most from the increased networking within the institution. With more than 40,000 students, it can be difficult to meet people outside one's unit. These programs provide opportunities for people to meet across discipline and responsibility lines to solve problems and to share information.

Evaluations for all four components are positive, and include many suggestions for speakers and topics. Academy graduates clamor for a second-tier program. Based on suggestions for additional topics for the Academy, ASU has developed new, stand-alone programs, including a five-day management skills institute (King 1990, 1991). Contact: Rita King, Assistant Human Resources Director, Staff Relations and Development, Arizona State University, Tempe, AZ 85287–1403, (602) 965–4798.

Boston College

In 1975, Boston College, under the leadership of Executive Vice President Frank B. Campanella, introduced a Management Development Program (MDP), for administrators and professional staff. Participants were chosen from among middle managers. The basic program included 14 five-hour sessions taught by faculty and administrators. The program's objectives were to help participants learn about the diverse university functions and components, examine the key elements of the management process and their application to the university environment, examine financial management in higher education, and explore human and organizational behavior. Its goal was to enable participants to develop new skills and knowledge in these areas, to enhance their effectiveness in their jobs.

The MDP was phased out in the spring of 1982 and reappeared in 1986 as part of the newly formed Professional Development Program (PDP) inspired by Frank Campanella. The purpose of the PDP was twofold: (1) to meet individual needs by enabling people to stretch to their best efforts both in the performance of their jobs and in the acquisition of new knowledge for their continued growth; and (2) to meet organizational needs requiring staff with specific managerial skills and competencies. Unlike the MDP, which was coordinated by two administrators and a faculty members as an "add-on" to their other responsibilities, the PDP was established as a formal Human Resources function, philosophically based and professionally staffed by a full-time director with a budget and other additional support services. This was an important transition. A highly successful "floating" enterprise became an established function offering programs, services, and consultation to a wide cross-section of employees and departments.

Dr. Alice Jeghelian was named Director of Professional Development and still serves in that capacity. Her first official act was to form an advisory committee of administrators, faculty, and staff who help her identify and evaluate program possibilities and who provide information and feedback regarding individual and institutional needs. The committee meets monthly throughout the year.

Programs are offered in supervisory and management development, general skills acquisition, career development, and in personal areas affecting family, health, and legal/financial matters. Regular subject categories include programs about Boston College's institutional character/mission; organizational structure and human resource systems; information technology; planning and organizing skills; communication skills; work style/work environment issues; multicultural environments; leadership and management; and supervisory skills. Programs are voluntary and vary from one-time, one-hour sessions to a seven-week series of half-day meetings. One of these series is called Management Perspectives, coordinated by Frank Campanella. It is today's scaled-down version of the MDP of the 1970s.

Since 1985 the PDP has expanded significantly in concept and in the number and diversity of its services and activities. In the beginning, "professional development" focused primarily on training individuals to perform better in their jobs and hopefully to advance. Soon the function also began looking at organizational needs and ways in which the PDP could benefit the work of institutional units. The concept of professional development began to shift from an individual- or career-centered focus to an increasingly work- or performance-centered approach with organizational development as the key focus, where both the individual and the institution are the beneficiaries. The PDP began to provide direct services to departments, upon request, with the aim of assisting them in achieving a specific learning goal (e.g., orienting new employees, conducting on-the-job-training, resolving problems, building teams, managing stress, etc.). This service was called "Have Program, Will Travel."

As a result of the expanded scope of professional development, its services today reflect what may more accurately be termed as human resource development, which has been described by the American Society for Training and Development (ASTD) as "the integrated use of training and development, organizational development, and career enrichment to improve individual, group, and organizational effectiveness." To reflect the change in the scope of this function at Boston College, the PDP was renamed the Human Resource Development Program in 1990 (Campanella 1981; Jeghelian 1990, 1991). Contact: Alice Jeghelian, Director of Professional Development, Boston College, Chestnut Hill, MA 02167, (617) 552-3338.

Eastern Illinois University

The Program for Professional Enrichment (PPE) was the brainchild of the university's Affirmative Action Advisory Committee. It was begun to provide more opportunities for minority and women employees to gain exposure to and experience in administrative positions, and to enhance their opportunities for future advancement. The program includes workshops on career advancement and a series of seminars on higher education administration, followed by an administrative internship program. The Advisory Committee decided that the program should be separate from the affirmative action unit to lay a broader base of support and to serve the professional development needs of all employees. The PPE is administered through the Office of the President. Each year, approximately 20 participants drawn from faculty, professional staff, and administrators are selected through an application process.

The workshop phase focuses on career planning within higher education administration, with topics such as self-assessment, analysis of career options, career mapping, goal setting, and career advancement strategies. Participants develop an individualized action plan as part of the program and have access to a consultant for follow-up after the program. Professors with expertise in career development and adult education designed the curriculum and facilitate the workshops. These workshops are offered over a six-week period and total approximately 20 hours. A committee of six senior officers designed the seminar series in higher education administration that follows; it is presented in 12 three-hour weekly seminars. This segment introduces trends and issues in higher education, organizational structures, financial management, human resources, leadership and management, student services, and institutional advancement. Presenters are drawn from all levels of higher education, primarily within Illinois, and include the university president and vice presidents.

After the workshop and seminar phases, participants may compete for a limited number of semester-long administrative internships. Participants submit a proposal for an internship, based on informational interviews and other research (strategies covered in the career workshops). Interns may receive partial release time during the internship, while PPE assists the intern's home department to cover the temporarily unmet duties.

Forty percent of the participants from the first three years of the program have moved into new positions at higher levels of responsibility. Participant evaluations have been extremely positive. Unexpected benefits have included the transmission of institutional culture and values through broad-based participation and networks built across professional staff, administrators, and faculty. Due to a clamor from PPE alumni for additional programming, follow-up seminars are organized periodically and reunions of classes are frequent (Anderson 1986; Anderson 1990, 1991). Contact: Judith Anderson, Director of Affirmative Action and Programs for Professional Enrichment, Eastern Illinois University, Charleston, IL 61920, (217) 581–5020.

Maricopa Community Colleges

The Visions Career Development Program grew from a 1984 effort to address the areas of retraining, renewal, and career development for all employees of the Maricopa Community College District. A committee composed of representatives from all employee groups assessed developmental needs through a survey to all employees. From this assessment, the committee developed a series of assumptions, a mission statement, and goals and objectives for programming. As a follow-up to this work, a strategic planning committee was formed to create a plan. The resulting programs are housed within the Human Resources Division, Department of Employee Development. The Maricopa effort is noteworthy for its efforts to address the needs of *all* employees, including administrators, professional staff, and faculty, as well as employees of the maintenance and operations, crafts, and food-service areas.

The cornerstone of Maricopa's employee development plan is the Visions Career Development Program. Through the program, employees identify their interests, aptitudes, and skills; explore internal and external career opportunities; identify and develop appropriate work-related behavior, skills, and knowledge that will assist in development of career action plans; learn the skills necessary for dealing with change and obsolescence in our technological society; and investigate and define options for retirement or change of career. All full-time employees of the Maricopa Colleges may participate. The annual program begins with workshops designed to facilitate the career development process. Separate workshops are offered for employees and supervisors. External career development specialists are available for individual consultation as a follow-up to the workshops. The goal of the program is to help participants identify and create projects for their own retraining and renewal, using the Human Resources Division for support. Other activities open to all employees include a wellness program, fitness centers, an internal employee exchange program (within the Maricopa Colleges' institutions or departments), external employee exchanges (with outside educational institutions or agencies), training programs for the use of computer hardware and software, and an employee assistance program. Also considered part of the employee development program are three employee recognition awards (innovator of the year, outstanding employees, and service anniversary awards).

Faculty may participate in a variety of additional programs, including faculty sabbaticals and support for course and program development and evaluation from the Center for Instructional Technology. Faculty interested in management may serve as management interns. Participants complete short-term projects with a management mentor and spend two weeks in the chancellor's office, three weeks in a college president's office, and four weeks in each vice chancellor's office. Through an open-ended Faculty/Staff Development Program, participants can extend their knowledge in their own and related disciplines. Department chairs explore problem-solving and leadership skills through the Management/Supervisory Training program.

Parallel programs exist for Management, Administrative, and Technological Personnel (MATP) and professional staff. Maintenance and Operations (M&O), Crafts, and Food Service Programs serve the needs of employees in these areas. The Professional Growth Program seeks to increase professional knowledge, update previous academic learning, and sharpen on-the-job thinking skills with the goal of preparation for greater responsibility. The M&O/Crafts Training Program provides opportunities for employees from these areas to become apprentices in areas such as carpentry; electrics; plumbing; heating, ventilation, and air conditioning; and electronics (Filan 1990; Maricopa Community Colleges 1986–87). Contact: Gary Filan, Manager, Organizational Development, Human Resources Division, Maricopa Community Colleges, District Offices, 3910 East Washington, Phoenix, AZ 85034, (602) 461–7324.

University of Nebraska–Lincoln

The Office of Professional and Organizational Development (OPOD) of the College of Agriculture at the University of Nebraska—Lincoln provides an extensive and comprehensive set of development activities. These can be divided into four areas: getting faculty started, supporting more-established faculty, supporting administrative development, and strengthening the institution through organizational development.

OPOD invests significant efforts in helping new faculty feel comfortable with their new positions. Contact begins with informal, individual meetings with OPOD associates. Group orientation sessions are scheduled at the beginning of each semester. Follow-up individual consulting focuses on teaching, a range of professional activities including scholarship, writing, career concerns and issues, and resource acquisition. A Pre-Tenure Support Group, for faculty on a tenure track who have not yet achieved tenure, meets once a month.

Additional activities support more-established faculty. Individual consulting on a range of specific issues is available to support career and life planning. NUPROF (an acronym that alternately stands for "New Professors" or "Nebraska University Professors"), a program for the professional renewal of faculty, is a systematic career reassessment process that provides the opportunity to change career directions. Each year a new NUPROF class is formed. After orientation sessions, all participate in the Faculty Development Institute, a three-day personal and professional assessment retreat. The Institute helps participants to understand themselves better in relation to change, to search for options, and to learn basic career-planning methods. Follow-up includes several months devoted to exploring options and gathering information. Working in trios, participants identify short- and long-term objectives, investigate alternatives, and interview resource people. All this work builds toward the development of a professional growth plan. In a special work session, participants are introduced to the concept of a growth plan (statement of goals, outcomes, and proposed activities) and learn to organize and then write one. After this session, each participant submits a growth plan to the campus steering committee for funding of up to $1,500. During the last phase of NUPROF, participants implement their growth plans. Twelve to 18 months after starting the program, participants evaluate their achievements, particularly regarding their growth plans, and define the next steps toward longer-range plans for additional study and career development.

More-established faculty can also participate in the NUPAGE (not an acronym) project supported by the Kellogg Foundation to develop new partnerships for building innovative, integrated curricula. OPOD also provides information and suggestions on designing faculty sabbaticals.

Equally dynamic programming supports administrators—in particular, department chairs and unit administrators. An annual series of workshops and seminars focuses on topics such as selecting personnel, with an emphasis on interviewing, evaluation, the theory and practice of performance appraisal, the personal and family side of international leaves, and legal issues. An administrative support group meets off campus with an open agenda to discuss topics of mutual interest and concern.

For this group, a centerpiece is the "Administrative Development Map," which is designed to provide a map of the administrative development process from hiring through various development activities across the administrative career. The program is based on the concept that an administrator confronts annually several critical periods and activities. A four-day management training seminar is provided annually for new department heads from a 13-state area. Individual meetings with OPOD associates to identify available resources related to the issues of faculty development are initiated. OPOD hosts new administrators on tours of the campus to introduce them to administrators in various offices and to orient them to campus resources. OPOD associates help to match new administrators with compatible mentors. New administrators are introduced to the policies and procedures of the university through a special workshop. Finally, OPOD provides each new administrator with a copy of its department chair handbook (published by the University of Nebraska Press and based upon research collected through the Lilly Endowment-TIAA/CREF Project on Department Chairs).

To support organizational development, OPOD associates work with units to develop support activities. Such programming helps to establish a common direction and to enhance team work initiatives (Wheeler 1990, 1991; NUPROF; OPOD). Contact: Daniel W. Wheeler, Coordinator, Office of Professional and Organizational Development, Institute of Agriculture and Natural Resources, University of Nebraska–Lincoln, College of Agriculture, 313 Agricultural Hall, Lincoln, NE 68583–0701, (402) 472–5558.

CONCLUSION

On-campus programming is an increasingly important form of leadership development. Because these programs typically originate to address some specifically felt campus needs, the resulting activities tend to be rooted in the culture of the organization. Such programs need to be flexible and grow with the needs of the institution and its faculty, professional staff, and administrators.

Formal on-campus programs are only one form of development. While they can have significant impact, they cannot replace individual development on the job. For faculty and administrators to grow professionally and improve their contributions to the institution, they must have multiple forms of development, including coaching, on-the-job development, and support from supervisors and the organizational structure.

REFERENCES

Anderson, Judith. ''Programs for Professional Enrichment.'' Paper presented at the national conference of the College and University Personnel Association, San Antonio, IL, 14 October 1986.

———. Telephone interview with Sharon A. McDade. 24 May 1990.

———. Letter to Sharon A. McDade. 12 March 1991.

Campanella, Frank B., Raymond F. Keyes, and Leo V. Sullivan. *Management Development for Colleges and Universities.* Boston: Boston College, 1981.

Filan, Gary. Telephone interview with Sharon A. McDade. 10 December 1990.

Jeghelian, Alice. Telephone interview with Sharon A. McDade. 23 August 1990.

———. Letter to Sharon A. McDade. 12 March 1991.

King, Rita. Telephone interview with Sharon A. McDade. 27 November 1990.

———. Letter to Sharon A. McDade. 8 March 1991.

Kotter, John P. *The Leadership Factor.* New York: The Free Press, 1988.

Maricopa Community Colleges. ''Visions: Strategic Plan with 1986–87 Work Plan.'' [Phoenix, AZ]: Maricopa Community Colleges, 1986–87.

———. ''A Summary of the Various Employee Development Programs Available to Employees of the Maricopa Community College District.'' [Phoenix, AZ]: Maricopa Community Colleges, [no date].

McCall, Morgan W., Jr. *Developing Executives through Work Experience.* Technical Report Number 33. Greensboro, NC: Center for Creative Leadership, May 1988.

McCall, Morgan W., Jr., Michael M. Lombardo, and Ann M. Morrison. *The Lessons of Experience: How Successful Executives Develop on the Job.* Lexington, MA: Lexington Books, 1988.

McCauley, Cynthia D. *Developmental Experiences in Managerial Work: A Literature Review.* Technical Report. Number 26. Greensboro, NC: Center for Creative Leadership, January 1986.

NUPROF. Brochure. [Lincoln, NB]: University of Nebraska, Office of Professional and Organizational Development, [no date].

Office of Professional and Organizational Development. ''Office of Professional and Organizational Development (OPOD): Areas of Activities.'' [Lincoln, NB]: University of Nebraska, Office of Professional and Organizational Development, [no date]. Photocopied.

OPOD [Lincoln, NB]: University of Nebraska, Office of Professional and Organizational Development, [no date].

Wheeler, Daniel W. Telephone interview with Madeleine F. Green. 23 February 1990.

———. ''Developmental Map for Unit Administrators—A Think Piece.'' [No date]. Photocopied.

———. Letter to Sharon A. McDade. 7 March 1991.

RESOURCES

Campanella, Frank B., Raymond B. Keyes, and Leo V. Sullivan. *Management Development for Colleges and Universities.* Boston: Boston College, 1981.

Campanella et al. were the officers of Boston College who created an in-house management development program that flourished during the 1970s and early 1980s. This book documents the evolution of the program, its goals and objectives, the curriculum, and the results of post-program evaluation. Although the book may now be difficult to find, it will be very useful reading for any institution that is considering launching its own in-house leadership or management development course for managers.

Cervero, Ronald M. *Effective Continuing Education for Professionals*. San Francisco: Jossey-Bass, 1988.

Although this book's focus is on continuing education within professions such as law and medicine, it has a great deal to say about the learning and development process for all professionals, including the leaders of colleges and universities. Chapters address how professionals learn and acquire expertise, how to foster participation in educational activities, and concepts of effective professional education. For higher education leaders who are considering launching on-campus programs for staff, the book includes insightful discussions on successful program development strategies that have just as much application to in-house development programs as they do to continuing education programming.

Kaplan, Robert E., Wilfred H. Drath, and Joan R. Kofodimos. *High Hurdles: The Challenge of Executive Self-Development*. Technical Report 25. Greensboro, NC: Center for Creative Leadership, April 1985.

A straightforward discussion about how executives can direct their own development. It addresses the issue of how powerful senior executives can obtain objective criticism and accomplish a self-evaluation through introspection. It also tackles the subject of why successful executives discount criticism and have little motivation to change. The report provides a variety of perspectives and tools to help executives understand their need for criticism and the necessity of change.

Kotter, John P. *The Leadership Factor*. New York: The Free Press, 1988.

Based on data from a survey of 900 senior executives in 100 corporations in the United States and in-depth interviews with 150 top managers in successful corporations, Kotter singles out the practices that develop superior leadership. The book analyzes the current corporate environment and relates effective leadership to that environment. The dozens of case histories are particularly instructive. He argues for realistic programs to attract, retain, and motivate leaders in mid-level and senior positions.

McCall, Morgan W., Jr. *Developing Executives through Work Experience*. Technical Report Number 33. Greensboro, NC: Center for Creative Leadership, May 1988.

This report summarizes a series of studies of successful, high-potential executives to discover what learning occurs through on-the-job experiences. It describes 16 developmental experiences, the elements that made them developmental, and the lessons executives learned from them. The report underscores the point that making better use of experience is a significant challenge for organizations that are serious about the development of leadership talent.

McCall, Morgan W., Jr., Michael M. Lombardo, and Ann M. Morrison. *The Lessons of Experience: How Successful Executives Develop on the Job*. Lexington, MA: Lexington Books, 1988.

McCall et al. have interviewed hundreds of corporate executives to understand how they learned to be effective managers and organizational leaders. They developed a template of five areas in which a successful manager must develop skills, and then explored the most effective mechanisms for acquiring those skills, such as learning from job assignments, interactions with other people such as bosses and mentors, and the learning challenges of hardships and crises. The Center for Creative Leadership, where this research was done, publishes technical reports that provide statistical back-up information on the research.

McCauley, Cynthia D. *Developmental Experiences in Managerial Work: A Literature Review*. Technical Report Number 26. Greensboro, NC: Center for Creative Leadership, January 1986.

The best literature review on the subject of developing managers and leaders through on-the-job training.

Schon, Donald A. *Educating the Reflective Practitioner*. San Francisco: Jossey-Bass, 1988.

This book is about the design and purpose of curricula in professions such as architecture, music, and counseling that have specific worlds of practice. While discussing these issues, Schon makes important observations on what he terms the "reflection-in-action" process involved in any professional development activity. This makes the book relevant to anyone thinking about the professional development of managers and faculty. Chapters focus on the coaching process, the development of professional skills, and the teaching and learning process of professional development.

PROGRAMS AND PRACTICES

On-Campus Fellowships, Internships, and Exchanges

The following fellowships, internships, and exchanges are not meant to be a complete listing, but rather a sampling of the range and variety of these types of programs.

Complete information on each program is provided in the *Appendix*. The letter and number in parentheses correspond to the section and entry number in the *Appendix*.

American Council on Education (ACE) (P7)

The Fellows Program *(P7b)*

Arizona State University (ASU) (S2)

Management Development Program Internship *(S2b)*

Beaver College (S4)

Faculty Fellow in Academic Affairs *(S4a)*

Board of Governors of State Colleges and Universities (Illinois) (S5)

Affirmative Action Administrative Fellows Program *(S5a)*

California State University System (CSU) (S7)

Administrative Fellows Program *(S7a)*

Chicago State University (S8)

Minority Administrative Fellow Program *(S8a)*

City University of New York (CUNY) (S9)

Chancellor's Academic Affairs Faculty Fellowship Program *(S9a)*

Committee for Institutional Cooperation (CIC) (S13)

Academic Leadership Fellows Program *(S13a)*

Faculty Exchange Center (P34)

League for Innovation in the Community College, the University of Texas–Austin, and the W. K. Kellogg Foundation (P46)

Expanding Leadership Diversity in Community Colleges *(P46a)*

National Faculty Exchange (NFE) (P58)

Pennsylvania State University (S21)

Administrative Fellows Program *(S21a)*

Tennessee Board of Regents (S26)

Minority Management Development Program *(S26a)*

University of Kansas (S31)

Office of Personnel Services *(S31a)*

University of Massachusetts—Boston (S32)

Staff Exchange Program *(S32a)*

University of South Carolina (S34)

Minority Administrative Fellowship *(S34a)*

University of Southern Colorado (S35)

Faculty Directors Program *(S35a)*

University of Wisconsin System (S39)

Administrative Associate Program *(S39a)*

W. K. Kellogg Foundation (P73)

National Fellowship Program *(P73a)*

State-Wide, System-Specific, and On-Campus Programs

This list of institutional programs is a sampling of the types and range of institution- and system-specific developmental efforts and is not meant to be a comprehensive tally of all programs available from every college or university.

The American University (AU) (S1)

Office of Training and Development Programs *(S1a)*

Arizona State University (ASU) (S2)

Academic Chairs *(S2e)*
Leadership Academy *(S2c)*
Management Development Program (MDP) *(S2a)*
President's Breakfast Series *(S2d)*

Boston College (S6)

Professional Development Programs *(S6a)*

City University of New York (CUNY) (S9)

Women's Leadership Institute *(S9b)*

Colorado State University (S10)

Administrative Women's Network *(S10d)*
Leadership Series *(S10c)*
Professional Development Institute *(S10b)*
Professional Development Programming *(S10a)*

Columbia University (S12)

Connections *(S12b)*
Front Line Leadership Program *(S12c)*
Middle Management Development Program *(S12d)*
Professional Development Programs *(S12a)*

Eastern Illinois University (S14)

Programs for Professional Enrichment (PPE) *(S14a)*

George Washington University (S15)

Training Division of Personnel Services *(S15a)*

Gordon College (S16)

Professional Development Through Growth Plans *(S16a)*

Indiana University—Bloomington (S17)

   Faculty Development Resources *(S17a)*

Kennesaw College (S18)

   Leadership Kennesaw College *(S18a)*

Lansing Community College (S19)

   Community Leadership Development Academy *(S19a)*

Maricopa Community College District (S20)

   M&O/Crafts Training Program *(S20b)*
   Professional Group Program *(S20c)*
   Visions Career Development Program *(S20a)*

Rochester Institute of Technology (RIT) (S22)

   Executive Leadership in an Academic Setting *(S22a)*

St. Norbert College (S25)

   Faculty Development Program *(S25a)*

Stanford University (S23)

   Administrative Development Program *(S23b)*
   Human Resources Development Programs *(S23a)*
   Management Development Program *(S23c)*
   Stanford Supervision and You *(S23d)*

State University of New York (SUNY) (S24)

   Affirmative Action Leave Program *(S24a)*

University of California–Los Angeles (UCLA) (S27)

   Management Enhancement Program *(S27a)*

University of California–Riverside (S28)

   Office of Instructional Development *(S28a)*

University of Iowa (S30)

   Administrative Seminar Program *(S30a)*

University of Kansas (S31)

   Office of Personnel Services *(S31a)*
   Workshops for University Managers *(S31c)*

University of Nebraska–Lincoln/Institute of Agriculture and Natural Resources (S33)

   Administrative Development Map *(S33e)*
   NUPAGE *(S33c)*
   NUPROF *(S33d)*
   Office of Professional and Organizational Development (OPOD) *(S33a)*
   Pre-Tenure Support Group *(S33b)*

University of Southern Colorado (S35)

   Faculty Directors Program *(S35a)*

University of Tennessee (S36)

   Institute for Leadership Effectiveness *(S36a)*

University of Texas–El Paso (S37)

   New Faculty and Staff Orientation Program *(S37a)*

University of Wisconsin–Eau Claire (S38)

   School for Graduate Studies and Office of University Research *(S38a)*

Washington State University (S40)

   Faculty Development and Support Services *(S40a)*

15

INEXPENSIVE DEVELOPMENT IDEAS

Leadership development activities need not be expensive or require extensive logistical support. The inexpensive development ideas listed in this chapter were collected from colleges and universities across the country.

Bring People Together Inside the Institution

- Institute a brown-bag lunch series for workers interested in improving their jobs or positions within the institution. For example, a lunch series for women in mid-level administrative positions could feature a representative from the personnel office to discuss the job search process and visits from various vice presidents to discuss the range of jobs within their units.

- Establish a higher education "book-of-the-month club" discussion composed of faculty, administrators, and even local trustees. Have the library secure sufficient copies of the selection through interlibrary loan so that all group members can read simultaneously.

- Encourage roundtable discussions on salient issues at the conclusion of advisory board committees.

- Conduct faculty luncheons about issues addressed in the *Chronicle of Higher Education*.

- Sponsor late-afternoon faculty forums in which professors make presentations to colleagues on their recent research or share teaching challenges. Advertise a different topic for each session or encourage faculty to prepare short vignettes.

- Encourage administrators to write case studies about management problems that they are currently facing. Then share the stories and solicit feedback from others in the unit or in a discussion group.

- Allow a few days between semesters for seminars by administrators and faculty on topics of professional interest.

- Ensure that one or two members of each committee or task force are new to the project or process. For example, assign a new faculty member to a search committee. The committee can benefit from the reflections of the new member on his or her recently completed search process and the new professor can both learn about how the institution searches for new faculty and develop expertise to serve on future search committees.

- Launch awards programs to recognize faculty, administrators, and staff who make significant contributions to the college and community. Use the awards to encourage leadership in service and community projects, especially projects that are linked to institutional goals.

- Print a booklet of profiles of outstanding faculty who have excelled in teaching, research, and service. Distribute the booklets widely to faculty, administrators, alumni, and students. This will convey the message that high standards of teaching, research, and service are expected and recognized.

- Involve emeriti faculty in campus committees, study groups, and informal discussion groups. Current faculty can benefit from their longer view of history and broad intellectual interests, while the emeriti faculty will enjoy the continued contact with colleagues and scholarship. Emeriti faculty can become an important resource for an institution when provided with continuing linkages and opportunities for mutual support.

- Take new faculty, administrators, and trustees on a tour of the campus to meet key officials in their offices. Such a tour provides vital orientation to the "who and how" of the campus beyond the traditional identification of buildings. Use the tour to identify resources and the processes to use those resources.

- Have emeriti professors, administrators, and staff in the new-employee orientation program explain the traditions and culture of the institution. Ask emeriti employees for anecdotes about the campus that capture key stories, profile leaders and renegades, or explain significant traditions.

- Initiate a faculty development newsletter that focuses on scholarly activities, works in progress, and announcements specifically related to teaching. There also may be benefit in a comparable newsletter for staff and other employees that highlights information on their jobs, institutional benefits, and tips for improving performance.

- Conduct periodic briefings on substantive issues vital to the institution. Although this may be a good forum for using an outside speaker, it also can be an opportunity to charge individuals or teams with preparing a briefing on an issue relevant to the campus. For example, create a team from the admissions, financial aid, government relations, and business offices to present a briefing on recent trends in federal, state, and institutional funding and the impact on institutional financial aid policies.

Expand Experiences

- Launch a "switch day" in which faculty, administrators, and students trade positions for a day. That is, a student spends a day trailing an administrator, an administrator spends a day trailing a professor. This provides people with an unusual opportunity to learn about the jobs of others and to see how the institution looks from their vantage points.

- Have faculty accompany the president and development officers on development visits. Faculty can be particularly effective at discussing their disciplines with potential donors, and the visits give faculty an opportunity to see the fund-raising process first-hand.

- Have faculty and administrators who usually are not involved accompany the hosts of VIPs on campus. They will add a new dimension to the conversation while learning about the institution from the interaction of the official host and the VIP.

- Give administrators, faculty, and trustees the opportunity to spend a weekend, a few days, or a night in a dormitory. Arrange informal sessions with students.

Reach Outside the Institution

- Send a team of faculty, administrators, or trustees to visit another nearby campus for a day to tour the campus, meet with counterparts and discuss common problems, and observe specialized academic programs and facilities.

- Explore group rates for subscriptions to relevant newsletters and journals—for example, a subscription to a department chair newsletter for all department chairs on campus. Use articles in the newsletter as the basis for discussion at department chair meetings and retreats.

- Set up a campus teleconferencing link or establish a relationship with a local television station to use its satellite link so that the institution can tap into the increasing number of teleconferences.

- Advocate involvement in professional organizations. Provide at least a minimum contribution toward the costs of conference participation if a professor or administrator has a leadership role in the organization. Put materials from associations in which the institution holds a membership on reserve in the library or resource center.

- Encourage administrators and professors to bring back materials from conferences they attend. Ask administrators and professors to commit in advance to a post-activity feedback session with colleagues and staff. At this session, suggest they share highlights of interesting sessions, or play an audio-tape of a particularly important session and then lead a discussion on it.

- Gather representatives from sister institutions to discuss common problems and share insights during a national convention.

- Take a team of faculty, administrators, trustees, and professional staff to a convention with a theme specifically related to an institutional objective or initiative. Identify people from among the presenters, members of the association's board, and other regular attenders to meet with the institutional group for private discussions specifically related to campus projects.

- Check for discounted group rates for convention registrations, travel, and lodging. Consider using an institutional van or station wagon for transportation. Could other attenders from the region share transportation costs? Suggest that area corporations make available seats on their airplanes as a donation to the institution.

- Organize a session with other attenders in the area of the campus as a follow-up to a convention. Such a session will reinforce the learning from the conference while building regional networks of people interested in the same topics.

- Add a side trip to another institution when attending a convention. Contact a counterpart at the institution and ask for an interview, tour of the campus, and access to others. Increasingly, associations are organizing group tours of area colleges in conjunction with their meetings. Go beyond the basic admissions tour to focus on a specific interest: for example, learning about efforts to support teaching development through a tour of the teaching center, or exploring computer-related support activities starting with a tour of the computer laboratories.

- Encourage trustees to attend educational meetings. Besides their participation in trustee-oriented events such as the annual meeting of the Association of Governing Boards of Universities and Colleges (AGB), support trustee attendance at other higher education meetings to develop a deeper understanding of the issues involved in that area. For example, the chair of the student affairs committee could attend the annual convention of the National Association of Student and Personnel Administrators (NASPA) with the chief student affairs officer; the head of the trustee academics committee could attend the convention of the American Association for Higher Education (AAHE) with deans and department chairs.

- Tap a consultant affiliated with an appropriate association to conduct a self-evaluation or planning retreat. For example, AGB provides trained board members to conduct board retreats for self-evaluation.

Other associations may not keep a roster of specially trained consultants, but can identify members with particular expertise and experience in evaluation and planning.

Create Relationships

- Team senior and novice administrators or professors as mentors and proteges so that they can share practices and policies that work and discuss campus culture and resource support. Match new department chairs with experienced chairs as mentors and provide a budget for weekly lunches together where new chairs can share problems and challenges. Other mentor pairings could include experienced professors with new faculty members, experienced trustees with new board members, and experienced administrators with new professional staff members.

- Pair new department chairs, faculty, or administrators. Although there is much to be learned from pairing veterans with new people, there are also advantages to pairing, for example, two new department chairs. It is useful to have a companion who is going through the same experiences, with whom one can share reactions and feelings.

Share Knowledge Through Classes and Courses

- Publicize opportunities within the institution to enroll in leadership, management, and job-development courses that are offered through the institution's regular curriculum and in the community. Provide tuition waivers to encourage administrators to attend such courses. Do not forget to include courses in areas such as public speaking, computers, communication, and even sociology or psychology.

- Encourage faculty interdisciplinary study by providing mechanisms that allow them to audit the courses of faculty in other departments.

- Enable trustees to attend classes in conjunction with their attendance at regular trustee meetings. For example, invite trustees to arrive a day early for the meeting and use that day to sit in on classes. Match trustees with classes in areas of their professional expertise, their undergraduate or graduate studies, or their current personal interests.

- Ask faculty members from areas such as management and psychology to present campus workshops on topics like time management, stress reduction, and negotiations. Ask faculty members to lead lunch discussions on management- or teaching-related topics.

- Create special sessions in the student computer laboratory for administrators to learn and experiment with management-assistance software. Invite software representatives to give demonstrations of programs to groups of campus administrators.

- Support special sessions in the student computer laboratory to introduce faculty to the new research, bibliography, relational data base, and memory-assistance programs. Invite software representatives to give demonstrations.

- Provide training to committee chairs on team building and conflict resolution in small groups. Identify members of the psychology, sociology, or business departments who have expertise in small group dynamics to serve as informal advisers to chairs of college committees.

Foster Exchanges

- Urge professors to create a partnership with a sister-campus faculty member who teaches similar courses. Have them schedule each other in their courses for guest lectures and for team-teaching some sessions.

- Support opportunities for faculty to trade teaching assignments with other professors who teach similar courses at a sister school. Both professors in a trade draw their salaries and receive paychecks from their home institutions, but teach at the other institution for a semester or year.

- Facilitate job exchanges in other jobs and places, both internal and external to the institution. Consider cross-training for employees in offices such as admissions and financial aid so that all employees of the office eventually learn how to do all the jobs. Organize mechanisms for job exchanges. Create rotating faculty internship positions in the offices of the president and vice presidents.

- Create interim developmental positions. When a job becomes vacant, do not immediately fill it with a long-term employee. Instead, use the vacancy, with an ''interim'' or ''acting'' designation, to develop people who are not quite ready for a full move but who could benefit from temporary experiences and responsibilities. Deliberately structure the opportunity as a developmental experience, with careful supervision and feedback as an integral part of the learning experience.

Collect Resources

- Assemble a special library of leadership development and management support materials collected at conferences and workshops. Locate it in an area close to where most administrators work. On a small campus, this may be in a reception area in the main administration building; on larger campuses, there may be a need for specialized libraries in the central office area of each unit such as student affairs and development. Encourage administrators to collect materials at conferences specifically for this library.

- Gather materials on teaching in a section of the library or in a special resource center. Encourage faculty to collect materials on teaching at the conferences they attend. Collect copies of syllabi used on the campus or in the unit. Invite faculty to lend to the center any personal materials on teaching. Circulate annotated bibliographies of these books to faculty. Include faculty comments and reviews of the most useful books.

- Make available cassettes from conferences so that others can listen to significant speeches and panel discussions as they drive to and from work.

Share Knowledge

- Encourage administrators within a unit to circulate articles, papers, and other materials of mutual professional interest. Allocate time at staff meetings for comments and observations on the materials. Select one of these articles or papers for deeper discussion at each meeting or initiate special monthly sessions for these discussions.

- Ask administrators and professors to present working papers to colleagues for their reaction before submitting the papers for reviews by journals.

- Persuade administrators or faculty who are going to present papers elsewhere to share their work on campus beforehand as a dress rehearsal. Invite critique of both the paper and its presentation as well as discussion of its content.

Learn in the Community

- Provide support for key administrators and faculty to join corporate or nonprofit boards both to represent the institution and to gain leadership experiences.

- Loan faculty and administrators to local nonprofits or businesses to spearhead special projects.

- Ask senior executives of area businesses to spend a week, month, term, or even a day a week "in residence" to meet with administrative leaders of the college, faculty who teach courses related to the industry, and students interested in business careers.

- Trade the opportunity for institutional officers to enroll in a corporate training program for the space to put on that program on your campus.

- Set up a consulting bank of professors and administrators who can help with problems of businesses and nonprofit groups in the community.

- Create a liberal arts ''great books'' program for local senior executives. Use faculty and resources from the institution to package the program. Formally invite area executives to participate with senior officers of the institution in a semester- or academic year-long program. Besides providing intellectual stimulation for the institution's officers, this activity provides networking opportunities with the community, showcases academic units of the institution that are usually not as visible to the business community, and provides an educational service to the community.

- Organize opportunities for faculty, administrators, professional staff, and technical employees to participate through the college in area public service activities. For example, college employees could serve food at a homeless shelter once a month, staff the ''Meals on Wheels'' program one night a week, or run the recycling project one Saturday a month. As student programs have shown, people are more inclined to become involved if an organizational structure is close at hand.

Involve the Human Resources Department

- Encourage administrators and faculty to submit personal professional development plans with their annual evaluations. Provide support for professional development initiatives, particularly activities organized on campus that will benefit others at the institution.

- Identify jobs with particular developmental potential across the institution. Keep track of the jobs, possible people to move into them, and benefits accrued by those who serve in the jobs. Pay particular attention to high performers who move into these jobs to make certain that support is provided and that obstacles are removed.

- Charge the Human Resources Department with preparing a personal assessment kit—forms and directions for conducting a self-assessment and a job assessment, and for developing short- and long-term professional goals. As in preparing a budget and long-term financial plan, people avoid self- and job assessment because of the initial difficulty of pulling all the information together and finding and then reading appropriate supporting materials. If the Human Resources Department does the organizational work and puts together a useful package, there is a greater possibility that employees will take the time for self-assessment.

- Prompt the Personnel or Human Resources office to keep lists of high performers, faculty and administrators who have indicated interest in new assignments, and those who may be ready for new challenges. When a job becomes vacant, consider filling it temporarily with someone from these lists while the search is conducted. Such short-term positions, with close supervision and coaching, can provide invaluable training and exposure as well as a test ground for emerging talent. The same lists may be useful to provide temporary fill-ins for people on vacation or attending long-term professional development programs.

- Request evidence of development of subordinates as part of supervisory evaluations. If development has institutional commitment, the responsibility for development should be included in the performance appraisal process.

RESOURCES

Lombardo, Michael M., and Robert W. Eichinger. *Eighty-Eight Assignments for Development in Place: Enhancing the Development Challenge of Existing Jobs*. Report Number 136. Greensboro, NC: Center for Creative Leadership, 1989.

This short booklet lays out on-the-job development activities in five categories relating to challenging jobs, working with other people, enduring hardships, coursework, and off-the-job-experiences. The activities involve small projects and start-ups, small-scope jumps and fix-its, small strategic assignments, coursework and coaching assignments, and activities away from work. Although the activities are designed for business and corporation employees, they are highly adaptable to those in colleges and universities.

Part Four:

APPENDICES

PROGRAMS AND PRACTICES

ASSOCIATIONS

The following list includes a representative sampling of major associations for faculty and administrators of colleges and universities. It is not meant to be a comprehensive listing, but rather is intended to provide information on major associations in a wide range of academic disciplines and administrative specializations. Regional organizations (academic or institutional) and associations for medical specializations are not included.

(A1) **Academy of International Business (AIB)**
A. B. Freeman School of Business, Tulane University, New Orleans, LA 70118–5669
(504) 865–5563
Gerard E. Watzke, Executive Secretary

(A2) **Academy of Management (AM)**
P. O. Box 39, Ada, OH 45810
(419) 772–1953
Ken Cooper, Secretary/Treasurer

(A3) **Academy of Marketing Science (AMS)**
School of Business Administration, P. O. Box 248012, University of Miami, Coral Gables, FL 33124
(305) 284–6673
Harold W. Berkman, Executive Vice President and Director

(A4) **Administrators and Teachers of English as a Second Language (ATESL)**
1860 19th Street, NW, Washington, DC 20009
(202) 462–4811
Colin Davies, Contact

(A5) **American Academy of Religion (AAR)**
Department of Religion, 401 Hall of Languages, Syracuse University, Syracuse, NY 13244–1170
(315) 443–4019
James B. Wiggins, Executive Director

(A6)   **American Alliance for Health, Physical Education, Recreation, and Dance (AAHPERD)**
1900 Association Drive, Reston, VA 22091
(703) 476-3400
Gil Brown, Executive Vice President

(A7)   **American Anthropological Association (AAA)**
1703 New Hampshire Avenue, NW, Washington, DC 20009
(202) 232-8800
Eugene L. Sterud, Executive Director

(A8)   **American Assembly of Collegiate Schools of Business (AACSB)**
605 Old Ballas Road, Suite 220, Saint Louis, MO 63141-7077
(314) 872-8481
William K. Laidlaw, Jr., Executive Vice President

(A9)   **American Association for Adult and Continuing Education (AAACE)**
1112 Sixteenth Street, NW, Suite 420, Washington, DC 20036
(202) 463-6333
Judith A. Koloski, Executive Director

(A10)   **American Association for Counseling and Development (AACD)**
5999 Stevenson Avenue, Alexandria, VA 22304
(703) 823-9800
Theodore P. Remley, Executive Director

(A11)   **American Association for Higher Education (AAHE)**
One Dupont Circle, NW, Suite 600, Washington, DC 20036
(202) 293-6440
Russell Edgerton, President

(A12)   **American Association for the Advancement of Science (AAAS)**
1333 H Street, NW, Washington, DC 20005
(202) 326-6400
Richard S. Nichelson, Executive Director

(A13)   **American Association for the Advancement of Slavic Studies (AAASS)**
128 Encina Commons, Stanford University, Stanford, CA 94305-6029
(415) 723-9668
Dorothy Atkinson, Executive Director

(A14)   **American Association of Bible Colleges (AABC)**
P.O. Box 1523, Fayetteville, AR 72702
(501) 521-8164
Randall E. Bell, Executive Director

(A15)   **American Association of Colleges for Teacher Education (AACTE)**
One Dupont Circle, NW, Suite 610, Washington, DC 20036-2412
(202) 293-2450
David G. Imig, Executive Director

(A16)   **American Association of Colleges of Nursing (AACN)**
One Dupont Circle, NW, Suite 530, Washington, DC 20036
(202) 463-6930
Geraldine Bednash, Executive Director

(A17)   **American Association of Colleges of Osteopathic Medicine (AACOM)**
6110 Executive Boulevard, Suite 405, Rockville, MD 20852
(301) 468-0990
Sherry R. Arnstein, Executive Director

(A18)   **American Association of Collegiate Registrars and Admissions Officers (AACRAO)**
One Dupont Circle, NW, Suite 330, Washington, DC 20036-1171
(202) 293-9161
Wayne E. Becraft, Executive Director

(A19)   **American Association of Community and Junior Colleges (AACJC)**
One Dupont Circle, NW, Suite 410, Washington, DC 20036
(202) 728-0200
David Pierce, President

(A20)   **American Association of Dental Schools (AADS)**
1625 Massachusetts Avenue, NW, Suite 502, Washington, DC 20036
(202) 667-9433
Preston Littleton, Executive Director

(A21)   **American Association of Philosophy Teachers (AAPT)**
1000 Stanton L. Young Boulevard, Library #418, University of Oklahoma, Oklahoma City, OK 73190-3046
(405)271-2111
Richard A. Wright, Executive Director

(A22)   **American Association of Phonetic Sciences (AAPS)**
63 Dauer Hall, University of Florida, Gainesville, FL 32611-2005
(904) 392-2046
W. S. Brown, Jr., Executive Secretary

(A23)   **American Association of Physics Teachers (AAPT)**
5112 Berwyn Road, College Park, MD 20740
(301) 345-4200
Bernard V. Khoury, Executive Officer

(A24) **American Association of Presidents of Independent Colleges and Universities (AAPICU)**
Pepperdine University, 24255 Pacific Coast Highway, Malibu, CA 90263
(213) 456–4888
David Davenport, President

(A25) **American Association of State Colleges and Universities (AASCU)**
One Dupont Circle, NW, Suite 700, Washington, DC 20036
(202) 293–7070
James B. Appleberry, President

(A26) **American Association of Teachers of Arabic (AATA)**
280 HRCB, Kennedy Center, Brigham Young University, Provo, UT 84602
(801) 378–3377
Delworth B. Parkinson, Jr., Executive Director

(A27) **American Association of Teachers of German (AATG)**
112 Haddontowne Court, Suite 104, Cherry Hill, NJ 08034
(609) 795–5553
Helene Zimmer-Loew, Executive Director

(A28) **American Association of Teachers of Slavic and East European Languages (AATSEEL)**
Department of Foreign Languages and Literature, Northern Illinois University, Watson Hall, Dekalb, IL 60115
(815) 753–9685
George Gutsche, Executive Director

(A29) **American Association of Teachers of Spanish and Portugese (AATSP)**
P. O. Box 6349, Mississippi State University, Mississippi State, MS 39762–6349
(601) 325–2041
James R. Chatham, Executive Director

(A30) **American Association of University Administrators (AAUA)**
George Washington University, 2121 I Street, NW, Rice Hall, 7th Floor, Washington, DC 20052
(202) 994–6503
Susan Kaplan, General Secretary

(A31) **American Association of University Professors (AAUP)**
1012 14th Street, NW, Suite 500, Washington, DC 20005
(202) 737–5900
Ernst Benjamin, General Secretary

(A32) **American Association of University Women (AAUW)**
1111 16th Street, NW, Washington, DC 20036
(202) 785–7700
Anne L. Bryant, Executive Director

(A33)   **American Association of Women in Community and Junior Colleges (AAWCJC)**
2907 N. Main Street, Anderson, SC 29621
(803) 226–5566
Leila Gonzales Sullivan, President

(A34)   **American Astronomical Society (AAS)**
2000 Florida Avenue, NW, Suite 300, Washington, DC 20009
(202) 328–2010
Peter B. Boyce, Executive Officer

(A35)   **American Business Law Association (ABLA)**
Western Carolina University, School of Business, Cullowhee, NC 28723
(704) 227–7401
Daniel J. Herron, Executive Secretary

(A36)   **American Chemical Society (ACS)**
1155 16th Street, NW, Washington, DC 20036
(202) 872–4589
John K. Crum, Executive Director

(A37)   **American College Personnel Association (ACPA)**
5999 Stevenson Avenue, Alexandria, VA 22304
(703) 823–9800
Leila Moore, President

(A38)   **American Comparative Literature Association (ACLA)**
Comparative Literature Department, Brigham Young University, Provo, UT 84602
(801) 378–5529
Larry H. Peer, Secretary/Treasurer

(A39)   **American Conference of Academic Deans (ACAD)**
1818 R Street, NW, Washington, DC 20009
(202) 387–3760
Maria-Helena Price, Executive Officer

(A40)   **American Council on Education (ACE)**
One Dupont Circle, NW, Suite 800, Washington, DC 20036
(202) 939–9300
Robert H. Atwell, President

(A41)   **American Council on Education/National Identification Program for the Advancement of Women in Higher Education (ACE/NIP)**
Office of Women in Higher Education, One Dupont Circle, NW, Suite 800, Washington, DC 20036
(202) 939–9390
Donna Shavlik, Director
Note: Each state has a state-based program with its own coordinator.

(A42) **American Economic Association (AEA)**
1313 21st Avenue South, Nashville, TN 37212
(615) 322–2595
Elton Hinshaw, Secretary/Treasurer

(A43) **American Educational Research Association (AERA)**
1230 17th Street, NW, Washington, DC 20036
(202) 223–9485
William J. Russell, Executive Officer

(A44) **American Forensic Association (AFA)**
North Dakota State University, Department of Communication,
  Minard Hall, Box 50–75, Fargo, ND 58105
(701) 237–7783
Robert Littlefield, Secretary

(A45) **American Historical Association (AHA)**
400 A Street, NE, Washington, DC 20003
(202) 544–2422
Samuel R. Gammon, Executive Director

(A46) **American Indian Higher Education Consortium (AIHEC)**
513 Central Court, NE, Suite 100, Washington, DC 20002
(202) 544–9289
Joseph McDonald, President

(A47) **American Institute of Biological Sciences (AIBS)**
730 11th Street, NW, Washington, DC 20001–4584
(202) 628–1500
Charles M. Chambers, Executive Director

(A48) **American Institute of Nutrition (AIN)**
9650 Rockville Pike, Bethesda, MD 20814
(301) 530–7050
Richard G. Allison, Executive Officer

(A49) **American Legal Studies Association (ALSA)**
341 Cushing Hall, Northeastern University, Boston, MA 02115
(617) 437–5211
Leonard G. Buckle, President

(A50) **American Library Association (ALA)**
50 E Huron Street, Chicago, IL 60611
(312) 944–6780
Linda L. Cresmen, Executive Director

(A51) **American Mathematical Association of Two Year Colleges
(AMATYC)**
Parkland College, 2400 West Bradley Avenue, Champaign, IL
  61821
(217) 351–2440
Dale Ewing, President

(A52) **American Mathematical Society (AMS)**
P. O. Box 6248, Providence, RI 02940
(401) 272–9500
William H. Jaco, Executive Director

(A53) **American Medical Association/Council on Medical Education
(CME-AMA)**
515 North State Street, Chicago, IL 60610
(312) 464–4933
William Areals, Chairman

(A54) **American Musicological Society (AMS)**
201 South 34th Street, University of Pennsylvania, Philadelphia,
PA 19104–6313
(215) 898–8698
Alvin H. Johnson, Executive Director

(A55) **American Philosophical Society (APA)**
University of Delaware, Newark, DE 19716
(302) 451–1112
David A. Hoekeman, Executive Director

(A56) **American Physical Society (APS)**
335 East 45th Street, New York, NY 10017
(212) 682–7341
William W. Havens. Jr., Executive Secretary

(A57) **American Political Science Association (APSA)**
1527 New Hampshire Avenue, NW, Washington, DC 20036
(202) 483–2512
Catherine E. Rudder, Executive Director

(A58) **American Psychological Association (APA)**
1200 17th Street, NW, Washington, DC 20036
(202) 955–7600
Raymond Fowler, Director

(A59) **American Society for Engineering Education (ASEE)**
Eleven Dupont Circle, NW, Suite 200, Washington, DC
20036–1207
(202) 293–7080
Frank L. Huband, Executive Director

(A60) **American Society for Microbiology (ASM)**
1325 Massachusetts Avenue, NW, Washington, DC 20005
(202) 737–3600
Michael Goldberg, Executive Director

(A61) **American Society for Theatre Research (ASTR)**
Theatre Arts Program, University of Pennsylvania, Philadelphia, PA 19104
(215) 898–7382
Cary M. Mazer, Secretary

(A62)   **American Society for Training and Development (ASTD)**
1640 King Street, Box 1443, Alexandria, VA 22313
(703) 683–8100
Curtis E. Plott, Executive Vice President

(A63)   **American Society of Allied Health Professions (ASAHP)**
1101 Connecticut Avenue, NW, Suite 700, Washington, DC
   20036
(202) 857–1150
Carolyn M. Del Polito Freelan, Executive Director

(A64)   **American Society of Cytology (ASC)**
1015 Chestnut Street, Suite 1518, Philadelphia, PA 19107
(215) 922–3880
Zuher M. Naib, President

(A65)   **American Society of International Law (ASIL)**
2223 Massachusetts Avenue, NW, Washington, DC 20008
(202) 265–4313
John Lawrence Hargrove, Executive Director

(A66)   **American Society of Parasitologists (ASP)**
Department of Biological Sciences, 500 West University Avenue,
   University of Texas—El Paso, El Paso, TX 79968
(915) 747–5844
Lilian F. Mayberry, Secretary/Treasurer

(A67)   **American Society of Zoologists (ASZ)**
104 Sirius Circle, Thousand Oaks, CA 91360
(805) 492–3585
Mary Adams-Wiley, Executive Officer

(A68)   **American Sociological Association (ASA)**
1722 North Street, NW, Washington, DC 20036
(202) 833–3410
William V. D'Antonio, Executive Officer

(A69)   **American Speech-Language-Hearing Association (ASLHA)**
10801 Rockville Pike, Rockville, MD 20852
(301) 897–5700
Frederick T. Spahr, Executive Director

(A70)   **American Statistical Association (ASA)**
1429 Duke Street, Alexandria, VA 22314
(703) 684–1221
Barbara A. Bailar, Executive Director

(A71)   **American Studies Association (ASA)**
2140 Taliaferro Building, University of Maryland, College Park,
   MD 20742
(301) 454–2533
John F. Stephens, Executive Director

(A72)   **American Veterinary Medical Association (AVMA)**
930 North Meacham Road, Schaumburg, IL 60196
(708) 605–8070
Roland Dommert, President

(A73)   **American Vocational Association (AVA)**
1410 King Street, Alexandria, VA 22314
(703) 683–3111
Charles H. Buzzell, Executive Director

(A74)   **Archaeological Institute of America (AIA)**
675 Commonwealth Avenue, Boston, MA 02215
(617) 353–9361
Mark Meister, Director

(A75)   **Association for Asian Studies (AAS)**
One Lane Hall, University of Michigan, Ann Arbor, MI 48109
(313) 665–2490
L. A. Peter Gosling, Secretary-Treasurer

(A76)   **Association for Biology Laboratory Education (ABLE)**
Department of Biology, 3401 South 39th Street, Alverno College,
   Milwaukee, WI 53215
(414) 382–6205
Leona Truckan, President

(A77)   **Association for Business Communications (ABC)**
Department of Management, College of Business Administration, University of North Texas, Denton, TX 76203
(817) 565–4423
John D. Pettit, Jr., Executive Director

(A78)   **Association for Communication Administration (ACA)**
311 Wilson Hall, Murray State University, Murray, KY 42071
(512) 762–3411
Vernon Gantt, Executive Director

(A79)   **Association for Continuing Higher Education (ACHE)**
Indiana University/Purdue University at Indianapolis,
   355 North Lansing Street, Indianapolis, IN 46202–5171
(317) 274–2637
Scott Evenbeck, Executive Vice President

(A80)   **Association for Institutional Research (AIR)**
314 Stone Building, Florida State University, Tallahassee, FL
   32306–3038
(904) 644–4470
Jean C. Chulak, Administrative Director

(A81)   **Association for Library and Information Science Education
(ALISE)**
5623 Palm Aire Drive, Sarasota, FL 34243
(813) 355–1795
Ilse Moon, Executive Secretary

(A82) **Association for School, College, and University Staffing, Inc. (ASCUS)**
1600 Dodge Avenue, S-330, Evanston, IL 60201–3451
(708) 864–1999
Charles A. Marshall, Executive Director

(A83) **Association for Theater in Higher Education (ATHE)**
Theater Service, P.O. Box 15282, Evansville, IN 47716
(812) 474–0549
Gil Lazer, President

(A84) **Association for the Study of Higher Education (ASHE)**
Texas A&M University, Department of Education and Administration, College Station, TX 77843–4226
(409) 845–0393
D. Stanley Carpenter, Executive Director

(A85) **Association of African Studies Programs (AASP)**
Department of Government and International Studies, University of South Carolina, Columbia, SC 29208
(803) 777–3108
Mark W. DeLancey, Chairman

(A86) **Association of American Colleges (AAC)**
1818 R Street, NW, Washington, DC 20009
(202) 387–3760
Paula P. Brownlee, President

(A87) **Association of American Geographers (AAG)**
1710 16th Street, NW, Washington, DC 20009–3198
(202) 234–1450
Ronald Adler, Executive Director

(A88) **Association of American Law Schools (AALS)**
1201 Connecticut Avenue, NW, Suite 800, Washington, DC 20036
(202) 296–8851
Betsy Levin, Executive Director

(A89) **Association of American Medical Colleges (AAMC)**
One Dupont Circle, NW, Suite 200, Washington, DC 20036
(202) 828–0400
Robert Petersdorf, President

(A90) **Association of American Universities (AAU)**
One Dupont Circle, NW, Suite 730, Washington, DC 20036
(202) 466–5030
Robert M. Rosenzweig, President

(A91) **Association of American University Presses (AAUP)**
584 Broadway, Room 410, New York, NY 10012
(212) 941–6610
Peter C. Grenquist, Executive Director

(A92)   **Association of Caribbean Studies (ACS)**
P. O. Box 22202, Lexington, KY 20502
(606) 257–6966
G. R. Dathorne, Executive Director

(A93)   **Association of Catholic Colleges and Universities (ACCU)**
One Dupont Circle, NW, Suite 650, Washington, DC 20036
(202) 457–0650
Alice Gallin, O.S.U., Executive Director

(A94)   **Association of Chairmen of Departments of Mechanics
(ACDM)**
Department of Engineering Mechanics, Ohio State University,
    209 Boyd Lab, 155 W. Woodruff Avenue, Columbus, OH 43210
(614) 292–2731
Sunder Advani, President

(A95)   **Association of College and University Auditors (ACUA)**
104 Coke Building, Texas A&M University, College Station, TX
    77843–6000
(409) 845–8112
Gary W. O'Neal, President

(A96)   **Association of College and University Housing Officers—
International (ACUHO-I)**
101 Curl Drive, Suite 140, Columbus, OH 43210–1195
(614) 292–0099
Jeannette Songer, Supervisor

(A97)   **Association of College Unions—International (ACU-I)**
400 East 7th Street, Bloomington, IN 47405
(812) 332–8017
Richard Blackburn, Executive Director

(A98)   **Association of Collegiate Schools of Architecture (ACSA)**
1735 New York Avenue, NW, Washington, DC 20006
(202) 785–2324
Richard McCommons, Executive Director

(A99)   **Association of Collegiate Schools of Planning (ACSP)**
Office of Academic Affairs, University of Toledo, Toledo, OH
    43606
(419) 537–2587
Carl V. Patton, President

(A100)   **Association of Community College Trustees (ACCT)**
1740 N Street, NW, Washington, DC 20036
(202) 347–1740
Raymond Taylor, Executive Director

(A101)   **Association of Conference and Events Directors—International (ACED-I)**
Colorado State University, Rockwell Hall, Ft. Collins, CO 80523
(303) 491–5151
Jill Lancaster, Director

(A102)   **Association of Departments of English (ADE)**
10 Astor Place, New York, NY 10003–6981
(212) 614–6317
David Laurence, Director

(A103)   **Association of Departments of Foreign Languages (ADFL)**
10 Astor Place, New York, NY 10003–6981
(212) 614–6319
David Goldberg, Associate Director

(A104)   **Association of Episcopal Colleges (AEC)**
805 Second Avenue, New York, NY 10017
(212) 986–0989
Linda A. Chisholm, President

(A105)   **Association of Governing Boards of Universities and Colleges (AGB)**
One Dupont Circle, NW, Suite 400, Washington, DC 20036
(202) 296–8400
Robert L. Gale, President

(A106)   **Association of Independent Colleges and Schools (AICS)**
One Dupont Circle, NW, Suite 350, Washington, DC 20036
(202) 659–2460
James Phillips, Executive Director

(A107)   **Association of Jesuit Colleges and Universities (AJCU)**
1424 Sixteenth Street NW, Suite 504, Washington, DC 20036
(202) 667–3889
Paul S. Tipton, S.J., President

(A108)   **Association of Military Colleges and Schools of the United States (AMCS)**
9115 McNair Drive, Alexandria, VA 22309
(703) 360–1678
Lt. Gen. Willard W. Scott (ret), Executive Director

(A109)   **Association of Physical Plant Administrators of Universities and Colleges (APPA)**
1446 Duke Street, Alexandria, VA 22314–3492
(703) 684–1446
Walter A. Schaw, Executive Vice President

(A110) **Association of Research Libraries (ARL)**
1527 New Hampshire Avenue, NW, 4th Floor, Washington, DC 20036
(202) 232–2466
Duane Webster, Executive Director

(A111) **Association of Schools of Journalism and Mass Communication (ASJMC)**
Association of Education of Journalism and Mass Communication (AEJMC)
1621 College Street, University of South Carolina, Columbia, SC 29208–0205
(803) 777–2005
Jennifer McGill, Executive Director

(A112) **Association of Southern Baptist Colleges and Schools (ASBCS)**
901 Commerce Street, Suite 600, Nashville, TN 37203–3630
(615) 244–2362
Arthur L. Walker, Jr., Executive Secretary

(A113) **Association of Teacher Educators (ATE)**
1900 Association Drive, Reston, VA 22091–1599
(703) 620–3110
Gloria Chernay, Executive Director

(A114) **Association of Teachers of Technical Writing (ATTW)**
Department of Rhetoric, University of Minnesota, 202 Haecker Hall, St. Paul, MN 55108
(612) 624–6206
Victoria M. Mikelonis, President

(A115) **Association of Theological Schools in the United States and Canada (ATS)**
10 Summit Park Drive, Pittsburgh, PA 15275–1103
(412) 788–6505
James Waits, Executive Director

(A116) **Association of University Summer Sessions (AUSS)**
Maxwell Hall 254, Indiana University, Bloomington, IN 47405
(812) 855–5048
Leslie J. Coyne, Recorder

(A117) **Association of Urban Universities (AUU)**
P.O. Box 33276, Washington, DC 20033
(301) 229–6037
James B. Harrison, President

(A118) **Broadcast Education Association (BEA)**
1771 North Street, NW, Washington, DC 20036–2891
(202) 429–5355
Louisa A. Nielsen, Executive Director

(A119) **CAUSE (Association for the Management of Information Technology in Higher Education)**
4840 Pearl East Circle, Suite 302E, Boulder, CO 80301–2487
(303) 449–4430
Jane N. Ryland, President

(A120) **College and University Computer Users Conference (CUCUC)**
1244 Blossom Street, Columbia, SC 29208
(803) 777–6890
Fred Goebler, Coordinator

(A121) **College and University Personnel Association (CUPA)**
1233 20th Street, NW, Suite 503, Washington, DC 20036
(202) 429–0311
Richard C. Creal, Executive Director

(A122) **College English Association (CEA)**
4245 East Avenue, Nazareth College of Rochester, Rochester, NY 14618
(716) 586–2525
John J. Joyce, Executive Director

(A123) **College Media Advisers (CMA)**
MJ-300, Department of Journalism, Memphis State University, Memphis, TN 38152
(901) 678–2403
Ronald E. Spielberger, Headquarters Manager

(A124) **College Placement Council (CPC)**
62 Highland Avenue, Bethlehem, PA 18017
(215) 868–1421
Warren E. Kauffman, Executive Director

(A125) **Cooperative Education Association (CEA)**
3311 Toledo Terrace, Suite A101, Hyattsville, MD 20782
(301) 559–8850
Dena Zook, Executive Secretary

(A126) **Council for Adult and Experiential Learning (CAEL)**
223 West Jackson Boulevard, Suite 510, Chicago, IL 60606
(312) 922–5909
Pamela Tate, President

(A127) **Council for Advancement and Support of Education (CASE)**
Eleven Dupont Circle, NW, Suite 400, Washington, DC 20036
(202) 328–5900
Peter Buchanan, President

(A128) **Council for Agricultural Science and Technology (CAST)**
137 Lynn Avenue, Ames, IA 50010–7197
(515) 292–2125
Stanley P. Wilson, Executive Vice President

(A129) **Council of 1890 College Presidents (CCP)**
Delaware State College, Dover, DE 19901
(302) 736–4901
William DeLauder, President

(A130) **Council of Colleges of Arts and Sciences (CCAS)**
Ohio State University, 186 University Hall, 230 North Oval Mall,
    Columbus, OH 43210–1319
(614) 292–1882
Richard J. Hopkins, Executive Director

(A131) **Council of Graduate Schools (CGS)**
One Dupont Circle, NW, Suite 430, Washington, DC 20036
(202) 223–3791
Jules B. LaPidus, President

(A132) **Council of Independent Colleges (CIC)**
One Dupont Circle, NW, Suite 320, Washington, DC 20036
(202) 466–7230
Allen P. Splete, President

(A133) **Council of Writing Program Administrators (CWPA)**
Department of English, Miami University, Oxford, OH 45056
(513) 424–4444
Jeffrey Sommers, Secretary-Treasurer

(A134) **Council on Governmental Relations (COGR)**
One Dupont Circle, NW, Suite 670, Washington, DC 20036
(202) 861–2595
Milton Goldberg, Executive Director

(A135) **Council on Social Work Education (CSWE)**
1600 Duke Street, Suite 300, Alexandria, VA 22314
(703) 683–8080
Donald Beless, Executive Director

(A136) **Ecological Society of America (ESA)**
Center for Environmental Studies, Arizona State University,
    Tempe, AZ 85287
(602) 965–3000
Duncan T. Patten, Business Manager

(A137) **Economic History Association (EHA)**
Department of History, George Washington University, Wash-
    ington, DC 20052
(202) 994–6052
William H. Becker, Secretary/Treasurer

(A138) **Entomological Society of American (ESA)**
9301 Annapolis Road, Lanham, MD 20706–3115
(301) 731–4535
W. Darryl Hansen, Executive Director

(A139) **Financial Management Association (FMA)**
College of Business Administration, Department of Finance,
   University of South Florida, Tampa, FL 33620
(813) 974–2084
Jack S. Rader, Executive Director

(A140) **Geological Society of America (GSA)**
P. O. Box 9140, 3300 Penrose Place, Boulder, CO 80301
(303) 447–2020
F. Michael Wahl, Executive Director

(A141) **Higher Education Resource Service (HERS)**
Cheever House, Wellesley College, MA 02181
(617) 235–0320
Cynthia Secor, Executive Director

(A142) **Hispanic Association of Colleges and Universities (HACU)**
411 SW 24th Street, San Antonio, TX 78207
(512) 433–1501
Antonio Rigual, President

(A143) **History of Science Society (HSS)**
35 Dean Street, Worcester, MA 01609
(508) 831–5712
Michael M. Sokal, Executive Secretary

(A144) **International Association of Campus Law Enforcement Administrators (IACLEA)**
638 Prospect Avenue, Hartford, CT 06105
(203) 233–4531
Peter J. Berry, Executive Director

(A145) **International Council of Fine Arts Deans (ICFAD)**
P. O. Box 1772, Department of Music, Southwest Texas State
   University, San Marcos, TX 78667–4616
(512) 245–2651
John E. Green, Executive Director

(A146) **International Technology Education Association (ITEA)**
1914 Association Drive, Reston, VA 22091
(703) 860–2100
Kendall N. Starkweathers, Executive Director

(A147) **Jesuit Association of Student Personnel Administrators
(JASPA)**
Broadway and Madison, Seattle University, Seattle, WA 98122
(206) 296–6274
Judith Sharpe, President

(A148) **Linguistic Society of America (LSA)**
1325 18th Street, NW, Suite 211, Washington, DC 20036–6501
(202) 835–1714
Margaret W. Reynolds, Executive Director

(A149) **Lutheran Educational Conference of North America (LECNA)**
122 C Street, NW, Suite 300, Washington, DC 20001
(202) 783–7505
Donald Stoike, Executive Director

(A150) **Mathematical Association of American (MAA)**
1529 18th Street, NW, Washington, DC 20036
(202) 387–5200
Marcia P. Sward, Executive Director

(A151) **Modern Language Association of America (MLA)**
10 Astor Place, 5th Floor, New York, NY 10003–6981
(212) 475–9500
Phyllis Franklin, Executive Director

(A152) **Music Educators National Conference (MENC)**
1902 Association Drive, Reston, VA 22091
(703) 860–4000
John J. Mahlmann, Executive Director

(A153) **National Academic Advising Association (NAcAcA)**
11300 Northeast Second Avenue, Barry University, Miami, FL
33161
(305) 899–3000
Eileen McDonough, Secretary

(A154) **National Association for Core Curriculum (NACC)**
404 White Hall, Kent State University, Kent, OH 44242
(216) 672–2792
Gordon F. Vars, Executive Secretary/Treasurer

(A155) **National Association for Equal Opportunity in Higher Education (NAFEO)**
Lovejoy Building, 400 12th Street, NE, 2nd floor, Washington,
DC 20002
(202) 543–9111
Samuel L. Myers, President

(A156) **National Association for Ethnic Studies (NAES)**
Department of English, Arizona State University, Tempe, AZ
85287–0302
(602) 965–2197
Christine Wilcox, Executive Director

(A157) **National Association for Women in Education (NAWE)**
Formerly National Association for Women Deans, Administrators, and Counselors (NAWDAC)
1324 18th Street, NW, Suite 210, Washington, DC 20036
(202) 659–9330
Patricia A. Rueckel, Executive Director
Note: Many states also have chapters.

(A158) **National Association of Academic Affairs Administrators (AcAfAd)**
Berklee College of Music, 1140 Boyleston Street, Boston, MA 02215
(617) 266–1400x212
Ronald C. Bentley, Roster/Membership Chair

(A159) **National Association of Biology Teachers (NABT)**
11250 Roger Bacon Drive, #19, Reston, VA 22090
(703) 471–1134
Patricia J. McWethy, Executive Director

(A160) **National Association of College Admission Counselors (NACAC)**
1800 Diagonal Road, Suite 430, Alexandria, VA 22314
(703) 836–2222
Frank E. Burnett, Executive Director

(A161) **National Association of College and University Attorneys (NACUA)**
One Dupont Circle, NW, Suite 620, Washington, DC 20036
(202) 833–8390
Phillip M. Grier, Executive Director

(A162) **National Association of College and University Business Officers (NACUBO)**
One Dupont Circle, NW, Suite 500, Washington, DC 20036
(202) 861–2500
Caspa L. Harris, President

(A163) **National Association of College and University Food Services (NACUFS)**
Michigan State University, 1405 South Harrison Road, Manly Miles Building, Suite 303, East Lansing, MI 48824
(517) 332–2494
Joseph Spina, Executive Director

(A164) **National Association of College Deans, Registrars, and Admissions Officers (NACDRAO)**
917 Dorset Avenue, Albany, GA 31701
(912) 435–4945
Helen Mayes, Executive Secretary

(A165) **National Association of Colleges and Teachers of Agriculture (NACTA)**
Delaware Valley College, Doylestown, PA 18901
(215) 345–1500
John C. Mertz, Executive Director

(A166) **National Association of Education Office Personnel (NAEOP)**
P. O. Box 12619, Wichita, KS 67277–2619
(316) 942–4822
Patricia Huggins, President

(A167) **National Association of Educational Buyers, Inc. (NAEB)**
180 Froeklick Farm Boulevard, Woodbury, NY 11797
(516) 364–6000
Neil D. Markee, Executive Vice President

(A168) **National Association of Geology Teachers (NAGT)**
Department of Geology, Western Washington, University,
Bellingham, WA 98225
(206) 676–3587
Robert Christman, Secretary/Treasurer

(A169) **National Association of Independent Colleges and Universities (NAICU)**
122 C Street, NW, Suite 750, Washington, DC 20001–2190
(202) 347–7512
Richard F. Rosser, President

(A170) **National Association of Personnel Workers (NAPW)**
Howard University, 2601 16th Street NW, Washington, DC 20089
(202) 806–4116
Nathaniel Thomas, President

(A171) **National Association of Schools and Colleges of the United Methodist Church (NASCUMC)**
P.O. Box 871, Nashville, TN 37202
(615) 340–7399
Kenjiro Yamada, Secretary/ Treasurer

(A172) **National Association of Schools of Art and Design (NASAD)**
National Association of Schools of Dance (NASD)
National Association of Schools of Music (NASM)
National Association of Schools of Theater (NAST)
11250 Roger Bacon Drive, Suite 21, Reston, VA 22090
(703) 437–0700
Samuel Hope, Executive Director

(A173) **National Association of State Universities and Land-Grant Colleges (NASULGC)**
One Dupont Circle, NW, Suite 710, Washington, DC 20036–1191
(202) 778–0818
Robert L. Clodius, President

(A174) **National Association of Student Financial Aid Administrators (NASFAA)**
1920 L Street, NW, Suite 200, Washington, DC 20036
(202) 785–0453
A. Dallas Martin, Jr., President

(A175) **National Association of Student Personnel Administrators (NASPA)**
1700 18th Street, NW, Suite 301, Washington, DC 20009–2508
(202) 265–7500
Elizabeth M. Nuss, Executive Director

(A176) **National Association of Trade and Technical Schools (NATTS)**
2251 Wisconsin Avenue, NW, Washington, DC 20007
(202) 333–1021
Dorothy C. Fenwick, Executive Director

(A177) **National Business Education Association (NBEA)**
914 Association Drive, Reston, VA 22091–1596
(703) 860–8300
Janet M. Treichel, Executive Director

(A178) **National Collegiate Athletic Association (NCAA)**
6201 College Boulevard, Overland Park, KS 66211
(913) 339–1906
Richard D. Schultz, Executive Director

(A179) **National Council for Geographic Education (NCGE)**
16A Leonard Hall, Indiana University of Pennsylvania, Indiana,
 PA 15705
(412) 357–6290
Norm Bettis, President

(A180) **National Council of University Research Administrators
 (NCURA)**
One Dupont Circle, NW, Suite 420, Washington, DC 20036
(202) 466–3894
Natalie Kirkman, Executive Director

(A181) **National Education Association (NEA)**
1201 16th Street, NW, Washington, DC 20036–3290
(202) 822–7749
Don Cameron, Executive Director

(A182) **National Orientation Directors Association (NODA)**
4123 West Main Street, Davenport College, Kalamazoo, MI
 49007
(616) 382–2833
Raymond A. Passkiewicz, Secretary/Treasurer

(A183) **National University Continuing Education Association
 (NUCEA)**
One Dupont Circle, NW, Suite 615, Washington, DC 20036
(202) 659–3130
Kay J. Kohl, Executive Director

(A184) **North American Association of Summer Sessions (NAASS)**
11728 Summerhaven Drive, Creve Coure, MO 63146
(314) 872–8406
Michael V. Nelson, Executive Director

(A185) **Society for College and University Planning (SCUP)**
2026M School of Education Building, University of Michigan,
  Ann Arbor, MI 48109–1259
(313) 763–4776
Joanne E. MacRae, Executive Secretary

(A186) **Society of Ethnic and Special Studies (SESS)**
Box 1652, Chemistry Building, Southern Illinois University—
  Edwardsville, Edwardsville, IL 62026
(618) 692–2042
Emil F. Jason, President

(A187) **Special Interest Group for University and College Computing
Services (SIGUCCS)**
P. O. Box 3842, Seal Beach, CA 90740–7842
(213) 985–9408
Penelope Crane, Chair

(A188) **Speech Communication Association (SCA)**
5105 Backlick Road, Building E, Annandale, VA 22003
(703) 750–0533
James L. Gaudino, Executive Director

(A189) **United Negro College Fund (UNCF)**
500 E. 62nd Street, New York, NY 10021
(212) 326–1118
Virgil Ecton, Acting Director

(A190) **University Council for Educational Administrators (UCEA)**
212 Rackley Building, Pennsylvania State University, University
  Park, PA 16802–3200
(814) 865–4700
Patrick B. Forsyth, Executive Director

NATIONAL PROGRAMS

(P1)   **AMERICAN ASSEMBLY OF COLLEGIATE SCHOOLS OF BUSINESS (AACSB)**
   Contact: Anita Craig, Director of Conferences, AACSB, 605 Old Ballas Road, Suite 220, Saint Louis, MO 63141–7077, (314) 872–8481

   (P1a)   **Associate Deans Seminar**
   This seminar helps new and experienced associate and assistant deans make a career of their jobs or prepare to move to deanships. Experienced deans and associate deans, augmented by specialists, lead the workshops, lectures, and small group discussions. The three-and-one-half-day seminar is scheduled during January of odd years. The program's fee does not include hotel or meals.

   (P1b)   **New Deans Seminar**
   This seminar's purpose is to train new deans of business schools for their positions and to link them with experienced deans for ongoing support. The goal of the three-and-one-half-day program is to explore models of leadership styles, to increase communications capacities, and to develop management expertise. A mentoring system matches new with experienced deans. Workshops, lectures, and small group discussions are led by experienced deans augmented by specialists. The seminar is scheduled in January of even years. The program's fee does not include housing or meals.

(P2)   **AMERICAN ASSOCIATION FOR HIGHER EDUCATION (AAHE)**
   Contact: Judy Corcillio, AAHE, One Dupont Circle, NW, Suite 600, Washington, DC 20036, (202) 293–6440

   (P2a)   **Annual Meeting**
   AAHE encourages campus teams to register for its annual meeting to explore higher education issues. AAHE provides complimentary working space in which teams may meet in separate sessions for briefings by convention speakers for in-depth discussions on topics of particular interest to them and their institutions. The four-day convention is held in late March or early April, rotating among Washington, DC, Chicago, and San Francisco. There is a reduced convention fee for team members who register together.

(P2b)   ***Conference on Assessment in Higher Education***
Annual national convention that focuses on issues of
assessment: communicating and using assessment
results; assessment in general education, the major,
and professional fields; methods and instruments;
diversity; national trends; developmental outcomes;
and the assessment process. Sessions include workshops, special interest groups, speakers, panel discussions, and case studies. Since AAHE believes that
assessment at its best means a campus-wide venture,
involving faculty, administrators, student affairs educators, and students, teams of these educators are
encouraged to attend. There is a reduced convention
fee for team members who register together and complimentary group work space is available. This four-
day forum is held each year in late June.

(P2c)   ***Faculty Senate Leadership Retreat***
Since 1989, the National Network of Faculty Senates
has sponsored a preconference leadership retreat in
conjunction with the AAHE National Conference. The
retreat features key resource persons in the areas of
faculty leadership and governance. Sessions concentrate on case-study approaches and emphasize the
ways successful faculty senates address institutional
challenge and change. Designed for both senate
leaders and administrators with responsibilities for
governance, the sessions stress collegial approaches to
such issues as strategic planning, multicultural programming, assessment, professional development,
faculty recruitment and orientation, and community
building.
Contact: Joseph G. Flynn, SUNY Distinguished Service Professor, State University of New York,
College of Technology, Alfred, NY 14802,
(607) 586–4185

(P2d)   ***Forum on Exemplary Teaching***
Started in 1989, this program, which runs parallel to
the annual AAHE convention, brings together exemplary teachers who teach other faculty on their campuses about teaching (although often without official
title or office) and promote good teaching on their
campuses. Forum participants attend special sessions
of the parallel AAHE convention between sessions in
which they discuss and explore aspects of teaching
and the teaching profession. Faculty are nominated by
chief academic officers to participate in the Forum.
Contact: Patricia A. Hutchings, Director, AAHE, One

Dupont Circle, NW, Suite 600, Washington,
DC 20036, (202) 293–6440

(P3) **AMERICAN ASSOCIATION OF COLLEGES FOR TEACHER EDUCATION (AACTE)**
Contact: Claude Goldberg, Program Manager, AACTE, One Dupont Circle, NW, Suite 610, Washington, DC 20036–2412, (202) 293–2450

(P3a) **New Deans Institute**
The goal of this seminar is to prepare new deans of schools and colleges of education for the challenges of their new jobs. The curriculum covers personal management style (using the Myers-Briggs Type Inventory), team building, channels of communications, internal and external relations, development, and fund raising. A core staff of three former deans of education, supported by guest speakers who are current or former education deans, teach the sessions through a variety of pedagogy, including workshops, small group activities, and speakers. The five-day seminar takes place in June. Hotel and meals are extra.

(P4) **AMERICAN ASSOCIATION OF COLLEGES OF NURSING (AACN)**
Contact: Anne Rhome, Senior Staff Specialist, AACN, One Dupont Circle, NW, Suite 530, Washington, DC, 20036, (202) 463–6930

(P4a) **Executive Development Series**
This workshop is designed to increase the knowledge base and skills that are necessary to lead a school or department of nursing in a complex and rapidly changing environment. Participants include nursing school deans, department chairs, faculty, or administrative staff who aspire to become dean or department chair. The program provides an overview of the administrative process and focuses on topics such as trends in higher education, strategic planning and evaluation, health science perspectives, and the role of the dean. New deans and chairs are encouraged to enter a mentoring program which is organized by AACN prior to the workshop.

(P5)   ***AMERICAN ASSOCIATION OF COMMUNITY AND JUNIOR COLLEGES (AACJC)***
Contact: Connie Odems, Vice President for Professional Services, AACJC, One Dupont Circle, NW, Suite 410, Washington, DC 20036 (202) 728–0200

(P5a)   ***Fellows Program***
Four participants are chosen each year from applicants from community, technical, and junior colleges for this fellowship program. Learning experiences can include one or more of the following settings: with AACJC or another higher education association in Washington, DC; with an AACJC member president in an institutional setting; with a state director of community, technical, and junior colleges; conducting independent research; or in a congressional internship. Fellows spend the first week of participation at the AACJC office in Washington, DC, for orientation. While there is no faculty in a formal sense, potential mentors include members of the AACJC staff, presidents of community colleges, directors of state community college organizations, and members of congressional delegations. The fellowship's timing during the year is at the discretion of the candidate and must last a minimum of three months but not more than one year. Participants must arrange their salary, housing expenses, and other individual costs. AACJC allocates a monthly stipend for incidentals.

(P5b)   ***Presidents Academy Workshop***
This five-day institute annually provides in-service, professional development for 50 new and experienced chief executive officers of AACJC member institutions. The workshop is held in Vail, Colorado, during July. The format utilizes mentors and case studies, and allows ample time for small group interaction. Participants are encouraged to reflect on their roles as institutional leaders. They also explore issues relating to presidential leadership and the CEO's role in academic, student, and community leadership. Presidents of member institutions and the AACJC staff lead the sessions. Spouses may participate in separate sessions or in any workshop sessions. If there are enough new presidents, AACJC sponsors a reception specifically for new presidents at its annual convention.
Contact: Carrole Wolin, Director of Professional Development, AACJC, One Dupont Circle, NW, Suite 410, Washington, DC 20036, (202) 728–0200

(P5c) ***Professional Development Workshop***
Patterned after the AACJC Presidents Academy annual summer workshop, the focus of this new five-day workshop is to broaden the leadership vision for senior administrators (excluding presidents) at AACJC member community, technical, and junior colleges. The seminar utilizes speakers, case studies, and small group discussions. Faculty include presidents and senior administrators of member institutions as well as members of the AACJC staff. Attention will be given to selecting participants who represent diversity in administrative positions and experiences, institutional size/type, geographic location, gender, and race/ethnicity. The workshop is held in Vail, Colorado, in late July/early August. Housing and most meals are extra; there are special fees for the attendance of spouses and children.

(P6) ***AMERICAN ASSOCIATION OF STATE COLLEGES AND UNIVERSITIES (AASCU)***
Contact: Christina Bitting, Director of Membership Services, AASCU, One Dupont Circle, NW, Suite 700, Washington, DC, 20036, (202) 293–7070

(P6a) ***Academic Leadership Institute***
This workshop provides administrative skills and professional renewal to chief academic affairs officers. Topics covered include legal issues in higher education, long range planning, and leadership styles. Faculty include associates of the AASCU Academic Affairs Resource Center (AARC) and experienced senior academic officers. Participants have typically held the position of senior academic officer for fewer than three years. The program is held in October, prior to the AARC meeting, which convenes in a different city each year.
Contact: AARC Director, AASCU, One Dupont Circle, NW, Suite 700, Washington, DC 20036–1192, (202) 293–7070

(P6b) ***New Presidents Sessions***
New presidents of member institutions may attend a morning orientation session and luncheon for new presidents and spouses preceding the annual Summer Council of Presidents. These special sessions, led by AASCU staff and experienced AASCU institutions, focus on launching the presidency and introduce AASCU. Spouses are included as full members of sessions.

(P6c)   ***Presidents' Academy***
This academy serves presidents of member institutions
who are within their first two years in office. The five-
day seminar, scheduled for June (before most new
presidents assume office), rotates to a different college
campus each year. Through in-depth discussion and
group interaction, AASCU staff and experienced presidents of AASCU institutions focus on the most critical
issues facing new presidents: networking with colleagues, setting priorities, meeting family obligations,
dealing with university constituencies, managing and
allocating resources, building relationships and influence, understanding campus culture, creating vision
for effective leadership, resolving conflict, and organizing the president's office. Spouses are included as
full members of all sessions.

(P6d)   ***Summer Council of Presidents***
This annual, five-day summer retreat provides leadership development for both new and experienced presidents of member institutions. AASCU staff and
experienced presidents of AASCU institutions lead the
workshop sessions and panel presentations. Morning
sessions are devoted to informal professional development seminars for presidents and spouses on topics of
current and major concern to higher education
leaders: leadership in the institutional culture, managing institutional investments, balancing priorities and
responsibilities, and fund raising. Additional sessions
address practical issues facing presidents, such as networking with colleagues, setting priorities, meeting
family obligations, dealing with university constituencies, and organizing the president's office. Afternoons
and evenings feature a wide range of recreational
activities for families. The program also includes a special half-day orientation session for new presidents.
The Council rotates to a different resort each July so
that presidents can incorporate the seminar into their
vacations.

(P6e)   ***Workshop for new member presidents/spouses during
annual meeting***
Sessions preceding AASCU's annual meeting introduce new presidents to AASCU's role and purpose.
These sessions are led by AASCU staff; the agenda
varies according to current higher education issues.
AASCU's annual four-day meeting is held in a different city each autumn.

(P7) **AMERICAN COUNCIL ON EDUCATION (ACE)**
Contact: Marlene Ross, Deputy Director, Center for Leadership
Development, ACE, One Dupont Circle, NW,
Suite 800, Washington, DC, 20036, (202) 939–9410

(P7a) ***Department Leadership Program***
ACE sponsors two types of leadership development
workshops for academic chairpersons and deans. Two-
day workshops can be arranged individually for a specific institution or consortium, and the program is
designed to fit the needs of the sponsoring institu-
tion(s). An experienced coordinator leads each workshop and specialists are brought to the campus to
address other topics of interest. Through these workshops, a significant number of department chairs and
deans can benefit from the program, and the shared
training experience helps create a support network
among chairs. National workshops are held twice each
year, in Washington in June and at a location in the
west in November. Participants for the national workshops include provosts, deans, and department
chairs. The workshop format allows for extensive
interaction with chairs/deans from institutions across
the country. For both types of seminars topics
addressed include faculty evaluation and development, roles and responsibilities of the department
chair, legal liabilities, and performance counseling.
Participants also receive materials that address timely
issues for and about chairpersons.
Contact: Rose-Marie G. Oster, Director, Department
Leadership Program, ACE, One Dupont
Circle, Suite 800, Washington, DC 20036,
(202) 939–9415

(P7b) ***The Fellows Program***
The premier fellowship program in higher eduction,
since 1965 the ACE Fellows Program has provided
higher education with an unique opportunity to identify and train future leaders. The fellowships prepare
promising individuals for progressively responsible
positions in higher education and enable them to test
their abilities and interest in administration. Approximately 30 fellows are selected each year through a
national competition for year-long internships in
which they work closely with presidents and senior
officers of colleges, universities, and other higher education organizations who serve as Mentors. Fellows
serve as interns either on their home campuses or at
host campuses. While the emphasis of the program is

on the Fellows and their fellowship experience, there also is considerable developmental learning for the senior administrators who serve as mentors to the Fellows. Mentors and Fellows meet regularly and mentors serve as guides for the Fellows as they observe and participate in all aspects of institutional administration. The ACE Fellows Project for Community Colleges: Leaders for Tomorrow is open to community college faculty and administrators. As an enhancement to the Fellows Program, this effort seeks to identify and train a pool of leaders for community colleges.

(P7c)   *Occasional colloquia for presidents*
These occasional seminars explore specific themes relating to leadership of colleges and universities: for example, moral leadership in higher education. Lectures, panel discussions and small group discussions, are presented by nationally known experts drawn principally from the professorate. Participation is by registration and is not limited by ACE membership or length of service. Spouses can participate fully in the seminar. These four-and-one-half-day seminars are typically scheduled for June in a resort.

(P7d)   *Sessions during annual meeting for presidents*
Special sessions are scheduled during the ACE annual meeting on topics of specific interest to presidents such as negotiating the presidential contract and legislative briefing. Traditionally, there is also a breakfast for presidential spouses.

(P8)   *AMERICAN MANAGEMENT ASSOCIATION (AMA)*
Contact: 135 West 50th Street, New York, NY 10020, (212) 296–8400, or AMA Extension Institute, P.O. Box 1026, Saranac Lake, NY 12983

The AMA offers an extensive and diverse array of seminars and workshops on issues of management. Topics range from basic accounting to staff supervision to team building to human resource management. Many programs are also available on video and audio tape.

(P9)   *ASPEN INSTITUTE*
Contact: Seminars Administration Office, The Aspen Institute, P.O. Box 222, Queenstown, MD 21658, (301) 820–5375

(P9a)   *The Executive Seminar*
This educational program for leaders from all professions uses the classics as beginning points for intensive roundtable discussions. The seminar explores

concepts vital to individuals, corporations, and society. Central are themes of democracy, freedom, equality, justice, property, and ethical conduct. The seminar is open to president and CEO level executives only. The program can also be offered on a consortial basis with four or five organizations each sending three to five participants. This arrangement encourages the exchange of ideas across organizations while allowing for team building among each group's administrators.

(P9b)   ***21st Century Leaders Program***
Presented as a series of intensive educational experiences designed to assist men and women who are now moving into general management and decision making positions in business, management, and academia. The program gives them perspective and context from which to address the traditional issues that confront them in their professions and communities. It also helps prepare them to face the unprecedented challenges emerging from a highly complex world where issues cross vocational, cultural, and national lines. All of the seminars in the program are offered each year, with maximum benefit coming from participating in the entire series over a two- to three-year period. Seminar topics include comparative cultures and values of east and west, ethics, science and technology, environment, cultural diversity, and leadership.

(P10)   **ASSOCIATION OF AMERICAN COLLEGES (AAC)**
Contact: Paula P. Brownlee, President, AAC, 1818 R Street, NW, Washington, DC 20009, (202) 387–3760

(P10a)   ***Specially designated presidential sessions at annual meetings***
Various sessions during the annual three-and-one-half-day January meeting are designated only for presidents of member institutions. The annual meeting is held in odd years in Washington, DC, and in even years in different major domestic cities. Presidential sessions include a breakfast, a hot-line response session organized around questions and problems submitted in advance by participating presidents, and presentations by college presidents and participant discussions. Each year, two or three sessions address specific themes such as presidential leadership in minority achievement or developing institutional leadership. Faculty include experienced presidents and scholars whose works address presidential leadership and higher education. There are specific activities for

spouses and partners; spouses are encouraged to attend any sessions. A reception for new presidents is held during the annual meeting.

(P11)   *ASSOCIATION OF AMERICAN LAW SCHOOLS (AALS)*
Contact: Jane LaBarbera, Associate Director, or Tracie Thomas, Conference Manager, AALS, 1201 Connecticut Avenue, NW, Suite 800, Washington, DC, 20036, (202) 296–8851

(P11a)   ***Deans and Librarians Workshop***
This workshop, for deans and aspiring deans, surveys issues associated with law libraries and media services that require decanal decision-making. Faculty include deans, senior administrators, and librarians of law schools. The one-day workshop is held in January in association with the annual meeting of the Association of American Law Schools. The fee for the annual meeting includes registration in this seminar.

(P11b)   ***Senior Administrators Workshop***
Goals for this seminar include helping law school deans and senior administrators better perform their duties while providing an opportunity for discussion and exploration of the latest issues affecting law schools. Experienced senior administrators of law schools and higher education and law specialists serve as faculty for the workshop. The three-day program is typically scheduled in the winter of every third year.

(P12)   *ASSOCIATION OF AMERICAN MEDICAL COLLEGES (AAMC)*
Contact: Marcie Foster, Program Manager, AAMC, One Dupont Circle, NW, Suite 200, Washington, DC 20036, (202) 828–0522

(P12a)   ***Executive Development Seminar for Deans***
New and experienced deans address the leadership and management skills needed to lead today's medical colleges. Sessions cover management skills, personnel, finance, governance, legal issues, dealing with the media, planning, organizational design, negotiation, and creating the search committee. Experienced deans, AAMC staff, and consultants teach through lectures, small groups, and class discussion. The five-day program is typically scheduled in late May/early June in Vermont.

(P13) *ASSOCIATION OF COLLEGIATE SCHOOLS OF ARCHITECTURE (ACSA)*
Contact: Richard McCommons, Executive Director, ACSA, 1735 New York Avenue, NW, Washington, DC 20006, (202) 785–2324

(P13a) *Administrators Conference*
Through hands-on activities, lectures, workshops, and small group discussion, this conference addresses current issues facing deans, department heads, and administrators of schools of architecture. Faculty include experienced deans and occasional outside experts. The two-and-one-half-day program is typically held in November. The registration fee does not include hotel or meals.

(P14) *ASSOCIATION OF COMMUNITY COLLEGE TRUSTEES (ACCT)*
Contact: Raymond Taylor, Executive Director, National Legislative Seminar and Regional Seminars, ACCT, 1740 N Street, NW, Washington, DC 20036, (202) 347–1740

(P14a) *National Legislative Seminar and Regional Seminars*
Through small group discussions, lectures, and briefings, these seminars give college presidents and trustees the chance to interact with Cabinet members, members of Congress, presidential appointees, and government staff members to discuss current higher education issues. In addition to the national seminars held in Washington, DC, ACCT also sponsors similar seminars in its five regions.

(P15) *ASSOCIATION OF GOVERNING BOARDS OF UNIVERSITIES AND COLLEGES (AGB)*
Contact: Jill Kennedy, Director of Programs, AGB, One Dupont Circle, NW, Suite 400, Washington, DC 20036, (202) 296–8400

(P15a) *Board-Mentor Service*
Since beginning in 1976 with the assistance of a grant from the Lilly Endowment, the AGB Board-Mentor Service has provided facilitators to over 350 board retreats and meetings. A retreat provides the opportunity for a board to step away from the pressures of regular meetings to discuss organization and performance. This service provides AGB-trained trustees from peer institutions to facilitate discussion. The goal is not for the facilitator to impose structure or process on a board, but rather to have an objective peer who

can help a board to investigate itself and to focus on its future operations.

Contact: Peter Hartman, Coordinator of On-Campus Programs, AGB, One Dupont Circle, NW, Suite 400, Washington, DC 20036, (202) 296–8400

(P15b) *Improving Board Performance*

This newly designed AGB workshop for trustees and presidents is based on a practical, research-tested model of board effectiveness that includes specific steps a board can take to enhance its operation and its value to the institution. Using a new model of board effectiveness formulated from an extensive three-year study on the subject, participants will learn strategies, tactics, and techniques that boards use to maintain and improve their performance.

(P15c) *Institute for Trustee Leadership: Program for Board Chairs and Chief Executive Officers of Independent Institutions*

The Institute explores issues of institutional governance. It creates the opportunity for the leadership team (president and board chair) to focus on team relationships and the way in which members can work together to strengthen the governance of the institution. Through case studies, class discussions, plenary sessions, team meetings, and consultation sessions, experts on trusteeship define the responsibilities of the board chair and CEO for educating and leading the board, strengthening the working relationship between the board chair and CEO, and assessing the relationship of the leadership team to the board, its committees, and various other constituencies. By the conclusion of the program, each team develops an action plan to improve institutional governance. There is no programming or housing for spouses; spouses are strongly discouraged from accompanying participants. The three-day institute runs each January at the Graylin Conference Center, Winston-Salem, North Carolina.

(P15d) *Introduction to AGB Services During National Conference on Trusteeship*

AGB staff, with the assistance of experienced trustees, present a one-hour information session before the annual AGB convention. The session is designed for first-time attenders of the AGB annual meeting, including new presidents and new trustees. The two-

and-one-half-day AGB annual meeting addresses issues of higher education relevant to presidents and trustees, whether new or experienced. Sessions include presentations, question-and-answer sessions, and group discussions. Although there is no specific programming for spouses, they may attend any session as registrants. The spring meeting is held in a different domestic major city each year.

(P15e) ***On-Campus Fundraising Workshop***
This self-assessment program, facilitated by a trustee from a comparable institution, provides a board with the opportunity to assess past fundraising performance and to look forward to future goals. Facilitators, who are long-time trustees specially trained by AGB, are matched with boards of similar institutions and characteristics.
Contact: Peter Hartman, Coordinator of On-Campus Programs, AGB, One Dupont Circle, NW, Suite 400, Washington, DC 20036, (202) 296–8400

(P15f) ***Program for Academic Affairs Committee Chairpersons and Senior Academic Officers***
This program focuses on strengthening governing board and institutional performance by enhancing the leadership capabilities of board and committee chairpersons and of chief executive officers and senior administrators. The program's goals include identification of academic leadership roles, exploration of institutional policies, instruction in designing and developing academic strategy and assessment of the academic affairs committee. Institutions are encouraged to send teams of the committee chairperson or vice chairperson, the academic administrators who work with the committee, and/or the institution's chief executive.

(P15g) ***Seminar for Chairpersons and Chief Executives of Theological Schools and Seminaries***
With the same format and goals as its sister program (Program for Board Chairs and Chief Executive Officers of Independent Institutions), this seminar addresses leadership issues specifically related to theological schools and seminaries. Special forums address topics such as the interaction of religious culture and governance.

(P15h) ***Seminar on Endowment Management***
This workshop is for teams of trustees, chief execu-

tives, and senior administrators involved with endowment management. It focuses on the history and development of endowment funds; the role of trustees in endowment management; developing investment objectives and guidelines; determining asset allocation and endowment spending policy; selecting and evaluating stocks, bonds, and cash; investing in foreign markets, real estate, and venture capital; and tactical asset allocation to enhance endowment growth. The seminar is typically scheduled in the autumn.

(P15i)   *Speaker Service*
AGB maintains a referral service of experts on governance and board operations who can serve as speakers for board retreats. The most frequent request is for speakers who can participate in orientation programs for trustees, particularly speakers who can address issues of the roles and responsibilities of trustees.
Contact: Peter Hartman, Coordinator of On-Campus Programs, AGB, One Dupont Circle, NW, Suite 400, Washington, DC 20036, (202) 296–8400

(P15j)   *Strategic Planning for Theological Schools*
This workshop for teams of trustees and administrators of theological schools focuses on the shared and distinctive planning roles of trustees and administrators and on the value of effective teamwork in ensuring successful strategic planning. Through informal small group discussions, participants are exposed to key issues facing the board's role in planning. Topics for the 1990 workshop included the nature and purposes of planning, problems and considerations in organizing a planning process, constituent involvement, and integrating academic, fiscal and facilities planning.

(P15k)   *Trustee Responsibility for Financial Affairs*
Designed to assist trustees, chief executives, and chief financial officers who comprise the financial affairs committee to monitor the financial climate of the institution. By learning to clarify the board's role in financial affairs, identify key institutional policies, work with constituents, set agendas and financial strategies, participants will develop the specific skills needed to work with the board in executing efficient and solid financial plans.

(P15l)   *Workshop for New Trustees*
AGB has conducted several workshops over the past

four years to help recently appointed trustees master the skills of trusteeship. The workshops are designed to orient new trustees to their complex roles and responsibilities in order to become contributing board members from the start. Through interaction among workshop faculty and participants, small group sessions, and case studies, the program considers topics such as governing board operation, responsibilities, fund-raising, board-president relations, academic and financial affairs, and policy making. The program is divided into separate sessions for public and private institutions.

(P16)   ***ASSOCIATION OF GOVERNING BOARDS OF UNIVERSITIES AND COLLEGES (AGB) IN COOPERATION WITH THE NATIONAL ASSOCIATION OF SYSTEM HEADS***
Contact: Jill Kennedy, Director of Programs, AGB, One Dupont Circle, NW, Suite 400, Washington, DC 20036, (202) 296–8400

(P16a)   ***Governing the Public Multicampus System***
This two-day workshop for trustees, chief executives, and campus executives is designed to address issues important to the governance of a multicampus system. Workshop topics include an overview of the day-to-day decision making process of the system CEO, points of tension within the roles and relationships of the system CEO, the structure and organization of university systems, and interrelationships among the board, CEO and campus heads, and external and internal constituencies. This workshop is open only to AGB member institutions.

(P17)   ***ASSOCIATION OF RESEARCH LIBRARIES (ARL)***
Contact: Training Program Manager, ARL, Office of Management Services, 1527 New Hampshire Avenue, NW, 4th floor, Washington, DC 20036, (202) 232–2466

The association offers a variety of programs for the development of leadership and management skills among librarians. The five-and-one-half-day **Advanced Management Skills Institute** *(P17a)* serves beginning or mid-level administrators (deans) by focusing on the development of goals, strategic planning, organizational problem solving, team development, decision making, communication mechanisms, leadership, and negotiation skills. Also for beginning or mid-level supervisors, the three-and-one-half-day

Basic Management Skills Institute *(P17b)* addresses the managerial role, explores the need for personal awareness, and stresses the ability to think conceptually with sessions on organizational diagnosis, motivation, interpersonal skills, values, decision making, working toward consensus in groups, conflict management, management style, and coaching. Designed to develop innovative thinking skills for individuals, the three-day **Creativity to Innovation Workshop** *(P17c)* seeks to help create structures and processes that maximize the creative skills of the individual, group, and organization. The program benefits library administrators and managers responsible for directing and providing leadership within libraries as well as staff members interested in developing their personal potential to contribute to library effectiveness. In the three-and-one-half-day **Project Planning Workshop** *(P17d)* library, professionals develop proficiency in organizational problem-solving and project planning skills. The three-and-one-half-day **Resources Management Institute** *(P17e)*, for librarians responsible for allocating, monitoring, or expending financial resources at the unit level or above, seeks to integrate and link financial and managerial processes. For librarians responsible for training, the three-and-one-half-day **Training Skills Institute** *(P17f)* provides a conceptual framework for the provision of training as well as methods and techniques to carry out the work.

(P18)   **THE BUSH FOUNDATION**
     Contact: John Archabal, Bush Leadership Program, 332 Minnesota Street, E-900, First National Bank Building, St. Paul, MN 55101, (612) 227–0891

     (P18a)   ***Leadership Program for Midcareer Development***
The Bush Leadership Fellowship program enriches the experience of mid-career administrators between the ages of 28 and 54 with five to seven years of full-time administrative experience and prepares them for higher levels of responsibility. The internships emphasize administrative training, and are available for residents of Minnesota, North and South Dakota, and northwest Wisconsin. The fellowships are available to applicants in all careers. The approximately 20 awards given each year include a monthly stipend, travel/moving allowance, and 50 percent of tuition or fees for participation in a specific program. Fellowship grants can be short (3–10 weeks) or long (4–18 months). Many

higher education administrators have used Bush Fellowships to attend Harvard's Institute for Educational Management, Carnegie Mellon's College Management Program, the HERS/Bryn Mawr Program, and the ACE Fellows Program.

(P19) **CARNEGIE MELLON UNIVERSITY/ SCHOOL OF URBAN AND PUBLIC AFFAIRS**

(P19a) **Academic Leadership Institute**
This five-and-one-half-day program is designed for provosts, academic vice presidents, deans of liberal arts colleges, and their assistants, as well as others in positions of academic leadership. Classes address topics such as academic planning, program development and assessment, future issues in higher education, assessing learning outcomes and teaching performance, faculty selection, fiscal planning, managing academic support services, and legal issues in higher education. Institute faculty use lectures, case studies, panel presentations, and small group discussions to address leadership-related issues confronting all facets of the academic program at colleges and universities. The annual institute is held in June.
Contact: Harry R. Faulk, Associate Dean for Executive Education, School of Urban and Public Affairs, Carnegie Mellon University, 5000 Forbes Avenue, Pittsburgh, PA 15213–9984, (412) 268–2194

(P19b) **College Management Program**
This three-week summer program introduces senior and upper-middle level college and university administrators to the strategies of higher education management and leadership. Courses address strategic planning, management, marketing, budgeting, financial analysis, situational leadership, decision making, and using the personal computer as a management tool. Classes include discussions, lectures, speeches, small group activities, role plays, and simulations, taught by scholars and practitioner experts in higher education, leadership development, and management. The program, held on the campus of Carnegie Mellon University, does not include provision for spouses. The fee includes tuition, housing, and meals.
Contact: Deborah Corsini, Director of Executive Education, School of Urban and Public Affairs, Carnegie Mellon University, 5000 Forbes Avenue, Pittsburgh, PA 15213–3890, (412) 268–6082

(P20)   **CENTER FOR CREATIVE LEADERSHIP**
Contact: Josie Donohue, Registrar, Leadership Development
Program, Center for Creative Leadership, 500 Laurinda Drive, P.O. Box P-1, Greensboro, NC
27438–6301, (919) 288–7210

The Center is a nonprofit educational institution
founded in 1970. Its mission is to encourage and
develop creative leadership and effective management
for the good of society overall. This mission is
accomplished through research, training, and
publication—with emphasis on the widespread, innovative application of the behavioral sciences to the
challenges facing the leaders of today and tomorrow.
Through its research, the Center has developed
models of management practice; through its training
programs, the Center applies these models as guides
for assessment and development. This combined
approach makes the Center's research accessible and
its training practical. Among the Center's many publications are *Breaking the Glass Ceiling: Can Women Reach
the Top of America's Largest Corporations?* and *The Lessons
of Experience*.

(P20a)   ***Dynamics of Strategy: Goals into Action***
This five-day program on the implementation of
organizational strategies, features a highly participa-
tive behavioral simulation. The program's design is
based on the principle that strategic leadership
requires anticipating, understanding, and responding
to the myriad issues affecting long-term business
viability. Effective high-level managers must think in
terms of the organizational whole, not just the sum of
the parts. This program provides the opportunity for
senior officers to examine their leadership styles and
enhance their skills in a risk-free environment.
Through a realistic simulation, assessment, case
studies, and back-home feedback, administrators can
determine and enhance their strengths and become
aware of and limit their deficiencies before costly mistakes occur.

(P20b)   ***Executive Women Workshop***
The Center's Executive Women Project was created to
find better ways to develop women for key executive
posts. The Workshop is backed by two years of
research, involving interviews with successful female
executives at or near the general manager level in For-
tune 500 companies. The workshop's goals include

drawing a picture of the leadership strengths and weaknesses of participants through testing and assessment exercises, reviewing the implications of research on the factors that lead to career success or derailment for high-level executive women, sharing experiences and ideas with other women managers in a unique supportive environment, weighing issues that arise in being both a successful woman and a successful manager, and formulating a plan for further self-directed development. A special feature of the workshop is individualized feedback based on the completion of a variety of assessment questionnaires by the participant and by colleagues at her company or institution.

(P20c)   ***Leadership and Teamwork: Increasing Team Leadership Capabilities***
This three-day seminar aims to increase the participant's ability to unify diverse people to work effectively as a team toward a common goal. The course is based on the premises that (1) effective teamwork produces superior results; and (2) skills of team-building and team-leading are increasingly required in the workplace. Prior to attending the course, observations are collected from the participant's "back-home team" to provide targeted feedback on the effectiveness of his/her leadership and teamwork behavior. The program includes a minimum of theory and a maximum of personal feedback and skill practice based on the application of proven leadership principles. Individuals in management positions who have demonstrated skills in the basic management functions of planning, organizing, and controlling material resources and who also want to improve their ability to lead people. The program is run several times throughout the year at the Center for Creative Leadership sites in Greensboro, North Carolina, or San Diego, California.

(P20d)   ***Leadership Development Program***
Senior and mid-level managers develop new approaches to leadership and obtain a clearer understanding of their effectiveness. Organizers provide factual data and advice on topics such as the creative leadership process, decision making, performance development, and using group resources. Besides simulations, classroom work, and evaluations, this program offers the opportunity for a two-and-one-half-hour one-on-one feedback session with a professional staff member who will interpret and discuss the results of several back-home feedback instruments taken

before the course. Faculty include specially trained members of the Center's staff. The six-day program is offered at the Center in Greensboro, North Carolina, or at program sites in several states and foreign countries at various times of the year. The registration fee includes all training materials and meals. Accommodations are extra. Scholarships are available to individuals from higher education. The Center also offers many other leadership development workshops and leadership publications.

(P21) CENTER FOR INTERNATIONAL EDUCATION
See Council for International Exchange of Scholars (CIES) for information on Fulbright programs.

(P22) CENTRAL ASSOCIATION OF COLLEGE AND UNIVERSITY BUSINESS OFFICERS (CACUBO)
Contact: Neil Smith, 212 Parker Hall, University of Missouri—Rolla, Rolla, MO 65401, (314) 341–4121

(P22a) Management Institute
The two-part CACUBO Management Institute is an intensive program designed to develop skills and promote professional, technical and personal growth of business and fiscal managers from all types of institutions. The Institute provides participants with hands-on experiences illustrating practical approaches to campus operations. Participants discuss work-related problems and solutions with colleagues from other institutions. The Level 1 program, lasting five days, emphasizes the development of creative leadership and management skills related to conducting fiscal operations and practices. Those who complete the Level 1 program receive a Certificate of Recognition allowing them to enroll in Level 2 to achieve the Professional Diploma. CACUBO sponsors several workshops for Level 2 participants to continue to develop and extend their knowledge of business-related concepts, with an emphasis on the application of those skills to business operations and management in higher education.

(P23) CHRISTIAN A. JOHNSON ENDEAVOR FOUNDATION
Contact: Nicholas H. Farnham, Director, The Troutbeck Program/Educational Leadership Project, Christian A. Johnson Endeavor Foundation, 109 East 89th Street, New York, NY 10128, (212) 534–2904

(P23a) Troutbeck Program/Educational Leadership Project
This one-week program for experienced presidents

and their spouses focuses on recharging the spirit of academic leadership in colleges and universities. Topics are explored through lectures and group discussions by academic scholars, and include philosophy, history, and politics as they relate to the values of institutional leadership. Discussion is focused on strengthening intellectual confidence and strategic planning ability. The aim of the seminar is to equip presidents to rethink and expand their vision of the academic mission, renew their sense of intellectual confidence, overcome the sense of isolation in their positions, and deepen their perception of what leadership entails. Spouses are invited to participate in all sessions. The seminar is named after the Troutbeck resort, where the program is held each summer.

(P24) ***COLLEGE AND UNIVERSITY PERSONNEL ASSOCIATION (CUPA)***
Contact: Jan Compton-Ouska, Manager of Professional Development, CUPA, 1233 20th Street NW, Suite 503, Washington DC 20036, (202) 429–0311

CUPA offers an array of two- and three-day intensive programs for human resource managers and personnel directors. Personnel from nearly every sector of higher education administration as well those who work closely with these institutions, such as lawyers and consultants, may apply for any of the ten workshops currently offered. The Senior Management Forum, for example, is open to those with at least five years of experience as human resource managers who wish to examine the current issues that have a major impact on their institutions. Other workshops cover wage and salary administration, effective personnel practices for small colleges, and employee relations.

(P25) ***COMMITTEE ON SCHOLARLY COMMUNICATION***
See Council for International Exchange of Scholars (CIES) for Fulbright Program information.

(P26) ***COUNCIL FOR ADVANCEMENT AND SUPPORT OF EDUCATION (CASE)***
Contact: Mary Kay Kreft, CASE, 11 Dupont Circle, NW, Suite 400, Washington, DC 20036, (202) 328–5923

(P26a) ***Forums for Women and Minorities in Institutional Advancement***
These CASE forums are designed for women or minorities who hold key positions in institutional

advancement. The program teaches participants to be active in seeking out advancement opportunities, and provides an opportunity to meet high-level advancement colleagues to establish important contacts.

Contact: Susan VanGilder, CASE, 11 Dupont Circle, NW, Suite 400, Washington, DC 20036, (202) 328–5942

(P26b)   *Presidential and Trustee Leadership in Fund Raising*
This two-day program is designed especially for the fund-raising leadership team—the president, trustees, and chief development officer. CASE encourages team participation for this workshop so that the team can explore its responsibilities in fund raising. Faculty assist participants in identifying strengths and defining areas of responsibility for the development team. Topics addressed include the capital campaign, donor cultivation, and board development. Experts in institutional advancement present the session through lectures, class discussions, and small group discussions. Held each spring in a different domestic city or resort, this seminar provides no specific programming for spouses.

(P26c)   *Presidents' Colloquium on Institutional Advancement*
Through lectures and group discussions, presidents with extensive experience in institutional advancement and experts in fund raising examine the presidential role in institutional advancement. The colloquium, which is beneficial for both new and experienced presidents, also provides spouse programming during some years. The two-day program rotates to a different resort each January.

(P26d)   *Summer Institute in Executive Management*
This summer program for senior managers aims to sharpen management skills by focusing on topics such as strategic planning and financial management. Experts in various areas of management teach the sessions through lecture, class discussion, small groups, role plays, and simulations. This one-week program takes place on the campus of the Owen School of Business of Vanderbilt University.

Contact: Vivienne Lee, Vice President, CASE, 11 Dupont Circle, NW, Suite 400, Washington, DC 20036, (202) 328–5929

(P27) **COUNCIL FOR ADVANCEMENT AND SUPPORT OF EDUCA-
TION (CASE), AND SNELLING, KOLB & KUHNLE**
Contact: Christine Barr, Snelling, Kolb & Kuhnle, Suite 500,
2100 M Street, NW, Washington, DC 20037, (202)
463–2111

(P27a) *Skills for Success: A Workshop for Getting Ahead*
This program is for officers of institutional advancement, development, alumni, media, government
affairs, and admissions. Its goals are to explore career
options; to develop a realistic understanding of participants' skills, talents, personalities, experiences, goals,
and ambitions; to understand the realities of the job
marketplace in higher education; to understand the
components of an effective resume; to explore the
skills of effective interviewing; to understand how to
negotiate a compensation package; and to learn how
to compare job offers. The workshop is led by Dr. John
Kuhnle, Senior Partner of Snelling, Kolb & Kuhnle.
This is an annual preconference seminar before the
CASE Annual Assembly.

(P28) **COUNCIL FOR INTERNATIONAL EXCHANGE OF
SCHOLARS (CIES)**
Contact: Steve Blodgett, CIES, 3400 International Drive, NW,
Suite M-500, Washington, DC 20008–3097, (202)
686–7870

(P28a) *Fulbright Scholar Program*
Although Fulbrights are known as faculty development opportunities, there are now three Fulbright programs available to administrators of all levels and
functions. Like the faculty programs, the goal of the
administrative programs is to provide reinvigoration
for teaching and leadership through cross-cultural
experiences. The **Seminars for International Education Administrators in Germany and Japan** *(P28b)* are
intensive, short-term programs of three to four weeks
to familiarize administrators with another higher education system. Each year, approximately 20 people participate in the German program, and five to six in the
seminar in Japan. Similar numbers of administrators
from these countries visit the U.S. for seminars on the
American higher education system. The **U.S./United
Kingdom College and University Academic Administrator Award** *(P28c)* sends three administrators to the
United Kingdom for a minimum of three months to
pursue individual professional programming initiatives. In turn, three administrators from the U.K. visit

the U.S. Additionally, administrators have participated in the traditional Fulbright programs, which run from a minimum stay of two months to a maximum stay of an academic year. Deadlines are November 1 for the administrative program, and June 15 and August 1 (depending on area of world applied for) for the faculty programs.

Fulbright Program grants are also available from:

Committee on Scholarly Communication with the People's Republic of China (CSCPRC), National Academy of Sciences, 2101 Constitution Avenue, NW, Washington, DC 20418, (202) 334–2718. (Research grants to China.)

Center for International Education, U.S. Department of Education, Washington, DC 20202, (202) 732–3283. (Faculty research, doctoral dissertation research, and group seminars and projects.)

Institute of International Education (IIE), 809 United Nations Plaza, New York, NY 10017, (212) 984–5329. (Grants for predoctoral study or research abroad.)

International Research and Exchanges Board (IREX), 126 Alexander Street, Princeton, NJ 08540–7102, (609) 683–9500. (Research grants to the Soviet Union and Eastern Europe.)

Fulbright Teacher Exchange Program, United States Information Agency, 301 4th Street, SW, Washington, DC 20547, (202) 485–2555. (Grants for teacher exchange and participation in summer seminars abroad.)

University Affiliations Program, United States Information Agency, 301 4th Street, SW, Washington, DC 20547, (202) 485–8489. (One-time institutional seed grants for faculty exchange between US and non-US postsecondary institutions.)

(P29)   **COUNCIL OF COLLEGES OF ARTS AND SCIENCES (CCAS)**
Contact: Richard J. Hopkins, Executive Director, CCAS, Ohio State University, 186 University Hall, 230 North Oval Mall, Columbus, OH 43210–1319, (614) 292–1882

(P29a)   **Annual Seminars**
These annual seminars for deans of colleges of arts and sciences examine practical issues associated with college or university administration. The seminar's theme is selected each year at the annual meeting. Seminars are organized so that deans spend time sharing and debating their approaches to common

problems. Seminar leaders include experienced deans and specialists in specific topics. The same two-day seminar runs in two different parts of the country (typically an eastern and western city) in March and April.

(P30) ***COUNCIL OF COLLEGES OF ARTS AND SCIENCES (CCAS) AND AMERICAN CONFERENCE OF ACADEMIC DEANS (ACAD)***
Contact: Richard J. Hopkins, Executive Director, CCAS, Ohio State University, 186 University Hall, 230 North Oval Mall, Columbus, OH 43210–1319 (614) 292–1882 or Maria-Helena Price, Executive Officer, ACAD, 1818 R Street, NW, Washington, DC 20009, (202) 387–3760

(P30a) ***Seminar for New Deans***
This seminar provides a forum in which new deans or deans moving to a new institution can familiarize themselves, in a controlled setting, with the art of college administration. Curriculum includes sessions on administrative philosophy, management style, planning, budgeting, curriculum and program development, grantsmanship, personnel recruitment, retention, development and fundraising, and relations with administration, faculty, and students. A specific, topical issue provides a special focus each year. Experienced college and university deans teach the sessions using presentations, discussion, lectures, small group activities. The College of William and Mary in Virginia hosts this four-day seminar each June. The fee does not include housing or meals.

(P31) ***COUNCIL OF GRADUATE SCHOOLS (CGS)***
Contact: Edna Khalil, Office Manager, CGS, One Dupont Circle, Suite 430, Washington, DC 20036, (202) 223–3791

(P31a) ***Summer Workshops for Graduate Deans***
Although designed primarily for new deans, associate deans, and assistant deans of graduate schools, many continuing deans and administrators involved in graduate affairs or research attend as well. The four-day workshop covers a broad range of topics—the current state of graduate education; governance and organization of graduate schools; student recruitment, admissions, and retention; academic program review; graduate information administration; legal issues; and legislative and government relations. Participants also meet in small teams to work through a case study about the graduate dean at a new institution who faces

all the challenges inherent in the topics above. The workshop provides participants with a broader sense of national issues in graduate education, suggestions for handling specific problems, and a national network of graduate school colleagues to call on for future information and support. Faculty include experienced deans and scholars in related fields who conduct classes using lectures, case studies, and small group activities. Hotel and meals are supplementary to the registration fee.

(P32) **COUNCIL OF INDEPENDENT COLLEGES (CIC)**
Contact: Mary Ann F. Rehnke, Director of Annual Programs, CIC, One Dupont Circle, NW, Suite 320, Washington, DC 20036, (202) 466–7230

(P32a) ***New Presidents Workshop preceding Annual Presidents Institute***
A one-day workshop for new presidents of member institutions preceding the annual two-and-one-half-day Presidents Institute introduces new presidents to the challenges and rewards of serving as leaders of independent institutions.

(P32b) ***Presidents Institute***
For presidents of member institutions, this institute explores the challenges facing leaders of independent institutions. Led by experienced presidents, the workshops, speeches, and group discussions focus on issues such as working with trustees, fund raising, budgeting, and enrollment management. Spouses are invited to participate. This institute also offers a luncheon and special sessions for new presidents and their spouses. The two-and-one-half day institute is held during the first week of January at a different resort each year.

(P33) **COUNCIL ON INTERNATIONAL EDUCATIONAL EXCHANGE (CIEE)**
Contact: Mark Gross, Department of Professional and Secondary Education Programs, CIEE, 205 East 42nd Street, New York, NY 10017, (212) 661–1414

(P33a) ***Development Seminars***
The CIEE seminars provide a unique opportunity for full-time administrators and faculty to spend time abroad and observe academic institutions overseas. Each seminar features several different activities during the week-long program: (1) lectures and

discussions organized around a specific theme (in English); (2) site visits related to lecture topics that allow participants opportunities to visit cultural and educational institutions; (3) a professional interchange that allows participants to meet with local academics in their same discipline; and (4) follow-up activities that are built into the operation of each seminar which may include studies, publications, or reports. The seminars are designed to enable participants to acquire information on current issues, develop discipline-specific data through interchange with foreign scholars and seminar participants, gain expertise on resources for institutional exchange possibilities, and influence home campus curricula on international issues. The seminar provides significant opportunity for personal interaction and networking. Total seminar costs (including roundtrip airfare) range from $1,500 to $3,000. Sponsoring institutions are expected to provide at least 50 percent support toward the fees.

(P34) **FACULTY EXCHANGE CENTER**
Contact: John Joseph, Executive Director, Faculty Exchange Center, 952 Virginia Avenue, Lancaster, PA 17603, (717) 393–1130

Started in 1973, the center serves as a clearinghouse and directory for faculty exchanges. The center supports two types of activities: exchanges in which two faculty replace each other for a semester or academic year at each other's institution, and making housing available for sabbaticals and long vacations to encourage travel among faculty. A faculty member interested in an exchange would identify institutions and jobs of interest from the directory, and then make the contact and arrange the swap privately. Both institutions and individual faculty can be members of the Center. Although listings are primarily in the United States, the directory does include several foreign institutions interested in exchanges.

(P35) **FULBRIGHT TEACHER EXCHANGE PROGRAM**
See Council for International Exchange of Scholars (CIES) for information on Fulbright programs.

(P36) **HARVARD UNIVERSITY/GRADUATE SCHOOL OF BUSINESS ADMINISTRATION**
Contact: AMP, Harvard Graduate School of Business Administration, Glass Hall, Boston, MA 02163, (617) 495–6161

(P36a)   ***Advanced Management Program (AMP)***
Harvard's Graduate School of Business Administration pioneered the campus executive development program. The AMP is the oldest of this type of programming, having been founded in the 1940s. The 13–week residential program provides a comprehensive and intensive look at management techniques and strategy. The program is taught almost entirely by the case study method by some of Harvard's most outstanding business school faculty. While most participants are from business and industry, several college and university presidents have attended, typically as part of a sabbatical after many years of service to their institutions.
Note: The business schools of many universities, such as the Massachusetts Institute of Technology's Sloan School, Northwestern University, and Cornell University, also offer major executive development programs.

(P37)   ***HARVARD UNIVERSITY/GRADUATE SCHOOL OF EDUCATION***

(P37a)   ***Harvard Seminar for New Presidents***
Designed for presidents within the first 12 months in office, this seminar prepares presidents to respond effectively to the multiple responsibilities and constituencies of their new office. Through case studies and small group discussion, it provides a practical and intellectual orientation to the presidency and support regarding the crucial first months in a new institution. Higher education experts and experienced presidents lead discussions on the contexts of leadership, trusteeship, key indicators of financial health, developing a plan of entry, building an administrative team, and articulating vision. This residential five-day program is scheduled in early June on the Harvard University campus. The program makes no provisions for spouses.
Contact: Greg Glover, Program Coordinator, Harvard Graduate School of Education, Gutman Library 339, Appian Way, Cambridge, MA 02318, (617) 495–2655

(P37b)   ***Institute for Educational Management (IEM)***
IEM develops leadership and management competencies with a specific focus on issues related to monitoring the environment, setting directions, marshalling resources and support, and managing implementation. Because of the rigorous, comprehensive nature of

the program, participants are required to be in residence throughout the Institute. Classes are highly interactive, using cases, small group discussions, role playing, and simulations. Classes are led by experts in higher education, leadership development, and management drawn primarily from the faculty of Harvard University. Participants are presidents and senior officers of higher education organizations from the United States and abroad. Presidential participants in IEM usually have completed several years in office before attending. There is no programming for spouses; spouses are strongly discouraged from accompanying participants and no housing is provided for them. This four-week summer program is held on the campus of Harvard University.

Contact: Inge-Lise Ameer, IEM Program Coordinator, Harvard Graduate School of Education, Gutman Library 339, Appian Way, Cambridge, MA 02318, (617) 495–2655

(P37c) ***Institute for the Management of Lifelong Education (MLE)***

MLE serves leaders concerned with the continuing and adult education process within colleges and universities, libraries, the military, professional associations, and the government; typical titles include Vice President and Dean for Continuing Education. The institute focuses on the role of officers of institutions that find themselves increasingly involved in serving the needs of adults and other "non-traditional" student populations. Through case study classes, small group discussions, role-playing, and simulations, experts in adult education, learning styles, and management, marketing, finance, and leadership drawn primarily from Harvard University lead highly interactive sessions. This two-week program is held on the campus of Harvard University each June. The all-inclusive fee includes room, board, tuition, and all curriculum materials. Because of the rigorous, comprehensive nature of the program, participants are required to be in residence throughout the Institute. There is no provision for spouses.

Contact: Clifford Baden, MLE Director, Harvard University, Gutman Library #339, Appian Way, Cambridge, MA 02138, (617) 495–3572

(P37d) ***Management Development Program (MDP)***

MDP develops the competencies of middle level administrators in leadership, management, and higher

education issues. The highly interactive sessions
employ case studies, small group discussions,
speakers, role-playing, and simulations. Faculty
include experts in higher education, leadership development, and management drawn primarily from Harvard University. This two-week summer program,
held on the campus of Harvard University, draws mid-
level administrators from the entire gamut of higher
education organizations from the United States and
abroad. The all-inclusive fee includes room, board,
tuition, and all curriculum materials. Scholarship
funds are available. Because of the rigorous, comprehensive nature of the program, participants are
required to be in residence throughout the Institute.
There are no provisions for spouses.

Contact: Tacy SanAntonio, MDP Program Coordinator, Harvard University, Gutman Library
#339, Appian Way, Cambridge, MA 02138,
(617) 495–2655

(P38) **HARVARD UNIVERSITY AND THE COLLEGE BOARD**

Contact: Jacquelyn R. Smith, Registrar, Harvard Summer Institute on College Admissions, 4 Clematis Road, Lexington, MA 02173 and Dean Whitla, Director, Harvard
University, Shannon Hall, Cambridge, MA 02138 (617)
495–1538

(P38a) **Summer Institute on College Admissions**

Begun in 1960, the program provides a reexamination
of past experience, a study of present practices, and a
review of predicted trends in the field of admissions
and counseling for college admissions officers and
high school guidance counselors who work primarily
with college bound students. Issues addressed include
recruiting, organizing the guidance function, enrollment management, minority admissions, parenting,
recommendations, score interpretation, test preparation, publications, use of staff resources, budgeting
and cost analysis, legal issues, and financial aid. The
format includes workshops, lectures, work sessions,
and information exchanges among participants. Faculty for this five-and-one-half-day institute include
admissions officers and higher education experts. Participants are required to be in residence on the Harvard campus for the program; many faculty members
are also in residence throughout the program.

(P39)   **HIGHER EDUCATION RESOURCE SERVICES (HERS) MID-AMERICA/ BRYN MAWR COLLEGE**
Contact: Cynthia Secor, Foote Hall, University of Denver, Colorado Women's College Campus, Denver, CO 80220, (303) 871–6866

> *(P39a)*   ***HERS Summer Institute for Women/Bryn Mawr Institute***
> HERS/Bryn Mawr provides an overview of higher education management and leadership for women mid-level managers and faculty, both academic and educational support, of colleges and universities. The program devotes significant attention to career development, surveying today's academic environment, academic governance, and institutional environment. During the four-week summer program, higher education leaders and scholars interact with participants through lectures, case studies, large and small group discussion, and individual consultations. The all-inclusive fee covers tuition, all curriculum materials, and room and board on the campus of Bryn Mawr College.

(P40)   **HIGHER EDUCATION RESOURCE SERVICES (HERS) NEW ENGLAND/ WELLESLEY COLLEGE**
Contact: Cynthia Secor, Cheever House, Wellesley College, Wellesley, MA 02181, (617) 235–0329

> *(P40a)*   ***HERS Institute for Women/Wellesley Institute***
> Like the HERS/Bryn Mawr program, the HERS/Wellesley program provides an overview of higher education management and leadership for women mid-level managers and faculty, both academic and educational support, of colleges and universities. It devotes significant attention to career development, surveying today's academic environment, academic governance, and institutional environment through lectures, case studies, large and small group discussions, and individual consultations with the higher education leaders and scholars who make up the program's faculty. This program is a series of five seminars held over the course of an academic year on the campus of Wellesley College.

(P41)   **INSTITUTE FOR EDUCATIONAL LEADERSHIP (IEL)**
Contact: Mara Ueland, Program Associate, IEL, 1001 Connecticut Avenue, NW, Suite 310, Washington, DC 20036, (202) 822–84714

> *(P41a)*   ***Educational Policy Fellowship Program***
> The goal of this program is to help leaders from

nonprofit organizations gain an understanding of public policy processes. Within higher education, participants are typically faculty and mid-level administrators who work in the public policy arena. Fellows examine the policy environments of their organizations while developing of leadership skills for current or future work-related endeavors. Besides weekly site meetings, the approximately 200 Fellows attend two issue-intensive national meetings that focus on national policy making and issues. Faculty include decision makers, policy analysts, and noted authorities and critics in policy-making and on policy issues. Participants remain in their full-time professional positions during the fellowship. The program involves 16 sites with an average of 20 Fellows per site who meet together approximately once a week from September through June to discuss specific topics assigned by IEL and other topics of interest to the group for personal rejuvenation. In addition to a fee, the Fellows' sponsoring organization must pay travel expenses.

(P42) **INSTITUTE OF INTERNATIONAL EDUCATION (IIE)**
See Council for International Exchange of Scholars (CIES) for information on Fulbright programs.

(P43) **INTERNATIONAL RESEARCH AND EXCHANGES BOARD (IREX)**
See Council for International Exchange of Scholars (CIES) for information on Fulbright programs.

(P44) **KANSAS STATE UNIVERSITY/CENTER FOR FACULTY EVALUATION AND DEVELOPMENT**
Contact: William Cashin, Conference Director, Academic Chairpersons Conference, Kansas State University, 1615 Anderson Avenue, Manhattan, KS 66502–1604, (800) 255–2757

(P44a) ***Annual Conference for Academic Chairpersons***
Since 1984, this seminar has brought together chairs from all disciplines for three days of discussion and exploration of the trials and tribulations, challenges and issues of this position. Topics range from teaching vs. research, service vs. advising, faculty vs. administration, leading vs. managing, ethical vs. legal issues, evaluation vs. development, to quality vs. quantity. There is an annual call for proposals each spring in preparation for the annual February event.

(P45) **LEAGUE FOR INNOVATION IN THE COMMUNITY COLLEGE**
Contact: Terry O'Banion, Executive Director, League for Innovation in the Community College, 25431 Cabot Road, Suite 204, Laguna Hills, CA 92653 (714) 855-0710

    (P45a) ***Executive Leadership Institute***
Begun in 1988, this program is designed to provide an opportunity for potential community college presidents to review their abilities and interests, to refine their skills, and to participate in discussions on leadership with community college leaders. Topics range from shaping the presidency, assessing personal qualifications, Board/CEO relations, internal leadership, politics and the CEO, collective bargaining and faculty relations, values and vision, and exercising leadership through the budget. Senior community college leaders serve as faculty. Participation in this one-week summer program is limited to 30. The program is held in Newport Beach, California.

    (P45b) ***Leadership 2000***
An international executive development conference that provides an opportunity for members of community college leadership teams to discuss issues, share views and solutions, and improve leadership skills and abilities. Keynote speakers, symposia, forums, and workshops address leadership development, governance, political/financial concerns, team building and collegiality, board/CEO effectiveness, access, and the quest for quality. The program is typically scheduled in the summer.

    (P45c) ***Minority Leadership Program***
Funded with a grant from the W. K. Kellogg Foundation, the League annually selects 10 Kellogg Fellows. Each fellow participates in a series of four seminars and professional development experiences in conjunction with a sponsoring mentor, other mentors, and project staff. Fellows may also participate in internships. Fellows also receive stipends to assist with travel and related expenses. The program is coordinated by the League and The University of Texas at Austin as part of the W. K. Kellogg Leadership project.

(P46) **LEAGUE FOR INNOVATION IN THE COMMUNITY COLLEGE, THE UNIVERSITY OF TEXAS—AUSTIN, AND THE W. K. KELLOGG FOUNDATION**
Contact: Brenda Marshall Beckman, Expanding Leadership Diversity, League for Innovation in the Community

College, 25431 Cabot Road, Suite 204, Laguna Hills, CA 92653, (714) 855–0710

(P46a)   ***Expanding Leadership Diversity in Community Colleges***
This program assists mid-level administrators and faculty such as division directors, department chairs, assistant deans, program coordinators, and other promising minority staff members to review their interests and abilities, participate in broadening experiences, and develop new skills in preparation for senior-level leadership as deans and vice presidents in community colleges. Ten Fellows are selected for this year-long experience. The program consists of a series of professional development seminars held at League for Innovation colleges and designed to allow Fellows to review their interests and abilities, participate in discussions with outstanding community college leaders, and develop familiarity with the range of issues facing community colleges. These experiences are designed for each Fellow in conjunction with a sponsoring CEO, other mentors, and project staff. The program's second major component includes the design and implementation of a year-long individual professional development plan for each fellow. The program also includes internships, special projects, focused study, opportunities to interact with CEOs of League member colleges, and participation in other League activities such as Leadership 2000.

(P47)   ***THE LILLY ENDOWMENT, INC.***
Contact: Ralph Lundgren, The Lilly Endowment, 2801 North Meridian Street, P.O. Box 88068, Indianapolis, IN 46208, (317) 924–5471

(P47a)   ***Workshop on the Liberal Arts***
This two-week summer workshop provides opportunities for teams of faculty and administrators from colleges and universities to explore in depth a problem associated with their institutions' liberal arts curricula. Each year, 25 institutions are invited to send a four-person team to the seminar at Colorado College in June. The workshop consists of 13 seminars. Participant teams enroll in one or two seminars related to their curriculum challenge while individually pursuing their interests in higher education and the liberal arts. Teams typically consist of a dean, department chair, and faculty leaders. Begun in 1958 by the Danforth Foundation, the program has been sponsored by the Lilly Endowment, Inc., since 1978.

(P48) **MASSACHUSETTS INSTITUTE OF TECHNOLOGY (MIT)/
SLOAN SCHOOL OF MANAGEMENT**

Contact: Alan F. White, Associate Dean for Executive Educa-
tion, Sloan School of Management, Massachusetts
Institute of Technology, Room E52–126, Cambridge,
MA 02139, (617) 253–7166

(P48a) ***Alfred P. Sloan Fellows Program***
The Sloan Fellows Program is designed to develop
the knowledge and skills of mid-level executives with
10 to 15 years of experience and to broaden their
values and attitudes for the additional responsibilities
of more senior management positions. Each year
approximately 55 Fellows are selected from both the
public and private sector for this 12–month program.
Through an intensive, graduate-level course load,
participants can expect to gain an understanding of
quantitative tools currently available to aid the
decision-making process, human behaviors and organizational environments, and the ''process of management'' that confers a general management
perspective for most kinds of organizations. The program helps Fellows develop an awareness of new
concepts and critical issues as well as provides a base
for continuing self-education. The fee, relocation, and
living expenses are usually paid by the sponsoring
organization.

(P49) **MODERN LANGUAGE ASSOCIATION (MLA)**

(P49a) ***Association of Departments of English (ADE) Summer
Seminars***
Each year three ADE Summer Seminars are held on
different campuses throughout the United States. Participants include English department administrators;
directors of writing, rhetoric, and communications
programs; and heads of humanities divisions, as well
as nominated colleagues. These four-day workshops
address topics important to faculty and administrators
in English studies, including curriculum and personnel change, dean-department chair relationships, and
interdisciplinary perspectives affecting English departments. There is also a pre-seminar workshop for new
chairs held the morning prior to the beginning of the
seminars. In the pre-seminar, two experienced ADE
chairs lead discussions on topics important to new
chairs, such as time management, budget, and personnel issues. Most meals, social events, and administra-

tive expenses are included in the registration fee.

Contact: David Laurence, Director, English Programs and ADE, MLA, 10 Astor Place, New York, NY 10003, (212) 614–6317

(P49b) *Association of Departments of Foreign Languages (ADFL) Summer Seminars*

Since 1971 the ADFL has sponsored summer workshops for department chairs and administrators of foreign language and literature departments to enable them to keep abreast of current activities in the field. Held each summer in locations in the east and west, these workshops are a forum for exchanging information and insights on departmental management and policy, curriculum and faculty development. The workshop format includes plenary sessions on topics such as new issues and methods in the curriculum, the academic reward system, and minority recruitment issues. These general sessions are followed by small group discussions to deal with the topics presented in an in-depth manner. The registration fee covers most meals and social events.

Contact: Judith Ginsberg, Director, Foreign Language Programs and ADFL, MLA, 10 Astor Place, New York, NY 10003, (212) 614–6320

(P50) *NATIONAL ASSOCIATION OF ACADEMIC AFFAIRS ADMINISTRATORS (AcAfAd)*

Contact: W. Peter Hood, Assistant Vice President for Academic Affairs/Director of the University Office of School-College Relations, University of Illinois, 312 Illena Tower, 409 East Chalmers, Champaign, IL 61820, (217) 333–2030

(P50a) *Management Development Seminar for Assistant and Associate Deans*

This three-day seminar was founded in 1978 to prepare assistant and associate deans for their management and leadership roles. Topics covered include grantsmanship, how to continue scholarship while in this new job, managing change, budgeting, career development, management styles and strategies, and management techniques. One of the most useful sessions is a free-flowing discussion on the nuts and bolts of academic management and leadership. Sessions are led by experienced deans, associate, and assistant deans. The seminar is held annually in November in Washington, DC. The registration fee includes materials and some meals; hotel costs are extra.

(P51)   **NATIONAL ASSOCIATION OF COLLEGE ADMISSION**
          COUNSELORS (NACAC)
          Contact: Joyce Smith, Associate Executive Director, NACAC,
          1800 Diagonal Road, Suite 430, Alexandria, VA 22314,
          (703) 836–2222

    (P51a)   **Admission Middle Management Institute**
          This three-day seminar is designed for experienced
          non-directors with at least three years of experience.
          Held each year in early June, the institute attempts to
          develop leadership skills through the exploration of
          topics such as management, supervision, communica-
          tion, and time management. The program also exam-
          ines issues of career paths in admissions.

(P52)   **NATIONAL ASSOCIATION OF COLLEGE AND UNIVERSITY**
          BUSINESS OFFICERS (NACUBO)
          Contact: Marie W. Klemann, Director, Professional Develop-
          ment Department, NACUBO, One Dupont Circle,
          NW, Suite 500, Washington, DC 20036–1178, (202)
          861–2520

          NACUBO offers a variety of programming oppor-
          tunities to enhance skills and share ideas among busi-
          ness officers and others who are involved with
          business-related activities of colleges and universities.
          Annual programs include the Accounting Roundtable,
          Law Institute for Business Officers, Senior Financial
          Officers Conference, Strategic Financial Management
          Issues for the 1990s, Strategic Planning and Budget-
          ing, Basic and Advanced Indirect Cost Rates, Fund
          Accounting and Reporting, Treasury/Cash Manage-
          ment Forum, Student Loan Management and Collec-
          tions, and Endowment Management. With its regional
          organizations CACUBO (Central), EACUBO (Eastern),
          SACUBO (Southern), and WACUBO (Western),
          NACUBO offers a wide range of professional develop-
          ment programs for business officers.

    (P52a)   **Senior Financial Officers Conference**
          This program for chief fiscal officers, comptrollers,
          treasurers, senior accounting officers, business man-
          agers, and internal audit managers provides the latest
          information on major issues in higher education finan-
          cial reporting. In addition to updating current account-
          ing principles and issues, the seminar provides a
          forum for the exchange of new ideas for fiscal manage-
          ment.

(P53)   *NATIONAL ASSOCIATION OF COLLEGE AND UNIVERSITY BUSINESS OFFICERS (NACUBO)/MARRIOTT EDUCATION SERVICES*
Contact: Mary Scohera, Program Manager for Professional Development, NACUBO, One Dupont Circle, NW, Suite 510, Washington, DC 20036 (202) 861–2520

     (P53a)   *Executive Leadership Institute*
This two-track program for chief business officers aims to enhance existing leadership skills, expand self-knowledge, and provide for an exchange of ideas regarding new approaches to management in a changing environment. Participation includes two summer sessions; each class includes 50 new participants and 50 returning participants. Participation is by invitation through the regional and national associations. Faculty include experienced chief business officers and business scholars and experts.

(P54)   *NATIONAL ASSOCIATION OF INDEPENDENT COLLEGES AND UNIVERSITIES (NAICU)*
Contact: Deborah Sykes, Coordinator of Membership Services, NAICU, 122 C Street, NW, Suite 750, Washington, DC 20001, (202) 347–7512

     (P54a)   *Public Policy Seminar for New Presidents*
This seminar introduces new presidents to public policy and the institution's role in affecting public policy. Sessions include briefings and speeches presented by the NAICU staff, public policy experts, and government leaders. Participation is by invitation. There is no specific programming for spouses. A one-and-one-half-day seminar is scheduled in Washington, DC, each autumn and spring.

(P55)   *NATIONAL ASSOCIATION OF STATE UNIVERSITIES AND LAND-GRANT COLLEGES (NASULGC)*
Contact: Alice Hord, Assistant to the President, NASULGC, One Dupont Circle, NW, Suite 710, Washington, DC 20036, (202) 778–0860

     (P55a)   *Council of Presidents*
This three-day conference for presidents of member institutions addresses the problems of succeeding in the presidency. Workshop sessions, led by NASULGC staff and experienced presidents, include intercollegiate athletics; working with private institutions, regents, and trustees; international education; public affairs; crisis management; and federal and state

management. Speaker and discussion sessions are incorporated into the council of presidents meetings at annual NASULGC conventions and include round tables with established presidents. There are special "Council of Presidential Spouses" sessions (For information on this Council, contact Joan Clodius at (202) 778-0860). The Council is held each autumn in a different domestic major city.

(P56) **NATIONAL ASSOCIATION OF STUDENT PERSONNEL ADMINISTRATORS (NASPA)**
Contact: Elizabeth Nuss, Executive Director, NASPA, 1700 18th Street, NW, Suite 301, Washington, DC 20009-2508, (202) 265-7500

(P56a) **Richard F. Stevens NASPA Institute**
The curriculum of this one-week summer program focuses on developing new perspectives for the chief student affairs officer and others with broad responsibilities in the student affairs area. Workshops, led by senior chief student services officers, scholars, and experts in student services issues, address a range of topics in management and contemporary issues, including leadership, skill development, strategic planning, budgeting, and total quality management. Instruction includes individual case study analysis combined with formal and small group discussion.

(P57) **NATIONAL CENTER FOR HIGHER EDUCATION MANAGEMENT SYSTEMS (NCHEMS)**
Contact: Arlene Barr, NCHEMS, P.O. Drawer P, Boulder, CO 80301-9752, (303) 497-0301

NCHEMS, a nonprofit corporation whose mission is to help colleges and universities improve their management capability, has for 20 years sought to bridge the gap between research and practice by placing the latest managerial concepts and tools in the hands of working administrators. It offers a variety of leadership and management development programs appropriate for college and university administrators of every level. Programs annually focus on themes such as strategic planning in the higher education setting, assessing quality and effectiveness, linking planning and budgeting, and enhancing administrative effectiveness. Each year, new programs are added to address current higher education challenges. Programs are usually offered several times each year in opposite parts of the country. Through its subsidiary, the NCHEMS

Management Services, Inc. (NMSI), offers individual consulting services. Although administrators can register individually for seminars, colleges and universities can benefit from institutional memberships in NCHEMS and from discounts on publications, the NCHEMS Annual Assembly, and Information Service reports and Data on Diskette orders.

(P58) ***NATIONAL FACULTY EXCHANGE (NFE)***
Contact: Bette Worley, President, 4656 West Jefferson Boulevard, Suite 140, Fort Wayne, IN 46804, (219) 436–2634

A consortium of colleges and universities, primarily from the United States, but also including Canada, and other foreign institutions, the Exchange serves as a broker or negotiators in the arrangement of faculty exchanges. The Exchange will help to find an appropriate place for a faculty member who seeks an exchange, and then assist the faculty member's institution in finding a replacement. Most exchanges are not direct swaps, but rather trades among several institutions, each having its teaching needs met through the arrangement. The Exchange can further help an institution extend its faculty resources by helping to fill short-term hiring needs to cover sabbaticals and leaves. The Exchange also supports an Emeriti Placement Program. It makes the credentials of emeriti faculty available within the consortium. They are often tapped to cover the short-term teaching needs of institutions. The Exchange is in the final stages of striking an agreement with the International Student Exchange Program to tap its contacts abroad to establish a network for international faculty exchanges. Initially, this service will be only a directory of opportunities. Later, the Exchange anticipates serving as a broker in these exchanges, as well. The Exchange does not cover house exchanges. The services of the Exchange are available only to member institutions and their faculty.

(P59) ***NATIONAL INSTITUTE FOR LEADERSHIP DEVELOPMENT***
Contact: Carolyn Desjardins, Director, The National Institute for Leadership Development, 640 North First Avenue, Phoenix, AZ 85003, (602) 223–4292

Founded in 1980 by the League for Innovation in the Community College with a grant from the Fund for the Improvement of Postsecondary Education (FIPSE), in cooperation with the American Association of Women in Community and Junior Colleges (AAWCJC), to develop women leaders. Since that time, the project has trained over 1,500 women for positions in community college administration. It has become self-supporting, under the direction of the Maricopa Community Colleges District.

(P59a)   ***Building a Better Team on Campus: Understanding Gender Issues***
This program explores gender issues and theories through a process of enabling campus teams to gain an awareness of themselves. Participant teams of male and female representatives from colleges and universities then return to their own campuses to run workshops on gender issues for their peers and for students. The five-day workshop will be introduced in 1991 and will be held on the campus of Arizona State University.

(P59b)   ***Leaders for Change***
This workshop prepares women for whom the Chief Executive Officer's position could be the next career step. The curriculum considers current issues in higher education and specific strategies for making the next career step. Faculty include women CEOs and higher education experts. The four-day seminar is held in February in Phoenix, Arizona. The registration fee does not include hotel or meals.

(P59c)   ***Leadership for a New Century***
This six-day intensive seminar brings together mid-level women administrators of academics, business, development and fund raising, and student development at four-year colleges and universities to strengthen their administrative leadership, and to build a national network of support and sharing. Other goals include examining important educational issues and enhancing management perspectives for women administrators within four-year institutions. The program is also appropriate for faculty who want to examine administration as a career. Workshop topics include budget and finance, institutional governance, organizational change and transformation, development, legal issues, and personnel management. Faculty include women CEOs and national experts. Participants work with a mentor to identify and complete a significant project for their institution. The seven-day seminar is held twice annually each October and January in Phoenix, Arizona. Hotel and meals are extra.

(P59d)   ***Leaders Project***
This program is directed at mid-level community college women administrators of academics, business, development and fund raising, and student development from around the country who want to strengthen their administrative, networking, and leadership skills and abilities. It is also appropriate for faculty who want to examine administration as a career. Goals include improving career skills and opportunities, focusing on major administrative issues, and developing mentoring for women interested in community college administration. After the workshop, participants continue to work on a campus project that facilitates seeing themselves more positively and provides campus visibility. The seven-day seminar runs four times during the spring semester (February through June) in Phoenix, Arizona. The registration fee does not include hotel or meals.

(P59e)   ***Workshop for Women Presidents***
This workshop, led by higher education experts, addresses timely issues for women presidents and provides opportunities for introspection. The two-day workshop is typically scheduled in January at a retreat area outside Phoenix, Arizona.

(P60)   ***NORTH CAROLINA STATE UNIVERSITY***
Contact: Terrence A. Tollefson, Director, Community College, Leadership Institute, Department of Adult and Community, College Education, P.O. Box 7801, North Carolina State University, Raleigh, NC 27695–7801, (919) 737–3590

(P60a)   ***Community College Leadership Institute***
The Community College Leadership Institute is designed to provide leadership development opportunities for approximately 25 current and potential community college leaders including vice-presidents, deans, program directors, and faculty. The program encourages participants to become intensely involved in various contemporary issues and prepares them for making decisions on these issues. The two-week workshop features several nationally prominent speakers and North Carolina practitioners. Frequently scheduled roundtable discussions and luncheons allow for extensive small-group interaction. Up to six hours of graduate credit are available for participating in the institute.

(P61)   *NTL INSTITUTE*
Contact: Registrar, NTL Institute, 1240 N. Pitt Street, Suite 100, Alexandria, VA 22314, (703) 548–1500/(800) 777–LABS

The purpose of the NTL (National Training Laboratories) Institute is to develop ways of improving the quality and effectiveness of relationships in all areas of human life. The Institute applies the findings and methods of the social sciences to improve the professions, extend basic and applied knowledge of society, and to develop leadership in directing social change. It particularly seeks to link the efforts of scholars and practitioners through programs of experience-based education, innovation in social change activities and programs, programs for the examination of personal and systems change efforts, and programs of research and development. Management and professional development programs focus on themes of conflict and transition; diversity; influence, negotiation, and communication; leadership/management; and team development. There are also programs on concepts and skills in organization development, consultation, and training. The NTL Institute offers masters degrees in Human Resource Development in conjunction with The American University and in Management with the John F. Kennedy University. There is also an extensive publication series. NTL also offers in-house consultation services and development programs.

(P61a)   ***Human Interaction Laboratory***
For anyone interested in learning more about themselves, how they relate to others, and to fine-tune their personal "style" of interaction. Activities, including T Groups, focus on concepts and theories to apply to other systems in daily life at work and at home. The program can be tailored to a general audience, middle managers, or senior executives. An Advanced Human Interaction Conference is also available.

(P61b)   ***Management Work Conference***
This program focuses on organizational issues and personal management style. The program is available for general audience, middle managers, and senior executives.

(P61c)   ***Senior Executive's Conference***
Designed for vice presidents, general managers, and other comparable high-level administrators who are concerned with understanding human interaction, group and individual relationships. The design is

planned around the managerial skill needs of top administrators in today's global workplace through small group discussions, large community sessions, and other experience-based activities.

(P61d)   *Other programs of potential interest to higher educa-tion administrators and faculty include:*
Becoming Whole: To Be Woman, Successful, and Black
Creating and Sustaining High Performing Teams
Developing High Performing Culturally Diverse Organizations
Developing Your Staff: How to Improve Your Morale, Motivation, and Productivity
Diversity Across Gender, Race, Nationality: A Look Into the Future
Effective Task-Group Leadership: Promoting Devel-opment in Management Teams and Task Forces
Facilitating and Managing Complex System Change
Leadership Excellence
Managing the Multicultural Workforce: A Bottom Line Issue
Negotiating and Building Good Working Relationships
Tavistock Workshop: Rethinking and Planning for Organizational Change
The Leading Edge: Advanced Team Building
Strategic Management and OD

(P62)   *OKLAHOMA STATE UNIVERSITY*
Contact: Thomas A. Karman, Educational Administration and Higher Education, 309 Gundersen, Oklahoma State University, Stillwater, OK 74078–0146, (405) 744–7244

(P62a)   *Annual National Conference of Academic Deans*
Perhaps the oldest continuous leadership develop-ment program in higher education, the "Stillwater Conference" (nicknamed after the site of the annual conference in Stillwater, Oklahoma) brings together academic deans for discussions on pertinent topics of higher education issues and management. The 1990 conference was the 44th annual meeting. A recent theme was "Keeping the Deans Human: Balancing Conflicting Demands." The four-day conference typ-ically includes plenary sessions, small group discus-sions, case studies, and panel discussions lead by experienced deans and higher education experts. Par-ticipants include all types of deans, assistant and asso-ciate deans, and academic vice presidents. The

conference is held in late July or early August. Hotel and meals are extra.

(P63)   ***PROFESSIONAL AND ORGANIZATIONAL DEVELOPMENT NETWORK IN HIGHER EDUCATION (POD)***
Contact: Delivee L. Wright, Executive Director, POD, Teaching and Learning Center, 121 Benton Hall, University of Nebraska—Lincoln, Lincoln NB 68588–0623, (402) 472–3079.

(P63a)   POD is a professional association of people who share a commitment to improving higher education. Typically, POD engages in faculty, administrative, instructional, or organizational development activities. Members of POD share the belief that learning, teaching, leadership, and institutional life are strengthened as opportunities for professional and personal growth. The Network helps its members to find resources for renewal, explore common interests and concerns, exchange information and ideas, forge supportive relationships, enhance professional skills, debate issues of ethics and strategies, and plan for the future. POD's principal goal is to make the idea of a network a reality for its members. This is achieved through an **Annual Fall Conference**, an annual book of readings, **To Improve the Academy**, a membership directory, **newsletters** four times a year, **regional meetings**, and a **summer institute** providing training in professional development issues.

(P64)   ***SOCIETY FOR VALUES IN HIGHER EDUCATION***
Contact: Charles Courtney, Executive Director, Society for Values in Higher Education, Box B-2814, Georgetown University, Washington, DC 20057, (202) 687–3653

(P64a)   ***The Fellows Meeting***
This August meeting provides a forum for the discussion of the values of higher education. Discussion topics have included "critical discourse," "education of women," "the relation of values to higher education," and "freedom of speech on campus." Fellows serve as conveners of small groups and discussions and present papers and lectures. Participants are drawn primarily from the membership of the Society, which includes approximately 1,400 active leaders in higher education including faculty leaders, deans, vice presidents, and presidents. The one-week program is scheduled on a different college campus each year. Housing and meals are not included in the fee. There

is also programming for spouses and children. Society members are elected through a nominations procedure. The Society also conducts specific projects on topics such as decision making in higher education, the practice of teaching, and institutional renewal through the improvement of teaching.

(P65) ***SOUTHERN ASSOCIATION OF COLLEGE AND UNIVERSITY BUSINESS OFFICERS (SACUBO)/UNIVERSITY OF KENTUCKY***
Contact: James Chapman, Assistant Vice Chancellor of Resource Management, (606) 257–1962, or Donna Hall, Director of Conferences and Seminars, CMBI, University of Kentucky, 204 Frazee Hall, Lexington, KY 40506–0031, (606) 257–3929

(P65a) ***College Management Business Institute (CMBI)***
Located on the campus of the University of Kentucky, this program for senior or mid-level officers in management, business, and financial affairs covers the major areas of business and financial management. Participants attend three one-week sessions over three summers. The first year covers fundamentals such as fund accounting, personnel administration, and purchasing, while the second and third years address a variety of subjects, such as the role of chief business officer, organizational structure, financial affairs and treasury, personnel administration and staff relations, auxiliary and business services, data processing, and planning. Faculty, who teach primarily through lectures and classroom discussion, include experts drawn from a wide-range of backgrounds and experiences. The registration fee does not include housing or meals.

(P66) ***TEXAS A&M UNIVERSITY/ COLLEGE OF EDUCATION***
Contact: Bryan R. Cole, Director, Summer Seminar on Academic Administration, Texas A&M University, College of Education, College Station, TX 77843, (409) 845–5364

(P66a) ***Summer Seminar on Academic Administration***
Since 1968, the Summer Seminar has provided a one-week training session for officers new to administration, including vice presidents, deans, and department chairs. With a focus on leadership development and managerial skills, the program is designed to give its 35 participants a thorough exposure to concepts and practices relevant to academic administration with particular emphasis on decision-making and

management in higher education. Instruction is carried on through case studies, seminars, open forum discussions, and lectures, in a format to prepare participants to meet the real problems of day-to-day campus life. The 500 individuals representing 132 institutions who have participated in the program have been primarily but not exclusively drawn from Texas. The fee includes registration, curriculum materials, housing, and meals.

(P67) **UNIVERSITY AFFILIATIONS PROGRAM**
See Council for International Exchange of Scholars (CIES) for information on Fulbright programs.

(P68) **UNIVERSITY OF CENTRAL FLORIDA**
Contact: University of Central Florida, College of Extended Studies, Orlando, FL 32816–0177

(P68a) ***Financial Management for Women in Higher Education***
This workshop is designed to develop an understanding of the processes and procedures attendant to the budget process and system of accounting utilized by institutions of higher education. Participants include individuals in colleges and universities interested in preparing for and seeking higher-level administrative positions that may require an understanding of fiscal management. Seminar leaders are partners in the higher education practices of major accounting companies. The seminar is held each March in Orlando, Florida.

(P69) **UNIVERSITY OF GEORGIA/INSTITUTE OF HIGHER EDUCATION AND THE GEORGIA CENTER FOR CONTINUING EDUCATION**
Contact: D. Parker Young, Institute of Higher Education, (404) 542–0574, or Amy S. Weir, Georgia Center for Continuing Education, The University of Georgia, Athens, GA 30602, (404) 542–1586

(P69a) ***Annual Conference on Higher Education and the Law***
This conference is designed to serve the needs of college and university presidents, deans, student affairs administrators, consulting attorneys, and other administrators concerned with the legal aspects of student, faculty, and administrative behavior. Typical topics addressed at this conference include personal liability of educators, civil rights law, employment issues, the litigious landscape of higher education, issues in student life, issues in academic affairs, and

legal and liability issues relating to health risks on campus. The conference was established in 1969.

(P70)   **UNIVERSITY OF MARYLAND**
Contact: William Thomas, Vice President for Student Affairs, University of Maryland, College Park, MD 20742, (301) 454–2925

   (P70a)   **Student Affairs Conference**
   Since 1974, the Student Affairs office of the University of Maryland has sponsored a major conference each February on the current challenges and issues in student affairs. Originally conceived as a development opportunity for members of the University of Maryland student affairs staff, the conference now attracts participants from as far away as Ohio, New York, and Tennessee. Among the approximately 400 annual participants are new professionals and veterans from student affairs, as well as representatives from other divisions of the University of Maryland. The one-day conference typically includes several speakers of national reputation, and a variety of invited and volunteer sessions utilizing panel discussions, lectures, and "how-to" applications. The theme of the 1991 conference was "Responding to Competing Priorities."

(P71)   **WESTERN ASSOCIATION OF COLLEGE AND UNIVERSITY BUSINESS OFFICERS (WACUBO)**

   (P71a)   **Executive Leadership and Management Institute**
   Focusing on the leadership and general management aspects of the business aspects of colleges and universities, this two-week program provides an intensive exploration of the challenges and issues facing senior business officers. In addition to reviewing accounting and business principles, the Institute focuses on the particular challenges of senior officers including strategic planning, negotiations, and administrative operations.
   Contact: Evelyn Broach, Assistant Controller for General Accounting, 857 Serra, Stanford University, Stanford, CA 94305–6205, (415) 723–0630

   (P71b)   **Business Management Institute**
   This four-year program is designed to advance the general fiscal and administrative skills of mid-level

business officers. The Institute meets for five days in August. Participants in the first-year curriculum focus on the basic functions of support services and other broad fiscal and management issues. Second-year participants focus on decision-influencing functions within colleges and universities. First- and second-year classes are taught primarily through lectures and class discussions. The third-year curriculum is designed for more experienced individuals and examines specific business issues and problems through case studies. The fourth-year curriculum is a culminating as well as continuing education experience in advanced management issues. The courses change annually to address pressing topics and problems. The fourth-year curriculum can be repeated for continuing education.

Contact: Donald W. Scoble, Associate Vice President for Business and Finance, San Francisco State University, 1600 Holloway Avenue, ADM 469, San Francisco, CA 94132, (415) 338–1323

(P72)   ***WILLIAMSBURG DEVELOPMENT INSTITUTE***
Contact: Jean A. Cogler, Director, Williamsburg Development Institute, 207 Mill Neck Road, Williamsburg, VA 23185, (804) 253–0033

   (P72a)   ***Williamsburg Development Institute***
   Assists those in educational and other tax-exempt institutions in improving their skills as organizers of institutional fundraising. The seminar covers a wide variety of topics, including institutional planning, foundation and corporate fund raising, record keeping, and time management. The program is particularly useful for development professionals with fewer than three years of experience, although it is also useful for presidents, trustees, and other senior officers new to fund raising. Experienced experts in fund raising provide intensive academic and practical instruction. The program takes place in Williamsburg, Virginia.

(P73)   ***W. K. KELLOGG FOUNDATION***
Contact: Larraine R. Matusak, Director, Kellogg National Fellowship Program, W. K. Kellogg Foundation, 400 North Avenue, Battle Creek, MI 49017–3398, (616) 969–2001

   (P73a)   ***National Fellowship Program***
   Initiated in 1980, this three-year Fellowship Program

provides an opportunity for individuals in the early
years of their professional careers to develop their professional skills and creativity. The program offers 50
outstanding young professionals an opportunity to
broaden their social and intellectual sensitivity, awareness, and leadership potential. Fellows are drawn
from business, education, human service agencies,
and private practice. Each Fellow is given a computer
and is required to communicate with the Foundation
and other fellows via a national computer network
called Confer. Fellows spend approximately 25 percent
of their time on fellowship-related activities, including
a self-designed learning plan for personal and professional development. In addition to time spent on the
self-designed learning plan, the program includes two
annual seminars of approximately five days each, plus
one mandatory two-week international seminar. Fellows are awarded $35,000 for the three-year period,
and $5,000 for travel expenses; 12.5 percent of their
annual salary (not to exceed an aggregate for the three
years of $24,000) is given to their employers.

(P74) **WOODROW WILSON NATIONAL FELLOWSHIP
FOUNDATION**
Contact: Richard O. Hope, Vice President, The Woodrow
Wilson National Fellowship Foundation, 330 Alex-
ander Street, P.O. Box 642, Princeton, NJ 08542, (609)
924–4666

(P74a)   *Administrative Fellows Program*
Established in 1967, the Administrative Fellows Program is designed to increase the pool of qualified professionals to address academic and financial concerns
in colleges serving disadvantaged groups. Colleges eligible to participate are those schools that have been
designated as "developing institutions" for the purposes of receiving Title III funds from the Department
of Education. The fellows are full-time administrators
who serve in positions such as assistant to the president, business manager, or director of research, planning, and development. Once selected as a finalist, the
Fellow's skills, expertise, and interests are matched
with position descriptions received from participating
institutions. Fellows' assignments focus on the crucial
problem of balancing cost and income while maintaining operational efficiency and educational effectiveness. Fellows are afforded the opportunity both to
contribute directly to the institution, and to work in an

environment in which their management skills may be honed and professional development accelerated. The Woodrow Wilson National Fellowship Foundation provides a salary subsidy to the participating institutions to supplement the negotiated salary of the Fellow.

STATEWIDE, SYSTEM-SPECIFIC, AND ON-CAMPUS PROGRAMS

Programs and activities on the following list typically are restricted to members of the sponsoring institution or organization.

(S1)   ***THE AMERICAN UNIVERSITY (AU)***
  Contact: Betsy Hostelter, Manager, Training and Development, AU, 4400 Massachusetts Avenue, NW, Washington, DC 20016, (202) 885–6206

  (S1a)   ***Office of Training and Development Programs***
    The Office of Training and Development offers three types of programs for AU faculty and staff. The **Specialized Programs** support a wide variety of training needs, from technical information to interpersonal skills and processes that impact the workplace. Topics covered include computer training, health and wellness, financial planning, and communication skills. The four-day **Management Development Program** *(S1b)* develops management and leadership skills for those employees of the university who supervise one or more full-time staff members. This core management program addresses topics such as leadership styles, problem solving, goal setting and planning, EEO issues and policy, and sexual harassment issues. Participants are selected by senior and executive staff.

(S2)   ***ARIZONA STATE UNIVERSITY (ASU)***
  Contact: Rita King, Assistant Human Resources Director, Staff Relations and Development, ASU, Tempe, AZ 85287–1403, (602) 965–4798

  (S2a)   ***Management Development Program (MDP)***
    In response to suggestions from a presidential task force, the human resource department created the MDP and its many initiatives. The **Management Internship** *(S2b)* is designed to provide developmental opportunities for potential managers while providing the university with qualified personnel to assist in the implementation of new initiatives and short-term projects. Interns are selected from faculty and professional staff applicants on a competitive basis and then assigned to specific vice presidential or other areas that have funded internship positions. Interns work in various administrative units and observe different

management and leadership styles. By completing short-term projects for a specific division, interns assist in management initiatives and learn ASU's management philosophy. The **Leadership Academy** *(S2c)* for mid-level administrators, faculty, and professional staff, meets bimonthly over an academic year. The seminars communicate ASU's management philosophy, provide an orientation to management and an overview of management skills, encourage communication among supervisors, and support the development and implementation of a promotional/management succession program. Participants, chosen from nominations made by the vice presidents, meet often with top-level speakers and complete group projects. A priority is placed on the recruitment of minority group members and women. The **President's Breakfast Series** *(S2d)* brings together vice presidents, academic deans, and senior administrators to hear nationally and internationally known speakers address issues related to institutional goals. Participants discuss cutting-edge issues while improving their decision-making skills and developing their networks among other top administrators. **Academic Chairs** *(S2e)* participate in a self-directed group that addresses necessary skills for department chairs identified by a series of focus groups. The program includes regular sessions throughout the year and a retreat that focuses on current issues, management skill-building, and networking. Session topics include stress management, leadership, faculty development, and new chair development.

(S3) ***ASSOCIATION OF CALIFORNIA COMMUNITY COLLEGE ADMINISTRATORS (ACCCA)***

Contact: Edward J. Valeau, Dean of Language Arts/Learning Resources, Association of California Community College Administrators, Skyline College, 3300 College Drive, San Bruno, CA 94066, (415) 355–7000 ext. 202

(S3a) *Mentor Program*
Participants in this program are placed with a mentor from another institution. Mentees may maintain their positions at their institutions or move to a host institution for the year. During the year, they meet with their mentor several times. Mentors work with the mentees through phone conferences, orientation sessions and activities throughout the year. The year-long program explores trends and practices in community college

administration by requiring the mentee to choose from
a list of study topics that range from board elections
and strategic planning procedures to affirmative action
and developing legislation. Participants periodically
review their lists and add areas they wish to explore or
develop. The program provides a professional development opportunity for those who aspire to higher
administrative positions in the California community
colleges.

(S4) **BEAVER COLLEGE**
Contact: Jean A. Dowdall, Vice President for Academic Affairs,
Beaver College, Glenside, PA 19038–3295, (215)
572–2924

(S4a) **Faculty Fellow in Academic Affairs**
A selected faculty member serves in the office of the
vice president for academic affairs to assist and provide leadership support for a wide range of projects
while continuing to teach one course each semester.
Responsibilities range from participation in organizing
retention studies, grant writing, and freshman year
programs to providing support for activities such as
planning and undergraduate academic programming.
The Fellow has the opportunity to observe and work
with senior administrative officers from student
affairs, college relations, and academic departments.
The appointment is renewable and compensation is
available for a Fellow who wishes to continue through
the summer.

(S5) **BOARD OF GOVERNORS OF STATE COLLEGES AND**
UNIVERSITIES (ILLINOIS)
Contact: Patricia K. Rea, Assistant Vice Chancellor for Legal
and Student Affairs, Board of Governors of State Col-
lege and Universities, 2040 Hill Meadows Drive,
Suite B, Springfield, IL 62702, (217) 782–6392

(S5a) **Affirmative Action Administrative Fellows Program**
The Administrative Fellows Program is a leadership
development program for female and minority faculty
and administrators and was initiated by the Chancellor
of the Illinois Board of Governors of State Colleges and
Universities, with the support of the presidents of the
Board's five universities. The program's objectives are:
(1) to increase the number of qualified minorities and
women in the applicant pools for upper-level administrative positions; (2) to identify and develop the

administrative talent of minority and women faculty and staff currently employed within the system; (3) to encourage successful Administrative Fellows to pursue careers in university administration; (4) to establish formal structures that will promote the mentoring of junior minority and women faculty and staff; and (5) to provide minority and women students with increased numbers of minority and women role models in leadership positions. At the heart of the Administrative Fellows program is the personalized Mentor/Fellow relationship. In addition to serving as an administrative staffperson to their primary Mentors and completing at least one major administrative project for the benefit of their host institutions, Fellows also help plan and attend a variety of administrative seminars designed to broaden their understanding of campus, system-wide, state, and national higher education administrative structures, issues and challenges.

(S6)   **BOSTON COLLEGE**
       Contact: Alice Jeghellian, Director of Professional Development, Boston College, Chestnut Hill, MA 02167, (617) 552–3338

(S6a)   *Professional Development Programs*
        As a function of the Department of Human Resources, the Human Resource Development Office offers a wide range of programs to the entire university community. The majority of individuals participating in these programs are professional/administrative workers (46 percent) and secretarial/clerical workers (36 percent), the remaining 18 percent divided between faculty (15 percent) and service/maintenance staff (3 percent). Although these programs are not billed as "faculty development," each year the number of faculty participants has been slowly increasing as more subjects relate to their interests—grant writing, advanced reading skills, etc. Faculty development per se is under the Academic Vice President. A Committee on Human Resource Development meets regularly and advises the Director on questions of program design and internal "marketability"; logistics of program delivery; the possibility of mandating certain programs in the future (i.e., having a core curriculum with certain programs described for certain positions, etc.); and implementing a new performance management system that will require a year-round cycle of

communication between supervisor and employee and that will include not only a performance appraisal but also periodic work plans and a required individual development plan. The new performance management system will apply to all non-faculty employees. An intensive training program to ''install'' the system began in 1991.

(S7) **CALIFORNIA STATE UNIVERSITY SYSTEM (CSU)**
Contact: Tim T. L. Dong, Assistant Vice Chancellor for Faculty and Staff Relations, California State University Chancellor's Office, 400 Golden Shore, Suite 222, Long Beach, CA 90802–4275, (213) 590–5603

(S7a) *Administrative Fellows Program*
Developed in 1978, this fellowship program provides administrative training to ethnic minority and women faculty and staff through mentor relationships and training workshops. Applicants are nominated by the campus presidents, and up to 12 full-time CSU faculty and staff members are selected each year by a system-wide committee. The Fellows are matched with CSU senior administrators who serve as their mentors for an academic year. The mentors provide guidance as well as opportunities for Fellows to be actively involved in the administration of campus programs. Throughout the year, Fellows attend workshops that provide additional training on various aspects of higher education administration. Of the 120 participants, 74 (62 percent), have advanced in educational administration.

(S8) **CHICAGO STATE UNIVERSITY**
Contact: Office of the Provost and Vice President for Academic Affairs, Chicago State University, 95th Street at King Drive, Chicago, IL 60628–1598, (312) 995–2410

(S8a) *Minority Administrative Fellow Program*
The Board of Governors of State Colleges and Universities, the governing board of five institutions in Illinois, established this fellowship program to identify and develop minority faculty for administrative leadership positions. Fellows are chosen through a screening process that includes interviews, then assigned to one of the five Board of Governors campuses (Chicago State University, Governors State University, Northeastern Illinois University, Eastern Illinois University, and Western Illinois University). The fellowships are for an academic year.

(S9)   **CITY UNIVERSITY OF NEW YORK (CUNY)**

(S9a)   ***Chancellor's Academic Affairs Faculty Fellowship Program***
CUNY initiated this program in 1979 to provide senior faculty members who are potential administrative leaders with a fellowship experience in the Office of Academic Affairs. This internship in academic administration provides Fellows with the opportunity to observe the University's overall management, and to participate in the formulation and implementation of University-wide academic programs and policies. Each year three Fellows spend a nine-month period working full-time with the Vice-Chancellor for Academic Affairs on special and ongoing projects. Fellows are introduced to concerns related to curriculum and programs, faculty, research, libraries, basic skills and skills assessment, and adult and continuing education. Each Fellow is assigned to work with a university dean of academic affairs who is responsible for one of these areas. In addition to the day-to-day experience with academic affairs, Fellows participate in seminars with college presidents and chief academic officers, take part in discussions of major issues of academic administration, and meet key members of the University community.
Contact: Jon Snuggs or Brenda Spatt, Office of Academic Affairs, CUNY, 535 East 80th Street, New York, NY 10021, (212) 794–5742/5423

(S9b)   ***Women's Leadership Institute***
The purpose of the CUNY Women's Leadership Institute is to identify, encourage, and train women leaders in higher education administration to bring to bear their considerable expertise and talent in shaping the future. The core of the Institute is a five-day residential program focused on the development of leadership skills. A follow-up component includes campus-based projects designed by the participants and guided by mentors. Curriculum topics include: staff supervision, budgeting and financial management, performance appraisal, team building, institutional management, decision making, and institutional culture and politics. The faculty of the Institute are drawn from among women leaders and specialists in higher education. A structured evaluation process, including a pre-Institute needs assessment and a quality assurance

component, is designed to ensure that the Institute
fulfills its stated objectives as well as meets the identified needs of the target population. A significant spin-
off from the Institute has been a support network for
women administrators who decide to pursue doctorate
degrees.

Contact: Marie J. Wittek, Women's Leadership Institute, CUNY, Office of Academic Affairs, 535
East 80th Street, New York, NY 10021, (212)
794–5554

(S10) *COLORADO STATE UNIVERSITY (CSU)*

Contact: Kay Herr, Associate Director, Office of Instructional
Services, Colorado State University, A71 Clark Building, Fort Collins, CO 80523, (303) 491–1325

(S10a) *Professional Development Programming*

The development programming of Colorado State University aims to enhance the understanding of administrative responsibilities, provide practical and
theoretical information, encourage campus awareness,
and train future academic administrators. Participants
include faculty, department chairs, professional staff,
and administrators. In addition to individual sessions
on specific topics, special annual programs include the
Professional Development Institute *(S10b)*, a three-
day intensive professional development program held
each January for department heads, administrators,
and persons preparing for academic administration
positions; the **Leadership Series** *(S10c)*, an annual
series of sessions on administrative and leadership
matters addressing topics such as "The Relationship
Between Deans and Chairpersons," and "Why the
Faculty Shortage?"; and the **Administrative Women's
Network** *(S10d)*, monthly discussions of administration and leadership issues affecting and of interest to
women. Each year approximately 35 workshops and
seminars are held on topics in teaching, research, service, administration, and personal career
development.

(S11) *COLORADO WOMEN IN HIGHER EDUCATION ADMINIS-
TRATION AND THE AMERICAN COUNCIL ON EDUCATION
NATIONAL IDENTIFICATION PROGRAM (ACE/NIP)*

Contact: Brangwyn Foote, Assistant Vice Chancellor for Academic Affairs, University of Colorado, Campus Box
40, Boulder, CO 80309, (303) 492–2962

(S11a)   ***Academic Management Institute for Women***
In a collaborative effort, the Colorado Women in
Higher Education Administration and its parent organization, the American Council on Education's
National Identification Program, formed a professional
development program designed specifically for
women in Colorado higher education administration.
This six-day seminar provides women administrators
with the opportunity to consider a variety of management issues and to strengthen their networks. Sessions address a broad range of career development
topics, from national trends to career planning strategies. National and state experts conduct sessions using
lectures, case studies, panel discussions, and small
group discussions. To complete the program, each participant completes an individual project at her home
institution. The class of 30 participants meet one or
two days a month from September through April in
Colorado. The registration fee does not include hotel
or meals. Participation requires nomination by a
campus Chief Executive Officer.

(S12)   ***COLUMBIA UNIVERSITY***
Contact: Rosalyn Hantman, Director of Personnel Planning and
Development, Columbia University, 311 Dodge, New
York, NY 10027, (212) 854–8336/3324

(S12a)   ***Professional Development Programs***
These workshops and seminars for academic and nonacademic officers and support staff are offered each
semester to help employees become more effective
workers, to support their career goals, and to make
them more aware of available health care resources.
Programs address management and supervision, quality service training, professional communication,
working in a multicultural environment, personnel
resources, computer training, administrative policies
and procedures, health and safety issues, and university benefits programs. Workshop leaders are faculty,
officers of the university, and outside consultants.
Workshops vary in length from one hour to eight
once-a-week, half-day sessions. A three-week **Connections** *(S12b)* program addresses issues of quality service for support staff, while a **Front Line Leadership
Program** *(S12c)* is for supervisors. A special **Middle
Management Development Program** *(S12d)*, designed
in conjunction with organizational experts from the
Columbia Business School, explores topics such as

strategy and strategic thinking, planning systems, decision making, conflict management and resolution, managerial negotiation, managing diversity, and implementing change.

(S13)   ***COMMITTEE FOR INSTITUTIONAL COOPERATION (CIC)***
Contact: Kenneth Anderson, Deputy Vice Chancellor for Academic Affairs, Committee for Institutional Cooperation, 2E Swanlund Administration Building, 601 E. John Street, University of Illinois, Champaign, IL 61820, (217) 333–8846

(S13a)   ***Academic Leadership Fellows Program***
This program is specifically oriented toward helping faculty address the challenges of academic administration at major research universities. Objectives are to identify faculty who have demonstrated exceptional ability and administrative promise and cultivate their leadership and managerial skills; to promote racial and gender diversity in administration; and to augment the ongoing professional development programs offered at CIC institutions. Each year four tenured faculty from each CIC institution are chosen to participate in the series of three two-day seminars on topics such as governance, human resources, planning, and budgeting. In addition, Fellows review assigned material and case studies, consult with mentors and academic leaders on their campuses, and participate in relevant campus administrative activities. Institutional members of CIC essentially include the Big 10 universities plus Pennsylvania State University and the University of Chicago.

(S14)   ***EASTERN ILLINOIS UNIVERSITY***
Contact: Judith Anderson, Director, Programs for Professional Enrichment, Old Main 108, Eastern Illinois University, Charleston, IL 61920, (217) 581–5020

(S14a)   ***Programs for Professional Enrichment (PPE)***
This is a three-phase program offering career development workshops, seminars in higher education administration, and administrative internships for faculty, mid-level administrators, and civil service staff. The program offers participants the opportunity to explore interests and options and gain valuable information about higher education administration. The career planning workshops focus on evaluating career goals while emphasizing higher education administration.

After completing the workshop, participants are invited to attend a seminar series designed to increase knowledge of issues and trends in administration. Finally, up to four participants are then selected for internship placement from those who have completed Phases I and II of the program. Internships are normally one semester and interns receive partial release time during the academic year. Through a separate external program, the PPE administers the University's application and selection process for faculty, administrators and staff interested in attending national external administrative development programs.

(S15) **GEORGE WASHINGTON UNIVERSITY**
Contact: Harvey Snyder, Training Manager, Personnel Services, George Washington University, 2110 G Street, N.W., Suite 101, Washington, DC 20052, (202) 994–4980

(S15a) *Training Division of Personnel Services*
Through workshops, seminars, discussions, and hands-on practicums, the Training Division of Personnel Services provides opportunities for employees to improve or obtain critical job skills necessary for functioning effectively in the complex University environment. The division presents approximately 20 different programs designed to meet specific work-related needs on a regular basis. Program content varies from general clerical training to contemporary higher education management issues. A typical schedule includes: AIDS seminar, career discussion, delegation skills, management forum, performance analysis, and supervisory training. The Training Division also offers its assistance to supervisors and managers in developing in-service training programs for their employees. New Employee Orientation is held twice per week and a specially designed program is offered to all new supervisory personnel. The division maintains a small library as well as a number of audiovisual resources. All programs are taught entirely by in-house personnel, including four professional staff trainers.

(S16) **GORDON COLLEGE**
Contact: R. Judson Carlberg, Dean of the Faculty, Gordon College, 255 Grapevine Road, Wenham, MA 01984, (508) 927–2300

(S16a) *Professional Development Through Growth Plans*
Gordon's growth planning program was initiated in

1976 as a way to link faculty rewards to demonstrated professional competence. Each participating faculty member writes a profile containing an assessment of strengths and weaknesses, a statement of current roles and perceived effectiveness in carrying out those roles, and a statement of long-range professional and personal goals spanning a period of three to five years. This profile forms the basis for a series of yearly individual development plans intended to cumulatively implement the participant's long-range goals. Each plan includes specific goals for the year, along with a description of intended means of accomplishment and assessment, and a budget request. The participant also chooses an advisory committee of faculty colleagues to help refine the growth plan, give advice during the implementation process, and write an assessment of goal accomplishment that accompanies the participant's self-assessment at the end of the calendar year. The program is supported by a grant from the W. K. Kellogg Foundation.

(S17)   ***INDIANA UNIVERSITY—BLOOMINGTON***
Contact: Deborah Olsen, Director, Faculty Development, Indiana University—Bloomington, Office of the Vice Chancellor for Academic Affairs, Bryan Hall 109, Bloomington, IN 47405, (404) 423-6033

(S17a)   ***Faculty Development Resources***
The Dean of Faculties Office sponsors annual competitions and ongoing programs for the career development of faculty and department chairs. Competitive programs include annual awards (stipends/release time) to young and mid-career faculty to pursue their scholarly interests, multidisciplinary seminars that allow faculty members to explore new disciplines, and a lecture award that rewards individuals who are outstanding teachers and scholars. Ongoing programs include tenure/promotion mentoring programs, a program for chairperson development, faculty exchange programs, and various career development workshops focusing on timely issues for personal and professional development.

(S18)   ***KENNESAW COLLEGE***
Contact: Betty L. Siegel, President, Kennesaw State College, P.O. Box 444, Marietta, GA 30061, (404) 423-6033

(S18a)   ***Leadership Kennesaw College***
To introduce faculty and department heads to the

larger leadership and management issues of the college. "Leadership Kennesaw College" is a year-long study program designed for faculty who want to prepare themselves for leadership challenges in higher education. A series of day-long monthly sessions begins and ends with retreats in September and May. Monthly programs address the various leadership challenges faced by faculty members, concentrating on topics such as personal dimensions of leadership, leadership in higher education, community outreach, politics and higher education, and challenges in human relations. Approximately 24 faculty members participate each year.

(S19) *LANSING COMMUNITY COLLEGE*
Contact: Bettye T. Gilkey, Community Leadership Development Academy, Business and Industry Institute, Lansing Community College, Room 210A North House, 534 North Capitol Avenue, P.O. Box 40010, Lansing, MI 48901–7210, (517) 483–1741

(S19a) *Community Leadership Development Academy*
Begun in 1982 to train potential leaders to effectively serve on boards, committees, and commissions for the college and in the community. The series of eight skills sessions begins in September and ends in December.

(S20) *MARICOPA COMMUNITY COLLEGES DISTRICT*
Contact: Gary Filan, Manager, Human Resources Division, Maricopa Community Colleges, District Offices, 3910 East Washington, Phoenix, AZ 85034, (602) 461–7324

(S20a) *VISIONS Career Development Program*
Designed to suit the needs of its employees, the professional development program offers a variety of opportunities for participants to develop their own action plans for achieving personal and professional goals. **Visions** is designed to address the areas of retraining, renewal, and career development for all District employees. The program covers six groupings: supervisory personnel, faculty, professional staff, management and administrative personnel, and maintenance and operations employees. Each group may choose from several workshops for career development assistance such as planning consultation and resume writing, personality profiles or retirement options. Personal enrichment courses such as fitness programs, service awards, and sabbatical

opportunities are among some of the other offerings. Parallel programs serve the needs of management, administrative, and technological personnel as well as employees of maintenance and operations (M&O), crafts, and food service. The **M&O/Crafts Training Program** *(S20b)* provides apprentice programs. The **Professional Group Program** *(S20c)* seeks to increase professional knowledge, update previous academic learning, and sharpen on-the-job thinking skills with the goal of preparation for greater responsibility.

(S21)   ***PENNSYLVANIA STATE UNIVERSITY***
Contact: Robert L. Kidder, Director, Employment and Development, Office of Human Resources, Pennsylvania State University, Rider Building, 120 South Burrowes Street, University Park, PA 16801, (814) 863–4606

(S21a)   ***Administrative Fellows Program***
This program is designed to provide an opportunity to enhance the administrative talents and qualifications of women and minority faculty and professional staff by involving them in mentorship experiences with senior-level administrators. Successful candidates are placed on a leave of absence and continue to receive a regular salary while participating in the program. Fellows are involved in a wide range of decision-making processes, learning activities, and programs that help create a pool of qualified women and minorities for senior-level administrative vacancies.

(S22)   ***ROCHESTER INSTITUTE OF TECHNOLOGY (RIT)***
Contact: Cynthia McGill, Assistant to the Provost, RIT, One Lomb Memorial Drive, P.O. Box 9887, Rochester, NY 14623–0887, (716) 475–6644

(S22a)   ***Executive Leadership in an Academic Setting***
Candidates for this seminar are nominated for participation by their supervisors and may include department chairs, faculty leaders, and heads of academic support units. In six sessions over an academic year, the 20 to 25 seminar participants explore topics such as strategic planning, resource allocation, academic culture, and legal issues. At the last session, participants report their recommendations on improving the teaching and learning environment at RIT to the President and Chairman of the RIT Board of Trustees. As a result of the program, alumni report having a broader perspective of the university as a complex organization

and encouragement to further develop their management and leadership skills.

(S23)   **STANFORD UNIVERSITY**
Contact: Judith Moss, Human Resource Development, Programs Manager, Stanford University, Stanford, CA 94305–6110,

(S23a)   ***Human Resources Development Programs***
Human Resource Services at Stanford offers three development programs for staff with administrative, managerial, or supervisory responsibilities. The **Administrative Development Program** *(S23b)* consists of 10 half-day sessions on topics such as organizational structure and environment, Stanford governance, the administrator's role, problem solving, and decision making. The program is intended to enhance administrative effectiveness by orienting participants to Stanford's organizational patterns and by providing skills development. The **Management Development Program** *(S23c)* is designed to provide a framework for understanding current management expectations, practices, and issues at Stanford, and for developing appropriate skills. Approximately 25 participants are nominated to attend these weekly sessions throughout the academic year, and the curriculum is updated annually to respond to changes in management emphasis. **Stanford Supervision and You** *(S23d)* is a required seminar for all staff in supervisory positions. This 12–week program develops skills critical to effective management and implementation of key human resource policies.

(S24)   **STATE UNIVERSITY OF NEW YORK (SUNY)**
Contact: Joyce Yaple Villa, Assistant Vice Chancellor for Employee Relations, Room N506, SUNY, State University Plaza, Albany, NY 12246, (518) 443–5684

(S24a)   ***Affirmative Action Leave Program***
Begun in 1987, this program provides a semester leave for faculty prior to tenure review, thus permitting recipients time away from campus to complete projects or study programs likely to improve their chances of attaining a permanent or continuing appointment. Persons targeted for assistance are minority individuals, women, disabled people and Vietnam-era veterans. Members of these groups are in short supply at many SUNY campuses, many of whom actively

participate in service activities at the expense of completing their own degrees, certifications, research, and publications. This program is designed to help them compensate for the disadvantage in the tenure review process that may result from their service commitments.

(S25)   **ST. NORBERT COLLEGE**
Contact: Kenneth J. Zahorski, Director, Office of Faculty Development, St. Norbert College, 320 Boyle Hall, De Pere, WI 54115, (414) 337–3093

> *(S25a)*   ***Faculty Development Program***
> St. Norbert College established an Office of Faculty Development (OFD) in 1985 to coordinate existing faculty development practices and to inaugurate new ones. Programs initiated at St. Norbert include a **Resource Center** *(S25b)* that provides faculty with information on professional development; a late-summer acclimation session, an orientation and mentor program for new faculty; a summer grants program; a noon discussion series about teaching and scholarship; a faculty development fund; a newsletter on faculty issues and professional development; and individual counseling. In 1988, the OFD helped form a 19–school consortial enterprise (the Wisconsin Association of Independent Colleges and Universities Faculty Development Network) dedicated to fostering faculty development through interinstitutional cooperation. The programs administered by the OFD are intended to create an environment conducive to growth, revitalization, and renewal.

(S26)   **TENNESSEE BOARD OF REGENTS**
Contact: James Vaden, Vice Chancellor for Business Affairs, Tennessee State Universities and Community College System, 1415 Murfreesboro Road, Suite 350, Nashville, TN 37217, (615) 366–4413

> *(S26a)*   ***Minority Management Development Program***
> This one-year internship program brings promising minority administrators into the central system office to work on projects with mentors. The goal is to provide these administrators with a foundation of management skills and a broadening of perspectives so that they can be placed in more senior positions on campuses within the system.

(S27)   ***UNIVERSITY OF CALIFORNIA—LOS ANGELES (UCLA)***
Contact: Deborah Raupp, Staff Development Coordinator, Office of the Vice Chancellor for Student Affairs, UCLA, 222 Murphy Hall, Los Angeles, CA 90024, (213) 206–1603

(S27a)   ***Management Enhancement Program***
This program has evolved significantly since its introduction in 1987. The program began as informational sessions to inform administrative members of the student affairs staff on activities and developments related to student affairs from the rest of the campus. From this beginning, the program has grown to meet the needs and interests of the department. The second year design included skills-oriented sessions, while in the third year administrators were assigned to groups and challenged to develop their own developmental project. For the 1990/91 academic year, administrators chose participation in one of a dozen areas, such as managing in a flattened hierarchy, handling communication between staff and managers, managing change, examining the organizational culture, putting strategic planning goals into practice, and gender-based leadership. Benefits of this ongoing development process have been the development of a departmental culture and the building of relationships across functional areas.

(S28)   ***UNIVERSITY OF CALIFORNIA—RIVERSIDE***
Contact: Curtis Grassman, Administrative Dean of Summer Programs and Instructional Development, University of California—Riverside, Office of Instructional Development, 2117 Administration Building, Riverside, CA 92521, (714) 787–4751

(S28a)   ***Office of Instructional Development***
The University of California—Riverside offers various grant-sponsored programs for faculty and undergraduates for the improvement of instructional leadership. Typically, faculty design and redevelop class materials for undergraduate courses. Student grants permit undergraduates to explore and work on projects with sponsored faculty. The central purpose of the program is to provide the opportunity to reevaluate the undergraduate curriculum while developing and expanding interdisciplinary and interdepartmental classes. Grants last from one academic quarter to one year.

(S29)   ***UNIVERSITY OF COLORADO—COLORADO SPRINGS***
Contact: Karen Earley, Director, The Colorado Exchange, Faculty and Staff Development, University of Colorado—Colorado Springs, 1861 Austin Bluffs Parkway, P.O. Box 7150, Colorado Springs, CO 80933–7150, (719) 593–3604

(S29a)   ***The Colorado Exchange***
Modeled after the National Faculty Exchange, this program extends an opportunity for staff, faculty, and administrators to exchange or work directly with their counterparts at participating colleges and universities throughout the state of Colorado. The program provides a unique avenue for gaining knowledge and new perspectives and enhancing skills and techniques. Exchanges can range from one day to one week for staff, from one semester to the duration of a special project for faculty, and from one week to a month or longer for administrators. Employees remain on their home campus payroll and benefits, while travel, food, and lodging are the responsibility of the exchange. Mini-grants are available on a limited basis.

(S30)   ***UNIVERSITY OF IOWA***
Contact: Jean Spector, Coordinator, Staff Development and Training, University of Iowa, 205 Eastlawn, Iowa City, IA 52242, (319) 335–2687

(S30a)   ***Administrative Seminar Program***
The Administrative Seminar Program is designed to expand opportunities for mid- and senior-level professional and scientific staff, and particularly for minorities and women at the University. The program enables participants to attend intensive professional development seminars on administrative/management as identified by the applicant. Seminar topics that may be funded include finance and budgeting, academic governance, computing, and human relations.

(S31)   ***UNIVERSITY OF KANSAS***
Contact: Judith A. Ramaley, Executive Vice Chancellor, University of Kansas, 231 Strong Hall, Lawrence, KS 66045, (913) 864–4946

(S31a)   ***Office of Personnel Services***
The Office of Personnel Services sponsors programs for mid-level managers and faculty members. The semester or summer-long **Faculty Fellows Program**

(S31b) taps the expertise of faculty members who can help study, evaluate, and offer solutions to campus problems. Fellows receive a small stipend and project expenses as well as some release time for their projects. Fellows are selected by the Executive Vice Chancellor and the participants may use their project results for publication. The **Workshops for University Managers** *(S31c)* are the first step in a long-range leadership development plan to provide opportunities for management development and to establish a qualified pool of managers at the university. Each one-day workshop has a follow-up session six months later. Seminar participants are nominated by the Vice Chancellors and University Directors to attend the seminars.

(S32) **UNIVERSITY OF MASSACHUSETTS—BOSTON**
Contact: Douglas Hartnagel, Dean of Enrollment Services, University of Massachusetts—Boston, Harbor Campus, Boston MA 02125, (617) 287–6020

(S32a) *Staff Exchange Program*
This staff exchange program began in 1983 to provide non-teaching professional employees from the Division of Enrollment Services with increased and effective interoffice management skills without leaving the campus. Participation is voluntary; participants are guaranteed return to their previous positions upon conclusion of the exchange. Each participant spends one calendar year in a new position within the Division of Enrollment Services' six departments. For the duration of the exchange, participants are not responsible for duties connected with their previous positions. Participants meet regularly with their supervisor and the dean to evaluate progress, to examine expectations, and to plan career goals. Participants establish a renewed sense of place within the university, a broader awareness of interdepartmental relations, and an increased sense of enthusiasm about the university.

(S33) **UNIVERSITY OF NEBRASKA—LINCOLN/INSTITUTE OF AGRICULTURE AND NATURAL RESOURCES**
Contact: Daniel W. Wheeler, Coordinator, OPOD, Institute of Agriculture and Natural Resources, University of Nebraska—Lincoln, 313 Agricultural Hall, Lincoln, NE 68583–0701, (402) 472–5558

(S33a)   ***Office of Professional and Organizational Development (OPOD)***
OPOD is a professional development unit designed to support and encourage faculty and administrative leadership. It offers various resources for faculty members including orientation for new faculty, individual consulting, a **Pre-Tenure Support Group** *(S33b)* for beginning faculty, consultation on a faculty leave program for established faculty, a curriculum development project supported by the Kellogg Foundation **(NUPAGE** *(S33c)*)**, and the **NUPROF** *(S33d)* career assessment program. NUPROF begins with a mandatory three-day Faculty Development Institute retreat, designed to help faculty understand the nature of change and the methods of career planning. Afterward, participants work in small groups to investigate career alternatives and personal needs to develop a growth plan. Plans are submitted to the campus steering committee for approval and implementation funds. Plans are evaluated after the first year. In addition to activities for faculty, OPOD sponsors several programs for administrators including an **Administrator Development Map** *(S33e)*, which outlines career paths and development activities; monthly seminars and workshops that address timely and important issues; and an informal unit administrator support group. Lastly, in order to establish a common direction for the College, OPOD assists in retreat planning and team building programs *(S33f)*.

(S34)   ***UNIVERSITY OF SOUTH CAROLINA***
Contact: Kenneth L. Schwab, Executive Vice President of Administration, University of South Carolina, Columbia, SC 29208, (803) 777–4245

(S34a)   ***Minority Administrative Fellowship***
Each year the University selects one minority faculty or professional staff member to participate in a one-year professional development program under the supervision of the Executive Vice President for Administration and the Provost. The fellowship is designed to increase understanding of the university system, to encourage and enhance the achievement of career goals in administration, to increase minority faculty retention rates, and to develop minority leadership in higher education by identifying and training individuals who show promise for responsible positions in administration. The program provides the opportunity

to study and gain valuable experience from observing the operation of the USC system. Applicants are chosen on a competitive basis and must have three years experience at the university. Funds are available for travel and professional development. Salary is funded through the fellowship, thereby allowing 100 percent release time.

(S35)   UNIVERSITY OF SOUTHERN COLORADO
Contact: Ernest Allen, Director of Faculty Development, University of Southern Colorado, 2200 Bonforte, Pueblo, CO 81001–4901, (719) 549-2313

(S35a)   *Faculty Directors Program*
This program provides opportunities for faculty members to gain experience in academic administration and to participate in institutional governance as representatives of campus-wide constituencies. A vacancy for an assistant vice president was converted into five positions for faculty directors, each receiving at least one-quarter release time from teaching, a $3,500 stipend, and a $2,000 operations budget to develop programs in instructional development, honors, academic advising, scholarly activities, and sponsored research. Faculty Directors work directly with department chairs, the Faculty Senate, and key governance units to fulfill institutional objectives; in addition, they function in advisory capacities to the Office of the Provost on important faculty and academic issues. All directors serve three-year terms.

(S36)   UNIVERSITY OF TENNESSEE
Contact: Katherine High, Associate Senior Vice President, University of Tennessee, 823 Andy Holt Tower, Knoxville, TN 37996–0184, (615) 974-3211

(S36a)   *Institute for Leadership Effectiveness*
This week-long institute is designed to provide mid- to senior-level administrators with insights and information concerning personal leadership styles and the principles and characteristics of organizations. This intensive workshop format immerses participants in an experiential learning situation that provides new information and perspectives. Through general sessions and small group interaction, participants address several topics including defining leadership, self-assessment, managing conflict, and campus culture. The Institute provides ample time for informal discussion and interaction with peers and colleagues.

(S37)   *UNIVERSITY OF TEXAS—EL PASO*
Contact: Laura Gomez, Personnel Specialist, The University of Texas—El Paso, El Paso, TX 79968–0507, (915) 747–5202

(S37a)   ***New Faculty and Staff Orientation Program***
This orientation is designed to develop sensitivity to the special nature of UT El Paso and the community it serves. The UT El Paso campus, located less than a mile from the U.S.-Mexico border, serves a student population that is about 55 percent Mexican-American and growing by 2 to 3 percent a year. This reality poses special challenges to the faculty and staff. This four-part orientation program begins with a session introducing demographic facts and implications as well as the University's long-term needs and goals. Afterwards, participants take a bus tour of El Paso to familiarize them with the city and environs, from which 85 percent of the student body is drawn. During the orientation's third segment, a pamphlet titled *Cómo se pronuncian?* is distributed. This booklet gives the pronunciation of many common Spanish names and places, helping new faculty and staff avoid embarrassment and alienation on the campus. The final part of the program is two semesters of an optional intensive Spanish language class. This orientation not only prepares newcomers for life in the community where Spanish is as prevalent as English but also increases faculty sensitivity to students' needs and problems. The program is extremely important to the success of new faculty and staff members in a Hispanic-majority environment. Faculty include the president, senior officers, and administrators of the university.

(S38)   *UNIVERSITY OF WISCONSIN—EAU CLAIRE*
Contact: Ronald N. Satz, Dean, University of Wisconsin—Eau Claire, Schofield Hall, Eau Claire, WI 54701, (715) 836–2721

(S38a)   ***School for Graduate Studies and Office of University Research***
The University of Wisconsin—Eau Claire offers several grant programs for faculty and academic staff. The programs are internally funded and administered by the School of Graduate Studies and the Office of University Research and provide support for professional development, curriculum improvement, research, and other scholarly and creative activities. In addition, the research office sponsors a variety of related scholarly

other scholarly and creative activities. In addition, the research office sponsors a variety of related scholarly activities including workshops, time reassignment incentives, and assistance with travel for professional purposes.

(S39) **UNIVERSITY OF WISCONSIN SYSTEM**
Contact: Stephen R. Portch, Vice President for Academic Affairs, The University of Wisconsin System Office, 1620 Van Hise Hall, 1220 Linden Drive, Madison, WI 53706, (608) 262–8778

(S39a) *Administrative Associate Program*
The semester or summer internship provides faculty and mid-level administrators from all University of Wisconsin campuses with an opportunity to learn about the operation of the Office of Academic Affairs. Through daily contact with the vice president, the associate observes the entire range of activities in the office and participates in joint projects of academic affairs and other system administration units, travels to campuses, attends meetings of the Board of Regents and other bodies, assumes increasingly responsible project assignments within the office, and works as a peer with other academic affairs staff. Associates learn a system-wide perspective on issues of higher education and become familiar with a variety of administrative activities. Interns are nominated by their institutions and selected through a competitive review process. Three appointments are made per year, one each for the fall, spring, and summer semesters.

(S40) **WASHINGTON STATE UNIVERSITY**
Contact: Donald W. Bushaw, Vice Provost for Instruction, Washington State University, 428 French Administration Building, Pullman, WA 99164–1046, (509) 335–5581

(S40a) *Faculty Development and Support Services*
This program focuses on faculty improvement and the development of competent teachers and scholars. There are four areas of support services offered: information technology, instructional and research development, personal well-being and career development. The services offered for academic enrichment range from computer training workshops to information on travel grants. Each service is available to university faculty on an ongoing basis throughout the year.

PARTICIPANTS IN THE REVIEW PROCESS

We are grateful to the many individuals who reviewed and commented on the manuscript, and who provided other valuable contributions to this book:

Dorothy de F. Abrahamse, Dean, Social and Behavioral Sciences, California State University—Long Beach

Andrew L. Abrams, Vice President for Legal Affairs, College of Charleston, SC

Eleanor Allen, Chair, Board of Trustees, Wilson College, PA

Judith Anderson, Director of Affirmative Action and Programs for Professional Enrichment, Eastern Illinois University

Artin Arslanian, Vice President for Academic Affairs, Belmont Abbey College, NC

Richard B. Artman, Vice President for Student Affairs, Nebraska Wesleyan University

Margaret A. Bacon, Resident Dean, School of Education, University of Colorado—Colorado Springs

Roger Baldwin, Assistant Professor, Higher Education, College of William and Mary, VA

Mercedes Basadre, Director of Educational Services, Georgetown University, Washington, DC

Joan Bean, Senior Development Officer, Fairleigh Dickinson University, NJ

Robert Beisner, Chair, History Department, The American University, Washington, DC

Howard Benoist, Vice President/Dean of Academic Affairs, Our Lady of the Lake University of San Antonio, TX

Paul N. Beyer, Director of Purchasing, The Johns Hopkins University, MD

Wanda Bigham, President, Marycrest College, IA

Carol Bland, Assistant to the President, University of Minnesota

E. Grady Bogue, former Chancellor, Louisiana State University, Shreveport, LA

Jerry M. Boone, President, Ferrum College, VA

Joseph Bouie, Executive Vice Chancellor, Southern University at New Orleans, LA

Donald Bowen, President, Stephen F. Austin State University, TX

Norman Bregman, Dean of Arts and Sciences, Henderson State University, AR

Thomas B. Brewer, President, Metropolitan State College, CO

Keith G. Briscoe, President, Buena Vista College, IA

H. Keith H. Brodie, President, Duke University, NC

Charles L. Brown, Assistant Vice President for Student Affairs, The University of Alabama

David G. Brown, Provost, Wake Forest University, NC

Joyce F. Brown, Vice Chancellor for Urban Affairs, City University of New York

William J. Brown, Jr., Associate Dean of Admissions, Lebanon Valley College, PA

Robert G. Cabello, Vice President of Student Affairs, Delta College, MI

Carol Cartwright, Vice Chancellor for Academic Affairs, University of California—Davis

Patrick A. Cashell, Assistant Registrar, University of Limerick, Ireland

Alfred L. Castle, Vice President for Development, Hawaii Pacific College

Richard P. Chait, Executive Director, National Center for Postsecondary Governance and Finance, University of Maryland

Brenda S. Cherry, Dean, College of Nursing, University of Massachusetts—Boston

Larry H. Christman, President, Association of Independent Colleges and Universities of Ohio

Stanley D. Clark, Dean, International Baptist Theological Seminary, Argentina

Thomasina Clemons, Director, Office of Affirmative Action Programs, The University of Connecticut

Harlan Cleveland, Professor of Public Affairs and Planning, Hubert Humphrey Institute for Public Affairs, University of Minnesota

Sanford Cohen, Provost, Senior Vice President for Academic Affairs, Wayne State University, MI

G. Jan Colijn, Dean of General Studies, Stockton State College, NJ

John S. Colley, Provost/Dean of the Faculty, Hampden-Sydney College, VA

Richard J. Collings, Dean, Liberal Arts and Sciences, Kutztown University, PA

Brian Copp, Assistant to the Vice Chancellor, University of Wisconsin—River Falls

Dagmar Cronn, Dean of Sciences, University of Maine

Margaret Curtis, Vice President for Academic Affairs, Livingstone College, NC

Craig Daniels, Dean of Arts and Sciences, Eastern Connecticut State University

Lawrence A. Davis, Jr., Dean, Arts and Sciences and Honors College, University of Arkansas at Pine Bluff

A. Robert DeHart, President, DeAnza College, CA

M. Kathleen Deignan, Associate Dean of Students, Princeton University, NJ

Albert A. Dekin, Jr., Associate Dean for Administration, School of Arts and Sciences, State University of New York—Binghamton

Carolyn Desjardins, Director, National Institute for Leadership Development, AZ

Nancy C. DeSombre, Vice President for Faculty and Instruction, Wright College, IL

Ann H. Die, Dean, Newcomb College, Tulane University, LA

Mark C. Dienhart, Associate Director, Department of Intercollegiate Athletics, University of Minnesota

Henry M. Doan, Director of Institutional Research, Adelphi University, NY

Kathleen Donofrio, Director of Personnel, Loyola College of Maryland

Walter Eggers, Vice President for Academic Affairs, University of New Hampshire

Elwood Ehrle, Professor of Biology, Western Michigan University

Thomas Ehrlich, President, Indiana University

Peggy Gordon Elliott, Chancellor, Indiana University Northwest

Paul Elsner, Chancellor, Maricopa County Community Colleges District Office, AZ

Alice Emerson, President, Wheaton College, MA

Mark Emmert, Associate Vice President for Academic Affairs, University of Colorado—Denver

Julius Erlenbach, Dean, College of Arts, Letters and Sciences, University of Wisconsin—La Crosse

Gary Filan, Manager, Organizational Development, Human Resources Division, Maricopa Community Colleges, AZ

Thomas F. Flynn, Dean of Undergraduate Studies, Mount Saint Mary's College, MD

Lowell L. Ford, Dean of Community Education and Student Services Division, Chemeketa Community College, OR

Suzanne Forsyth, Director of Human Resources, American Council on Education, Washington, DC

Thomas W. Fryer, Jr., Chancellor, Foothill-DeAnza Community College, CA

Juliet V. Garcia, President, Texas Southmost College

Mildred Garcia, Assistant Vice President for Academic Affairs, Montclair State College, NJ

Thomas A. Gaylord, Director, Planning and Information Systems, University of Alaska—Fairbanks

Patricia L. Geadelmann, Director of Governmental Relations, University of Northern Iowa

Charles Gibley, Jr., Dean, Graduate School of Arts and Sciences, Philadelphia College of Pharmacy and Science, PA

George T. Gilmore, University Registrar, New York University

Elsa Gomez, President, Kean College, NJ

Neil R. Grabois, President, Colgate University, NY

William H. Gray, Campus Director, Washington State University—Spokane

Richard E. Greene, President, St. Thomas University, FL

Janet Greenwood, President, University of Bridgeport, CT

Kenneth R. R. Gros Louis, Vice President and Chancellor, Indiana University

Mary E. Gutting, Dean of Student Life, Gettysburg College, PA

Anne C. Hall, Dean, Faculty of Music, Wilfrid Laurier University, Canada

John R. Halstead, Vice President for Student Affairs, University of Maine

Grace Hampton, Vice Provost, The Pennsylvania State University

Rosalyn F. Hantman, Director, Personnel, Planning and Development, Columbia University, NY

Marilyn Haring-Hidore, Dean, School of Education, University of Massachusetts—Amherst

Bernard W. Harleston, President, The City College of the City University of New York

Mary W. Harris, Dean, Center for Teaching and Learning, University of North Dakota

James A. Hayes, Associate Dean for Academic Affairs/Registrar, Union Theological Seminary, NY

George C. Heider, Vice President for Academic Affairs, Concordia College, NE

Neil R. Heighberger, Dean, College of Social Sciences, Xavier University, OH

Peggy Heim, Senior Research Officer, TIAA-CREF, NY

Kay U. Herr, Director, Office of Instructional Services, Colorado State University

Barbara J. Hetrick, Vice President and Dean of Academic Affairs, Hood College, MD

Emita B. Hill, Vice President for Institutional Advancement, Lehman College of the City University of New York

Ewell James Hindman, Associate Vice President for Academic Affairs, University of Northern Colorado

Carol L. Hinds, Academic Dean, Saint Mary College, KS

Kimberly Hokanson, Office of Development, Harvard University, MA

Michael K. Hooker, President, University of Maryland—Baltimore County

Ellen S. Hurwitz, Provost/Dean of the Faculty, Illinois Wesleyan University

R. Kenneth Hutchinson, Associate Vice President for Human Resources, University of Missouri System

Marianne Inman, Vice President/Dean of the College, Northland College, WI

Jerry Israel, Vice President/Academic Dean, Simpson College, IA

Jane M. Jameson, Senior Vice President for Personnel, University of South Carolina—Columbia

Alice Jeghelian, Director of Professional Development, Boston College, MA

Lynn G. Johnson, President, Hudson-Mohawk Association of Colleges and Universities, NY

Joel M. Jones, President, Fort Lewis College, CO

Steven W. Jones, President, Phillips County Community College, AR

Wiley F. Jones, Business Manager, Alcorn State University, MS

Sheila Kaplan, Chancellor, University of Wisconsin—Parkside

Leroy Keith, President, Morehouse College, GA

Shirley Strum Kenny, President, Queens College of the City University of New York, NY

Rita King, Assistant Personnel Director, Arizona State University

Allen E. Koenig, President, Chapman College, CA

Judy Kuipers, Vice President of Academic Affairs, California State University—Fresno

Jack G. Kuszaj, Associate Dean of Students, Wheaton College, MA

Richard A. Lacey, Vice President for Development, Louisiana College, LA

Bette E. Landman, President, Beaver College, PA

Marjorie W. Lavin, Assistant Vice President for Academic Affairs, State University of New York—Empire State College, NY

William D. Law, Jr., President, Lincoln Land Community College, IL

Frank Lazarus, Vice President for Academic Affairs, Marquette University, WI

Robert Learman, Chair, Economics Department, The American University, Washington, DC

Mary F. Lenox, Dean, School of Library and Informational Science, University of Missouri, Columbia

Ruth P. Li, President, Provincial Tai-Tung Teachers' College, Taiwan

Michael Loux, Dean of Arts and Letters, University of Notre Dame, IN

James W. Lucas, Dean, School of Strategic Intelligence, Defense Intelligence College, Washington, DC

Dorothy I. MacConkey, President, Davis and Elkins College, WV

Charles Mackey, Dean of Humanities, Simmons College, MA

Peggy L. Maki, Dean of Continuing Education, Beaver College, PA

James D. McComas, President, Virginia Polytechnic Institute and State University

LeVerne McCummings, President, Cheyney University of Pennyslvania

Patrick D. McDonough, President, Marietta College, OH

Laurel A. McLeod, Dean of Students, Colorado College

Joseph T. McMillan, President, Huston-Tillotson College, TX

Irving P. McPhail, President, LeMoyne-Owen College, TN

Paula Allen Meares, Acting Dean of the School of Social Work, University of Illinois at Urbana—Champaign

David Merkowitz, Director of Public Affairs, American Council on Education, Washington, DC

Juan Mestas, Visiting Associate, American Council on Education, Washington, DC

Richard S. Meyers, President, Western Oregon State College

Alfredo B. Montes, Acting Vice President for Student Affairs, Pima Community College, AZ

Barbara Moody, Dean, Montserrat College of Art, MA

Page S. Morahan, Chair, Microbiology and Immunology, The Medical College of Pennsylvania

Kenneth P. Mortimer, President, Western Washington University

Robert L. Mulder, Dean, School of Education, Pacific Lutheran University, WA

Paige E. Mulhollan, President, Wright State University, OH

Carol B. Muller, Assistant Dean, Thayer School of Engineering, Dartmouth College, NH

Jeanne Neff, Vice President for Academic Affairs, Susquehanna University, PA

George Newkome, Vice President for Research, University of South Florida

Bethany Oberst, Dean, College of Arts and Sciences, Southwest Missouri State University

G. Dennis O'Brien, President, University of Rochester, NY

Rose-Marie Oster, Director, Department Leadership Program, American Council on Education, Washington, DC, and Professor, Germanic and Slavic Languages and Literatures, University of Maryland—College Park

Betty J. Overton, Dean, Graduate School, University of Arkansas—Little Rock

Cynthia Pace, Vice President/Dean of Instruction, Waterbury State Technical College, CT

Elaine S. Padilla, Executive Assistant to the President, Rockland Community College, NY

David Payne, Vice President for Academic Affairs, Emporia State University, KS

James Pence, Vice President for Academic Affairs and Dean of the Faculty, Wartburg College, IA

Erbel S. Perkins, Personnel Director, Rice University, TX

Daniel Perlman, President, Webster University, MO

Roy P. Peterson, Assistant to the Director for Educational Attainment, Kentucky Council of Higher Education

Lawrence K. Pettit, Chancellor, Southern Illinois University

Sally Pickert, Professor, Department of Education, The Catholic University of America, Washington, DC

Charles Ping, President, Ohio University

Patricia R. Plante, former President, University of Southern Maine

Jeffrey E. Porter, Assistant Dean/Director of General Education, National Technical Institute for the Deaf, Rochester Institute of Technology, NY

Judith S. Prince, Director, Graduate Regional Studies, University of South Carolina— Spartanburg

Carol DeLong Pyles, Dean, College of Health, Physical Education and Recreation, Eastern Illinois University

Carla J. Raatz, Director, Office of Human Resources, University of Wisconsin—Madison

Jean C. Ramage, Dean, College of Education and Psychology, James Madison University, VA

Blandina Cardenas Ramirez, Director, Office of Minorities in Higher Education, American Council on Education, Washington, DC

Robert Rasch, Director of Personnel, Dickinson College, PA

Richard Reilly, Dean, School of Arts and Sciences, St. Bonaventure University, NY

Olivia Rivas, Dean of Student Personnel Services, Texas Southmost College

Jerry H. Robbins, Dean, College of Education, Georgia State University

Piedad F. Robertson, President, Bunker Hill Community College, MA

Raymond J. Rodrigues, Associate Vice President for Academic Affairs, Colorado State University

William R. Rogers, President, Guilford College, NC

Bernard Ross, Chair, Public Administration, The American University, Washington, DC

Marlene Ross, Acting Director, Center for Leadership Development, American Council on Education, Washington, DC

Richard R. Rush, Executive Vice President, California State University—San Marcos

Nancy Schlossberg, Professor, Counseling and Personnel Services, University of Maryland—College Park

Rosemary S. J. Schraer, Chancellor, University of California—Riverside

Jack Schuster, Professor, Education and Public Policy, Claremont Graduate School, CA

Gloria D. Randall Scott, President, Bennett College, NC

Maurice J. Sevigny, Chairman, Department of Art, The University of Texas—Austin

Adib A. Shakir, President, Tougaloo College, MS

Donna Shavlik, Director, Office of Women in Higher Education, American Council on Education, Washington, DC

Ruth G. Shaw, President, Central Piedmont Community College, NC

Fred R. Sheheen, Commissioner of Higher Education, South Carolina Commission on Higher Education

Martha K. Shouldis, Dean, College of Technology and Applied Science, West Virginia Institute of Technology

James M. Shuart, President, Hofstra University, NY

George M. Shur, University Legal Counsel, Northern Illinois University

Betty Lentz Siegel, President, Kennesaw State College, GA

John A. Sims, Associate Dean, Business and Industry, Portland Community College, OR

C. Jane Snell, Dean, Division of Professional Studies, State University of New York College at Cortland

R. Eric Staley, Executive Director, Development and College Relations, Mary Baldwin College, VA

Conrad Stanitski, Vice President for Academic Affairs, Mount Union College, OH

John C. Stockwell, Vice Chancellor, University of Wisconsin—Parkside

Kala M. Stroup, President, Southwest Missouri State University

Ann Stuart, Provost/Vice President for Academic Affairs, Alma College, MI

Stephen J. Sweeny, Senior Vice President for Academic Affairs, College of New Rochelle, NY

John S. Swift, Jr., Associate Dean, University College, The University of Toledo, OH

Barbara Taylor, Director of Programs and Research, Association of Governing Boards of Colleges and Universities, Washington, DC

John A. Taylor, Vice President for Academic Affairs, Lincoln University, MO

Charles Tidball, Member, Board of Trustees, Wilson College, PA

John Toller, Director of Personnel, University of Connecticut

Theodore G. Tong, Associate Dean, Academic Affairs, The University of Arizona

Judith Touchton, Deputy Director, Office of Women in Higher Education, American Council on Education, Washington, DC

Arthurlene G. Towner, Dean, School of Education, California State University—Hayward

Martha Turnbull, Director of Personnel Services, Ithaca College, NY

Whitney G. Vanderwerff, Dean of the College, Greensboro College, NC

James A. Van Dyke, Vice President for Educational Services, Portland Community College, OR

Quintin Vargas, III, Vice President for Academic Affairs, Laredo State University, TX

George B. Vaughan, Director, Center for Community College Education, George Mason University, VA

Donald C. Wade, Executive Director, Southern University Alumni Federation, LA

Acie L. Ward, Assistant to the Chancellor for Legal Affairs, North Carolina Central University

Beth I. Warren, Associate Vice President for Human Resources, University of Southern Maine

Doris W. Weathers, Vice President for Student Affairs, LeMoyne-Owen College, TN

Karen Welter, Training Program Manager, Association of Research Libraries, Office of Management Services, Washington, DC

Daniel W. Wheeler, Coordinator, Office of Professional and Organizational Development, University of Nebraska—Lincoln

Tolor E. White, Vice President for Finance and Business Affairs, Southern University and A&M College, LA

Lee J. Williames, Assistant Provost, University of Scranton, PA

Shirley Stennis Williams, Senior Academic Planner, University of Wisconsin System

Gerald W. Williamson, Vice President for Student Services, East Central Oklahoma State University

Reginald Wilson, Senior Scholar, American Council on Education, Washington, DC

Judy Wittenberg, Dean of Arts and Sciences, Hood College, MD

Andrew Wolvin, Chair, Speech Communications Department, University of Maryland—College Park

Jean Wyld, Dean of Academic Affairs, Colby-Sawyer College, NH

Neil Wylie, Executive Officer, Council of Presidents of New England Land-Grant Universities, NH

Kenneth J. Zahorski, Director of Faculty Development, St. Norbert College, WI

Index

21st Century Leaders Program—Aspen Institute 76, 94, 276

Academic Affairs Administrators (AcAfAd)—Management Development Seminar for Assistant and Associate
    Deans 114, 116, 150, 264, 303

Academic Chairs Group—Arizona State University 152, 232, 320

Academic Deans, National Conference of—Oklahoma State University 117, 311

Academic Leadership Fellows Program—Committee For Institutional Cooperation (CIC) 173, 231, 327

Academic Leadership Institute—Carnegie Mellon University. 95, 115, 211, 284

Academic Leadership Institute—American Association of State Colleges and Universities (AASCU) 272

Academic Management Institute for Women (Colorado ACE/NIP) 96, 114, 117, 131, 150, 158, 251, 325

Academic vice president 79–96

Academy of International Business (AIB) 169, 247

Academy of Management (AM). 169, 247

Academy of Marketing Science (AMS) 169, 247

ACE National Identification Program 96, 114, 117, 131, 150, 158, 251, 325

ACE/NIP—See American Council on Education National Identification Program

Academic Management Institute for Women—Colorado ACE/NIP 96, 114, 117, 131, 150, 158, 251, 325

Addressing needs and concerns of related constituencies 111

Administrative Associate Program—University of Wisconsin System 117, 153, 174, 232, 340

Administrative Development Map—University of Nebraska/Institute of Agriculture and Natural
    Resources 136, 153, 233, 337

Administrative Development Program—Stanford University 136, 233, 332

Administrative Fellows Program—California State University System 135, 152, 173, 231, 323

Administrative Fellows Program—Pennsylvania State University 135, 174, 231, 331

Administrative Fellows Program—Woodrow Wilson Foundation 134, 317

Administrative Seminar Program—University of Iowa 136, 233, 335

Administrative vice president 79–96

Administrative Women's Network—Colorado State University 117, 135, 153, 173, 232, 325

Administrators and Teachers of English as a Second Language (ATESL). 150, 169, 247

Administrators Conference—Association of Collegiate Schools of Architecture (ACSA) 115, 151, 278

Admission Middle Management Institute—National Association of College Admissions Counselors
    (NACAC) 134, 304

Advanced Management Program (AMP)—Harvard University Business School 33, 69, 77, 295

Advanced Management Skills Institute—Association of Research Libraries (ARL). 115, 133, 188, 282

Advancement officer, chief 79–96

Affirmative Action Administrative Fellows Program—
    Board of Governors of State Colleges and Universities (Illinois) 117, 135, 152, 173, 231, 321

Affirmative Action Leave Program—State University of New York (SUNY) 174, 233, 332

Alfred P. Sloan Fellows Program—Massachusetts Institute of Technology (MIT). 33, 69, 77, 95, 116, 302

American Academy of Religion (AAR) 169, 247

American Alliance for Health, Physical Education, Recreation, and Dance (AAHPERD) 169, 248

American Anthropological Association (AAA) 169, 248

American Assembly of Collegiate Schools of Business (AACSB) 113, 115, 248, 268

    Associate Deans Seminar 115, 268

    New Deans Seminar 115, 268

American Association for Adult and Continuing Education (AAACE). .113, 131, 248

American Association for Counseling and Development (AACD) 131, 248

American Association for Higher Education (AAHE). 32, 113, 131, 150, 170, 172, 187, 238, 248, 268

    Annual Meeting 150, 172, 187, 268

    Conference on Assessment in Higher Education 150, 172, 187, 269

    Faculty Senate Leadership Retreat 172, 269

    Forum on Exemplary Teaching. 172, 269

American Association for the Advancement of Science (AAAS). 170, 248

American Association for the Advancement of Slavic Studies (AAASS) 170, 248

American Association of Bible Colleges (AABC) 76, 248

American Association of Colleges for Teacher Education (AACTE). 114, 115, 249, 270

    New Deans Institute 115, 270

American Association of Colleges of Nursing (AACN) 114, 115, 150, 249, 270

Executive Development Series 115, 150, 270
American Association of Colleges of Osteopathic Medicine (AACOM) .76, 114, 249
American Association of Collegiate Registrars and Admissions Officers (AACRAO) 131, 249
American Association of Community and Junior Colleges (AACJC) 32, 67, 75, 76, 94, 114, 115,
    133, 150, 151, 172, 211, 249, 271
    Fellows Program 94, 115, 133, 151, 172, 271
    Presidents Academy Workshop 76, 271
    Professional Development Workshop 94, 115, 133, 151, 211, 272
American Association of Dental Schools (AADS) 114, 249
American Association of Philosophy Teachers (AAPT) 170, 249
American Association of Phonetic Sciences (AAPS) 170, 249
American Association of Physics Teachers (AAPT) 170, 249
American Association of Presidents of Independent Colleges and Universities (AAPICU) 76, 250
American Association of State Colleges and Universities (AASCU) 32, 67, 69, 76, 94, 250, 272
    Academic Leadership Institute 94, 272
    New Presidents Sessions 76, 272
    Presidents' Academy 76, 273
    Summer Council of Presidents 76, 273
    Workshop for new member presidents/spouses during annual meeting 76, 273
American Association of Teachers of German (AATG) 170, 250
American Association of Teachers of Slavic and East European Languages (AATSEEL) 170, 250
American Association of Teachers of Spanish and Portuguese (AATSP) 170, 250
American Association of University Administrators (AAUA) 114, 131, 150, 250
American Association of University Professors (AAUP) 170, 250
American Association of University Women (AAUW) 114, 131, 150, 170, 250
American Association of Women in Community and Junior Colleges (AAWCJC) 114, 131, 150, 251
American Astronomical Society (AAS) 170, 251
American Business Law Association (ABLA) 170, 251
American Chemical Society (ACS) 170, 251
American College Personnel Association (ACPA) 87, 131, 251
American Comparative Literature Association (ACLA) 170, 251
American Conference of Academic Deans (ACAD) 32, 114, 116, 251, 292
    Seminar for New Deans 116, 292
American Council on Education (ACE) 31, 32, 67, 75, 76, 94, 114, 115, 133, 151, 172, 187,
    211, 231, 251, 274
    Department Leadership Program 94, 115, 151, 158, 187, 211, 274
    Fellows Program 32, 76, 94, 115, 138, 151, 158, 172, 211, 231, 274
    Occasional colloquia for presidents 76, 275
    Sessions during annual meeting for presidents 76, 275
American Council on Education/National Identification Program (ACE/NIP) 96, 114, 117, 131, 150,
    158, 251, 325
American Economic Association (AEA) 170, 252
American Educational Research Association (AERA) 71, 170, 252
American Forensic Association (AFA) 170, 252
American Historical Association (AHA) 170, 252
American Indian Higher Education Consortium (AIHEC) 76, 252
American Institute of Biological Sciences (AIBS) 170, 252
American Institute of Nutrition (AIN) 170, 252
American Legal Studies Association (ALSA) 170, 252
American Library Association (ALA) 131, 252
American Management Association (AMA) 31, 76, 94, 115, 133, 151, 275
American Mathematical Association of Two Year Colleges (AMATYC) 170, 252
American Mathematical Society (AMS) 170, 252, 253
American Medical Association (AMA) 170, 253
American Musicological Society (AMS) 170, 253
American Philosophical Society (APA) 170, 253
American Physical Society (APS) 170, 253
American Political Science Association (APSA) 170, 253
American Psychological Association (APA) 170, 253
American Society for Engineering Education (ASEE) 170, 253
American Society for Microbiology (ASM) 170, 253
American Society for Theatre Research (ASTR) 170, 253

American Society for Training and Development (ASTD)................................131, 254
American Society of Allied Health Professions (ASAHP)....................................170, 254
American Society of Cytology (ASC)..170, 254
American Society of International Law (ASIL)...170, 254
American Society of Parasitologists (ASP)...170, 254
American Society of Zoologists (ASZ)..170, 254
American Sociological Association (ASA)...170, 254
American Speech-Language-Hearing Association (ASLHA) 170, 254
American Statistical Association (ASA)...171, 254
American Studies Association (ASA)..171, 254
American University, The...135, 232, 319
    Office of Training and Development Programs 135, 232, 319
American Veterinary Medical Association (AVMA) 171, 255
American Vocational Association (AVA) 171, 255
Annual Seminars—Council of Colleges of Arts and Sciences (CCAS) 116, 291
Archaeological Institute of America (AIA)..171, 255
Arizona State University (ASU) 78, 96, 117, 135, 152, 173, 221–222, 231, 232
    Academic Chairs Group 152, 232, 320
    Internship 135, 152, 173, 231, 319
    Leadership Academy 117, 135, 152, 173, 221–222, 232, 320
    Management Development Program (MDP) 96, 135, 152, 173, 221–222, 231, 232, 319
    President's Breakfast Series 78, 96, 117, 221–222, 232, 320
Armed Services 213
Aspen Institute 76, 94, 275
    The Executive Seminar 76, 275
    21st Century Leaders Program 76, 94, 276
Assessment, job 217
Assessment, self 92, 217
Assistant/associate deans...97–116
Associate Deans Seminar—American Assembly of Collegiate Schools of Business (AACSB) 115, 268
Association for Asian Studies (AAS) 171, 255
Association for Biology Laboratory Education (ABLE).....................................171, 255
Association for Business Communications (ABC) 171, 255
Association for Communication Administration (ACA) 171, 255
Association for Continuing Higher Education (ACHE)...............................114, 131, 255
Association for Institutional Research (AIR) 131, 255
Association for Library and Information Science Education (ALISE)..........................171, 255
Association for School, College, and University Staffing, Inc. (ASCUS) 131, 256
Association for the Management of Information Technology (CAUSE) 131, 260
Association for Theater in Higher Education (ATHE)....................................171, 256
Association for the Study of Higher Education (ASHE) 71, 171, 256
Association of African Studies Programs (AASP) 171, 256
Association of American Colleges (AAC)....................................75, 77, 256, 276
    Specially designated presidential sessions at annual meetings 77, 276
Association of American Geographers (AAG)...171, 256
Association of American Law Schools (AALS)............................114, 115, 256, 277
    Deans and Librarians Workshop..115, 277
    Senior Administrators Workshop 115, 277
Association of American Medical Colleges (AAMC)......................114, 115, 256, 277
    Executive Development Seminar for Deans 115, 277
Association of American Universities (AAU) 75, 256
Association of American University Presses (AAUP) 131, 256
Association of California Community College Administrators
    (ACCCA) 117, 135, 152, 320
    Mentor Program 117, 135, 152, 320
Association of Caribbean Studies (ACS) 257
Association of Catholic Colleges and Universities (ACCU)..............................67, 76, 257
Association of Chairmen of Departments of Mechanics (ACDM) 150, 257
Association of College and University Auditors (ACUA) 131, 257
Association of College and University Housing Officers—International (ACUHO-I) 131, 257
Association of College Unions—International (ACU-I)...................................131, 257
Association of Collegiate Schools of Architecture (ACSA) 114, 115, 151, 257, 278

Administrators Conference 115, 151, 278
Association of Collegiate Schools of Planning (ACSP) 114, 257
Association of Community College Trustees (ACCT) 58, 76, 77, 257, 278
   National Legislative Seminar and Regional Seminars 58, 77, 278
Association of Conference and Events Directors—International (ACED-I) 131, 258
Association of Departments of English (ADE). 150, 258
   Summer Seminars 150, 258
Association of Departments of Foreign Languages (ADFL) 150, 258
   Summer Seminars 150, 258
Association of Education of Journalism and Mass Communication (AEJMC) .171, 259
Association of Episcopal Colleges (AEC) 76, 258
Association of Governing Boards of Universities and Colleges (AGB) 31, 53, 54, 76, 77, 94, 187, 188,
   238, 258, 278–282
   Board-Mentor Service. 53, 58, 187, 278
   Governing the Public Multicampus System 58, 77, 188, 282
   Improving Board Performance 58, 77, 187, 279
   Institute for Trustee Leadership: Program for Board Chairs and Chief Executive Officers of
      Independent Institutions 58, 77, 187, 279
   Introduction to Services during National Conference on Trusteeship 58, 77, 279
   On-Campus Fundraising Workshop 58, 187, 280
   Program for Academic Affairs Committee Chairpersons and Senior Academic Officers 58, 94, 187, 280
   Seminar for Chairpersons and Chief Executives of Theological Schools and Seminars 58, 77, 187, 280
   Seminar on Endowment Management 58, 77, 94, 187, 280
   Speaker Service 58, 281
   Strategic Planning for Theological Schools 58, 77, 94, 187, 281
   Trustee Responsibility for Financial Affairs 58, 77, 94, 187, 281
   Workshop for New Trustees 58, 281
Association of Independent Colleges and Schools (AICS) 76, 258
Association of Jesuit Colleges and Universities (AJCU) 76, 258
Association of Military Colleges and Schools of the United States (AMCS). .76, 258
Association of Physical Plant Administrators of Universities and Colleges (APPA). 131, 258
Association of Research Libraries (ARL) 114, 115, 131, 133, 188, 259, 282
   Advanced Management Skills Institute 115, 133, 188, 282
   Basic Management Skills Institute 115, 133, 283
   Creativity to Innovation Workshop. 115, 133, 283
   Project Planning Workshop. 115, 133, 283
   Resources Management Institute 115, 133, 283
   Training Skills Institute 115, 133, 283
Association of Schools of Journalism and Mass Communication (ASJMC) 114, 259
Association of Southern Baptist Colleges and Schools (ASBCS) 76, 259
Association of Teacher Educators (ATE) 171, 259
Association of Teachers of Technical Writing (ATTW) 171, 259
Association of Theological Schools in the United States and Canada (ATS). .76, 259
Association of University Summer Sessions (AUSS). 114, 132, 259
Association of Urban Universities (AUU) 67, 76, 259
Association programs 231–251
Associations. 247–267
Awards, awards programs 236

Balancing personal and professional life. 91, 179
Basic Management Skills Institute—Association of Research Libraries (ARL) 115, 133, 283
Beaver College 173, 231, 321
   Faculty Fellow in Academic Affairs. 173, 231, 321
Benefits of leadership development programs 13–17, 33
Board of Governors of State Colleges and Universities (Illinois) 117, 135, 152, 173, 231, 321
   Affirmative Action Administrative Fellows Program 117, 135, 152, 173, 231, 321
Board of regents/trustees. 6, 9, 41–58
Board retreats 52
Board-Mentor Service—Association of Governing Boards (AGB). 53, 58, 187, 278
Boston College 135, 222, 224, 232, 322
   Professional Development Programs 135, 222, 224, 232, 322
Broadcast Education Association (BEA) 171, 259

Brown-bag lunches, series. 235
Bryn Mawr College—HERS Summer Institute for Women 32, 95, 116, 133, 151, 158, 172, 212, 298
Budgets and budgeting. 13, 20, 63, 82, 100, 122, 141
Building a Better Team on Campus: Understanding Gender Issues—National Institute for Leadership
    Development 116, 134, 152, 172, 188, 212, 308
Burnout 85
Bush Foundation 77, 94, 115, 133, 151, 283
    Leadership Program for Midcareer Development 77, 94, 115, 133, 151, 283
Business affairs. 14, 84, 85, 129
Business Management Institute—Western Association of College and University Business Officers
    (WACUBO). 96, 134, 315

California State University System 135, 152, 173, 231, 323
    Administrative Fellows Program 135, 152, 173, 231, 323
Campus tour. 236
Career development. 160–162, 205
Career mobility 71, 124, 213
Career paths. 80, 160
Career plateau 160
Career planning, preparation. 60–61, 79–81
Carnegie Mellon University 95, 115, 133, 151, 211, 284
    Academic Leadership Institute. 95, 115, 211, 284
    College Management Program 95, 115, 133, 151, 211, 284
CAUSE (Association for the Management of Information Technology) 131, 260
Center for Creative Leadership 31, 95, 115, 133, 151, 188, 211, 285
    Dynamics of Strategy: Goals into Action. 95, 115, 285
    Executive Women Workshop 95, 115, 285
    Leadership and Teamwork: Increasing Team Leadership Capabilities 95, 115, 188, 286
    Leadership Development Program 95, 115, 133, 151, 211, 286
Center for International Education 287, 291
Central Association of College and University Business Officers (CACUBO) 95, 133, 211, 287
    Management Institute 95, 133, 211, 287
Chair, department—see department chair
Chairpersons, Conference for Academic—Kansas State University/Center for Faculty Evaluation and
    Development 151, 299
Chamber of Commerce 83
Chancellor's Academic Affairs Faculty Fellowship Program—City University of New York (CUNY). 173,
    231, 324
Chicago State University 152, 173, 231, 323
    Minority Administrative Fellow Program 152, 173, 231, 323
Christian A. Johnson Endeavor Foundation 77, 287
    Troutbeck Program/Educational Leadership Project 69, 77, 287
Chronicle of Higher Education. 70, 109, 147, 205
City University of New York (CUNY) 117, 135, 152, 173, 231, 232, 324
    Chancellor's Academic Affairs Faculty Fellowship Program 173, 231, 324
    Women's Leadership Institute 117, 135, 152, 173, 232, 324
Collective bargaining. 29
College and University Computer Users Conference (CUCUC) 132, 260
College and University Personnel Association (CUPA) 132, 133, 260, 288
College Board, The—Summer Institute on College Admissions 133, 297
College English Association (CEA) 171, 260
College Management Business Institute (CMBI)—Southern Association of College and University Business
    Officers. 96, 134, 212, 313
College Management Program—Carnegie Mellon University 95, 115, 133, 151, 211, 284
College Media Advisers (CMA). 132, 260
College Placement Council (CPC) 132, 260
Colorado ACE/NIP—Academic Management Institute for Women 96, 114, 117, 131, 150
Colorado Exchange—University of Colorado-Colorado Springs 335
Colorado State University 117, 135, 153, 173, 232, 325
    Administrative Women's Network. 117, 135, 153, 173, 232, 325
    Leadership Series 117, 135, 153, 173, 232, 325
    Professional Development Institute 117, 135, 153, 173, 232, 325

Professional Development Programming. 153, 173, 232, 325
Colorado Women in Higher Education Administration (ACE/NIP) 96, 114, 117, 131, 135, 150, 153,
    158, 251, 325
    Academic Management Institute for Women. 96, 117, 135, 153, 326
Columbia University. 135, 153, 232, 326
    Connections 135, 153, 232, 326
    Front Line Leadership Program 135, 232, 326
    Middle Management Development Program 135, 153, 232, 326
    Professional Development Programs 135, 153, 232, 326
Committee for Institutional Cooperation (CIC) 173, 231, 327
    Academic Leadership Fellows Program 173, 231, 327
Committee on Scholarly Communication with the People's Republic of China—Fulbright Programs . . .288, 291
Common agenda 15, 176
Common experiences 176
Common rewards. 177
Common language, vocabulary 15, 176
Communication, communication skills and abilities. 8, 15, 30, 65, 104, 239
Community activities, service 70, 90, 195, 241–242
Community College Leadership Institute—North Carolina State University 96, 116, 152, 173, 309
Community Leadership Development Academy—Lansing Community College. . .117, 135, 153, 174, 233, 330
Competitive culture 175
Computer skills 239
Conference for Academic Chairpersons—Kansas State University 151, 299
Conference of Academic Deans—Oklahoma State University. 117, 311
Conference on Assessment in Higher Education—American Association for Higher Education
    (AAHE) 150, 172, 187, 269
Conference on Higher Education and the Law—University of Georgia/Institute of Higher Education 78,
    96, 117, 134, 314
Conflict resolution 8, 29, 196
Connections—Columbia University. 135, 153, 232, 326
Consultants, consulting 67, 68, 89, 238
Cooperative Education Association (CEA) 132, 171, 260
Cornell University—Executive Development Program 33
Corporate education, training programs 213
Council for Adult and Experiential Learning (CAEL). 132, 171, 260
Council for Advancement and Support of Education (CASE) 32, 58, 68, 77, 86, 95, 115, 133, 188, 260,
    288
    Forums for Women and Minorities in Institutional Advancement 95, 133, 288
    Presidential and Trustee Leadership in Fund Raising 58, 77, 188, 289
    Presidents' Colloquium on Institutional Advancement 77, 289
    Skills for Success: A Workshop for Getting Ahead 290
    Summer Institute in Executive Management 95, 115, 133, 289
Council for Advancement and Support of Education (CASE) and Snelling, Kolb & Kuhnle. 133, 290
    Skills for Success: A Workshop for Getting Ahead 133, 290
Council for Agricultural Science and Technology (CAST) 171, 260
Council for International Exchange of Scholars (CIES) 77, 95, 115, 133, 151, 172, 211, 290, 291
    Fulbright Scholar Program 77, 95, 115, 133, 151, 172, 211, 290
    Seminars for International Education Administrators in Germany and Japan 115, 133, 151, 211, 290
    U.S./United Kingdom College and University Academic Administrator Award 115, 133, 151, 211, 290
Council of 1890 College Presidents (CCP). 76, 261
Council of Colleges of Arts and Sciences (CCAS) 114, 116, 261, 291
    Annual Seminars 116, 291
    Seminar for New Deans 116, 292
Council of Graduate Schools (CGS). 114, 116, 261, 292
    Summer Workshops for Graduate Deans 116, 292
Council of Independent Colleges (CIC). 75, 77, 261, 293
    New Presidents Workshop preceding Annual Presidents Institute 77, 293
    Presidents Institute 77, 293
Council of Medical Education (CME) 170, 253
Council of Presidents—National Association of State Universities and Land-Grant Colleges
    (NASULGC) 77, 305
Council of Writing Program Administrators (CWPA) 150, 261

Council on Governmental Relations (COGR) 132, 261
Council on International Educational Exchange (CIEE). 95, 116, 133, 151, 172, 293
   Development Seminars 95, 116, 133, 151, 172, 293
Council on Social Work Education (CSWE) 171, 261
Creating the working environment for administrators and staff 82
Creativity to Innovation Workshop—Association of Research Libraries (ARL) 115, 133, 283
Curriculum 8, 43, 163

Dean 97–117
Dean of instruction 97–117
Dean of the faculty 97–117
Deans and Librarians Workshop—Association of American Law Schools (AALS) 115, 277
Decision making 8, 29, 46, 59, 84, 104, 147
Department chair. 9, 137–153
Department Leadership Program—American Council on Education (ACE) 94, 115, 151, 187, 211, 274
Development 28
Development plan 163, 217
Development Seminars—Council on International Educational Exchange (CIEE) . .95, 116, 133, 151, 172, 293
Developmental programming 213
Developmental stages within a job 84–86, 104–106
Diversity 7, 9, 16–17, 62
Dormitory, spending a night in 237
Dynamics of Strategy: Goals into Action—Center for Creative Leadership 95, 115, 285

Eastern Illinois University 135, 153, 173, 224–225, 232, 327
   Programs for Professional Enrichment (PPE) 135, 153, 173, 224–225, 232, 327
Ecological Society of America (ESA). 171, 261
Economic History Association (EHA) 171, 261
Educational Leadership Project/Troutbeck Program—Christian A. Johnson Endeavor Foundation. . .69, 77, 287
Educational Policy Fellowship Program—Institute for Educational Leadership (IEL) 116, 134, 151, 172,
   212, 298
Emeriti faculty 236
Endowment 43
Entomological Society of America (ESA) 121, 171
Evaluation 42, 53, 123, 147, 189–202, 217
Exchanges. 89, 240
Executive Development Seminar for Deans—Association of American Medical Colleges (AAMC). . . .115, 277
Executive Development Series—American Association of Colleges of Nursing (AACN) 115, 150, 270
Executive Leadership and Management Institute—Western Association of College and University Business
   Officers (WACUBO) 96, 134, 315
Executive Leadership in an Academic Setting—Rochester Institute of Technology 136, 153, 174, 233, 331
Executive Leadership Institute—League for Innovation in the Community College. 95, 300
Executive Leadership Institute—National Association of College and University Business Officers (NACUBO)/
   Marriott Education Services 95, 212, 305
Executive Seminar—Aspen Institute. 76, 275
Executive Women Workshop—Center for Creative Leadership 95, 115, 285
Expanding Leadership Diversity in Community Colleges—League for Innovation in the Community College,
   University of Texas-Austin, W. K. Kellogg Foundation. 116, 134, 151, 172, 231, 300–301
External relations 15, 61–63

Faculty 6, 9, 140, 155–174, 235, 242
Faculty and staff development 140, 155–174
Faculty Development and Support Services—Washington State University 174, 234, 340
Faculty Development Program—St. Norbert College 165–167, 174, 233, 333
Faculty Development Resources—Indiana University-Bloomington 153, 173, 233, 329
Faculty Directors Program—University of Southern Colorado 174, 232, 233, 338
Faculty Exchange Center 172, 294
Faculty Fellow in Academic Affairs—Beaver College. 173, 321
Faculty Fellows Program—University of Kansas 174
Faculty Senate Leadership Retreat—American Association for Higher Education (AAHE) 172, 269
Faculty, emeriti 236
Fellows Meeting—Society for Values in Higher Education 77, 96, 117, 152, 173, 312

Fellows Program—American Association of Community and Junior Colleges (AACJC)........94, 115, 133, 151, 172, 271

Fellows Program—American Council on Education (ACE) 32, 76, 94, 115, 133, 151, 158, 172, 211, 231, 274

Fellows Program—California State University System...........................135, 152, 173, 231, 323

Fellowship Program—W. K. Kellogg Foundation 117, 134, 152, 173, 212, 232, 316

Female leadership styles 62

Financial Management Association (FMA) 171, 262

Financial Management for Women in Higher Education—University of Central Florida   96, 117, 134, 152, 314

Follow up to a leadership development activity 208, 210

Forum on Exemplary Teaching—American Association for Higher Education (AAHE) 172, 269

Forums for Women and Minorities in Institutional Advancement—Council for Advancement and Support of Higher Education (CASE) 95, 133, 288

Front Line Leadership Program—Columbia University 135, 232, 326

Fulbright Programs 77, 95, 115, 133, 151, 172, 211, 287, 290, 291

   Center for International Education 287, 291

   Committee on Scholarly Communication with the People's Republic of China 288, 291

   Council for International Exchange of Scholars (CIES) 77, 95, 115, 133, 151, 172, 211, 290, 291

   Fulbright Teacher Exchange Program...291, 294

   Institute of International Education (IIE) 291, 299

   International Research and Exchanges Board (IREX) 291, 299

   University Affiliations Program, United States Information Agency 291, 314

Fund raising 43, 101

Geological Society of America (GSA) 171, 262

George Washington University 135, 153, 173, 232, 328

   Training Division of Personnel Services....................................135, 153, 173, 232, 328

Gordon College...173, 232, 328

   Professional Development Through Growth Plans 173, 232, 328

Governing boards—See Boards

Governing the Public Multicampus System—Association of Governing Boards (AGB) and National Association of System Heads 58, 77, 188, 282

Government and legislative relations 82

Graduate programs 80

Great books programs 242

Growth contract 198

Harvard Seminar for New Presidents—Harvard Graduate School of Education 66, 77, 295

Harvard University and the College Board 133, 297

   Summer Institute on College Admissions...133, 297

Harvard University/Graduate School of Business Administration..........................69, 77, 294

   Advanced Management Program (AMP)...33, 69, 77, 295

Harvard University/Graduate School of Education 77, 95, 116, 133, 151, 188, 211, 295

   Harvard Seminar for New Presidents 66, 77, 295

   Institute for Educational Management (IEM).......................32, 77, 88, 95, 116, 188, 211, 295

   Institute for the Management of Lifelong Education (MLE)..................95, 116, 133, 151, 211, 296

   Management Development Program (MDP)............................95, 116, 133, 151, 211, 296

Higher Education Resource Service (HERS)........32, 95, 114, 116, 132, 133, 150, 151, 172, 212, 262, 298

   HERS Bryn Mawr Institute/Summer Institute for Women........32, 95, 116, 133, 151, 158, 172, 212, 298

   HERS Wellesley Institute/Institute for Women....................32, 95, 116, 133, 151, 172, 212, 298

Hispanic Association of Colleges and Universities (HACU)....................................76, 262

History of Science Society (HSS) 171, 262

Human Interaction Laboratory—NTL Institute 96, 116, 134, 152, 310

Human resource development plan 35

Human Resource Development Program—Boston College 322

Human Resources Development Programs—Stanford University 136, 332

IBM 213

Identifying new leaders 5, 6, 14, 24, 125, 158, 190

Improving Board Performance—Association of Governing Boards (AGB) 58, 77, 187, 279

In-house courses and workshops...23, 33, 232-233

Indiana University—Bloomington 153, 173, 233, 329

Faculty Development Resources 153, 173, 233, 329
Institute for Educational Leadership (IEL) 116, 134, 157, 172, 212, 298
    Educational Policy Fellowship Program 116, 134, 157, 172, 212, 298
Institute for Educational Management (IEM)—Harvard University 32, 77, 88, 95, 116, 188, 211, 295
Institute for Leadership Effectiveness—University of Tennessee 96, 117, 136, 233, 338
Institute for the Management of Lifelong Education (MLE)—Harvard University/
    Graduate School of Education 95, 116, 133, 151, 211, 296
Institute for Trustee Leadership: Program for Board Chairs and Chief Executive Officers of Independent
    Institutions—Association for Governing Boards (AGB) 58, 77, 187, 279
Institute for Women/Wellesley Institute—Higher Education Resource Services (HERS) 32, 95, 116,
    133, 151, 172, 212, 298
Institute of International Education (IIE)—Fulbright Programs 291, 299
Institutional advancement vice president. 79–96
Institutional climate, culture 7, 28, 33, 63, 146, 157, 191
Institutional development plan 20
Institutional effectiveness 13
Institutional objectives. 61
Institutional renewal 16
Instructional methods 206
International Association of Campus Law Enforcement Administrators (IACLEA). 132, 262
International Business Machines (IBM) 213
International Council of Fine Arts Deans (ICFAD) 114, 262
International Faculty Development Seminars—Council on International Educational Exchange (CIEE) 95,
    116, 133, 151, 172, 293
International Research and Exchanges Board (IREX)—Fulbright Programs 291, 299
International Technology Education Association (ITEA) 171, 262
Internship—Arizona State University 135, 152, 173, 231, 319
Internships 32
Interpersonal skills. 30, 65, 83, 104, 142, 196, 216
Introduction to AGB Services During National Conference on Trusteeship—Association of Governing Boards
    (AGB) 58, 77, 279
Isolation. 120, 125

Jesuit Association of Student Personnel Administrators (JASPA) 132, 262
Job assessment. 217
Job cycles 84–86, 104–106
Job exchanges 89, 219, 240
Job phases 84–86, 104–106
Job rotation 128, 213

Kansas State University/Center for Faculty Evaluation and Development 151, 299
    Annual Conference for Academic Chairpersons. 151, 299
Kellogg Foundation. .116, 117, 134, 151, 152, 172, 173, 212, 231, 232, 300, 316
    Expanding Leadership Diversity in Community Colleges 116, 134, 151, 172, 231, 301
    National Fellowship Program 117, 134, 152, 173, 212, 232, 316
    NUPAGE 174, 233, 337
Kennesaw College 153, 174, 233, 329
    Leadership Kennesaw College 153, 174, 233, 329

Lansing Community College. 117, 135, 153, 174, 233, 330
    Community Leadership Development Academy. 117, 135, 153, 174, 233, 330
Law, Conference on Higher Education and the—University of Georgia/Institute of Higher Education 78,
    96, 117, 134, 314
Leaders for Change—National Institute for Leadership Development 96, 116, 134, 212, 308
Leaders Project—National Institute for Leadership Develop 116, 134, 152, 172, 212, 309
Leadership 2000—League for Innovation in the Community College. 95, 116, 188, 300
Leadership Academy—Arizona State University 117, 135, 152, 173, 221–222, 232, 320
Leadership and Teamwork: Increasing Team Leadership Capabilities—Center for Creative Leadership 95,
    115, 188, 286
Leadership capacities 9, 27–38, 44–46, 64–65, 83–84, 103–104, 125–126, 141–143, 175–177
    Creating a working environment. 62, 82
    Knowledge of higher education 45, 83, 103, 142

Knowledge of the institution 45, 125
Management and decision making 29, 64, 84, 104, 141
Mastery of specialized information 125
Mental vigor, physical vitality, dealing with stress 65, 84, 104
Maximizing people's strengths 14
Providing vision and setting goals 28, 45, 64, 83, 103, 125, 142, 176, 195
Team building (See also Team building) 68, 126, 140
Understanding leadership roles 45, 142
Understanding oneself 30
Willingness to learn 46
Working with people 29, 68, 83, 104, 142, 196, 216
Leadership development 5-10, 13-25, 49-52, 66-73, 107-111, 126-128, 143-147,
    158, 163, 166, 169, 182
Leadership Development Program—Center for Creative Leadership 95, 115, 133, 151, 211, 286
Leadership for a New Century—National Institute for Leadership Development . .116, 134, 152, 172, 212, 308
Leadership Kennesaw College—Kennesaw College 153, 174, 233, 329
Leadership Program for Midcareer Development—Bush Foundation 77, 94, 115, 133, 151, 283
Leadership responsibilities
    Academic priorities, instruction, academic programs 62, 99, 121-122, 140
    Budget and resources 63, 82, 102, 122, 140
    Court of Appeal 44
    Facilities, space, and equipment 102, 122
    Faculty, faculty development, promotion and tenure 100
    Governance 139
    Institutional autonomy 44
    Institutional and unit environment, climate 62, 81, 82
    Linkage to external constituencies, unit to institution, across institution, to mission 15, 61, 63,
        81-83, 102, 122, 140
    Operations 81, 100
    Personnel development, issues, conflicts, evaluations 101
    Planning 102, 121
    Students and student issues 63, 140
    Supervising the office 100, 101
Leadership Series—Colorado State University 117, 135, 153, 173, 232, 325
Leadership temperament 36
League for Innovation in the Community College 95, 116, 134, 151, 172, 188, 231, 300
    Executive Leadership Institute 95, 300
    Expanding Leadership Diversity in Community Colleges 116, 134, 151, 172, 231, 300-301
    Leadership 2000 . . . . .95, 116, 188, 300
    Minority Leadership Program 134, 151, 172, 300
Lilly Endowment, Inc. 116, 151, 172, 188, 228, 301
    Workshop on the Liberal Arts 116, 151, 172, 188, 301
Linguistic Society of America (LSA) 171, 262
Loss of anonymity 91
Loyola College of Maryland 24-25
Lutheran Educational Conference of North America (LECNA) 76, 263

Maintenance & Operations (M&O)/Crafts and Food Service Training Program—Maricopa Community College
    District 135, 233, 330-331
Management Development Program—Arizona State University 96, 135, 152, 173, 221-222, 231, 232, 319
Management Development Program (MDP)—Boston College 322
Management Development Program (MDP)—Harvard Graduate School of Education 95, 116, 133,
    151, 211, 296
Management Development Program—Stanford University 136, 233, 332
Management Development Seminar for Assistant and Associate Deans—National Association of Academic
    Affairs Administrators (AcAdAf) 114, 116, 150, 264, 303
Management Enhancement Program—University of California Los Angeles (UCLA) 136, 233, 334
Management Institute—Central Association of College and University Business Officers (CACUBO) 95,
    133, 211, 287
Management Work Conference—NTL Institute 96, 116, 134, 152, 310
Management/Supervisory Training Program—Maricopa Community Colleges 117, 135, 153, 174, 233, 331
Maricopa Community Colleges District 117, 135, 153, 174, 225-226, 233, 330

M&O/Crafts Training Program 135, 233, 331
   Professional Group Program 117, 135, 153, 174, 233, 331
   Visions Career Development Program 117, 135, 153, 174, 225–226, 233, 330
Married and single administrators 91
Marriott Education Services 95, 212, 305
   Executive Leadership Institute 95, 212, 305
Massachusetts Institute of Technology (MIT) 33, 69, 77, 95, 116, 302
   Alfred P. Sloan Fellows Program 33, 69, 77, 95, 116, 302
Mathematical Association of America (MAA) 171, 263
Mentors and mentoring 67, 90, 110, 144, 216, 218
Mentor Program—Association of California Community College Administrators (ACCCA) 117, 135, 152, 320
Middle Management Development Program—Columbia University 135, 153, 232, 326
Military—See armed services
Minorities 7, 9, 15, 17, 44, 127, 163
Minority Administrative Fellow Program—Chicago State University 152, 173, 231, 323
Minority Administrative Fellowship—University of South Carolina 136, 174, 232, 337
Minority Leadership Program—League for Innovation in the Community College 134, 151, 172, 300
Minority Management Development Program—Tennessee Board of Regents 136, 174, 231, 333
Mission 28, 37, 42, 45, 54, 63, 82, 123, 130
Modern Language Association of America (MLA) 151, 171, 263, 302
   Association of Departments of English (ADE) Summer Seminars 151, 302
   Association of Departments of Foreign Languages (ADFL) Summer Sessions 151
Moral support 142
Multicultural environments 62
Music Educators National Conference (MENC) 171, 263
Myers-Briggs Type Indicator (MBTI) 177

National Academic Advising Association (NAcAdA) 132, 263
National Association for Core Curriculum (NACC) 114, 263
National Association for Equal Opportunity in Higher Education (NAFEO) 75, 132, 263
National Association for Ethnic Studies (NAES) 171, 263
National Association for Women Deans, Administrators, and Counselors (NAWDAC)—
   See National Association for Women in Education
National Association for Women in Education (NAWE) 114, 132, 150, 171, 263
National Association of Academic Affairs Administrators (AcAfAd) 114, 116, 150, 264, 303
   Management Development Seminar for Assistant and Associate Deans 116, 303
National Association of Biology Teachers (NABT) 264
National Association of College Admission Counselors (NACAC) 132, 264, 304
   Admission Middle Management Institute 134, 304
National Association of College and University Attorneys (NACUA) 132, 264
National Association of College and University Business Officers (NACUBO) 31, 95, 132, 212, 264, 304
   Executive Leadership Institute 212, 305
   Senior Financial Officers Conference 95, 304
National Association of College and University Food Services (NACUFS) 132, 264
National Association of College Deans, Registrars, and Admissions Officers (NACDRAO) 132, 264
National Association of Colleges and Teachers of Agriculture (NACTA) 171, 264
National Association of Education Office Personnel (NAEOP) 132, 264
National Association of Educational Buyers, Inc. (NAEB) 132, 265
National Association of Geology Teachers (NAGT) 171, 265
National Association of Independent Colleges and Universities (NAICU) 68, 75, 77, 265, 305
   Public Policy Seminar for New Presidents 77, 305
National Association of Personnel Workers (NAPW) 132, 265
National Association of Schools and Colleges of the United Methodist Church (NASCUMC) 76, 265
National Association of Schools of Art and Design (NASAD) 114, 265
National Association of Schools of Dance (NASD) 114, 265
National Association of Schools of Music (NASM) 114, 265
National Association of Schools of Theater (NAST) 114, 265
National Association of State Universities and Land-Grant Colleges (NASULGC) 75, 77, 265, 305
   Council of Presidents 77, 305
National Association of Student Financial Aid Administrators (NASFAA) 132, 265
National Association of Student Personnel Administrators (NASPA) 86, 87, 95, 132, 134, 212, 238, 265, 306
   Richard F. Stevens Institute 95, 134, 212, 306

National Association of System Heads...58, 77, 188, 282
  Governing the Public Multicampus System.....................................58, 77, 188, 282
National Association of Trade and Technical Schools (NATTS)...............................76, 266
National associations...59, 80, 124, 141, 164, 186
National Business Education Association (NBEA).......................................171, 266
National Cash Register (NCR)...213
National Center for Higher Education Management Systems (NCHEMS)........95, 116, 134, 152, 212, 306
National Collegiate Athletic Association (NCAA)....................................132, 266
National Conference of Academic Deans—Oklahoma State University.........................117, 311
National Council for Geographic Education (NCGE)...................................172, 266
National Council of University Research Administrators (NCURA)...........................132, 266
National Education Association (NEA)...172, 266
National Faculty Exchange (NFE)...172, 231, 307
National Fellowship Program—Kellogg Foundation...............116, 117, 134, 152, 173, 212, 232, 316
National Institute for Leadership Development..................77, 96, 116, 134, 152, 172, 188, 212, 307
  Building a Better Team on Campus: Understanding Gender Issues.......116, 134, 152, 172, 188, 212, 308
  Leaders for Change..96, 116, 134, 212, 308
  Leaders Project...116, 134, 152, 172, 212, 309
  Leadership for a New Century...........................116, 134, 152, 172, 212, 308
  Workshop for Women Presidents..77, 309
National Legislative Seminar and Regional Seminars—Association of Community College Trustees (ACCT) 58, 77, 278
National Orientation Directors Association (NODA)....................................132, 266
National programs..268–318
National University Continuing Education Association (NUCEA)...........................132, 266
Negotiating, negotiations..8, 30, 36
Networks and networking......................................34, 108, 128, 207, 219
New assignments..214
New Deans Institute—American Association of Colleges for Teacher Education (AACTE)..........115, 270
New Deans Seminar—American Assembly of Collegiate Schools of Business (AACSB).............115, 268
New employee...202
New Faculty and Staff Orientation Program—University of Texas-El Paso...........136, 153, 174, 233, 339
New Presidents Sessions—American Association of State Colleges and Universities (AASCU)........76, 272
New Presidents Workshop preceding Annual Presidents Institute—Council of Independent Colleges (CIC) 77, 293
New-employee orientation program..236
Newsletter, faculty development...236
North American Association of Summer Sessions (NAASS)...........................114, 132, 266
North Carolina State University.................................96, 116, 152, 173, 309
  Community College Leadership Institute.......................96, 116, 152, 173, 309
Northwestern University..69
NTL Institute...96, 116, 134, 152, 310
  Human Interaction Laboratory.............................96, 116, 134, 152, 310
  Management Work Conference.............................96, 116, 134, 152, 310
  Senior Executive's Conference...96, 310
NUPAGE—University of Nebraska...174, 233, 337
NUPROF—University of Nebraska/Institute of Agriculture and Natural Resources 153, 174, 227–228, 233, 337

Obstacles to leadership development...............................18–20, 156–157
Occasional colloquia for presidents—American Council on Education (ACE)....................76, 275
Off-campus programs...107, 144, 205–212
Office of Instructional Development—University of California Riverside....................174, 233, 334
Office of Personnel Services—University of Kansas.......................136, 153, 174, 231, 233, 335
Office of Professional and Organizational Development (OPOD)—University of Nebraska 136, 153, 174, 226–228, 233, 337
Office of Training and Development Programs—American University.....................135, 232, 319
Oklahoma State University...117, 311
  Annual National Conference of Academic Deans.......................................117, 311
On-Campus Fundraising Workshop—Association of Governing Boards (AGB)...............58, 187, 280
On-campus programs...............................33, 34, 107, 109, 158, 213–234
On-the-job learning, training.............................10, 33, 36, 66, 68, 214
Organizational structure...178

Orientation, orientation programs 49, 54, 144, 220
Outward Bound 70

Peers 216
Pennsylvania State University 135, 174, 231, 331
    Administrative Fellows Program 135, 174, 231, 331
Performance appraisal, evaluation 91, 189–202
Personal lives. 104
Planning 19–22, 122, 196
Planning and organizing skills. 196
Pluralism. 7, 9, 16–17, 62, 170
Power 8, 103, 179
Pre-Tenure Support Group—University of Nebraska/Institute of Agriculture and Natural Resources. 153,
    174, 227, 233, 337
Presidency. 54–56, 61–80, 84–90, 92, 96–100, 104–106, 108, 114, 122, 124, 129, 196, 198, 201–205
President's Breakfast Series—Arizona State University 78, 96, 117, 221–222, 232, 320
Presidential and Trustee Leadership in Fund Raising—Council for Advancement
    of Higher Education (CASE) 58, 77, 188, 289
Presidential spouse—See spouses
Presidents 9, 42, 56, 59–78
Presidents Academy Workshop—American Association of Community and Junior Colleges (AACJC) . .76, 271
Presidents Institute—Council of Independent Colleges (CIC) 77, 293
Presidents' Academy—American Association of State Colleges and Universities (AASCU) 76, 273
Presidents' Colloquium on Institutional Advancement—Council for Advancement and Support of Education
    (CASE) 77, 289
Professional and Organizational Development Network in Higher Education (POD) 117, 152, 173, 312
Professional associations 128, 237, 247–267
Professional development. 6, 10, 195
Professional Development Institute—Colorado State University 117, 135, 153, 173, 232, 325
Professional development, growth plan 146
Professional Development Program (PDP)—Boston College 135, 222, 224, 232, 322
Professional Development Programming—Colorado State University 153, 173, 232, 325
Professional Development Programs—Columbia University 135, 153, 232, 326
Professional Development Through Growth Plans— Gordon College 173, 232, 328
Professional Development Workshop—American Association of Community and Junior Colleges
    (AACJC) 94, 115, 133, 151, 211, 272
Professional Group Program—Maricopa Community Colleges District 117, 135, 153, 174, 233, 331
Professional organizations 207, 237, 247–267
Professors, emeriti 236
Program for Academic Affairs Committee Chairpersons and Senior Academic Officers—Association of
    Governing Boards (AGB) 58, 94, 187, 280
Program for Professional Enrichment (PPE)—Eastern Illinois University . . .135, 153, 173, 224–225, 232, 327
Project Planning Workshop—Association of Research Libraries (ARL) .115, 133, 283
Provosts—See academic vice presidents
Public Policy Seminar for New Presidents—National Association of Independent Colleges and Universities
    (NAICU) 77, 305
Public relations 83
Public service activities—See community service

Quality of life. 90

Reading 69
Renewal. 34, 68–71, 89
Resources Management Institute—Association of Research Libraries (ARL) 115, 133, 283
Retirement 71
Retreats 52, 128, 182
Reward structures 178
Richard F. Stevens Institute—National Association of Student Personnel Administrators (NASPA). 95, 134,
    212, 306
Rochester Institute of Technology (RIT) 136, 153, 174, 233, 331
    Executive Leadership in an Academic Setting 136, 153, 174, 233, 331
Role models 62, 67, 90, 110, 144, 216, 218

Rotating employees 219
Roundtable discussions 236

Sabbaticals...89, 128
School for Graduate Studies and Office of University Research—University of Wisconsin-Eau Claire 153, 174, 234, 449
Self-assessment 142, 146, 217
Seminar for Chairpersons and Chief Executives of Theological Schools—Association of Governing Boards (AGB)..58, 77, 187, 280
Seminar for New Deans—Council of Colleges of Arts and Sciences (CCAS) and American Conference of Academic Deans (ACAD) 116, 292
Seminar on Endowment Management—Association of Governing Boards (AGB).........58, 77, 94, 187, 280
Seminars for International Education Administrators in Germany and Japan—Council for International Exchange of Scholars (CIES) 115, 133, 151, 211, 290
Senior administrators, officers 6, 79–96
Senior Administrators Workshop—Association of American Law Schools (AALS) 115, 277
Senior Executive's Conference—NTL Institute 96, 310
Senior Financial Officers Conference—National Association of College and University Business Officers (NACUBO) 95, 304
Sessions during annual meeting for presidents—American Council on Education (ACE) 76, 275
Sessions for presidents at annual meetings—Association of American Colleges (AAC) 77, 276
Single administrators 91
Skills for Success: A Workshop for Getting Ahead—Council for Advancement and Support of Education (CASE) and Snelling, Kolb & Kuhnle 133, 290
Sloan School of Management Executive Development Programs—Massachusetts Institute of Technology (MIT) 33, 69, 77, 95, 116, 302
Social interaction, socialization..184
Society for College and University Planning (SCUP) 132, 267
Society for Values in Higher Education....................77, 96, 117, 152, 173, 312
   The Fellows Meeting.............................77, 96, 117, 152, 173, 312
Society of Ethnic and Special Studies (SESS)..........................171, 267
Southern Association of College and University Business Officers (SACUBO)...........96, 134, 212, 313
   College Management Business Institute (CMBI)................96, 134, 212, 313
Speaker Service—Association of Governing Boards (AGB) 58, 281
Special Interest Group for University and College Computing Services (SIGUCCS)...............132, 267
Specialization 15, 120, 125, 178
Specially designated presidential sessions at annual meetings—Association of American Colleges (AAC) 77, 276
Speech Communication Association (SCA).............................171, 267
Spouses 42, 72–73
Staff, staff development 25, 220
Staff Exchange Program, University of Massachusetts-Boston 136, 232, 336
Stanford University...136, 233, 332
   Administrative Development Program 136, 233, 332
   Human Resources Development Programs 136, 233, 332
   Management Development Program 136, 233, 332
   Stanford Supervision and You 136, 233, 332
Starting from scratch 215
State University of New York (SUNY) 174, 233, 332
   Affirmative Action Leave Program 174, 233, 332
Statewide, system-specific and on-campus development programs 319–340
St. Norbert College...165, 174, 233, 333
   Faculty Development Program 165–167, 174, 233, 333
Strategic Planning for Theological Schools—Association of Governing Boards (AGB) 58, 77, 94, 187, 281
Strategies for development
   Adventure programs 70
   Assessment—See assessment, self, and evaluation
   Association meetings...67, 87
   Committees, task forces 70
   Consultants, consulting (See also Consulting)....................67, 68, 70, 183
   Develop breadth 89, 129
   Discipline, stay active in 165

Evaluation 92
Exchanges, job rotations (See also Exchanges) 89, 219
Experiences outside higher education 129
Expertise, develop areas of 120
Exposure to the wider world of higher education 108
Growth plan, contract. 195, 198
Informal activities 86
Institutional crises, learning from 88
Learn the institution's culture 146
Learn the basics—managing and leading 107
Manage time with an eye on the future 147
Mentoring (See also Mentoring) 90, 144
Networks (See also Networks) 87, 88, 108, 110
Nonacademic activities 90
On-the-job development, on-campus development (See also On-the-job-learning) 66, 107, 109, 127
Orientation programs (See also Orientation programs 49, 50, 144
Participate in institutional deliberations 129
Problem-solving techniques, develop alternative 110
Professional organizations, associations (local, regional, and national) 129
Professional service. 90
Reading, research, writing, reflection 69, 87, 107
Responsibilities outside the institution 140
Responsibility for one's own development. 129, 146, 158, 164
Reach out on behalf of others 109
Retreats, workshops (get-away from campus activities) (See also Retreats) 52, 128, 182
Sabbaticals (See also Sabbaticals) 89
Specialized seminars and workshops. 88
Staff assignments. 163
Teaching 89, 110
Travel (visits to other institutions and international) (See also International) 51, 69, 70, 85
Stress, management, reduction. 68, 104, 110
Student affairs, life, services. 140
Student Affairs Conference—University of Maryland 134, 315
Student affairs officers 81
Summer Council of Presidents—American Association of State Colleges and Universities (AASCU) . . .76, 273
Summer Institute for Women/Bryn Mawr Institute—Higher Education Resource Service (HERS) 32, 95,
    116, 138, 151, 158, 172, 212, 298
Summer Institute in Executive Management—Council for Advancement and Support of Education
    (CASE) 95, 115, 133, 289
Summer Institute on College Admissions—Harvard University and The College Board 133, 297
Summer Seminar on Academic Administration—Texas A&M University 96, 117, 152, 313
Summer Workshops for Graduate Deans—Council of Graduate Schools (CGS) 116, 292
Sunshine laws 41, 53
Switch day 237

Task forces—See committees
Teaching 89, 110
Teams 144, 175–188, 208, 238
Team building 8, 9, 15, 123, 125, 175–188
Teleconferences. 237
Temporary assignments. 219
Tennessee Board of Regents. 136, 174, 231, 333
    Minority Management Development Program 136, 174, 231, 333
Texas A&M University/College of Education. 96, 117, 152, 313
    Summer Seminar on Academic Administration 96, 117, 152, 313
TIAA/CREF 228
Title VII of the Civil Rights Act of 1964. 193–194
Town/gown relations. 43
Training Division of Personnel Services—George Washington University. 135, 153, 173, 232, 328
Training Skills Institute—Association of Research Libraries (ARL) 115, 133, 283
Travel 51, 69, 70, 88
Troutbeck Program/Educational Leadership Project—Christian A. Johnson Endeavor Foundation. . .69, 77, 287

Trust 196, 200, 203, 206
Trustee Responsibility for Financial Affairs—Association of Governing Boards (AGB) 58, 77, 94, 187, 281
Trustees 41–59
Turf 120, 179

U.S./United Kingdom College and University Academic Administrator Award—Council for International
    Exchange of Scholars (CIES) 115, 133, 151, 211, 290
United Negro College Fund (UNCF) 76, 267
University Affiliations Program, United States Information Agency—Fulbright Programs 291, 314
University Council for Educational Administrators (UCEA) 114, 132, 267
University of California—Los Angeles (UCLA) 136, 233, 334
    Management Enhancement Program 136, 233, 334
University of California—Riverside 174, 233, 334
    Office of Instructional Development 174, 233, 334
University of Central Florida 96, 117, 134, 152, 314
    Financial Management for Women in Higher Education. 96, 117, 134, 152, 314
University of Colorado-Colorado Springs. 335
    Colorado Exchange 335
University of Georgia/Institute of Higher Education. 78, 96, 117, 134, 314
    Annual Conference on Higher Education and the Law 78, 96, 117, 134, 314
University of Iowa 136, 233, 335
    Administrative Seminar Program 136, 233, 335
University of Kansas 136, 153, 174, 231, 233, 335
    Faculty Fellows Program. 174
    Office of Personnel Services 136, 153, 174, 231, 233, 335
    Workshops for University Managers 153, 233, 336
University of Kentucky and the Southern Association of College and University Business Officers
    (SACUBO). 96, 134, 212, 313
    College Management Business Institute (CMBI) 96, 134, 212, 313
University of Maryland 134, 315
    Student Affairs Conference 134, 315
University of Massachusetts—Boston 136, 232, 336
    Staff Exchange Program 136, 232, 336
University of Nebraska—Lincoln/Institute of Agriculture and Natural Resources 136, 153, 174, 226–228, 233,
    336
    Administrative Development Map 136, 153, 233, 337
    NUPAGE 174, 233, 337
    NUPROF 153, 174, 227–228, 233, 337
    Office of Professional and Organizational Development (OPOD) 136, 153, 174, 226–228, 233, 337
    Pre-Tenure Support Group 153, 174, 227, 233, 337
University of South Carolina 136, 174, 232, 337
    Minority Administrative Fellowship 136, 174, 232, 337
University of Southern Colorado 174, 232, 233, 338
    Faculty Directors Program 174, 232, 233, 338
University of Tennessee 96, 117, 136, 233, 338
    Institute for Leadership Effectiveness 96, 117, 136, 233, 338
University of Texas—Austin 116, 134, 151, 172, 231, 300
    Expanding Leadership Diversity in Community Colleges 116, 134, 151, 172, 231, 301
University of Texas—El Paso. 136, 153, 174, 233, 339
    New Faculty and Staff Orientation Program 136, 153, 174, 233, 339
University of Wisconsin—Eau Claire. 153, 174, 234, 339
    School for Graduate Studies and Office of University Research 153, 174, 234, 339
University of Wisconsin System 117, 153, 174, 232, 340
    Administrative Associate Program. 117, 153, 174, 232, 340

Values. 18, 27, 28, 36, 45, 69
Vision 4, 7, 27, 37, 42, 44, 81, 103, 141, 142, 176, 195
Visions Career Development Program—Maricopa Community College District 117, 135, 153, 174, 225–226,
    233, 330

W. K. Kellogg Foundation. 116, 117, 134, 151, 152, 172, 173, 212, 231, 232, 300, 316
    Expanding Leadership Diversity in Community Colleges 116, 134, 151, 172, 231, 300–301

Fellowship Program...117, 134, 152, 173, 212, 232, 316
    NUPAGE 174, 233, 337
Washington State University...174, 234, 340
    Faculty Development and Support Services...174, 234, 340
Wellesley College/Higher Education Resource Service (HERS)—Institute for Women 32, 95, 116, 133, 151, 172, 212, 298
Western Association of College and University Business Officers (WACUBO).................96, 134, 315
    Business Management Institute...96, 134, 315
    Executive Leadership and Management Institute......................................96, 134, 315
Williamsburg Development Institute 58, 78, 96, 134, 212, 316
Wisconsin Association of Independent Colleges and Universities (WAICU)............................165
Women 7, 9, 17, 62, 127, 160
Women's Leadership Institute—City University of New York (CUNY) 117, 135, 152, 173, 232, 324
Woodrow Wilson National Fellowship Foundation 134, 317
    Administrative Fellows Program 134, 317
Working environment 62, 82
Workshop for new member presidents/spouses at annual meeting—American Association of State Colleges and
    Universities (AASCU) 76, 273
Workshop for New Trustees—Association of Governing Boards (AGB) 58, 281
Workshop for Women Presidents—National Institute for Leadership Development 77, 309
Workshop on the Liberal Arts—Lilly Endowment, Inc. 116, 151, 172, 188, 301
Workshops for University Managers—University of Kansas 153, 233, 336

Xerox Corporation...213